REVISED SECOND EDITION

INTERNATIONAL STUDIES: PERSPECTIVES ON A RAPIDLY CHANGING WORLD

Edited by Greta Uehling
University of Michigan, Ann Arbor

Bassim Hamadeh, CEO and Publisher
Carrie Montoya, Acquisitions Editor
Kaela Martin, Project Editor
Jeanine Rees, Production Editor
Jess Estrella, Senior Graphic Designer
Alexa Lucido, Licensing Supervisor
Joyce Lue, Interior Designer
Natalie Piccotti, Director of Marketing
Kassie Graves, Vice President of Editorial
Jamie Giganti, Director of Academic Publishing

Cover image copyright © 2014 iStockphoto LP/Bubaone.

Printed in the United States of America.

ISBN: 978-1-5165-3849-2 (pbk) 978-1-5165-4521-6 (al) / 978-1-5165-3850-8 (br) / 978-1-5165-3851-5 (pf)

CONTENTS

What is International Studies?   v

Chapter One: Globalization   1

Seanon Wong. "What's in a Dumpling? The Chinese Fast-Food Industry and
the Spread of Indigenous Cultures under Globalization" in *Stanford Journal of
East Asian Affairs*   17

Stanley Hoffmann. "Clash of Globalizations" in *Foreign Affairs*   27

Suzanne Staggenborg. "Introduction"   35

Chapter Two: International Organizations and Relations   45

Karen A. Mingst and Margaret P. Karns. "The United Nations in World Politics"
in *United Nations in the 21st Century*   53

John McCormick and Jonathan Olsen. "Introduction" in *The European Union:
Politics and Policies*   67

Chapter Three: Human Rights and Humanitarianism   81

Claude Welch. "The Universal Declaration of Human Rights at Sixty,"
U.S. Department of State e-publications   99

Susan Waltz. "Who Wrote the Universal Declaration of Human Rights?"
U.S. Department of State e-publications   107

Eric Posner. "The History of International Human Rights Law"
in *The Twilight of Human Rights Law*   115

António Guterres. "Remarks to the General Assembly" from the
United Nations   127

Jayshree Bajoria and Robert McMahon. "The Dilemma of Humanitarian
Intervention" from the Council on Foreign Relations   133

Chapter Four: Global Health and Environment   **139**

Debra DeLaet and David DeLaet. "Key Concepts in Global Health" in
Global Health in the 21st Century: The Globalization of Disease and Wellness   145

Scott Stonington. "On the (F)utility of Pain" in *The Lancet*   163

Scott Stonington. "Whose Autonomy?" in the *Journal of the
American Medical Association*   167

Regina Axelrod and Stacy Vandeveer. "The Global Environment: Institutions,
Law and Policy" in CQ Press   179

Juliette Jowit. "Bjørn Lomborg: The Dissenting Climate Change Voice Who
Changed His Tune" from *The Guardian*   191

Chapter Five: Human Development   **197**

Chimamanda Ngozi Adichie, "The Danger of a Single Story"   204

Andy Baker. "Introduction: Underdevelopment and Diversity in the
Global South" in *Shaping the Developing World: The West, the
South, and the Natural World*   205

United Nations Human Development Report 1990   231

Kennedy Odede. "Slumdog Tourism" from *The New York Times*   243

Chapter Six: Culture and Identity   **245**

Sarah Riley. "Identity, Community, and Selfhood: Understanding the
Self in Relation to Contemporary Youth Cultures"   257

Amin Maalouf. "In the Name of Identity: Violence and the Need to Belong"   273

Benjamin Shingler. "The Next Hot Sound? Powwow Step,
Aboriginal Hip-Hop" from *Al Jazeera America*   281

Lila Abu-Lughod. "Do Muslim Women Really Need Saving?
Anthropological Reflections on Cultural Relativism and its Others"
from *American Anthropologist*   285

What is International Studies?

In the past few decades, global interdependence has been increasing. This volume explores some of the many ways that people, ideas, capital, and technology flow across political, economic, and cultural borders, as well as perspectives on those flows. The interconnected quality of the world we live in suggests a strict disciplinary approach may no longer be ideal for understanding complex global problems. The field of international studies has developed to meet this challenge. It has evolved from a subtopic within political science into an interdisciplinary and comparative approach to questions of global significance. There is a closely related field you may have heard of, global studies, which focuses more on the role of race, class, and gender in international affairs. This closely related field places less emphasis on the importance of the nation-state. Both international and global studies are inspired by looking at the world from the perspective of different geographical areas and academic disciplines, and both fields are inspired to nurture the development of global citizens.

International studies is a relatively new field. The International Studies Association (ISA) has played a crucial role in the field's rapid growth and development. The ISA was formed in 1959 when scholars and practitioners saw a need for greater international and interdisciplinary dialogue (http://www.isanet.org). The association continues to connect scholars and practitioners around the world and even has nongovernmental consultative status at the United Nations (http://www.isanet.org). The seven journals that the association publishes are valuable sources of information for students of international studies.[1] This is a great time to be interested in international studies: individuals have never been as affected by events far from their homes as they are today.

International studies is a very broad field, and this volume can only provide an introduction. In spite of this breadth, there are some connecting themes that readers will find throughout the selections. First, globalization, as a central and organizing concept, is explored from a different angle in each chapter. Human rights, human security, and human development are other key concepts you will take with you from the readings and links that follow. The first chapter on globalization will give readers a sense of the main debates about this central topic. Chapter two will explore international organizations and relations and relies predominantly on the discipline of political science. In chapter three, we

---

1   The journals students at the undergraduate level will find most helpful are *The International Studies Review*, *International Studies Perspectives*, and *Foreign Policy Analysis* http://www.isanet.org/Publications/ISP.

consider two answers to the weaknesses of states and organizations: human rights and humanitarianism. Chapter four includes readings from the sciences as we consider global health and environment. Human development came about in part to help solve issues of global health and environment and this is the topic of chapter five. The field of human development aspires to reduce inequalities within and between countries and enhance health and well-being for all people. The sixth and last chapter brings us back to the central problem of globalization with which we began the course: understanding continued cultural heterogeneity in spite of the homogenizing forces of globalization. In this chapter, we consider these tendencies from the perspective of refugees and indigenous peoples. As a whole, the volume aims to provide a clearer understanding of an increasingly international world; a better understanding of a selection of important international issues; and some conceptual tools that will help you analyze events long after your introduction to international studies.

Globalization: What's in a Word?

The Merriam Webster Dictionary defines globalization as "the act or process of globalizing; the state of being globalized."[2] While the word "globalization" first appeared in the dictionary in 1961 (MacGillivray 2006: 11), the word "global" has been used as an adjective for much longer. MacGillivray traces the first use of the adjective "global" all the way back to 1892, when a Frenchman named Monsieur de Vogue was described in Harper's Magazine as having "global ambitions." The magazine describes him as a person who is hungry to experience colors, tastes, and ideas from all over the world, a person whose interests were "as wide as the universe" (McGillivray 2006: 10).

Global Intent

In his book, McGillivray suggests that a necessary prerequisite to the globalization we see today was the intent at first to know and then circumnavigate the globe (2006: 26). The history of globalization is in many ways the history of competition for the knowledge and power to encompass the world. Distinguishing the global from the international, and zeroing in on a precise definition, is helpful because the word "global" is too often used casually, as a synonym for "great." For the purpose of this volume, globalization will be defined as the processes through which regions have become more interdependent through communication, transportation, and trade facilitated by intensified transnational movement of ideas, information, people, goods, and capital.

A useful tool for exploring the usage of particular words is the Google Ngram[3] viewer. Google Ngram viewer is a free, online search engine that measures the frequency of a given word (or words) in published

---

2   http://www.merriam-webster.com/dictionary/globalization
3   You can access the Google Ngram viewer to perform your own searches at https://books.google.com/ngrams.

Image 0.1 Google Books Ngram Viewer

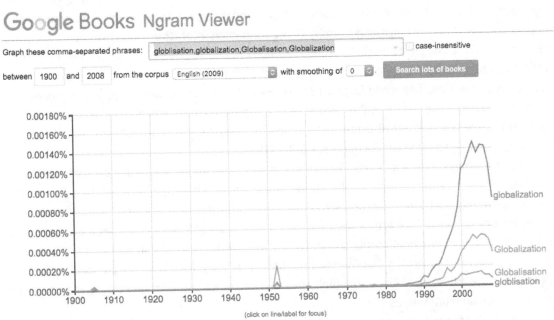

Source: https://books.google.com/ngrams.

sources. It is possible to perform searches in eight different languages: American English, British English, French, German, Spanish, Russian, Hebrew, and Chinese. What is visible in the screen capture of a search for American English sources using globalization is the precipitous rise of the term in the 1990s and the first decade of the twenty-first century. You can see from the figure below just how rapidly use of the term expanded.

When sifting through titles of books on globalization, some interesting patterns appear. One tendency is to make normative assessments about whether globalization is good or bad. This often entails painting globalization in a stark way using opposites. *Jihad vs. McWorld* (Barbar 1995) and *The World Is Flat* (Friedman 2005) are two titles that are typical of the unequivocal way that many people talk about globalization. This may be a reflection of the insecure place the topic holds in contemporary scholarship. Another strong tendency is to see the phenomenon as negative—to fear globalization. Throughout the late 1990s, the word was most often seen in print with the "anti-" prefix (McGillivray 2006). Globalization has vocal critics. Although the media has characterized these critics as "anti-globalization," few among them would be against globalization itself. After all, protesters benefit from the same communication and transportation networks as people who see globalization as a beneficial process. What they object to is the specific ways that international institutions have promoted globalization to the detriment of the world's most poor and vulnerable people.

The word *globalization* has come to the center of attention in the last two decades, but academic discussion of its distinguishing features has been going on for the last two centuries. Given the interdisciplinary nature of international studies, it is worthwhile to consider the intellectual history of globalization. Academic writing in the nineteenth and twentieth centuries points to the distinct awareness that new forms of transportation and communication technology were transforming people's experience of distance and thereby changing human interaction. Karl Marx, well known as the author of *The Communist Manifesto*, argued capitalist modes of production would inevitably result in the reduced significance of space. Capitalism, he thought, had a tendency to spread to and create all kinds of connections (Marx and Engels 1848 [1964]). Marx was ambivalent about this process that contained seeds of exploitation at the same time that it presented the potential to be a positive force. Marx penned the first theoretical explanation of how and why geographical distances were seemingly becoming compressed (*Stanford Encyclopedia:* 2002 [2014]: 2)

Academic ambivalence about transformations in communications and transportation technology continued in the twentieth century. John Dewey, an American philosopher known best for his support of democracy, was concerned about the implications for democracy if the temporal and spatial characteristics of human interaction were fundamentally changed. He thought that a proliferation of cross-border interactions would seriously undermine the efficacy of local and participatory democracy (Dewey 1927 [1954]). In writing that foreshadowed contemporary discussions of global citizenship, he asked how citizenship would function if high-speed technologies made for less stable and geographically fixed human relationships.

In the 1960s Marshall McLuhan proposed the idea that we live in a "global village" (McLuhan 1967). McLuhan used the expression to describe how the world was, metaphorically speaking, shrinking as a result of electronic media. To his way of thinking, the media can be compared to an electronic nervous system that integrates the globe. McLuhan postulated that consuming information passively, such as from television, would change human thinking itself. McLuhan was concerned that as people transcended their physical neighborhood, it would lead to "maximal disagreement on all points" (McLuhan 1967: 272). He saw technology as leading to a social breakdown of sorts if one is continuously bombarded with new patterns of relationship and new friends. McLuhan also introduced the concept of "global theatre" to emphasize the positive interactive potential of new technologies (McLuhan and Nevitt 1972). Every place becomes a potential performance space with advanced communication technology. An increasingly networked culture leads to a situation in which people have the ability to "do their own thing" for others to witness. Anyone can be an actor on a global stage. McLuhan and Nevitt write "The population of the world is both the cast and content of this new theatre" 1972: 145). Remarkably, McLuhan was preoccupied by this before software for downloading and uploading was available, presaging the capacities of individuals to be producers as well as consumers of knowledge so clear today. McLuhan would be unsurprised by the current propensity to disseminate photos of ourselves engaged in a perpetual flow of mundane activities. These three examples—Marx, Dewey, and McLuhan—demonstrate that although the word "globalization" gained wide circulation recently, scholars have been concerned about the phenomenon since at least the 1800s.

CHAPTER ONE

Globalization

Key Features of Contemporary Globalization

There are at least three key features that characterize the process of globalization: time–space compression, disembedding (sometimes called deterritorialization), and interdependence.

It is fairly obvious that globalization makes geographic distance less important, sometimes obliterating its significance altogether. In *The Condition of Postmodernity*, human geographer David Harvey (1990) expanded on Marx's thinking to theorize that the relationship between time and space is changing by becoming more "compressed." Harvey associated this compression with changes to capitalism in which production and consumption of products have become accelerated. What time–space compression means for daily life is that one's expectations about navigating geographical space and chronological time are revised. This acceleration is believed to change the way one perceives reality itself. New expectations shape desires, motivations, and frustrations. One's ability to accomplish tasks accelerates, making increased velocity a concomitant feature of globalization. Social interaction is increasingly characterized—paradoxically—by absence. People can be "present" in two places at the same time. One may FaceTime a friend in Japan at the same time that one chats with a roommate, or has a meal with one's family. With the advent of home technologies, one may do one's laundry while dining out. Increased velocity is sometimes associated with success and prosperity. Space–time compression provides a way for some people to transcend isolation, poverty, and social exclusion. However, technologies that compress time and space, whether they be jet planes or cell phones, are not universally available, making this process incomplete. Space–time compression is thus also a way inequalities of wealth and power can be reinforced.

A related term is disembedding. Something is disembedded when it is "moved from a singular, concrete, tangible, and local context to an abstract or virtual state" (Eriksen 2014: 19). Something is disembedded if it can be accessed from anywhere. For example, when you share information on Google drive, that information is independent of your physical location and therefore disembedded. Facebook disembeds friendship from a local context. Money disembeds economic transactions by making wealth convertible. As more and more aspects of life are disembedded, the world becomes more abstract.

Social relations are lifted from familiar places and restructured (Eriksen 2014). One reason this is significant is that the origins of ideas, texts, and products are more difficult to identify as they become disconnected from their creators. Another reason this is significant is that everything, becomes commodifiable. Disembedding therefore raises anxieties about globalization possibly leading to greater social alienation. To take the Facebook example, however, technology obviously has the capacity to link people by making things, people, and ideas more accessible.

Interdependence is another defining feature of globalization. Globalization is a process that establishes consequential relationships among regions, countries, and people. An important criterion for distinguishing globalization from a phenomenon that is merely widespread is the extent to which a geographically distant person, government, or phenomenon has the ability to make an impact on a geographically distant place. If the government of a developed and industrialized country places as tax or tariff on an agricultural product coming from a less developed country, the latter will be affected. The economies of the two countries profoundly influence one another.

Though "globalization" has become one of the most widely used terms in the contemporary international studies lexicon, scholars disagree about when the process began, what drives it, and whether or not it is making the world a more peaceful or prosperous place. One debate concerns how the process is understood historically. Just how long has globalization been going on? This is a thought-provoking question because setting the beginning at human migration out of the African continent, as some do, equates globalization with migration and dilutes the concept—perhaps to the point of rendering it useless. For the purpose of international studies, the word "globalization" is best reserved for the processes that bring parts of the world into greater interdependence and for projects that aim to be truly global.

A second debate is about the extent to which globalization fosters economic prosperity. Champions of the phenomenon, such as Thomas Friedman, contend globalization offers poor countries an opportunity to develop economically and achieve greater well-being. Opponents of this view counter that the specific ways in which the global economy is organized have benefitted primarily multinational corporations based in the Western world, not the world's poor. The best way to set this debate to rest is to avoid overly broad generalizations and engage in a detailed and country-by-country analysis—something many scholars, including Pankaj Ghemawat, are endeavoring to do. He has created the Global Connectedness Index, which was designed to measure the various impacts of globalization.[1]

A third debate has to do with the extent to which globalization facilitates democracy. As scholars Peter Leeson and Andrea Dean (2009) point out, the factors are complex. One way that globalization spreads democracy is that when people travel or use communication technology, they become more aware of how their lives could be different. In some cases, this may cause them to demand a more accountable, democratic government that is responsive to their needs and desires. It is also true, however, that technological advances associated with globalization have made terrorism more possible and likely (Hoffman 2002: 111). Hoffman emphasizes that when marginalized and economically destitute people become more aware of the opportunities they are missing, the feelings of exclusion and resentment can inspire social and political movements that seek revenge in violent ways (2002: 3).

---

1 https://www.youtube.com/watch?v=5YHZna0ENLY

A fourth debate is whether globalization is leading to cultural homogenization or Americanization. Scholars differ markedly on this topic. There are certainly some striking trends that point to a loss of diversity. For example, the United Nations Educational, Scientific and Cultural Organization (UNESCO) states on its website that of the approximately 6,000 languages that are spoken today, as many as half will disappear by the end of this century.[2] But more often than not, global trends acquire unique local expressions. The most reasonable arguments avoid the untenable extremes that globalization will lead to homogeneity or, on the contrary, clashes of cultures and civilizations.

The history of the world is a history of cultural borrowing and mixing. No doubt the scope of cultural mixing has intensified as a result of globalization. The concept of cultural creolization (Hannerz 1992) or hybridity (Bhabha 2004) is helpful. The term was taken from biology and initially used to critique forms of colonial racism in which there was an effort to keep White Europeans separate from non-European "others," leading people of mixed heritage to be stigmatized.

Hybridity is now used to describe any intermingling of two previously separate traditions or cultures that results in something new. A useful contrast can be made with multiculturalism, which places an emphasis on respecting and maintaining cultural differences. The flows of goods, capital, and people associated with globalization lead to cultural mixing. The dominance of English on the Internet, and the standardization of time zones, measurements, and currencies such as the euro, further accelerate these processes. Cultural anthropologists note that fear of homogenization frequently triggers attempts to differentiate oneself or one's group.

Hybridity became a useful concept for postcolonial studies because it provided a way to conceptualize how African, Asian, and European cultures have been influencing one another since at least the fifteenth century. In contrast to the argument that Western colonialism and imperialism rolled right over the indigenous cultures they came in contact with, postcolonial studies was able to demonstrate that even if people in the colonies were exploited economically or politically dominated, they retained their agency in the cultural realm (Mercer 2016: 6). Colonized peoples made strategic choices about the elements of culture they adopted and those they resisted. A focus on hybridity reveals globalization is a much more complicated and multidirectional process. From colonialism onwards, it has been characterized by negotiation and selective appropriation. The concept of appropriation opened up a new way of thinking about the relations between the West and the rest. As Mercer puts it: "what was once a monologue about otherness became a dialogue about difference" (Mercer 2016:2).

A common misconception is that cultural mixing implies a prior state in which cultures had firm boundaries and were "pure" or untouched. Another misconception to dispel is that mixing means everything is in flux and subject to change. Fluid identities exist amidst cultural stability, and conversely, just because there are stable identities or fixed cultural boundaries it does not mean cultural mixing is impossible.

---

2   http://www.unesco.org/new/en/culture/themes/endangered-languages/

Cultural Globalization

We can examine the question about homogenization by considering cultural flows a bit more closely. Hip hop in East Africa provides classic example of the cultural flows inherent in globalization. Globalization in East Africa has considerable historic depth, beginning with the process of contact and conquest—the system of colonialism—that brought African economies into contact with European powers (Cooper 2001). Hip hop in East Africa combines traditional forms of African expressive culture, especially praise singing (Ntarangwi 2009: 26), with melodies and beats from the United States. Thus, ethnomusicologists point out the pattern of call and response, short repeated phrases, and rhythmic patterns that loop and interlock effectively connect musical forms in Africa and the United States (2009: 26). This is an example of how music styles are adapted to local sensibilities in a way that meshes the local and the global (Mugubane 2006).

Hip hop can be used as a means to understand how music makers see themselves in relation to globalization. It can be variously used to connect musicians and audience to their local place, to craft an image of their nation, and to represent that nation to global audiences (Appert 2016: 280). Musical hybridity affords musicians a way to select, reconfigure and transform sounds into new meanings. For example, Appert points out musicians incorporate varying degrees of traditional music, and choose their language to reach specific local and global audiences. In East Africa, lyrics are used to criticize the effects of economic globalization, especially the destructive forms of globalization practiced by international financial institutions. At the same time, musicians are self-consciously aware that they take advantage of globalization when they sell their music to a wide audience. Hip hop music careers give artists agency to both shape their own lives and comment on the social and political issues that concern them. Hip hop is an example of something that can both be a product of globalization, as well as serve as a medium to critique globalization. This underscores the point that globalization is a complex process that can't be reduced to "helpful" or "harmful."

Film offers additional insights into the process of cultural globalization. Films, and the technology to produce them, have been crossing borders since they were invented in the early 1900s: the technology of sound developed in a competition among French, German, and American innovators. On one hand, film is an *agent* of globalization: it brings people (actors and film crews) and ideas (in the form of the plot and cinematography) as well as forms of technology from one region to another. However, it is also true that this cross-fertilization would not have been possible in the first place without the intensified transportation and communication links of globalization. Hence it is fair to say the global film industry is both a cause and an effect of globalization (Herbert 2015).

The global film industry demonstrates how anxieties may be raised by globalization. Schlosser (2001) describes the "dumping" of American cultural products, such as Hollywood films, as damaging to local cultures. Part of the concern has to do with films dominating screens in places where smaller film industries lack the finances or finesse to compete with larger studios. The content of the film may also be troubling, particularly if the film portrays lifestyles that are unobtainable, or if the lifestyles are undesirable to the leadership of a country. These concerns are very real in countries like China and

United Arab Emirates—China limits the number of foreign films that can be released, and United Arab Emirates bans specific films.

Cultural theorists see this as more complicated. They put forward the idea that what matters most is the viewer's interpretation or "reception" of a cultural product such as film. Umberto Eco coined the term "aberrant decoding" to describe how a viewer's or reader's interpretation can differ from what an author intends (Eco 1972). Stuart Hall further developed this idea by arguing it would be too simplistic to think that audiences passively receive the meaning that is intended by a film's producers. It is possible for an audience both to understand the intended message and interpret it in a contrary way (Hall 1973: 18). There is therefore reason to question the extent of Hollywood's dominance.

Most recently, some analysts have found evidence that Hollywood producers are paying more attention to preferences in foreign markets (Walls and McKenzie 2012). Hollywood producers are recognizing that just because a film does well in box offices in the United States does not necessarily mean it will do well overseas. The Hollywood film industry may be changing in the direction of better accommodation of foreign tastes and requirements (Walls and McKenzie 2012).

Economic Globalization

The United Nations Monetary and Financial Conference at Bretton Woods

The international economic institutions created after World War II are important drivers of economic globalization. A key moment in this progression occurred when delegates from the Allied nations convened a meeting in Bretton Woods, New Hampshire. The conference was officially called the United Nations Monetary and Financial Conference, but most people use "Bretton Woods" as an abbreviated way of referring to the pivotal decisions made at the Mount Washington Hotel in July 1944. Bretton Woods was central to the process of globalization because the institutions it created have integrated what were previously more autonomous economic systems.

The main idea behind the gathering at Bretton Woods was that collective action at the global level would be required for the creation of economic stability in the wake of the Great Depression and World War II (Stiglitz 2003: 12). As a result of the gathering, two institutions were created: the International Monetary Fund (IMF) and the International Bank of Reconstruction and Development (IBRD).

The IMF had a difficult task: preventing another global depression (Stiglitz 2003: 10). Economists took note of the massive unemployment resulting from the Great Depression. According to the prevailing doctrine at the time, free markets should automatically lead to full employment. The thinking on the part of John Maynard Keynes, the "father" of economics, was that fiscal and monetary policy would be required. Taking measures to boost aggregate demand, he thought, would cause the economy to grow again (Image 1.1). The IMF aimed to stimulate growth by encouraging countries with weak economies to do more to contribute to aggregate demand. The IMF also worked to stabilize currencies and

Image 1.1 White and Keynes

Assistant Secretary of the US Treasury Dexter White and father of economics John Maynard Keynes at Bretton Woods

prevent the volatility that had jeopardized a smoothly functioning economy in the past. The dollar became the world's global currency and was backed with gold. Stiglitz points out that at its inception, the IMF recognized that intervention in markets is often necessary to provide social goods and protect national economies (2003: 12). Subsequently, the IMF became known for its policies based on the idea that markets are best left to regulate themselves. Thinking on the best course to international financial cooperation is continually evolving.

Economists at Bretton Woods attempted to include the Soviet Union. The idea was that the use of gold, which the Soviet Union had in abundance, could enable the Soviet Union to participate. Harry Dexter White, the United States Treasury official who was not incidentally also a Soviet spy, debated with Keynes, the British economist, about how best to do this. White kept the Soviets apprised of the conversations taking place at Bretton Woods. The Kremlin endorsed the agreements reached at the end of the Bretton Woods conference, but never ratified them.

A second institution created at the gathering was the International Bank for Reconstruction and Development (IBRD). This organization was created to administer grants and loans to countries (primarily European) whose economies were devastated by the war. Stiglitz remembers the word "development" was tacked on at the end of the name of the bank without reflection (2003: 11). This was a time when most of the countries in the developing world were still colonies. Very little development was foreseen because these countries were thought to be the responsibility of their colonizers. That changed dramatically with time. Today, the IBRD is the world's largest bank devoted to development, and provides policy advice and a wide range of financial products to a vastly greater number of countries.[3] The bank also expanded its activity to an increasing array of economic sectors that have an impact on countries' development.

A third institution was planned at the Bretton Woods conference but failed to materialize. Organizers of the conference envisioned an international trade organization to promote fair rules. Though they were not able to agree on the establishment of this organization, a less comprehensive agreement was signed, called the General Agreement on Tariffs and Trade (GATT). Decades passed before a round of negotiations, the Uruguay Round in 1995, founded the World Trade Organization (WTO). Together, these

---

3   http://www.worldbank.org/en/who-we-are/ibrd

organizations provided the basic economic institutions or "architecture" that created greater economic interdependence.

Globalization has helped countries that were previously less prosperous gain new and different opportunities to carry out trade and commerce. Considering the lack of a broad consensus on the policies that are most useful to manage debt, alleviate poverty, and stabilize financial markets, students of international studies are likely to see interesting changes in the years to come.

Perspectives on the Scope of Globalization

Globalization is often discussed in normative terms that attempt to pin down whether the process is good or bad. One of the prominent and often-quoted voices is that of Thomas Friedman (also see the video), a *New York Times* columnist. He has written a number of books on the topic of globalization that have put him on the best seller list—and aroused the bemusement of scholars in the social sciences.

Friedman's central argument is that globalization is profoundly and irrevocably changing the world. Most of these changes are allegedly for the better. He argues that globalization has changed the way the economy works and that as a result, more people can compete and collaborate. His list of forces that "flatten" the world, by which he means reducing socioeconomic inequality, has become famous, even though the "forces" he identifies are far from commensurable, starting with the Berlin Wall and progressing through technological developments and social phenomena. He is especially interested in the role of technology, and chronicles how the Internet, software that manages workflows, and phenomena such as outsourcing and offshoring have enabled people in previously isolated or low-income countries to benefit from an increasingly global market.

Outsourcing is an arrangement in which a corporation contracts some portion of its activity to another company. It was a significant trend in human resources when corporations determined they could save on production costs by having labor in a country with lower expectations about wages provide a subset of services such as online technical support. Outsourcing has been supplemented by other trends such as offshoring, in which a corporation moves its entire operation to another country. In recent years, the offshoring trend has been offset by onshoring, the practice of transferring a business operation that was previously located overseas back to the original country.

One weakness of Friedman's argument is that his is a distinctly American perspective. It does not fully account for the still large numbers of people who lack Internet access and do not see a global market as something they may benefit from (including hip hop artists in parts of East Africa). Criticism of the universal benefits of globalization is supported by facts about Internet penetration. According to the United Nations International Telecommunications Union, the differences in the percentage of the population that uses the Internet are stark, ranging from Iceland, where the figure is 98.2 to Chad and Niger, where the percentage is less than 3. According to the report, there are 3.9 billion people in the world who do not use the Internet. While Friedman is accurate that the Internet creates new opportunities, this argument should not be overextended.

Pankaj Ghemawat (see video) argued against Friedman in an article published in *Foreign Policy* in 2007. Ghemawat contends that impressions of globalization as a great equalizer are just that—impressions. What is needed is an examination of the data on transborder flows, which he takes as indicators interconnectedness. Examining three metrics—migrants as the percentage of the population, foreign direct investment, and exports of goods and services—he demonstrates that these figures are much lower than most expect and Friedman's claims are exaggerated.

The Trump presidency raises important doubts about the future course of globalization. Headlines to the effect that globalization will now come to an end have appeared in major newspapers. Ghemawat argues that claims that globalization will become a thing of the past as a result of the Trump presidency and Brexit are exaggerated.[4] Ghemawat tries to use reason and evidence to make more grounded claims. He finds that while international business transactions on the part of the United States are significant, they are much less significant than the amount of domestic business transactions. President Trump may support policies that limit international trade, but this can have only a limited impact on globalization as a whole.[5] Although President Trump campaigned with "anti-globalization" rhetoric, it is important to keep in focus other parts of the world where new trading relationships are being created and already existing ones maintained.

Ghemawat and Friedman exemplify different perspectives on globalization that are worthwhile to explore more deeply. There are three, originally laid out by David Held and Anthony McGrew (1999), that will be considered. Hyperglobalists consider the integration of markets and erosion of the nation-state a foregone conclusion (Dickens 2003). They see globalization as an irreversible and profoundly transformative process that is moving us to a novel chapter of human history. For hyperglobalists, the world is essentially borderless. These scholars tend to place a great deal of importance on the peaks of globalization, or the phases in which the world was most globalized. The first of these peaks was at the beginning of the twentieth century, and the second occurred in the 1990s following the dismantling of the Berlin Wall. According to Held and McGrew, hyperglobalist authors argue there is a global economy that transcends state borders (1999: 3-5). It follows that a state's ability to regulate its economy is diminished: the decisions that shape trade and investment are made by large multinational corporations (MNCs) with the support of intergovernmental organizations (IGOs) such as the WTO and the World Bank. In the hyperglobalists' world, MNCs and IGOs intervene in governments' decision-making process. Economic outcomes are a result of world forces rather than the internal decisions of particular countries. Good examples of hyperglobalists are Thomas Friedman and Kenichi Ohmae, who wrote *Borderless World* and *The End of the Nation State*.

Skeptics contest the novelty of globalization, preferring to think about it as something that has been occurring for centuries. In *Globalization in Question*, Paul Hirst and Grahame Thompson (1999) point out that investment and trade were higher in 1890–1914 than when they were writing in the late 1990s (1999: 5–7). Skeptics believe that globalization is limited to the wealthy (Organisation for Economic Cooperation and Development [OECD]) countries that also have a great deal of power to shape globalization itself, having influenced the trading regulations that shape economic globalization.

---

4   https://hbr.org/2017/07/globalization-in-the-age-of-trump
5   https://hbr.org/2017/07/globalization-in-the-age-of-trump

These authors believe that far from disappearing, old divisions between wealthy Western countries and poorer, less developed countries are becoming deeper. Skeptics think that the existence of a global economy is something of a myth. Rather, there are three main trading blocs of a regional nature (Americas, Europe, and Asia). Skeptics reject the notion that state governments' decisions have lost significance: in this view, government policymaking retains its significance and national governments remain powerful. If you are interested in the skeptical position you may want to read *Globalization in Question* by Hirst and Thompson (1999).

David Held and his colleagues have attempted to carve out a position, a transformationalist one, between the hyperglobalists and the skeptics (1999; 2001). Transformationalists disagree that globalization is a myth covering over the reality that the international economy is increasingly segmented. They take the position that the significance of national governments is simply changing. They see that the distribution of power in the world is neither fully integrating the globe (the hyperglobalist position) nor completely dividing the world (the skeptical position). They argue that globalization is very uneven and does both, depending on the location. Unlike the other positions, they maintain that the outcome of globalization is not determined. Globalization can advance or be reversed. The transformationalists argue there is no single cause of globalization and shift their attention away from the economy to dynamics such as space–time compression and social relations. If you are interested in the typology of Held et al. you can turn to Held and McGrew's entry in the *Oxford Companion to the Politics of the World* titled "Globalization" (2001).

All typologies are simplifications, and any typology of scholarly positions is inherently limited. Nonetheless, it provides a useful way to begin to make sense of the diversity of perspectives on globalization. Considering that globalization has cultural, economic, and political dimensions, it is an enormous topic of study that defies easy categorization.

Global Citizenship

Historically, primary political loyalties were unquestionably based on a connection to a particular place, and these places were defined in terms of territorial boundaries. But with globalization, there is a growing sense of global citizenship. Global citizenship has a deep philosophical history. Diogenes was the first person to speak of being a citizen of the world, in the fourth century BCE. Diogenes was critical of the society he lived in and sought to embody higher values through a simple lifestyle. When asked from where he came, he replied he was a citizen of the world. This is a remarkable claim because at the time, identity was closely tied to citizenship in a specific city-state. Of course, this was a philosophical statement: Diogenes is likely to have had very little knowledge of the world outside his region of Greece of this time. After Diogenes used the term, Stoic philosophers developed the concept that one has two communities: one's local community and the human community. The Stoic philosophers used the word *cosmopolitan* to refer to the idea that whatever one's political loyalties or ethnic allegiance may be, one's overarching moral obligations stem from one's

Image 1.2 Diogenes

The Book of Moralities of Jacques Legrand. "How the state of poverty is agreeable". Diogenes in his barrel and Crates of Thebes who gives up wealth for virtue.

membership in humanity. Cosmopolitans like Appiah (see video) emphasize that these moral obligations to other human beings exist regardless of social, economic, religious, or other differences. Communitarian philosophers dispute this stance. They agree with the idea that one should be concerned about social justice but argue that one's moral obligations to foreigners are very different than the obligations one has toward people in one's own community. They disagree that attempts to enhance the well-being of distant strangers are likely to be effective.

The concept of global citizenship has drawn on philosophy and has developed into an identity with practical applications. Nigel Dower and John Williams define global citizenship as self-conscious membership in the community of all humanity, something much wider than the traditional sense of citizenship. "This membership is important in the sense that it involves ... a significant loyalty or commitment beyond the nation state" (2016: 1). Translated into practice by organizations such as Oxfam, global citizenship is a constellation of attitudes. A global citizen:

- Is respectful of diversity
- Strives to understand how the world works
- Is against social injustice
- Participates in the communities around him or her, from local to global
- Is willing to act to make the world a more equitable, sustainable place
- Takes responsibility for his or her own actions.[6]

Given this list, global citizenship at first appears unobjectionable. A closer examination reveals the concept has some weaknesses. One important criticism is that it is vague. For example, what does it mean to be respectful of diversity? Few have the temerity to argue that diversity should not be respected. Global citizenship does not provide much guidance on how diversity is to be managed, or how the value placed on it is to be expressed. The counterargument to this criticism is that the concept must remain vague to accommodate the full spectrum of people and viewpoints it is intended to encompass.

---

6   https://www.oxfam.org.uk/education/who-we-are/what-is-global-citizenship

A second and related criticism is that it lacks institutional support and is therefore of little pragmatic value. Claiming to be a global citizen does not legitimize passage across an international border or through airport security. How can this status be actualized if there are no institutions to confer such citizenship? The counterargument to this criticism is that global citizenship is not a literal form of citizenship. Rather it is intended to signal a frame of mind. To call it "citizenship" is to use a metaphor. Further, global citizenship is not intended to *replace* national citizenship. As a way of thinking, it offers an additional outlet for expression and action.

A third criticism is that elitism is inherent in this self-ascribed identity, and this elitism renders it ineffective for accomplishing its stated objectives. The notion of global citizenship does not have much meaning to people who lack the time and resources to act globally, from this vantage point. It is more difficult to rebut this argument. A weak rebuttal is that taking the stance of a global citizen is at least preferable to the forms of ethnic nationalism and particularism that appear to be on the rise. This is therefore perhaps the most trenchant critique.

Proponents of "critical global citizenship" (Mikander 2016) hold that the underlying assumptions inherent in global citizenship warrant scrutiny. Global citizens, as exemplified in "voluntourism" and gap year tourism, assume people in less wealthy and developed countries want and perhaps even need their assistance. Proponents of global citizenship, they argue, have a biased and even ethnocentric interpretation of history in which European and other Western developed countries are the sole source of civilization and modernity. From this perspective, the notion of global values embodied by global citizens is not terribly different from the colonial project in which it was the "white man's burden" to help other nations. What are your thoughts?

Global Social Movements

A paradigmatic expression of global citizenship is the formation of transnational social movements. Transnational activist networks or transnational social movements are an important component of how global citizenship is practiced. This represents the development of what Habermas (1989 [1962]) described as an expanding "public sphere"—a new area of activity in which it is rational critical discussion by citizens, rather than state power, that determines a course of action. Some scholars make a distinction between the "new" movements seen since the 1960s, which tend to be focused on human rights and those that came before, focused more on socioeconomic issues and material well-being (Scott 1990; Pichardo 1997).

What distinguishes transnational social movements today from those of the past are the number, size, professionalism, and speed with which they accomplish their objectives. They are an excellent example of time–space compression because physical distance loses some of its significance and activities are accelerated, with ideas also sometimes going "viral" as a result of networks. Transnational social movements are an example of disembedding in the sense that campaigns can be—and often are—designed and organized from a number of places simultaneously between people who don't know each other and are unlikely to ever meet in person.

Advocacy movements are most likely to become inter- or transnational when communication channels between a group of people wanting change and their government are blocked. Of course, political entrepreneurs must have a goal and see a chance that activism will be successful for a network to form. To describe how a local issue is projected onto a global stage, Keck and Sikkink (1998) use the term "the boomerang effect". They argue that when authorities are unresponsive to desired changes, activists move the issue past these authorities with the assistance of their networks. These networks may consist of foreign nongovernmental organizations (NGOs), international organizations, or governments. A "boomerang" effect takes place when the demand comes back to the activists' domestic arena with the force of international opinions and sanctions behind it. Recalcitrant and nonresponsive governments face more severe consequences if they do not change their stance. Networks are powerful, but not in the same way as states. Rather, they harness the power of communication and symbols through processes of globalization to exert an influence.

Readings

In "What's in a Dumpling?" **Seanon Wong** uses the example of fast food in China to show that globalization does not always lead to homogenization. Rather than devastating local business, the arrival of American-style fast food, in Wong's estimation, inspired local entrepreneurs to innovate. Wong, Seanon. 2006. "What's in a Dumpling" *Stanford Journal of East Asian Affairs,* Vol. 6(1): 25–32

Stanley Hoffman's essay titled "Clashing Globalizations" provides a brief tour of key debates about globalization. This article appeared in a leading journal of international relations, *Foreign Affairs.* Hoffman wrote the article in response to the terrorist attacks of September 11, 2001, but his observations concerning the debates about globalization, what he calls "the sound and the fury," remain relevant today. He points out that globalization presents a challenge to the study of international relations, which had previously contented itself with studying interstate relations.

Hoffman explores the weaknesses of various models of globalization that gained currency in the 1990s. He takes issue with Francis Fukuyama's idea that ideological conflicts are a thing of the past and Samuel Huntington's idea that "civilizational" conflicts are likely to erupt. Both Fukuyama and Huntington see globalization affecting politics in such a way that the nation-state is becoming less important. Hoffman argues that this fails to take into account the continued relevance of nationalism and national identity. Hoffman explores the significant effects of globalization on politics, as well as globalization's connection to terrorism. Hoffman, Stanley. 2002. "Clash of Globalizations," *Foreign Affairs,* Vol. 81(4):104–115.

Pankaj Ghemawat (video) disagrees with Friedman and provides economic data to refute some of Friedman's more sweeping generalizations. One useful takeaway from Ghemawat's talk is that the world is not as globalized as one may think. He provides quantitative evidence that international trade, migration, and communication are limited. Thus overstatements, when they lead to irrational fears of globalization, are counterproductive. Whereas Friedman is a hyper-globalist, Ghemawat is a skeptic. Skeptics acknowledge that globalization is occurring, but see it as a more regionalized phenomenon. They emphasize that industrialized nations have built regionalized trading blocs (Schiff and Winters 2003: 209) rather than a truly global economy. Skeptics contend that the endurance of the nation-state system is evidence that globalization has not resulted in the complete erosion of borders and therefore emphasize the distinct limits of globalization. Ghemawat, Pankaj. 2012. "World 3.0: Why it's not as flat as you might think" NUS Business School, May 12, 2012. https://www.youtube.com/watch?v=m1mlFsk836Y.

Kwame Anthony Appiah (video) is a philosopher and cultural theorist who is best known for his writing on the topic of cosmopolitanism. He has taught at the University of Ghana, Cornell, Yale, Harvard, and Princeton. In a short YouTube video, Appiah takes his listeners back to the Greek Cynics of the fourth century BCE and Diogenes' proposition that he is a citizen of the world, even though he knew nothing of the world outside the Greece of his time. He contrasts cosmopolitanism with fundamentalism and considers what one may owe to strangers. Appiah, Kwame. "Thought Leader Kwame Anthony Appiah on Cosmopolitanism" Carnegie Council for Ethics in International Affairs, November 12, 2012. https://www.youtube.com/watch?v=inyq_tfm8jc.

In *Social Movements*, **Suzanne Staggenborg** explains the main theoretical approaches used by scholars to understand social movements. She provides a brief synopsis of concepts such as contentious politics and repertoires of collective action that have informed the study of social movements. Staggenborg also explains how new social movement theory proposes that contemporary social movements differ from traditional ones in consequential ways. Staggenborg, Suzanne. 2008. *Social Movements*. Ontario, Canada: Oxford University Press.

References

Appert, Catherine. 2016. "On Hybridity in African Popular Music: The Case of Senegalese Hip Hop Authors" *Ethnomusicology* Vol. 60 (2): 279–299.

Bell, Clare, Okwui Enwezor, Danielle Tilkin, and Octavio Zaya, eds. 1996. *In/sight: African Photographers, 1940 to the Present*. Exhibition catalogue. New York: Guggenheim Museum.

Bhabha, Homi K. 2004. *The Location of Culture*. Abingdon, UK: Routledge.

Cooper, Fredrick. 2001. "What is the Concept of Globalization Good For? An African Historian's Perspective." *African Affairs* 100 (399): 189–213.

Dewey, John. 1927 [1954]. *The Public and Its Problems*. Athens, OH: Swallow Press.

Dicken, Peter. 2003. *Global Shift: Reshaping the Global Economic Map in the 21st Century*. New York: Guilford Press.

Dower, Nigel, and John Williams. 2016. *Global Citizenship: A Critical Introduction*. New York: Taylor and Francis.

Eco, Umberto. 1972. "Towards a Semiotic Inquiry into the Television Message." In Ackbar Abbas and John Nguyet Erni (eds.), *Internationalizing Cultural Studies: An Anthology*. London: Blackwell, 238.

Eriksen, Thomas Hylland. 2014. *Globalization: The Key Concepts*. London and New Delhi: Bloomsbury.

Habermas, Jürgen. 1989 [1962]. Thomas Burger and Frederick Lawrence, trans. *The Structural Transformation of the Public Sphere: An Inquiry into a Category of Bourgeois Society.* Cambridge, MA: MIT Press.

Hall, Stuart. 1973. *Encoding and Decoding in the Television Discourse.* Birmingham: Centre for Contemporary Cultural Studies.

Hannerz, Ulf. 1992. *Cultural Complexity: The Social Organization of Meaning.* New York: Columbia University Press.

Harvey, David. 1990. *The Condition of Postmodernity: An Enquirey into the Origins of Cultural Change.* Malden, MA: Wiley and Oxford: Blackwell.

Held, David, and A. McGrew. 2001. "Globalization." In *Oxford Companion to the Politics of the World Globalization.* Oxford: Oxford University Press.

Held, David, Anthony McGrew, David Goldblatt, and Jonathan Perraton. 1999. *Global Transformation: Politics, Economics and Culture.* Stanford: Stanford University Press, 32–86.

Herbert, Danile. 2015. Lecture to International Studies 101, University of Michigan, Ann Arbor.

Hirst, Paul, and Grahame Thompson. 1999. *Globalization in Question*: The International Economy and the Possibilities of Governance. Cambridge: Polity Press and Malden, MA: Blackwell.

Hoffman, Stanley. 2002. "Clash of Globalizations," *Foreign Affairs*, Vol. 81(4): 104–112.

Keck, Margaret E., and Kathryn Sikkink. 1998. *Activists Beyond Borders: Advocacy Networks in International Politics.* Ithaca, NY: Cornell University Press.

Leeson, Peter T., and Andrea M. Dean. 2009. "The Democratic Domino Theory: An Empirical Investigation." *American Journal of Political Science* 53 (3): 533–551.

Marx, Karl, and Friedrich Engels. 1848 [1964]. *The Communist Manifesto.* New York: Pocket Books.

McLuhan, Marshall. 1967. *Hot & Cool: A Primer.* New York: Dial Press.

McLuhan, Marshall, and Barrington Nevitt.. 1972. *Take Today: The Executive as Dropout.* New York: Harcourt Brace.

Mercer, Kobena. 2016. *Travel and See: Black Diaspora Art Practices since the 1980s.* Durham: Duke University Press.

Mikander, Pia. 2016. "Globalization and Continuing Colonialism: Critical Global Citizenship Education in an Unequal World." *Journal of Social Science Education* 15 (2):70–79.

Mugubane, Zine. 2006. "Globalization and gangster rap: Hip hop in the post-apartheid city." in Dipannita Basu and Sidney J. Lemelle, eds. *The vinyl ain't final: Hip hop and the globalization of Black popular culture.* London: Pluto Press, 208–209.

Ntarangwi, Mwenda. 2009. *East African Hip Hop: Youth Culture and Globalization.* Urbana and Chicago: University of Illinois Press.

Ohmae, Ken'ichi. 1990. *Borderless World: Power and Strategy in the Interlinked World Economy.* New York: Harper & Row.

Ohmae, Kenichi. 1995. *The End of the Nation State*: The rise of regional economies. New York: Free Press.

Ortner, Sherry. 2006. *Anthropology and Social Theory: Culture, Power, and Acting Subject.* Durham, NC: Duke University Press.

Pichardo, Nelson. 1997. "New Social Movements: A Critical Review." *Annual Review of Sociology* 23: 411–430.

Schiff, Maurice, and Alan Winters. 2003. *Regional Integration and Development.* Washington, DC: World Bank.

Schlosser, Eric. 2001. *Fast Food Nation: The Dark Side of the All-American Meal.* Boston: Houghton Mifflin.

Scott, A. 1990. *Ideology and the New Social Movements.* London: Unwin Hyman.

Stanford   Encyclopedia   of   Philosopy,   2002/2014.   "Globalization,"   https://plato.stanford.edu/entries/
    globalization/

Stiglitz, Joseph. 2003. *Globalization and its Discontents*. Norton, W. W. & Company.

Walls, William David, and Jordi McKenzie. 2012. "The Changing Role of Hollywood in the Global Movie Market."
    Journal of Media Economics 25 (4): 198–219, http://dx.doi.org/10.1080/08997764.2012.729544.

United Nations International Telecommunications Union https://www.itu.int/en/Pages/default.aspx Accessed July 8.
    2018

Image Credits

What's in a Dumpling?
The Chinese Fast-Food Industry and the Spread of Indigenous Cultures under Globalization

by Seanon Wong

Critics of globalization who bemoan the corruptive effects of McDonald's and KFC on fragile local cuisines often overlook the interesting corollary that globalization also serves to export local cuisines, stimulating instead of stifling cultural diversity. Taking as her major example Chinese fast-food, Wong makes a strong case that, far from being subsumed, local cultures have thrived in today's globalized environment by benefiting from enlarged markets and modern business management.

The impact of globalization on indigenous cultures has been hotly debated in recent years. Proponents of globalization celebrate it as the ultimate order of humanity. David Rothkopf, an international trade scholar, for example, argues that the "homogenizing influences of globalization ... [are] positive; globalization promotes integration and the removal not only of cultural barriers but of many of the negative dimensions of culture." Being the primary sponsors of globalization, Americans should not hesitate to promote their culture worldwide because it is "fundamentally different" and provides "the best model for the future."[1] On the other hand, critics condemn globalization as a new form of domination. The cultural imperialism thesis claims that "authentic, traditional and local culture in many parts of the world is being battered out of existence by the indiscriminate dumping of large quantities of slick commercial and media products, manly from the United States."[2] Regardless of one's take on this debate, one common assumption prevails: Indigenous cultures, as Barber famously proclaims, are giving way to the uniform culture of "McWorld."

Commentators have rightly observed that in China, as in other countries opening up to global exchanges, the entry of Western fast food (American in particular) has altered the dietary habits of many Chinese. However, it would be a grave oversight to conclude that Chinese culinary practices are in peril on the course towards cultural homogenization. In this article, I take a revisionist standpoint on the cultural effects of globalization. Using the culinary cultures of China as illustration, I refute the claim

Seanon Wong, "What's in a Dumpling?" *Stanford Journal of East Asian Affairs*, vol. 6, no. 1, pp. 25–32. Copyright © 2006 by Stanford Journal of East Asian Affairs. Reprinted with permission.

that globalization is simply cultural homogenization by highlighting that globalization has provided for the promotion and exportation of certain local cuisines; it can thus be understood as a means of propagating elements of traditional cultures in novel ways. The increasing awareness of Chinese culinary cultures worldwide offers a case in point: thanks to the proliferation of Chinese fast food establishments globally, Australians, Europeans and Americans can savor Chinese dumplings, Mongolian hotpots, Cantonese *dimsum* and northwestern Chinese noodles—cuisines that were mostly unheard of in the West before China lifted the "bamboo curtain" and resumed foreign contact in the 1970s—with as much convenience as hamburgers and pizzas are found in China nowadays.

My arguments are presented in three sections. First, I provide an overview of past discussions on China's experience with cultural globalization. Second, I argue that the extant literature is flawed by a theoretical misconception about globalization. As the experience of other developing countries confirms, globalization allows indigenous cultures to grow through participation in one important institution of modernity—the global market. To conclude, I discuss the origin and evolution of China's fast food industry. I select several notable chains to illustrate how China is contributing to global cultural diversity by reviving and exporting its culinary cultures abroad.

The Advent of McWorld?

As recently as two to three decades ago, it was assumed that hamburgers, French fries, pizza and other fast food products would never succeed in China. When McDonald's opened its first restaurant in Hong Kong in 1975, "few thought it would survive more than a few months."[3] American fast food chains brought products and services that bore little resemblance to the local culinary interests. In a region where rice is the traditional staple, fast food was largely perceived as a snack rather than a proper meal.[4] Besides, fast food table manners typically oppose traditional eating etiquette. For example, in Japan, eating while standing or with one's bare hands were social taboos.[5] Chinese societies shared similar attitudes, as formal meals are traditionally consumed with chopsticks and other utensils. How could Western companies such as KFC market its "finger-lickin'" chicken in such an adverse environment?

As a result, many were surprised when Western fast food became an enormous success in China. The industry expanded into mainland China in 1987 when KFC set up its first franchise in downtown Beijing. At that time, the restaurant was the world's largest fast food outlet, drawing up to 3,000 customers daily during its first year of operation and subsequently setting numerous company records.[6] The Golden Arches first appeared when McDonald's arrived at Shenzhen in 1990, and American fast food chains experienced a spectacular boom thereafter. When Beijing's first McDonald's opened in 1992, the restaurant—equipped with 700 seats and 29 cash registers—served 40,000 customers on its first day.[7] Currently, there are approximately 700 McDonald's all over mainland China. Hong Kong alone boasts over 200 with more than 10,000 employees. The company proudly declares on its website that in 2003, "McDonald's Hong Kong cracked 32.5 million U.S.A. Grade A eggs, prepared over 25 million pounds of French fries, and grilled over 4.4 million pounds of beef patties to serve its customers." KFC has been even more ambitious. From 2001 to 2003, the number of KFC franchises in the mainland doubled from 400 to over 800. Today, it has 1,400 in more than 200 Chinese cities, with a presence in every province save Tibet.

What does this phenomenal success of Western fast food reveal about cultural globalization? As anthropologist James Watson points out, Chinese cuisines "are not small-scale cultures under imminent threat of extinction; we are dealing with ... societies noted for their haute cuisines. If McDonald's can make inroads in these societies ... it may indeed be an irresistible force for world culinary change."[8] Indeed, at first glance, the introduction of American-style fast food in China may suggest that indigenous cultures will soon be tossed into the trash heap of history. In Beijing, people reacted with a mixture of surprise and anxiety. Some Chinese restaurants, including ones that have been local favorites for generations, were soon driven out of business as customers opted for Western food. The "invasion" was seen as "an alarming threat to both the local food industry and the national pride of Chinese culinary culture."[9]

This viewpoint is echoed by other academics: humanity, as some suggest, is on an irreversible track towards cultural homogenization. Benjamin Barber, for instance, foresees the future as "a busy portrait of onrushing economic, technological, and economic forces that demand integration and uniformity and that mesmerize peoples everywhere with fast music, fast computers, and fast food—MTV, Macintosh, and McDonald's—pressing nations into one homogeneous global theme park, one McWorld tied together by communications, information, entertainment, and commerce."[10] In his international bestseller, *Fast Food Nation*, journalist Eric Schlosser claims that the end of the Cold War "has led to an unprecedented 'Americanization' of the world, expressed in the growing popularity of movies, CDs, music videos, television shows, and clothing from the United States."[11]

The Western media has also sided with academic wisdom. According to the *Washington Post*, "China's cuisine is increasingly being altered by the growing consumption of fast food, with Chinese now more likely than Americans to eat takeout meals." Ironically, as China strives to assert its stature as an autonomous and distinctive power, it finds itself being integrated into the "Filet-O-Fish-eating, Pepsi-drinking cosmos."[12] Globalization has made the country susceptible to foreign ideas, and culinary preferences have shifted accordingly. For example, cheese traditionally had been too pungent to be palatable for many Chinese. But in recent years, aggressive marketing by multinational suppliers of dairy products—along with their allies in the supermarket and fast food industries—are gradually recasting Chinese tastes. The demand for cheese is growing.[13]

Chinese lifestyle has changed so dramatically that some even call into question the meaning of being Chinese. The *New York Times* notes that "ordinary people in China's cities have found much common ground with Americans, with the way they live converging rapidly in the marketplace ... Europeans may be wont to view every Big Mac as a terrifying sign of American cultural imperialism, but Chinese have mostly welcomed the invasion—indeed they have internalized it."[14] Studies show that receptiveness to American fast food has little to do with the taste of the food itself. Rather, most Chinese visit the Golden Arches or KFC because the experience satisfies their curiosity about, if not yearning for, American culture. The Big Mac, in the words of Yunxiang Yan, is "a Symbol of Americana." Especially to the younger generations, eating fast food is "an integral part of their new lifestyle, a way for them to participate in the transnational cultural system."[15]

Globalization and the Spread of Indigenous Cultures

Has the extant literature aptly described and explained the dynamics of globalization and its impact on the culinary cultures of China?[16] Those who lament the end of cultural diversity base their reasoning on two assumptions. The first is that globalization on the one hand and the persistence of indigenous cultures on the other are inherently antithetical; as Barber puts it, their relationship constitutes the "dialectic of McWorld".[17] The second assumption is that local identities exist *a priori*. A culture must already be recognized by both members within and without a community before being brought under the impact of globalization. For instance, to make the case that KFC is uprooting Beijing's native identity by ousting the city's famed roast duck from its restaurant menus, one must argue that people were conscious of a Beijing identity in the first place, and that Beijing delicacies are an essential component of this identity. Identity erosion would not be an issue if this identity never existed.

Both of these assumptions are flawed, as cultural identities are more a modern creation than a primordial conception. "Globalization," according to Tomlinson,

> is really the globalization of modernity, and modernity is the harbinger of identity ... Modernity ... means, above all, the *abstraction* of social and cultural practices from contexts of local particularity ... [It] institutionalizes and regulates cultural practices, including those by which we imagine attachment and belonging to a place or a community. The *mode* of such imagination it promotes is what we have come to know as 'cultural identity'. (italics in original)[18]

Contrary to popular belief, globalization is not a unilateral process in which a "McWorld" culture spreads, erodes and ultimately supplants indigenous cultures. Globalization produces—rather than victimizes—people's consciousness of their cultural environment. As in the case of Chinese culinary cultures, by successfully incorporating an important institution of modernity—a market economy—"globalizing" societies are empowered to repackage and promote their cultures beyond their geographical confines.

The experiences of Japan and India are instructive. According to Tulasi Srinivas, while the forces of "cultural globalization ... do enter India, cultural models are also increasingly emitted *from* India." The most prominent example is the rise of New Age culture, as reflected by the widespread practice of meditation, yoga and spiritual healing, and by the consumption of Indian cultural artifacts all over the world.[19] Furthermore, the "entry of multinational food companies has been widely reported ... but the concurrent boom in local foods and indigenous cuisine has been ignored." Inspired by the efficiency of Western management, the Indian catering sector "takes Indian recipes, simplifies them for quick production, and decreases time and cost to the consumer."[20] Indian society, as Srinivas succinctly posits, is experiencing "a restructuring of cultural concepts and institutions, incorporating the global and modern with the traditional and local."[21]

In addition, a culture's influence abroad has less to do with its inherent "strength"—a notion Huntington adopts in his famous analysis of civilization conflict—than with a society's level of economic development and integration with the global order. According to Tamotsu Aoki, the success of

American fast food in Japan since the 1960s only in part reflected a dietary revolution that transformed Japanese society. As the number of foreign restaurants grew exponentially, "a simultaneous process of fast-foodization of traditional Japanese food was occurring."[22] Nowadays, hamburgers have to compete with sushi in many Western countries.

Economic development also enabled Japanese corporations to promote their native cultures internationally. Suntory, for instance, pioneered "the penetration of Japanese mass culture and Japan's image in Asia" through the aggressive marketing of its beverages. Shiseido managed to infiltrate the saturated European market and compete on par with the European cosmetic giants because the company highlighted its Japanese origin. The exoticism associated with Japanese aesthetics bolstered Shiseido's popularity among European consumers. The case of Japan shows that globalization "progresses in accordance with the degree of development in each society, and the traditions and culture of each country and society are reflected in the process."[23]

Similar observations can be made for other Asian societies. For example, economic prosperity has provided the material foundation for Hong Kong and Taiwan to develop their entertainment sectors. Combining traditional Chinese with modern elements, Hong Kong and Taiwanese popular cultures have been enormously influential in mainland China[24] and also globally. Despite its history as a British colony and its cosmopolitan outlook, Hong Kong retained its Chinese roots. The city became an exemplar of Chinese culture as it became the chief producer and exporter of products ranging from Chinese *qipao* (cheongsams) to movies glorifying Shaolin martial arts.

Noodles vs. Sesame Seed Buns

Considering the omnipresence of McDonald's, KFC and Pizza Hut, American fast food has been a revolutionary force in China's everyday culture. They have yet to become the most popular dining locations, however. Indigenous cultures, including culinary traditions, are on the rise in China. Paradoxically, globalization is responsible for their revival.

The evolution of Hong Kong's culinary scene offers an ideal starting point for discussion, since the city has been on the forefront of global integration for a much longer time than mainland China. As American fast food chains have boomed in Hong Kong over the last three decades, the demand for fast food—American or otherwise—has grown even faster. Currently, Hong Kong ranks first in the world for frequency of fast food consumption. Over 60 percent of the city's denizens eat at takeway restaurants at least once a week, compared to only 41 percent and 35 percent in mainland China and the United States respectively.[25] Hong Kong's fast food industry, nevertheless, is dominated by Chinese companies such as Café de Coral, Fairwood and Maxim. Chinese dishes accounted for over 70 percent of fast food supplied in Hong Kong in 2002.

Just as India underwent a trend of "fastfoodization" as it joined the global economy, the success of Café de Coral in Hong Kong epitomized the mass commoditization of Chinese cuisines. Before the company was established in 1969, Hong Kong already had a long history of eating out. Café de Coral, however, was among the first to put Chinese food into large-scale production and consumption. Its initial strategy was simple: "It moved Hong Kong's street foods indoors, to a clean, well-lighted cafeteria that offered instant services and moderate prices...",[26] and business expanded steadily thereafter. Ironically, the real boost for Café de Carol came when the Golden Arches arrived in 1975. According to Michael Chan, the company's current chairman, "McDonald's landing ... inspired [Café de Coral's] confidence in self-service catering."[27] In the late-1970s, Café de Coral started using television commercials for mass advertising, and learning from McDonald's production model, established its first central food processing plant. Café de Coral is now Hong Kong's largest supplier of fast food.

Recently, Café de Coral extended its ambition beyond Hong Kong. The company's mission is to become "a distinguished corporation in the food and catering industry as the world's largest Chinese quick service restaurant group ..."[28] In 2000, it acquired Manchu Wok, Canada's largest Chinese fast food supplier and second largest in the United States. With over 200 restaurants throughout North America and the number rising constantly, Café de Coral prides itself "as a menu innovator specializing in fast and fresh Chinese cuisine, ranging in style from Cantonese to Szechwan." Chan boasts that eventually, "Chinese [food] will displace the burger and the pizza". The future of fast food, as *The Economist* predicts, "may be congee, tofu and roast duck."[29]

The recent flourish of local fast food restaurants in mainland China is reminiscent of Hong Kong's experience, as challenges posed by American fast food since the late-1980s have compelled many Chinese restaurateurs to react and innovate. It was against this backdrop of foreign competition that the genesis of Chinese fast food occurred. The industry's nascent phase—which lasted until the early-1990s—was marked by constant attempts by local entrepreneurs to imitate their foreign challengers. Numerous copy-cat restaurants, with names such as "McDuck's," "Mcdonald's" and "Modormal's", appeared in the major cities. Most of them have posed little threat to the Western fast food giants. One outstanding exception, however, is Ronghuaji, or "Glorious China Chicken".

Ronghuaji was founded in 1989 after two Shanghai entrepreneurs were inspired by KFC's business model. Since its inception, emulating KFC has been Ronghuaji's *modus operandi*. Franchises were set up in downtown Beijing and Shanghai, usually right next to existing KFC restaurants, selling chicken products prepared with a wide variety of Chinese recipes. Although all of its Beijing outlets failed to be consistently profitable and eventually went out of business, Ronghuaji's moment of success "demonstrated that Chinese entrepreneurs could employ Western technology and create an industry with 'Chinese characteristics.'"[30]

Throughout the 1990s, Chinese entrepreneurs learned that reinvention of Chinese cuisine in the form of fast food—rather than blind imitation of foreign recipes—provided a better path to business success. Alarmed by the popularity of the American chains, the Chinese government promulgated state policy in 1996 to foster a local fast food industry.[31] As Yan observes, the "fast-food fever" jumpstarted by the Western restaurants in Beijing "has given restaurant frequenters a stronger consumer consciousness and has created a Chinese notion of fast food and an associated culture."[32] By the end of 1996, over 800 local fast food companies were doing business in China, operating over 4,000 restaurants. The annual revenue was over RMB40 billion, accounting for one-fifth of the catering industry's total revenue. By 1999, annual revenue surged to RMB75 billion, 20 percent higher than the previous year, and accounted for one-third of the industry's total. The growth rate for fast food was 7 percent higher than the average growth rate of the catering industry as a whole. Furthermore, contrary to the myth of foreign domination, Chinese-style fast food occupied a much larger portion of the market. As of 2002, four out of five fast food operators are Chinese restaurants. Business turnover of fast food restaurants serving Western dishes in 2000 accounted for only one-third of the industry's total volume.[33]

The extraordinary growth of the Chinese fast food market is the direct result of rising consumerism. As in Café de Coral's success in Hong Kong, however, the real impetus to growth was the introduction of fast food management to aspiring Chinese entrepreneurs. Several of the industry's leading figures were former employees of McDonald's and KFC—an experience which equipped them with Western management concepts and techniques. The success of their business owed much to their ability to combine "modern methods of preparation and hygiene with traditional Chinese cuisine ..." Beijing's most famous restaurant, Quanjude Roast Duck Restaurant, even sent its management team to McDonald's in 1993. A year later, it introduced its own roast duck fast food.[34]

An important business concept that helped Chinese chains to proliferate is franchising. Today, nearly all fast food restaurants in China publicize telephone hotlines for franchise information. With the friendly denomination of *jiameng rexian* (literally, "the hotline to join the league") these numbers are usually posted in prominent places, such as restaurant entrances. For instance, in 1996, Daniang Dumplings was merely a community restaurant in Changzhou in Jiangsu province with only six employees selling arguably the most prototypical of northern Chinese food—*shuijiao* (boiled dumplings). Within the next nine years, it expanded into an empire of over 150 franchises throughout the country and as far as Indonesia and Australia.

The phenomenal success of Café de Coral, Daniang Dumplings and others is of great significance not only to the preservation of Chinese culinary cultures at home, but also their influence abroad. When a new restaurant is established in a foreign territory, not only is its food consumed, but its associated culture is also propagated among the host community. The case of Mongolian hotpot illustrates how a culture that was once found in a restricted geographical region can spread through market expansion. In the past, Mongolian hotpot was found mostly in northern China; it was considered an exotic cuisine even to Chinese of other regions. In the past six years, however, Xiaofeiyang—a chain enterprise started at the turn of the century with just one outlet in Inner Mongolia—transformed hotpot into a regular repast throughout the country. Today, the chain owns franchises in as far south as Guangdong and Hong Kong—the geographical opposite of the cuisine's origin in China. It has an aggressive plan to expand overseas, with outlets already set up in North America.

Another remarkable example is Malan Hand-Pulled Noodles. The company opened its first restaurant in 1993, serving traditional dishes from northwestern China in a fast food setting. By the end of 2002 it had multiplied into 436 outlets nationwide. By 2004, it had expanded outside of China, into Singapore, Western Europe, and California.[35] On the opening day of its first restaurant in the United States, company manager Frank Wang declared that by "inheriting the essence of traditional beef noodles, and maintaining the original taste of Chinese food culture, Malan Noodle achieves further development by applying the modern fast food concept, thus making the national snack flourish."[36]

Conclusion

The primary lesson one can learn from the thriving Chinese fast food sector is that globalization is facilitating the spread of cultural diversity, rather than—as the word "globalization" so misleadingly suggests—a tendency towards cultural homogeneity. The opening up of Chinese society cultivated a population curious about outside ideas, values and cultures. A taste for foreign lifestyle, however, is not the same as cultural submission. As the Chinese learned to become "modern," globalization also nurtured a class of outward-looking entrepreneurs who extracted elements of Chinese culture and combined them with modern business management to compete in the global economy.

The arguments presented in this article serve to rectify the misconception of cultural homogenization that underpinned intellectual exchanges in the past. The case of Chinese culinary cultures, however, represents only the tip of the iceberg of China's contribution to global cultural trends. Other areas of Chinese traditions are also experiencing a revival. The production, research and development of Chinese medicine, for example, have been modernized; its practice is gaining wide acceptance in many Western countries. Various types of *qigong*—the Chinese art of self-healing that combines meditation and body movements—are also proliferating. To truly understand the fate of indigenous cultures under globalization, analysts should pay more attention to China as a cultural emitter, rather than simply labeling it a passive follower of a purported global culture.

Endnotes

1. David Rothkopf, "In Praise of Cultural Imperialism? Effects of Globalization on Culture," *Foreign Policy*, June 22, 1997, 39, 48–49.

2. John Tomlinson, *Cultural Imperialism: A Critical Introduction* (Baltimore: Johns Hopkins University Press, 1991), 8.

3. James L. Watson, "McDonald's in Hong Kong: Consumerism, Dietary Change, and the Rise of a Children's Culture," in James L. Watson, ed., *Golden Arches East: McDonald's in East Asia* (Stanford: Stanford University Press, 1997), 78.

4. Ibid., 84.

5. Emiko Ohnuki-Tierney, "McDonald's in Japan: Changing Manners and Etiquette," in James L. Watson, ed., *Golden Arches East: McDonald's in East Asia* (Stanford: Stanford University Press, 1997), 175–180.

6. Eriberto P. Lozada, Jr., "Globalized Childhood?: Kentucky Fried Chicken in Beijing," in Jun Jing, ed., *Feeding China's Little Emperors: Food, Children, and Social Change* (Stanford: Stanford University Press, 2000), 117.

7. Yunxiang Yan, "McDonald's in Beijing: The Localization of Americana," in James L. Watson, ed., *Golden Arches East: McDonald's in East Asia* (Stanford: Stanford University Press, 1997), 39.

8. James L. Watson, "Introduction: Transnationalism, Localization, and Fast Foods in East Asia," in James L. Watson, ed., *Golden Arches East: McDonald's in East Asia* (Stanford: Stanford University Press, 1997), 6.

9. Yunxiang Yan, "Of Hamburger and Social Space: Consuming McDonald's in Beijing," in Deborah S. Davis, ed., *The Consumer Revolution in Urban China* (Berkeley and Los Angeles: University of California Press, 2000), 205.

10. Benjamin Barber, *Jihad vs. McWorld* (New York: Ballantine Books, 1995), 4.

11. Eric Schlosser, *Fast Food Nation: The Dark Side of the All-American Meal* (New York: Perennial, 2002), 239–240.

12. Peter S. Goodman, "Fast Food Takes a Bit Out of Chinese Culture," *Washington Post*, December 26, 2004.

13. Rebecca Buckman, "Let Them Eat Cheese," *Far Eastern Economic Review*, December 11, 2003.

14. Elisabeth Rosenthal, "Buicks, Starbucks and Fried Chicken. Still China?," *New York Times*, February 25, 2002.

15. Yan, "McDonald's in Beijing: The Localization of Americana," 40–53.

16. Watson and his team have proposed a rebuttal to the cultural homogenization thesis. They claim that albeit its popularity in East Asia, McDonald's has been more or less detached from its American root. In order to cater to the particular needs of local markets, the food and services of McDonald's have changed so much that the company has ceased to be a fast food supplier in the American sense. For further details, see James L. Watson, ed., *Golden Arches East: McDonald's in East Asia* (Stanford: Stanford University Press, 1997).

17. Barber, op.cit., 6.

18. John Tomlinson, "Globalization and Cultural Identity," in David Held and Anthony McGrew, eds., *The Global Transformations Reader: An Introduction to the Globalization Debate* (Cambridge: Polity Press, 2003), 60.

19. Tulasi Srinivas, "'A Tryst with Destiny': The Indian Case of Cultural Revolution," in Peter L. Berger and Samuel P. Huntington, eds., *Many Globalizations: Cultural Diversity in the Contemporary World* (New York: Oxford University Press, 2002), 90.

20. Ibid., 94–99.

21. Ibid., 106.

22. Tamotsu Aoki, "Aspects of Globalization in Contemporary Japan," in Peter L. Berger and Samuel P. Huntington, eds., *Many Globalizations: Cultural Diversity in the Contemporary World* (Oxford University Press, 2002), 68–80.

23. Ibid., 74.

24. Thomas Gold, "Go With Your Feelings: Hong Kong and Taiwan Popular Culture in Greater China," *China Quarterly*, vol. 136 (December 1993), 907–925.

25. ACNielsen, *Consumers in Asia Pacific—Our Fast Food/Take Away Consumption Habits*, 2nd Half, 2004.

26. Watson, "McDonald's in Hong Kong: Consumerism, Dietary Change, and the Rise of a Children's Culture," 81.

27. Café de Coral company profile, Hong Kong Chamber of Commerce, available online at <www.chamber.org.hk/info/member_a_week/member_profile.asp?id=80>.

28. Company website, <www.cafedecoral.com.>.

29. "Fast Chinese Cuisine: Junk Food?," *The Economist*, December 7, 2002.

30. Lozada, Jr., op. cit., 125.

31. Yan, "Of Hamburger and Social Space," 207.

32. Ibid., 201.

33. *Fast Food Market Report* (Friedl Business Information, 2002)

34. Yan, "McDonald's in Beijing," 74–75.

35. Malan Noodle Corporate Website, "Introduction," <http://www.malan.com.cn/introduce_en.htm>

36. Malan Noodle Corporate Website, "Grand Opening of Malan Noodle Outlet Restaurant in Monterey Park, USA," <http://www.malan.com.cn/ news/73147200312264325_en.htm>

Clash of Globalizations

by Stanley Hoffmann

A New Paradigm?

What is the state of international relations today? In the 1990s, specialists concentrated on the partial disintegration of the global order's traditional foundations: states. During that decade, many countries, often those born of decolonization, revealed themselves to be no more than pseudostates, without solid institutions, internal cohesion, or national consciousness. The end of communist coercion in the former Soviet Union and in the former Yugoslavia also revealed long-hidden ethnic tensions. Minorities that were or considered themselves oppressed demanded independence. In Iraq, Sudan, Afghanistan, and Haiti, rulers waged open warfare against their subjects. These wars increased the importance of humanitarian interventions, which came at the expense of the hallowed principles of national sovereignty and nonintervention. Thus the dominant tension of the decade was the clash between the fragmentation of states (and the state system) and the progress of economic, cultural, and political integration—in other words, globalization.

Everybody has understood the events of September 11 as the beginning of a new era. But what does this break mean? In the conventional approach to international relations, war took place among states. But in September, poorly armed individuals suddenly challenged, surprised, and wounded the world's dominant superpower. The attacks also showed that, for all its accomplishments, globalization makes an awful form of violence easily accessible to hopeless fanatics. Terrorism is the bloody link between interstate relations and global society. As countless individuals and groups are becoming global actors along with states, insecurity and vulnerability are rising. To assess today's bleak state of affairs, therefore, several questions are necessary. What concepts help explain the new global order? What is the condition of the interstate part of international relations? And what does the emerging global civil society contribute to world order?

Sound and Fury

Two models made a great deal of noise in the 1990s. The first one—Francis Fukuyama's "End of History" thesis—was not vindicated by events. To be sure, his argument predicted the end of ideological conflicts, not history itself, and the triumph of political and economic liberalism. That point is correct in a narrow sense: the "secular religions" that fought each other so bloodily in the last century are now dead. But Fukuyama failed to note that nationalism remains very much alive. Moreover, he ignored the explosive potential of religious wars that has extended to a large part of the Islamic world.

Fukuyama's academic mentor, the political scientist Samuel Huntington, provided a few years later a gloomier account that saw a very different world. Huntington predicted that violence resulting from international anarchy and the absence of common values and institutions would erupt among civilizations rather than among states or ideologies. But Huntington's conception of what constitutes a civilization was hazy. He failed to take into account sufficiently conflicts within each so-called civilization, and he overestimated the importance of religion in the behavior of non-Western elites, who are often secularized and Westernized. Hence he could not clearly define the link between a civilization and the foreign policies of its member states.

Other, less sensational models still have adherents. The "realist" orthodoxy insists that nothing has changed in international relations since Thucydides and Machiavelli: a state's military and economic power determines its fate; interdependence and international institutions are secondary and fragile phenomena; and states' objectives are imposed by the threats to their survival or security. Such is the world described by Henry Kissinger. Unfortunately, this venerable model has trouble integrating change, especially globalization and the rise of nonstate actors. Moreover, it overlooks the need for international cooperation that results from such new threats as the proliferation of weapons of mass destruction (WMD). And it ignores what the scholar Raymond Aron called the "germ of a universal consciousness": the liberal, pro-market norms that developed states have come to hold in common.

Taking Aron's point, many scholars today interpret the world in terms of a triumphant globalization that submerges borders through new means of information and communication. In this universe, a state choosing to stay closed invariably faces decline and growing discontent among its subjects, who are eager for material progress. But if it opens up, it must accept a reduced role that is mainly limited to social protection, physical protection against aggression or civil war, and maintaining national identity. The champion of this epic without heroes is *The New York Times* columnist Thomas Friedman. He contrasts barriers with open vistas, obsolescence with modernity, state control with free markets. He sees in globalization the light of dawn, the "golden straitjacket" that will force contentious publics to understand that the logic of globalization is that of peace (since war would interrupt globalization and therefore progress) and democracy (because new technologies increase individual autonomy and encourage initiative).

Back to Reality

These models come up hard against three realities. First, rivalries among great powers (and the capacity of smaller states to exploit such tensions) have most certainly not disappeared. For a while now, however, the existence of nuclear weapons has produced a certain degree of prudence among the powers that have them. The risk of destruction that these weapons hold has moderated the game and turned nuclear arms into instruments of last resort. But the game could heat up as more states seek other WMD as a way of narrowing the gap between the nuclear club and the other powers. The sale of such weapons thus becomes a hugely contentious issue, and efforts to slow down the spread of all WMD, especially to dangerous "rogue" states, can paradoxically become new causes of violence.

Second, if wars between states are becoming less common, wars within them are on the rise—as seen in the former Yugoslavia, Iraq, much of Africa, and Sri Lanka. Uninvolved states first tend to hesitate to get engaged in these complex conflicts, but they then (sometimes) intervene to prevent these conflicts from turning into regional catastrophes. The interveners, in turn, seek the help of the United Nations or regional organizations to rebuild these states, promote stability, and prevent future fragmentation and misery.

Third, states' foreign policies are shaped not only by realist geopolitical factors such as economics and military power but by domestic politics. Even in undemocratic regimes, forces such as xenophobic passions, economic grievances, and transnational ethnic solidarity can make policymaking far more complex and less predictable. Many states—especially the United States—have to grapple with the frequent interplay of competing government branches. And the importance of individual leaders and their personalities is often underestimated in the study of international affairs.

For realists, then, transnational terrorism creates a formidable dilemma. If a state is the victim of private actors such as terrorists, it will try to eliminate these groups by depriving them of sanctuaries and punishing the states that harbor them. The national interest of the attacked state will therefore require either armed interventions against governments supporting terrorists or a course of prudence and discreet pressure on other governments to bring these terrorists to justice. Either option requires a questioning of sovereignty—the holy concept of realist theories. The classical realist universe of Hans Morgenthau and Aron may therefore still be very much alive in a world of states, but it has increasingly hazy contours and offers only difficult choices when it faces the threat of terrorism.

At the same time, the real universe of globalization does not resemble the one that Friedman celebrates. In fact, globalization has three forms, each with its own problems. First is economic globalization, which results from recent revolutions in technology, information, trade, foreign investment, and international business. The main actors are companies, investors, banks, and private services industries, as well as states and international organizations. This present form of capitalism, ironically foreseen by Karl Marx and Friedrich Engels, poses a central dilemma between efficiency and fairness. The specialization and integration of firms make it possible to increase aggregate wealth, but the logic of pure capitalism does not favor social justice. Economic globalization has thus become a formidable cause of inequality among and within states, and the concern for global competitiveness limits the aptitude of states and other actors to address this problem.

Next comes cultural globalization. It stems from the technological revolution and economic globalization, which together foster the flow of cultural goods. Here the key choice is between uniformization (often termed "Americanization") and diversity. The result is both a "disenchantment of the world" (in Max Weber's words) and a reaction against uniformity. The latter takes form in a renaissance of local cultures and languages as well as assaults against Western culture, which is denounced as an arrogant bearer of a secular, revolutionary ideology and a mask for U.S. hegemony.

Optimism regarding globalization rests on very fragile foundations.

Finally there is political globalization, a product of the other two. It is characterized by the preponderance of the United States and its political institutions and by a vast array of international and regional organizations and transgovernmental networks (specializing in areas such as policing or migration or justice). It is also marked by private institutions that are neither governmental nor purely national—say, Doctors Without Borders or Amnesty International. But many of these agencies lack democratic accountability and are weak in scope, power, and authority. Furthermore, much uncertainty hangs over the fate of American hegemony, which faces significant resistance abroad and is affected by America's own oscillation between the temptations of domination and isolation.

The benefits of globalization are undeniable. But Friedmanlike optimism rests on very fragile foundations. For one thing, globalization is neither inevitable nor irresistible. Rather, it is largely an American creation, rooted in the period after World War II and based on U.S. economic might. By extension, then, a deep and protracted economic crisis in the United States could have as devastating an effect on globalization as did the Great Depression.

Second, globalization's reach remains limited because it excludes many poor countries, and the states that it does transform react in different ways. This fact stems from the diversity of economic and social conditions at home as well as from partisan politics. The world is far away from a perfect integration of markets, services, and factors of production. Sometimes the simple existence of borders slows down and can even paralyze this integration; at other times it gives integration the flavors and colors of the dominant state (as in the case of the Internet).

Third, international civil society remains embryonic. Many nongovernmental organizations reflect only a tiny segment of the populations of their members' states. They largely represent only modernized countries, or those in which the weight of the state is not too heavy. Often, NGOs have little independence from governments.

Fourth, the individual emancipation so dear to Friedman does not quickly succeed in democratizing regimes, as one can see today in China. Nor does emancipation prevent public institutions such as the International Monetary Fund, the World Bank, or the World Trade Organization from remaining opaque in their activities and often arbitrary and unfair in their rulings.

Fifth, the attractive idea of improving the human condition through the abolition of barriers is dubious. Globalization is in fact only a sum of techniques (audio and videocassettes, the Internet, instantaneous communications) that are at the disposal of states or private actors. Self-interest and ideology, not humanitarian reasons, are what drive these actors. Their behavior is quite different from the vision of globalization as an Enlightenment-based utopia that is simultaneously scientific, rational, and universal.

For many reasons—misery, injustice, humiliation, attachment to traditions, aspiration to more than just a better standard of living—this "Enlightenment" stereotype of globalization thus provokes revolt and dissatisfaction.

Another contradiction is also at work. On the one hand, international and transnational cooperation is necessary to ensure that globalization will not be undermined by the inequalities resulting from market fluctuations, weak state-sponsored protections, and the incapacity of many states to improve their fates by themselves. On the other hand, cooperation presupposes that many states and rich private players operate altruistically—which is certainly not the essence of international relations—or practice a remarkably generous conception of their long-term interests. But the fact remains that most rich states still refuse to provide sufficient development aid or to intervene in crisis situations such as the genocide in Rwanda. That reluctance compares poorly with the American enthusiasm to pursue the fight against al Qaeda and the Taliban. What is wrong here is not patriotic enthusiasm as such, but the weakness of the humanitarian impulse when the national interest in saving non-American victims is not self-evident.

Imagined Communities

Among the many effects of globalization on international politics, three hold particular importance. The first concerns institutions. Contrary to realist predictions, most states are not perpetually at war with each other. Many regions and countries live in peace; in other cases, violence is internal rather than state-to-state. And since no government can do everything by itself, interstate organisms have emerged. The result, which can be termed "global society," seeks to reduce the potentially destructive effects of national regulations on the forces of integration. But it also seeks to ensure fairness in the world market and create international regulatory regimes in such areas as trade, communications, human rights, migration, and refugees. The main obstacle to this effort is the reluctance of states to accept global directives that might constrain the market or further reduce their sovereignty. Thus the UN's powers remain limited and sometimes only purely theoretical. International criminal justice is still only a spotty and contested last resort. In the world economy—where the market, not global governance, has been the main beneficiary of the state's retreat—the network of global institutions is fragmented and incomplete. Foreign investment remains ruled by bilateral agreements. Environmental protection is badly ensured, and issues such as migration and population growth are largely ignored. Institutional networks are not powerful enough to address unfettered short-term capital movements, the lack of international regulation on bankruptcy and competition, and primitive coordination among rich countries. In turn, the global "governance" that does exist is partial and weak at a time when economic globalization deprives many states of independent monetary and fiscal policies, or it obliges them to make cruel choices between economic competitiveness and the preservation of social safety nets. All the while, the United States displays an increasing impatience toward institutions that weigh on American freedom of action. Movement toward a world state looks increasingly unlikely. The more state sovereignty crumbles under the blows of globalization or such recent developments as humanitarian intervention and the fight against terrorism, the more states cling to what is left to them.

Second, globalization has not profoundly challenged the enduring national nature of citizenship. Economic life takes place on a global scale, but human identity remains national—hence the strong resistance to cultural homogenization. Over the centuries, increasingly centralized states have expanded their functions and tried to forge a sense of common identity for their subjects. But no central power in the world can do the same thing today, even in the European Union. There, a single currency and advanced economic coordination have not yet produced a unified economy or strong central institutions endowed with legal autonomy, nor have they resulted in a sense of postnational citizenship. The march from national identity to one that would be both national and European has only just begun. A world very partially unified by technology still has no collective consciousness or collective solidarity. What states are unwilling to do the world market cannot do all by itself, especially in engendering a sense of world citizenship.

Third, there is the relationship between globalization and violence. The traditional state of war, even if it is limited in scope, still persists. There are high risks of regional explosions in the Middle East and in East Asia, and these could seriously affect relations between the major powers. Because of this threat, and because modern arms are increasingly costly, the "anarchical society" of states lacks the resources to correct some of globalization's most flagrant flaws. These very costs, combined with the classic distrust among international actors who prefer to try to preserve their security alone or through traditional alliances, prevent a more satisfactory institutionalization of world politics—for example, an increase of the UN's powers. This step could happen if global society were provided with sufficient forces to prevent a conflict or restore peace—but it is not.

Globalization, far from spreading peace, thus seems to foster conflicts and resentments. The lowering of various barriers celebrated by Friedman, especially the spread of global media, makes it possible for the most deprived or oppressed to compare their fate with that of the free and well-off. These dispossessed then ask for help from others with common resentments, ethnic origin, or religious faith. Insofar as globalization enriches some and uproots many, those who are both poor and uprooted may seek revenge and self-esteem in terrorism.

Globalization and Terror

Terrorism is the poisoned fruit of several forces. It can be the weapon of the weak in a classic conflict among states or within a state, as in Kashmir or the Palestinian territories. But it can also be seen as a product of globalization. Transnational terrorism is made possible by the vast array of communication tools. Islamic terrorism, for example, is not only based on support for the Palestinian struggle and opposition to an invasive American presence. It is also fueled by a resistance to "unjust" economic globalization and to a Western culture deemed threatening to local religions and cultures.

If globalization often facilitates terrorist violence, the fight against this war without borders is potentially disastrous for both economic development and globalization. Antiterrorist measures restrict mobility and financial flows, while new terrorist attacks could lead the way for an antiglobalist reaction comparable to the chauvinistic paroxysms of the 1930s. Global terrorism is not the simple extension of war among states to nonstates. It is the subversion of traditional ways of war because it does not care about the sovereignty of either its enemies or the allies who shelter them. It provokes its victims to take measures that, in the name of legitimate defense, violate knowingly the sovereignty of those states accused of encouraging terror. (After all, it was not the Taliban's infamous domestic violations of human rights that led the United States into Afghanistan; it was the Taliban's support of Osama bin Laden.)

But all those trespasses against the sacred principles of sovereignty do not constitute progress toward global society, which has yet to agree on a common definition of terrorism or on a common policy against it. Indeed, the beneficiaries of the antiterrorist "war" have been the illiberal, poorer states that have lost so much of their sovereignty of late. Now the crackdown on terror allows them to tighten their controls on their own people, products, and money. They can give themselves new reasons to violate individual rights in the name of common defense against insecurity—and thus stop the slow, hesitant march toward international criminal justice.

Another main beneficiary will be the United States, the only actor capable of carrying the war against terrorism into all corners of the world. Despite its power, however, America cannot fully protect itself against future terrorist acts, nor can it fully overcome its ambivalence toward forms of interstate cooperation that might restrict U.S. freedom of action. Thus terrorism is a global phenomenon that ultimately reinforces the enemy—the state—at the same time as it tries to destroy it. The states that are its targets have no interest in applying the laws of war to their fight against terrorists; they have every interest in treating terrorists as outlaws and pariahs. The champions of globalization have sometimes glimpsed the "jungle" aspects of economic globalization, but few observers foresaw similar aspects in global terrorist and antiterrorist violence.

Finally, the unique position of the United States raises a serious question over the future of world affairs. In the realm of interstate problems, American behavior will determine whether the non-super-powers and weak states will continue to look at the United States as a friendly power (or at least a tolerable hegemon), or whether they are provoked by Washington's hubris into coalescing against American preponderance. America may be a hegemon, but combining rhetorical overkill and ill-defined designs is full of risks. Washington has yet to understand that nothing is more dangerous for a "hyperpower" than the temptation of unilateralism. It may well believe that the constraints of international agreements and organizations are not necessary, since U.S. values and power are all that is needed for world order. But in reality, those same international constraints provide far better opportunities for leadership than arrogant demonstrations of contempt for others' views, and they offer useful ways of restraining unilateralist behavior in other states. A hegemon concerned with prolonging its rule should be especially interested in using internationalist methods and institutions, for the gain in influence far exceeds the loss in freedom of action.

In the realm of global society, much will depend on whether the United States will overcome its frequent indifference to the costs that globalization imposes on poorer countries. For now, Washington is too reluctant to make resources available for economic development, and it remains hostile to agencies that monitor and regulate the global market. All too often, the right-leaning tendencies of the American political system push U.S. diplomacy toward an excessive reliance on America's greatest asset—military strength—as well as an excessive reliance on market capitalism and a "sovereigntism" that offends and alienates. That the mighty United States is so afraid of the world's imposing its "inferior" values on Americans is often a source of ridicule and indignation abroad.

Odd Man Out

For all these tensions, it is still possible that the American war on terrorism will be contained by prudence, and that other governments will give priority to the many internal problems created by interstate rivalries and the flaws of globalization. But the world risks being squeezed between a new Scylla and Charybdis. The Charybdis is universal intervention, unilaterally decided by American leaders who are convinced that they have found a global mission provided by a colossal threat. Presentable as an epic contest between good and evil, this struggle offers the best way of rallying the population and overcoming domestic divisions. The Scylla is resignation to universal chaos in the form of new attacks by future bin Ladens, fresh humanitarian disasters, or regional wars that risk escalation. Only through wise judgment can the path between them be charted.

We can analyze the present, but we cannot predict the future. We live in a world where a society of uneven and often virtual states overlaps with a global society burdened by weak public institutions and underdeveloped civil society. A single power dominates, but its economy could become unmanageable or distrupted by future terrorist attacks. Thus to predict the future confidently would be highly incautious or naive. To be sure, the world has survived many crises, but it has done so at a very high price, even in times when WMD were not available.

Precisely because the future is neither decipherable nor determined, students of international relations face two missions. They must try to understand what goes on by taking an inventory of current goods and disentangling the threads of present networks. But the fear of confusing the empirical with the normative should not prevent them from writing as political philosophers at a time when many philosophers are extending their conceptions of just society to international relations. How can one make the global house more livable? The answer presupposes a political philosophy that would be both just and acceptable even to those whose values have other foundations. As the late philosopher Judith Shklar did, we can take as a point of departure and as a guiding thread the fate of the victims of violence, oppression, and misery; as a goal, we should seek material and moral emancipation. While taking into account the formidable constraints of the world as it is, it is possible to loosen them.

Introduction

by Suzanne Staggenborg

Social movements around the world have used a wide variety of protest tactics to bring about enormous social changes, influencing cultural arrangements, public opinion, and government policies. Consider the following examples:

- At the beginning of the twentieth century British suffragists, impatient with the failure of their government to give women the vote, protested in Parliament, marched in the streets, chained themselves to the railings outside the Prime Minister's residence, and went on hunger strikes. Numerous suffragists were jailed and force-fed, and many were beaten by police when they participated in demonstrations. The militancy and bravery of the suffragists inspired movement activists around the world. By the 1920s suffrage movements had won the vote for women in many different countries, but struggles for a full range of women's rights continued. Today, the women's movement continues to combat problems such as violence against women and to fight for access to education, employment, and citizenship rights for women around the world.

- In the southern United States, civil rights activists in the 1950s and 1960s used boycotts, sit-ins, mass demonstrations, 'freedom rides' on public transportation, and voter registration drives to secure basic rights for blacks. Activists were jailed, beaten, and murdered as they combatted a society in which African Americans were denied service in many public establishments, forced to sit in the back of buses and give up their seats to whites, and disenfranchised by threats of violence when they attempted to vote. After the civil rights movement won battles over desegregation of public facilities and voting rights, blacks became a political force in the South and African Americans served as mayors of cities that once denied them basic rights, such as Atlanta, Georgia, and Jackson, Mississippi.

- In Canada, a group calling itself the Association for Social Knowledge formed in Vancouver in 1964 to begin the long process of creating a positive gay identity at a time when gays and lesbians were denied basic rights such as employment and often arrested simply for socializing together in bars and other public places. By 1971, the low-key approach of the early activists gave way to a gay liberation movement that marched on Parliament Hill to demand the 'freedom to love'. Since the 1970s, gay and lesbian rights groups have lobbied for inclusion in human rights codes, filed lawsuits to secure legal protections, and staged numerous 'gay pride' parades and demonstrations. In 2005, after many years of equality-seeking work by the lesbian and gay rights movement, same-sex marriage became legal throughout Canada.

- In 1999, a seemingly new movement for global justice burst on the scene with large demonstrations against the World Trade Organization meetings in Seattle, which virtually closed down the WTO conference. In Quebec City in 2001, activists stormed the fence that had been erected to keep protestors from disrupting meetings to establish a Free Trade Area of the Americas (FTAA). These and other demonstrations around the world helped to raise public consciousness about the impacts of the trade and monetary policies of global institutions. The global justice movement works to unite local and international activists and organizations from a variety of different social movements and attempts to influence international labour, environmental, and human rights standards.

In all of these examples, individuals have banded together in collective efforts to create social change by presenting demands for justice and pressuring authorities to respond. Movements have organized to protect the environment, oppose wars, and advocate for the rights of more and more groups, including workers, women, gay men and lesbians, students, disabled people, senior citizens, and many racial and ethnic groups. Social movements are important vehicles for social and political change, yet it is not always apparent how it is possible to bring together a variety of groups and individuals with varying interests and ideologies to form a cohesive movement capable of effecting real changes. Thus, social movement theorists attempt to answer a variety of questions about the growth and impact of movements, which are relevant to activists and policy-makers as well as to social scientists. Key questions include why movements originate when they do, how they attract and maintain support, how they present issues and formulate strategies and tactics, how they structure organizations, how they change cultures, why they generate opposition and sometimes decline, and how and why they succeed or fail in achieving their objectives.

The Origins of the Social Movement

The social movement, as we know it today, is a relatively recent means of organizing for social change. Charles Tilly, who has done extensive historical research on the origins of the social movement in the Western world, quotes from an account of a 'movement' in 1682 in Narbonne, France, to make this point:

> [T]here was a little movement in Narbonne on the occasion of the collection of the cosse tax, which had been ordered by an act of the royal council. Many women gathered with the common people, and threw stones at the tax collectors, but the Consuls and the leading citizens hurried over and put a stop to the disorder. (Quoted in Tilly, 1984: 297)

Although this seventeenth-century incident is referred to as a 'little movement', it bears scant resemblance to what we think of today as a 'social movement'. The term *petit mouvement* was part of the vocabulary of the time, used to refer to 'a localized collective action by ordinary people which the authorities considered necessary and proper to end by force' (ibid., 298). Tilly points out that today we would not consider this type of action a **social movement** unless it were more enduring, part of a series of collective actions rather than one incident, and enacted by participants with common interests and a distinct identity, who had broader goals than stopping a particular tax. He uses the concept of a **repertoire of collective action** to get at the idea that limited forms of protest are familiar during a given time. Our protest repertoire has changed dramatically since the women of Narbonne stoned their tax collectors.

Collective action in Western countries such as France and England (see Tilly, 1986, 1995, 2004a) was once localized and defensive. People got together within their communities to defend local interests, using protest forms drawn from local culture and typically directed at particular individuals. For example, the **charivari** was a traditional form of collective action directed towards individuals who had transgressed community norms, such as a married man who got a single woman pregnant. The guilty party would be subject to a noisy demonstration designed to humiliate him or her before the community. As historian Edward Shorter (1975: 219) describes, there were many variations of the charivari, based on local tradition:

> Sometimes the demonstration would consist of masked individuals circling somebody's house at night, screaming, beating on pans, and blowing cow horns (which the local butchers rented out). On other occasions the offender would be seized and marched through the streets, seated perhaps backwards on a donkey or forced to wear a placard describing his sins. Sometimes the youth would administer the charivari; on other occasions villagers of all ages and sexes would mix together.

Despite such variations, the charivari shared characteristics in common with other forms of protest in the traditional repertoire, which also included food riots, grain seizures, and land revolts (Tarrow, 1998: 32–6). All of these traditional forms of action were short in duration and local in scope; even when a national issue such as taxation was involved, the targets of the protest were local authorities and the actions were particular to the local community (Tilly, 1995: 45). In contrast to this traditional repertoire, a new repertoire of collective action, consisting of tactics such as large-scale demonstrations, strikes, and boycotts, began to develop in Europe and North America in the late eighteenth century and became firmly established in the nineteenth century. The new repertoire was cosmopolitan rather than parochial, with protests often targeted at national rather than local authorities. The tactics of the new repertoire were 'modular' (Tarrow, 1998) in that they could easily be transported to many locales and situations, rather than being tied to local communities and rituals. For example, the boycott and the mass petition were tactics that could be aimed at any target with regard to any type of grievance. The nineteenth-century abolition movement was one of the first social movements to use these tactics, organizing a boycott of sugar grown with slave labour and sending petitions signed by large numbers of supporters to the British Parliament (Tarrow, 1998: 38–9).

The story of how this shift in repertoires came about is a complicated one (see Tilly, 1995, 2004a, 2004b; Tarrow, 1998), but it involved the expansion of nation-states and the spread of capitalism. With the development of national electoral politics, special-purpose associations formed to represent the interests of various groups, including dissident aristocrats and bourgeois activists who sometimes formed alliances with dissatisfied workers. These coalitions adopted new means of making claims, such as mass petitions and disciplined marches, to replace the often violent direct actions, such as food riots and grain seizures, which had been central to the older repertoire and were more likely to be repressed by authorities. With the spread of wage labour, workers gained independence from particular landlords and masters, and were freer to engage in political activities (Tilly, 2004b: 27). The repertoire of collective action gradually changed, and the social movement became part of the new repertoire.

Thus, the social movement emerged in a particular historical period as a result of large-scale social changes and political conditions that made it possible. Although there have been some innovations in protest forms, social movements still select tactics from essentially the same repertoire of contention that became established in the nineteenth century. Tilly notes, however, that the social movement and its repertoire are products of historical circumstances and could change as political conditions change. For example, insofar as centralized nation-states are replaced with transnational bodies, the national social movement may become a less effective form of political organization (ibid., 14). Indeed, transnational movements and organizations are already significant, and new forms of action, such as Internet-based protests, have developed with new technologies and processes of globalization.

Defining Social Movements

Research by Charles Tilly and others on the origins of the social movement has been influential in promoting a political view of social movements (see McAdam et al., 2001). In this view, social movements are one form of **contentious politics:**

> contentious in the sense that social movements involve collective making of claims that, if realized, would conflict with someone else's interests, political in the sense that governments of one sort or another figure somehow in the claim making, whether as claimants, objects of claims, allies of the objects, or monitors of the contention. (Tilly 2004b: 3)

According to Tilly, social movements as they developed in the West after 1750 came to consist of sustained **campaigns** that made collective claims aimed at authorities. They typically created special-purpose associations or coalitions and engaged in strategies such as demonstrations, petition drives, public statements, and meetings—various tactics that make up the modern *social movement repertoire*. Movement actors attempt to represent themselves publicly as worthy, unified, numerous, and committed (ibid., 3–4).

Based on this contentious politics approach, Sidney Tarrow (1998: 4) provides a succinct definition of social movements as '*collective challenges, based on common purposes and social solidarities, in sustained interaction with elites, opponents, and authorities.* Social movements are *sustained* in that they consist of multiple campaigns or at least multiple episodes of collective action within a single campaign. Movement campaigns consist of *interactions* among movement actors, their targets, the public, and other relevant actors. The targets of movement claims are often government authorities, but may also be other types of authorities, such as business owners or religious leaders (Tilly, 2004b: 4).

Social movements are not the only form of contentious politics. McAdam, Tarrow, and Tilly (2001) include in their definition of contentious politics various public and collective political struggles, such as revolutions, nationalism, and strike waves, as well as social movements. They also consider actions by established political actors within institutions as contentious politics, provided the action is episodic and departs from the everyday, non-collective action that goes on within institutions. For example, the activities of the National Commission on Terrorist Attacks Upon the United States (also known as the 9/11 Commission), backed by collective action on the part of family members of victims of the 11 September 2001 terrorist attacks, might be considered a form of contentious politics, though perfectly legal and using an established political forum. McAdam et al. (2001: 7–8) distinguish between *contained contention* by established political actors and *transgressive contention*, which involves at least some 'newly self-identified political actors' and/or 'innovative collective action' by at least some parties.

Although the distinction between social movements and other phenomena such as *political parties* and *interest groups* is not always sharp, movement scholars have generally regarded movements as *challengers* that are at least in part *outsiders* with regard to the established power structure (Tilly, 1978; Gamson, 1990 [1975]). Political parties and interest groups, in contrast, are *insiders* with at least some degree of access to government authorities and other elites. However, political insiders may engage in (usually) contained contention, and movements may become **professionalized** in the sense that they include fairly stable organizations, often headed by paid leaders, and may have memberships consisting largely of financial contributors, or 'paper members', rather than activists (McCarthy and Zald, 1973). It may be difficult to distinguish between a professional movement organization and an established interest group.

Some social movement theorists have distinguished between social movements and the organized entities that typically populate movements. John McCarthy and Mayer Zald (1977: 1217–18) define a social movement as 'a set of opinions and beliefs in a population which represents preferences for changing some elements of the social structure and/or reward distribution of a society' and a **countermovement** as 'a set of opinions and beliefs in a population opposed to a social movement'. In this view social movements are 'preference structures' or sets of opinions and beliefs, which may or may not be turned into collective action, depending on preexisting organization and opportunities and costs for expressing preferences. Movements supported by populations that are internally organized through communities or associations are most likely to generate organized structures (ibid.; Oberschall, 1973). A **social movement organization (SMO)** is defined as 'a complex, or formal, organization which identifies its goals with the preferences of a social movement or a countermovement and attempts to implement those goals' (McCarthy and Zald, 1977: 1218). Movements differ from one another in the extent to which they are organized by formal organizations and in the extent to which they trigger organized opposition or countermovements. McCarthy and Zald refer to the collection of organizations within a movement as a **social movement industry** and to all of these 'industries' in a society as the **social movement sector.**

McCarthy and Zald's definition of the social movement as a preference structure differs from most other definitions, including the contentious politics view of movements as collective challenges, in that McCarthy and Zald separate preferences for change from organized collective action. They argue that this approach has the advantage of recognizing that movements are 'never fully mobilized' and that the size or intensity of preferences may not predict the rise and fall of the organized movement (ibid., 1219). Collective action may depend less on the grievances of unorganized groups than on social movement leaders who act as 'entrepreneurs' in mobilizing—and perhaps even creating—preferences (McCarthy and Zald, 1973). Moreover, McCarthy and Zald's approach leads us to focus on social movement organizations and the interactions of these organizations within the context of a particular social movement. Organizations have different structures, which affect their strategies and longevity, and they may cooperate or compete with one another. In some instances, organizational interests may interfere with the attainment of movement goals or preferences.

The distinction between a social movement and a social movement organization is important because major social movements typically include multiple organizations, and internal organizational dynamics and inter-organizational alliances are critical to movement strategies and outcomes. For example, the environmental movement in North America includes organizations such as Greenpeace, the Sierra Club, the Nature Conservancy, the World Wildlife Fund, and Earth First!, to name only a few of the many active organizations. These organizations have different ideologies and strategic approaches and may compete with one another for members and funding, despite their common commitment to environmental protection. Coalitions of movement organizations are often difficult to form and maintain, particularly among those with different structures and strategic preferences. However, many movements face organized countermovements, which increase the urgency of coalition work (Staggenborg, 1986). Movement-countermovement interactions, as well as interactions with the state, are an important topic for social movement research and often involve organizational dynamics (see Zald and Useem, 1987; Meyer and Staggenborg, 1996).

At the same time that analyses of social movement organizations are critical to social movement theory, scholars have recognized that movements consist of more than politically motivated organizations with an explicit mandate to seek change in public policy. The notion of a **social movement community** captures the idea that movements consist of networks of individuals, cultural groups, alternative institutions, and institutional supporters as well as political movement organizations (see Buechler, 1990; Staggenborg, 1998). Moreover, movements also consist of more than the public protest events emphasized by the contentious politics approach. Although the contentious politics approach recognizes that movements can target authorities other than the state, critics charge that movements such as religious and self-help movements tend to be neglected along with less visible forms of collective action, such as efforts to change institutions and create new forms of culture. Consequently, a number of theorists have called for broadening our conception of social movements.

Mayer Zald (2000) suggests that we should view **ideologically structured action** as movement activity. He argues that movement-related activity occurs within such organizations as political parties and government agencies, and that families and schools are important in socializing movement supporters. In short, action shaped by movement ideology can be found in a variety of institutions and structures of everyday life. David Snow (2004) argues that movements can be conceived as 'collective challenges to systems or structures of authority', including various types of organizations and institutions and also sets of cultural beliefs and understandings. These theorists and others argue that movement activity occurs in a wide range of venues, through a variety of forms of collective action. Movements consist of informal networks as well as formal organizations and they produce culture and collective identity as well as political campaigns (cf. Armstrong, 2002; Diani, 1992; Melucci, 1989, 1996; Polletta and Jasper, 2001; Rupp and Taylor, 1999).

The danger, as Tilly (2004b: 10) points out, is that 'one may see social movements everywhere.' He argues that it is better to stick to a definition of movements as consisting of sustained campaigns directed at authorities, which use the social movement repertoire and create public displays of worthiness, unity, numbers, and commitment. Then, movements can be compared to other forms of contentious politics such as conflict over policy within institutions. This approach has the merit of keeping the definition of social movements tied to the historical origins of the social movement that Tilly has so carefully documented. Nevertheless, studies of contemporary social movements such as the women's movement show that we cannot completely understand the maintenance and outcomes of important social movements without looking broadly at their cultural, institutional, and political manifestations (Staggenborg and Taylor, 2005).

As the above discussion shows, the area of social movement study is one in which there are disagreements even about the very definition of social movements. Rather than seeing this as a weakness, however, we can view it as a sign of a lively field in which new perspectives and ideas compete with existing approaches. Different definitions of social movements lead to different emphases in the study of particular movements. The contentious politics definition of the social movement as a sustained challenge to elites or other opponents by shifting coalitions of collective actors through a series of public campaigns points to the political nature of social movements and their role in putting issues on the public agenda and changing public policies. McCarthy and Zald's view of social movements as preference structures leads us to focus on how preferences get transformed into organized movements through the enterprise of leaders and the creation of different types of movement organizations. Conceptualizations of social movements as including ideologically structured action, social movement communities, and challenges to different types of institutional authorities all point to the multiple arenas in which movements operate. These different emphases are not necessarily incompatible, and their usefulness depends in part on the nature of the movement being studied.

References

Armstrong, Elizabeth A. 2002. *Forging Gay Identities: Organizing Sexuality in San Francisco, 1950–1994.* Chicago: University of Chicago Press.

Buechler, Steven M. 1990. *Women's Movements in the United States.* New Brunswick, NJ: Rutgers University Press.

————. 1995. 'New Social Movement Theories', *Sociological Quarterly* 36, 3: 441–64.

————. 2000. *Social Movements in Advanced Capitalism*. New York: Oxford University Press.

————. 2002. 'Toward a Structural Approach to Social Movements', *Research in Political Sociology* 10: 1–45.

Diani, Mario. 1992. 'The Concept of Social Movement', *Sociological Review* 40, 1: 1–25.

Gamson, William A. 1990. *The Strategy of Social Protest*, 2nd edn. Belmont, Calif.: Wadsworth. (First edition 1975.)

————. 1998. 'Social Movements and Cultural Change', in Marco G. Giugni, Doug McAdam, and Charles Tilly, eds, *From Contention to Democracy*. Lanham, Md: Rowman & Littlefield, 57–77.

McAdam, Doug. 1983. 'Tactical Innovation and the Pace of Insurgency', *American Sociological Review* 48,6: 735–54.

————, Sidney Tarrow, and Charles Tilly. 2001. *Dynamics of Contention*. Cambridge: Cambridge University Press.

McCarthy, John D., and Mayer N. Zald. 1973. *The Trend of Social Movements in America: Professionalization and Resource Mobilization*. Morristown, NJ: General Learning Press.

———— and ————. 1977. 'Resource Mobilization and Social Movements: A Partial Theory', *American Journal of Sociology* 82, 6: 1212–41.

———— and ————. 2002. 'The Enduring Vitality of the Resource Mobilization Theory of Social Movements', in H.T. Jonathan, ed., *Handbook of Sociological Theory*. New York: Kluwer Academic/ Plenum, 533–65.

————. 1989. *Nomads of the Present: Social Movements and Individual Needs in Contemporary Society*, ed. John Keane and Paul Mier. Philadelphia: Temple University Press.

————. 1996. *Challenging Codes: Collective Action in the Information Age*. Cambridge: Cambridge University Press.

Oberschall, Anthony. 1973. *Social Conflict and Social Movements*. Englewood Cliffs, NJ: Prentice-Hall.

———— and James M. Jasper. 2001. 'Collective Identity and Social Movements' *Annual Review of Sociology* 27: 283–305.

Rupp, Leila J. 1997. *Worlds of Women: The Making of an International Women's Movement*. Princeton, NJ: Princeton University Press.

———— and Verta Taylor. 1987. *Survival in the Doldrums: The American Women's Rights Movement, 1945 to the 1960s*. New York: Oxford University Press.

Shorter, Edward. 1975. *The Making of the Modern Family*. New York; Basic Books.

————. 2004. 'Social Movements as Challenges to Authority: Resistance to an Emerging Conceptual Hegemony', *Research in Social Movements, Conflicts and Change 25*: 3–25.

————. 1998. 'Social Movement Communities and Cycles of Protest: The Emergence and Maintenance of a Local Women's Movement', *Social Problems* 45, 2: 180–204.

———— and Verta Taylor. 2005. 'Whatever Happened to the Women's Movement?', *Mobilization* 10, 1: 37–52.

Tarrow, Sidney. 1989. *Democracy and Disorder: Protest and Politics in Italy, 1965–1975*. Oxford: Oxford University Press.

_____. 1998. *Power in Movement: Social Movements and Contentious Politics,* 2nd edn. Cambridge: Cambridge University Press.

Tilly, Charles. 1978. *From Mobilization to Revolution.* Reading, Mass.: Addison-Wesley.

_____. 1984. 'Social Movements and National Politics', in H. Charles Bright and Susan Harding, eds, *Statemaking and Social Movements.* Ann Arbor: University of Michigan Press, 297–317.

_____. 1986. 'European Violence and Collective Action Since 1700', *Social Research* 53, 1: 159–84.

_____. 1988. 'Social Movements, Old and New' *Research in Social Movements, Conflicts and Change* 10: 1–18.

_____. 1995. *Popular Contention in Great Britain, 1758–1834.* Cambridge, Mass.: Harvard University Press.

_____. 2004a. *Contention and Democracy in Europe, 1650–2000.* New York: Cambridge University Press.

_____. 2004b. *Social Movements, 1768–2004.* Boulder, Colo.: Paradigm.

Zald, Mayer N. 2000. 'Ideologically Structured Action: An Enlarged Agenda for Social Movement Research', *Mobilization* 5, 1: 1–16.

_____ and Bert Useem. 1987. 'Movement and Countermovement Interaction: Mobilization, Tactics, and State Involvement', in M.N. Zald and J.D. McCarthy, eds, *Social Movements in an Organizational Society.* New Brunswick, NJ: Transaction Books, 247–72.

CHAPTER TWO

International Organizations and Relations

In the famous treatise *Leviathan*, first published in 1651, Thomas Hobbes argues that in the absence of strong leadership to maintain order, humans would resort to killing one another and life would be "solitary, poor, nasty, brutish, and short" (Hobbes 2012). His interpretation of human nature as self-interested cooperation, and the need to base political communities on a "social contract" continues to be a core theme in political philosophy today. With authors such as John Locke, Montesquieu, and Jean-Jacques Rousseau, Hobbes advanced the field of political philosophy during the European Enlightenment. These theorists debated both the reasons to form states and the ideal form of the state.

International organizations provide a means of cooperation among states and, along with nongovernmental organizations (NGOs), will be explored in the readings for this chapter. In what follows, a variety of efforts to achieve greater international cooperation are explored. The Peace of Westphalia was an especially critical time in the formation of the international state system. The Peace of Westphalia, signed in 1648, brought both the Eighty Years' War and the Thirty Years' War between the Dutch and the Germans to a close. These wars, concerned fundamentally with religion, had taken many lives in Europe for decades. The treaty placed states at the center of a new system based on a territorial definition of politics. Under the terms of the agreement, some countries were granted territory and others had their previously contested or ambiguous sovereignty over territory confirmed. The agreement included an ecclesiastical settlement that ensured mutual tolerance for the three predominant religious communities in the European region at the time: Calvinists, Roman Catholics, and Lutherans. The principle that peace can be maintained if states refrain from interfering in one another's domestic affairs became a stable way of organizing politics. The agreement provided a basis for state interaction, all the way through the twentieth century. In many ways, supranational organizations challenge this order.[1]

The study of international organizations and relations finds its disciplinary home in political science. Political science is a broad field comprising a number of subfields including: political theory, comparative politics, political ideology, international relations, and others, according to the American Political Science Association.[2] Political science is interested in both the theory and practice of government and politics. The field seeks to understand political community and institutions, and how power, authority, and resources are allocated in society. The methodologies used by political scientists are drawn from both the sciences and the humanities.

---

1   https://www.britannica.com/event/Peace-of-Westphalia
2   http://www.apsanet.org/RESOURCES/For-Students

International Organizations

The first truly international organization arose from the Congress of Vienna, which took place in 1814–1815 after the Napoleonic Wars. The Congress redrew the borders of European countries and created the Central Commission for Navigation on the Rhine. The primary mandate of this organization was to establish security for navigating the Rhine River. How did an agreement about the navigation of a single river become the center of evolving international jurisprudence? The Rhine touches on the interests of multiple states in multiple sectors. The Rhine begins in Switzerland, forms part of the border between France and Germany, and flows through Germany and the Netherlands. Security on the river was therefore an important component of both security and economic prosperity.

The first international organization focused primarily on maintaining world peace was the League of Nations. The League brought previously vague affirmations about the importance of preventing war in philosophy to the practical realm of politics.[3] The League of Nations was established by the Paris Peace Conference that ended World War I. The organization enjoyed some significant successes. Most notably, it led to the creation of the Permanent Court of International Justice (PCIJ) that worked from 1922 to 1946 from The Hague in the Netherlands. The PCIJ was the first permanent international tribunal enjoying general jurisdiction. It paved the way for the International Court of Justice to be created, and clarified aspects of international law.[4] The League also led to the creation of the International Labor Organization (ILO), which is active today. The ILO promotes social justice through protecting and harmonizing workers', governments', and employers' rights. It applies itself to ending the drug trade, promoting child welfare, the abolition of slavery, and refugee protection. The ILO would become the first specialized agency of the United Nations. The League has also been criticized, however, for being unable to fulfill its primary purpose: preventing a second world war. Without its own, separate military force, the League relied on the Great Powers of World War I to carry out its resolutions, something they were not always in an advantageous position to do. The efficacy of the League was hampered by significant issues of commitment. The United States never joined; Germany, Japan, and Italy, major protagonists in World War II, withdrew; and the Soviet Union was only very briefly a member.

Efforts to establish an effective collective security organization continued after World War II, when leaders came together to create the United Nations (UN). The UN is the only international intergovernmental organization with nearly universal membership. As such, it occupies a special place in international studies. The UN was formed as a collective security organization by a coalition of the great powers emerging from World War II. That configuration still shapes the UN and the work it is able to do today. The UN is an example of political globalization: nation-states come together to give up some of their power in the interest of cooperation.

The European Union is also an instructive example of the way international organizations provide platforms for cooperation. The European Union evolved out of the European Coal and Steel Community (ECSC), an organization that envisioned sharing strategic natural resources as one way to avoid future conflict. This was the idea of Robert Schuman, French Foreign Minister. The ECSC also marked the

---

3   https://www.britannica.com/topic/League-of-Nations
4   http://www.icj-cij.org/en/pcij

Image 2.1. United Nations Structure

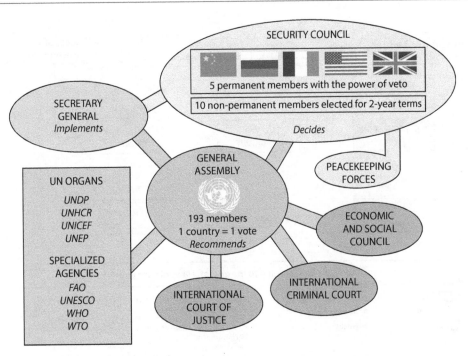

end of punishing the losers of a conflict by making them pay for damages. The key thinkers behind the formation of the European Union believed this practice led to more conflict.[5] More than fifty years of integration have transformed the economic and political landscape of Europe and given unprecedented power to a new set of supranational institutions. Still, there are remaining questions. From the beginning, there have been competing visions regarding the form and optimal level of integration. As Staab has written, "Regardless of the outcome of this debate, the European Union represents a hugely influential vehicle for organizing Europe and constitutes a unique experiment of 'deep international cooperation'" (2011: ix).

The Tools of International Relations

An important way for states to cooperate is through implementing the tools of international relations. The essence of diplomacy is convincing other state parties that it is in their interest to support your country's policies and activities (Livitsky 2018). Diplomacy is at its most powerful when the country with which one is negotiating believes its interests will suffer—potentially through a credible use of force—if your proposed policy is not supported. As the practice of communication and negotiation between the representatives of states, diplomacy is the least interventionist and most preferred tool.

---

5   https://europa.eu/european-union/about-eu/history/founding-fathers_en

Image 2.2. Political System of the European Union

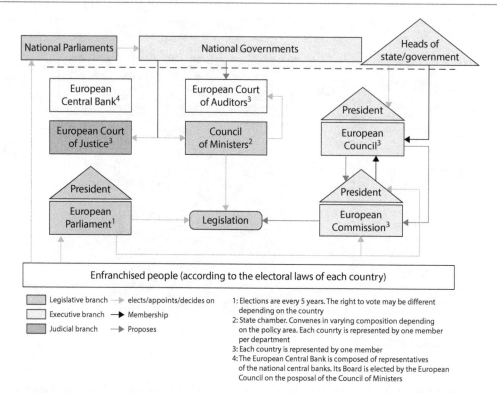

Legislative branch — elects/appoints/decides on

Executive branch → Membership

Judicial branch → Proposes

1: Elections are every 5 years. The right to vote may be different depending on the country
2: State chamber. Convenes in varying composition depending on the policy area. Each counrty is represented by one member per department
3: Each country is represented by one member
4: The European Central Bank is composed of representatives of the national central banks. Its Board is elected by the European Council on the posposal of the Council of Ministers

When the practice of negotiation fails, sanctions are usually the tool of next resort. The primary purpose of sanctions is, however, still to bring about a change of behavior. Sometimes that change of behavior is simply a return to the negotiating table. There are many types of sanctions: economic sanctions focus on limiting trade and financial aid; political sanctions take the form of imposing restrictions on the travel of the citizens of the country targeted by sanctions, imposing restrictions on international sports or cultural activities, and expelling diplomats. Military sanctions focus on limiting the sale or purchase of military equipment. The overarching purpose of all sanctions is to focus attention on a country's inappropriate behavior in order to change it. Pressuring a country to alter its behavior by shaming it is more effective in countries where leaders are accountable and vulnerable to the force of public opinion.

Sanctions are far from a precise tool of international relations. Care must be taken that they have the intended impact. When innocent civilians are harmed by sanctions, their leaders may blame the sanctioning country and be emboldened to continue objectionable activities, defeating the purpose of sanctions. Care must also be taken that they have a greater effect on the country that is being sanctioned than on the country that is doing the sanctioning.

The allotment of a benefit is also considered a tool. Perhaps the best example of this will be studied in the readings that follow: the European Union. Countries that are candidates to become member states have a strong incentive to bring their policies and practices into alignment with those of the European Union. Among other measures, they must end internal conflicts and improve their human rights record. In exchange, there are many benefits ranging from collective security to advantageous trading relationships and reduced travel restrictions for citizens.

War is considered the "ultimate" tool of international relations. A statement by Clausewitz (1989) [1832] that is often quoted is that war is "the continuation of politics by other means." There are many considerations to take into account in embarking on this step. A primary one is whether or not the matter has been brought before the UN Security Council. The Security Council remains the most legitimate arbitrator of collective action for mutual security. Chapter VII is frequently invoked as a guiding principle. The use of force is legitimate, but only under a limited set of agreed-upon circumstances. "All Members of the United Nations, in order to contribute to the maintenance of international peace and security, undertake to make available to the Security Council, on its call and in accordance with a special agreement or agreements, armed forces, assistance, and facilities, including rights of passage, necessary for the purpose of maintaining international peace and security"[6].

Flows

Globalization is changing what it means to be a nation-state. The process of globalization has created new networks of power that cut across the territorial boundaries of nation-states. These networks have been called "polycentric forms of governance" and "networks of governance" in the political science literature (Kacowicz and Mitrani 2016: 193). What this means in plain language is that for a variety of reasons, the post-Cold War world has been characterized by a diffusion of power away from states— leading to a very different equilibrium between states and the international organizations, markets, and civil societies that interact with them. Some portend the demise of the nation-state (Reich 2014). The flow to pay attention to in this chapter is therefore the flow of power and authority. Attention to this flow will help decipher the changing nature of the state in world politics.

There are at least three ways the power and authority of the nation-state could be challenged by globalization. First, the creation and proliferation of *international intergovernmental organizations* has changed the decision-making process in world politics (Seymour 2014). New forms of collective decision making mean that states must consider the views of other states, as well as listen to the professionals who lead intergovernmental and nongovernmental organizations. One example of this is the International Monetary Fund (IMF), which can insist that a country reduce spending on welfare programs or devalue its currency as a condition of a loan. Without losing their sovereignty, then, states are encouraged to relinquish some of their authority as part of interacting in the international arena. The growth of international intergovernmental organizations does not necessarily translate into the demise of the nation-state. Intergovernmental organizations depend on the presence of states for their very existence. It is unlikely that nation-states will be entirely replaced by larger political units because publics oppose this move on a number of grounds. In the European Union, euro-skeptics point

---

6   http://www.un.org/en/sections/un-charter/chapter-vii/index.html

to the "democratic deficit" when a country relinquishes decisions to EU authorities who are acting with some impunity, and in a manner that is removed from an electorate.

A second way power may diffuse is through the expanding field of *international law* that exposes states to new systems of regulation. Increasingly, there are rights and duties that supersede the claims of states. Though they may not always have coercive powers of enforcement, new international laws are changing state behavior. One of the first examples of this trend was the International Tribunal at Nuremburg between 1945 and 1949.[7] The Tribunal established a precedent for the international trial of war criminals. The trials were conducted according to the laws not of a single country, but of several: Britain, France, the United States, and the Soviet Union. Since Nuremburg, the International Court of Justice and, more recently, the International Criminal Court have continued the trend. The International Criminal Court has the power to discipline the behavior of states by punishing perpetrators of the most serious crimes. This spread of global governance is significant, but still limited. As Hirst and Thompson point out, international law depends on a set of states where the rule of law is firmly established (1995: 190).

A third way that power appears to have ebbed from the nation-state is through the growing importance of international flows of capital, goods, and services—in short, an increasingly globalized economy. The sheer number of economic transactions that cross nation-state borders, according to this thinking, has left the state weakened as an economic actor. Multinational corporations have the freedom to produce, market, and distribute goods and services without a great deal of regard for national loyalty. To put it slightly differently, their loyalty is dependent on the advantages and disadvantages of operating in a particular country. Likewise, financial institutions such as banks are increasingly global in their operations and portfolios. With communications technology, they can both monitor and respond to changes around the world with flexibility. This technology has increased the mobility of currencies, stocks, and shares for financial and commercial organizations. Private financial institutions are significant players in all this: if the economic behavior of a state is considered ill advised by private financial traders, the state will see the value of its currency decline and its access to capital decrease. The way that states make policy is shaped by this kind of international disciplining. On the whole, technological advances have had the effect of integrating markets, eroding previously clear economic boundaries. The ability of individual nation-states to regulate their economies is inevitably affected.

This development does not spell the end of the nation-state, but changes in the way it behaves. There are also dynamics that protect of the continued importance of the nation state. First, whether any given territory is included in global production networks or ignored by them depends on policy decisions made by governments. The choice to facilitate flows of capital and trade is significant: states can, of course, resist the integration process by isolating themselves in a variety of ways. States may not be able to dictate the structure of trade networks or supply chains, but they can make their territories more attractive to influential economic actors.

Second, contrary to expectations, an increase in international trade and commerce is often correlated with an increased, as opposed to decreased, role for a state government (Evans 2009: 249). Why? Because governments are required to balance and calculate the flows as well as mitigate negative

7 https://www.britannica.com/event/Nurnberg-trials

effects. (Rodrik 2009: 265). The highly open and very small European economies have large governments to facilitate cooperation and simultaneously minimize the adverse effects impacts of openness to the international economy (Rodrik 2009: 265). The correlation holds outside of Europe as well. This is part of expanding demands placed on governments since the late nineteenth century (Rodrik 2009: 264). At that time, providing for the poor through safety nets such as medical insurance, social security insurance, and various forms of welfare were not expectations as they are today. Prior to World War II, government expenditure averaged around 20 percent of Gross Domestic Product.[8] A decade ago, that figure had already climbed to 47 percent (Rodrik 2009: 264). Thus, the more open to trade a country is (e.g., the Netherlands) the more likely it is that a high proportion of government spending will be devoted to social protection.

These trends demonstrate the future of the nation-state in the context of globalization is yet to be determined. Discussing the "failure," "end," or "demise" of the nation-state is premature. While it is undeniable that the balance of power and authority is shifting, the nation-state is still the most enduring way of organizing politics. States are likely to remain the main actors in world affairs, and state sovereignty is likely to remain the fundamental principle on which these relations are based. The power of intergovernmental organizations lies in the ability to help states cooperate, pursue shared goals, and manage conflict. Given the shifting balance of power, the best line of inquiry is to consider not whether the nation-state is obsolete, but how exactly the exercise of state power has changed with the increased presence of nonstate actors.

---

8 Gross Domestic Product is the sum of all the goods and service produced in a nation in a year.

The United Nations in World Politics

by Karen A. Mingst and Margaret P. Karns

I t is hard to imagine a world without the United Nations. Despite many ups and downs over more than sixty-five years, the UN has not only endured but also played a key role in reshaping the world as we know it. It has embodied human-kind's hopes for a better world through the prevention of conflict. It has promoted a culture of legality and rule of law. It has raised an awareness of the plight of the world's poor, and it has boosted development by providing **technical assistance**. It has promoted concern for human rights, including the status of women, the rights of the child, and the unique needs of indigenous peoples. It has formulated the concept of environmentally sustainable development. It has contributed immensely to making multilateral diplomacy the primary way in which international norms, public policies, and law are established. It has served as a catalyst for global policy networks and partnerships with other actors. It plays a central role in **global governance**. Along the way, the UN has earned several Nobel Peace Prizes, including the 2005 award to the International Atomic Energy Agency (IAEA) and its chief, Mohamed ElBaradei; the 2001 prize to the UN and Secretary-General Kofi Annan; the 1988 award to UN peacekeepers; and the 1969 honor to the International Labour Organization (ILO).

In the many areas of UN activity, we can point to the UN's accomplishments and also to its shortcomings and failures. More than sixty-five years after its creation, the UN continues to be the only **international organization (IO)** or, more correctly, **international intergovernmental organization (IGO)** of global scope and nearly universal membership that has an agenda encompassing the broadest range of governance issues. It is a complex system that serves as the central site for multilateral diplomacy, with the UN's General Assembly as center stage. Three weeks of general debate at the opening of each fall assembly session draw foreign ministers and heads of state from small and large states to take advantage of the opportunity to address the nations of the world and to engage in intensive diplomacy.

As an intergovernmental organization, however, the UN is the creation of its member states; it is they who decide what it is that they will allow this organization to do and what resources—financial and otherwise—they will provide. In this regard, the UN is very much a political organization, subject to the winds of world politics and the whims of member governments. To understand the UN today, it is useful to look back at some of the major changes in world politics and how they affected the UN.

The United Nations in World Politics: Vision and Reality

The establishment of the United Nations in the closing days of World War II was an affirmation of the desire of war-weary nations for an organization that could help them avoid future conflicts and promote international economic and social cooperation. ... [T]he UN's Charter built on lessons learned from the failed League of Nations created at the end of World War I and earlier experiments with international unions, conference diplomacy, and dispute-settlement mechanisms. It represented an expression of hope for the possibilities of a new global security arrangement and for fostering the social and economic conditions necessary for peace to prevail.

The United Nations and Politics in the Cold War World

The World War II coalition of great powers (the United States, the Soviet Union, Great Britain, France, and China), whose unity had been key to the UN's founding, was nevertheless a victim of rising tensions almost before the first General Assembly session in 1946. Developments in Europe and Asia between 1946 and 1950 soon made it clear that the emerging Cold War would have fundamental effects on the UN. How could a **collective security** system operate when there was no unity among the great powers on whose cooperation it depended? Even the admission of new members was affected between 1950 and 1955 because each side vetoed applications from states that were allied with the other.

The Cold War made Security Council actions on threats to peace and security extremely problematic, with repeated sharp exchanges and frequent deadlock. Some conflicts, such as the French and American wars in Vietnam and the Soviet interventions in Czechoslovakia and Hungary, were never brought to the UN at all. The UN was able to respond to the North Korean invasion of South Korea in 1950 only because the Soviet Union was boycotting the Security Council at the time.

In order to deal with a number of regional conflicts, the UN developed something never mentioned in its charter, namely, **peacekeeping**; this has involved the prevention, containment, and moderation of hostilities between or within states through the use of lightly armed multinational forces of soldiers, police, and civilians.

Peacekeeping was a creative response to the breakdown of great-power unity and the spread of East-West tensions to regional conflicts. UN peacekeeping forces were used extensively in the Middle East and in conflicts arising out of the decolonization process during the Cold War period. Thirteen operations were deployed from 1948 to 1988. The innovation of peacekeeping illustrates what the Cold War did to the UN: "It had repealed the proposition that the organization should undertake to promote order by bringing the great powers into troubled situations. ... Henceforward, the task of the United Nations was to be defined as that of keeping the great powers out of such situations."[1]

The Effects of the Nuclear Revolution

The UN Charter had just been signed when the use of two atomic bombs on Japan on August 6 and 10, 1945, began a scientific and technological revolution in warfare that would have a far-reaching impact on the post-World War II world. At the United Nations, the earliest and most obvious effect of nuclear weapons was to restore the issue of disarmament (and its relative, arms control) to the agenda. Disarmament as an approach to peace had been discredited during the interwar era. The UN almost from its inception in early 1946 became a forum for discussions and negotiations on **arms control and disarmament**. Hence, the nuclear threat not only transformed world politics but also made the UN the key place where statespersons sought to persuade each other that war had become excessively dangerous, that disarmament and arms control were imperative, and that they were devoted to peace and restraint.

The Role of the United Nations in Decolonization and the Emergence of New States

At the close of World War II, few would have predicted the end of colonial rule in Africa and Asia. Yet twenty-five years after the UN Charter was signed, most of the former colonies had achieved independence with relatively little threat to international peace and security. Membership in the UN more than doubled from 51 states in 1945 to 118 in 1965 and had tripled by 1980 (see Figure 2.1.1), the vast majority of these new members being newly independent states. The UN played a significant role in this remarkably peaceful transformation, much of which took place during the height of the Cold War.

Figure 2.1.1. Growth in UN Membership, 1945–2011

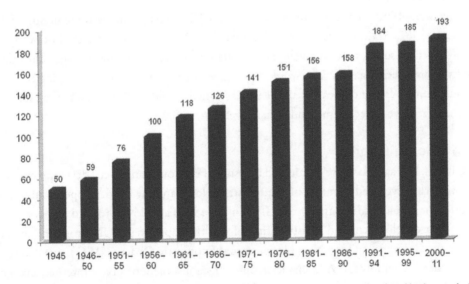

Source: Compiled from Robert E. Riggs and Jack C. Plano, *The United Nations: International Organization of World Politics*, 2nd ed. (Belmont, CA: Wadsworth, 1994), 45, and updated.

Twenty-six new states were later seated in the UN after the Cold War's end, mostly as a result of the dissolution of the Soviet Union and Yugoslavia.

The UN Charter endorsed the principle of **self-determination**. Already independent former colonies, such as India, Egypt, Indonesia, and the Latin American states, used the UN as a forum to advocate an end to colonialism and independence for territories ruled by Great Britain, France, the Netherlands, Belgium, Spain, and Portugal. Success added new votes to the growing anti-colonial coalition.

By 1960 a majority of the UN's members favored decolonization. General Assembly Resolution 1514 that year condemned the continuation of colonial rule and preconditions for granting independence (such as a lack of preparation for self-rule) and called for annual reports on the progress toward independence for all remaining colonial territories. The UN provided an important forum for the **collective legitimation** of a change in international norms (that is, colonialism and imperialism were no longer acceptable patterns of state behavior, and colonial peoples had a right to self-determination). The international system was fully internationalized to include all sovereign, independent states that sought membership.

The consequences of decolonization and the expanded number of independent states were manifold. The less developed, often newly independent states of Africa, Asia, and Latin America formed a strong coalition within the UN known as the **Group of 77 (G-77)**; after 1960 this coalition commanded a majority of votes on a broad range of issues. Whereas the Cold War had shaped politics in the UN until 1960, the G-77, and what became known as "North-South issues," shaped much of the politics thereafter. The two sets of issues became entwined in complex ways, and political divisions changed. The Soviet Union and many Western European states often sided with the G-77, and the United States frequently found itself in a small minority.

Beginning in the 1960s, new issues proliferated on the UN's agenda, many at the urging of the G-77. For example, in 1967, Arvid Pardo, the representative from Malta, argued on behalf of newly independent states that the resources found on the deep seabed were the "common heritage of mankind," not the property of any specific nation. This would subsequently have an impact on emerging environmental issues as well as on the law of the sea. Of all the issues pushed by the G-77, however, none received more attention than the drive for economic and social development.

The North-South Conflict

By the late 1960s, UN agendas were dominated by issues of economic and social development and the relations between the developed countries of the industrial North and the less developed countries (LDCs) of the South. The ideological leaning of the G-77 in the 1960s and 1970s toward a heavy government role in economic development and redistribution of wealth shaped many UN programs and activities. In the 1970s the G-77 pushed for a **New International Economic Order (NIEO)**, marshaling support in the UN General Assembly for "A Declaration on the Establishment of a New International Economic Order" and "A Charter of Economic Rights and Duties of States." For most of the decade, the NIEO debates dominated and polarized the UN system, with the deep divide between North and South at times making agreement on both economic and security issues impossible to achieve.

The North-South conflict continues to be a central feature of world politics, and hence of the UN, although the rhetoric and issues of the NIEO sharply diminished in the late 1980s and 1990s. For example, the UN's treatment of environmental issues, which first began with the Stockholm Conference on the Human Environment in 1972, has been permeated by North-South differences. The 1997 Kyoto Conference on Climate Change heard echoes of the North-South conflict when developing countries insisted that industrial countries make the first reductions in carbon dioxide emissions. Those echoes still persisted at the 2009 Copenhagen conference on climate change. The G-77, however, is no longer as cohesive a group; its members' interests increasingly diverged in the 1980s when some states, especially in Southeast Asia, achieved rapid economic growth and as many developing countries shifted from statis-toriented economic policies to neoliberal ones, calling for open markets and privatization. Chapter 5 discusses these shifts further as well as the increased emphasis on poverty alleviation that accompanied the **Millennium Development Goals (MDGs)** approved in 2000.

World Politics Since the Cold War's End

The Cold War's end in 1990 meant not only new cooperation among the five permanent members of the Security Council but also a resurgence of nationalism, civil wars, and ethnic conflicts; the new phenomenon of failed states; and a related series of humanitarian crises. The consequence was greater demands than ever before on the United Nations to deal with threats to peace and security as well as environmental and developmental issues, democratization, population growth, humanitarian crises, and other problems. UN peacekeepers were called on to rebuild Cambodia; create peace in Bosnia; organize and monitor postconflict elections in Nicaragua, Namibia, and many other places; monitor human rights violations in El Salvador; and oversee humanitarian relief in Bosnia, Somalia, Rwanda, Kosovo, the Democratic Republic of the Congo (DRC), East Timor, and Afghanistan. Beginning with Iraq's invasion of Kuwait in 1990, the UN's enforcement powers were used more in the post–Cold War era than at any previous time.

With the spread of **democratization** to all regions of the globe from Latin America, Eastern Europe, and states created from the former Soviet Union to Africa and Asia, many authoritarian governments in the late 1980s and 1990s were forced to open their political processes to competing political parties, adopt more stringent human rights standards, and hold free elections. Since 1990 the UN has been in heavy demand to provide observers for elections in countries around the world. UN-sanctioned intervention in Haiti in 1993 marked the first time the UN took action to restore a democratically elected government. In Namibia, Kosovo, Bosnia, and East Timor, the UN was called upon to assist with organizing the elements of newly independent states, including the provision of transitional administrations, writing of constitutions, training of police and judges, and organization of elections.

By 1995, however, the early post–Cold War optimism about the United Nations had faded. The peacekeepers in Somalia, Bosnia, and Rwanda found little peace to be kept, although their presence did alleviate much human suffering. Despite almost continuous meetings of the UN Security Council and numerous resolutions, the UN's members lacked the political will to provide the military, logistical, and financial resources needed to deal adequately with these and other complex situations. In addition, the UN faced a deep financial crisis in the late 1990s caused by the increased cost of peacekeeping and other activities and the failure of many members, including the United States, to pay their assessed contributions. The organization clearly needed significant reforms to meet the increased demands and address weaknesses in its structures and operations, but member states failed to use either the occasion of the UN's fiftieth anniversary in 1995 or the UN's sixtieth anniversary in 2005 to approve many of the necessary changes. The UN did not stand still, however. Some changes could be made without member states' approval; other reforms were approved at the 2005 World Summit. And, in its responses to many complex conflicts, humanitarian crises, new threats to peace posed by nuclear weapons proliferation and terrorism, as well as persistent global poverty, the UN demonstrated that it was still central to many aspects of global governance, as discussed in subsequent chapters.

Well before the Cold War's end, the UN played an important role on a nexus of **interdependence** issues by convening global conferences and summits on topics ranging from the environment, food, housing, the law of the sea, disarmament, women, and water to human rights, population and development, and social development. These conferences have articulated new international norms; expanded international law; set agendas for governments, as well as for the UN itself, through programs of action; and promoted linkages among the growing communities of **nongovernmental organizations (NGOs)** active on different issues, the UN, and member states' governments.

Still, the UN has never played a central role in international economic relations. Although economic topics have appeared on the agendas of the General Assembly and the United Nations Economic and Social Council (ECOSOC), the major decisionmaking has always taken place in institutions that have never really been part of the UN system: the World Bank, the International Monetary Fund (IMF), the World Trade Organization (WTO), and the **Group of 7 (G-7)**, as well as in Washington, Tokyo, London, and the headquarters of major corporations and banks. The UN has, however, been active from its earliest years in efforts to promote economic and social development, introducing the ideas of development aid in the 1950s, sustainable development in the 1980s, and human development in the 1990s. Many of the global conferences contributed other ideas and reinforced understanding of the way development overlaps with the status of women, population, food, and other problems. UN Secretary-General Kofi Annan used the occasion of the new millennium to convene a Millennium Summit in 2000. In suggesting the special gathering, the secretary-general hoped "to harness the symbolic power of the millennium to the real and urgent needs of people everywhere."[2] His special report, *We the Peoples*, provided his views of the state of the world, the major global challenges, and the need for structural reform of the UN itself. The three days of meetings drew the largest gathering of world leaders ever: There were 147 heads of state or government and representatives from forty-four other countries.

The Millennium Declaration adopted at the close of the extraordinary summit reflected the high degree of consensus on two priorities: peace and development. Different leaders had stressed different aspects of the issues, ranging from globalization and nuclear weapons to fairer economic systems, ethnic tolerance, and human immunodeficiency syndrome (HIV/AIDS). They had disagreed about how to restructure the UN, but not about the importance of the world organization; they concurred with lofty language about values and principles and also committed themselves to the series of specific objectives known as the MDGs that include halving the number of people living on less than one dollar a day by the year 2015 and reversing the spread of HIV/AIDS, malaria, and other major diseases. The declaration outlined special measures to meet the needs of Africa, and it intensified efforts to reform the Security Council, to strengthen ECOSOC and the International Court of Justice (ICJ), to make the General Assembly a more effective deliberative and policymaking body, and to ensure that the UN has the resources to carry out its mandates. ...

Rising globalization has been a major feature of world politics since the Cold War's end. **Globalization** is the process of increasing worldwide integration of politics, economics, social relations, and culture that often appears to undermine state sovereignty. In the 1990s this process of increased connectivity greatly accelerated, especially in the area of economic activities across state borders with the rapid growth in flows of finance, goods and services (trade), and investment, as well as diffusion of technology. Many regard globalization as desirable because it has fueled greater prosperity and higher standards of living in many parts of the world. Others, however, point to the growing inequality among and within nations and the ways in which globalization creates both winners and losers, such as those whose jobs in developed countries are lost to workers in developing countries who are paid lower wages. There is also the dark side of globalization that has facilitated the growth of trafficking in drugs, persons, and other criminal enterprises.

The UN itself and various **specialized agencies** within the UN system have struggled to address globalization issues. Although the International Labour Organization, World Health Organization (WHO), and World Intellectual Property Organization (WIPO) are very much involved in globalization-related issues of labor, health, and intellectual property rights, the fact that the targets of antiglobalization protesters have been the World Bank, IMF, G-7, and WTO underscores the UN's marginal role in international economic relations. Yet globalization has fueled the growth of NGOs. Subsequent chapters illustrate how the UN and NGOs, which represent what some have called global civil society, are working out new partnerships that will make each more responsive to globalization issues.

The emergence of the United States as the world's sole superpower has been a related aspect of post–Cold War world politics, the era of globalization, and the early twenty-first century. The economic and military capabilities of the United States have far exceeded those of any other state, and, with the collapse of the Soviet Union, the United States had no serious rival. Many worried that this development would result in the UN's marginalization, particularly if, or when, the United States chose to act unilaterally. This view was borne out when the United States invaded Iraq in 2003 in defiance of international opposition. An alternative view was that the UN could become a puppet of the sole superpower, dependent upon its goodwill for funding and subservient in authorizing US actions. Yet in the late 1990s and first decade of the twenty-first century, we have seen groups of states and of NGOs willing to push ahead with policy initiatives even when the United States has opposed them, examples being the International Criminal Court, the Convention on Landmines, the Kyoto Protocol on Climate Change, and its successor. Although its support has fluctuated, in fact, the United States has always been important to the United Nations ... .

Now, with the rapid rise of China, India, South Africa, Brazil and other emerging powers as well as the reassertiveness of Russia (a group collectively known as the **BRICS**), world politics is again shifting, and the years ahead will likely see significant changes in how these shifts play out within the UN. Already in international economic relations, the G-7 has been effectively replaced by the **Group of 20 (G-20)**, and the emerging powers have pushed for changes in their voting shares within the World Bank and IMF. The reform of UN Security Council membership will gain new attention and urgency with these power shifts.

To understand the links between world politics and the United Nations, it is also important to examine the major international relations theories to see how they explain global changes and the roles of IGOs such as the UN.

Contending International Relations Theories

For much of the post–World War II era, **realist theory**, or **realism**, provided the dominant explanation for international politics. Realists see states as the most important actors in the international system. They view states as unitary actors that define their national interests in terms of maximizing power and security. States' **sovereignty** means that they coexist in an anarchic international system and, therefore, must rely primarily on themselves to manage their own insecurity through balance of power, alliances, and deterrence. International rules (law) and norms, as well as international organizations, do not carry much weight with realists because they lack enforcement power. In realists' view, IGOs and NGOs are marginal actors. IGOs, in particular, do not enjoy autonomy or capability for independent action on the world stage. Rather, they reflect the interests of their members, especially the most powerful ones. In this view, the UN is constrained by its members' willingness to work through it in dealing with specific problems, to comply with and support its actions, to provide peacekeeping contingents (military or civilian), and to pay for its regular operations and special programs. In realist theory, cooperation among states is not impossible, but states have little incentive to enter into international arrangements, and they are always free to exit from them.[3]

For many international relations scholars, however, realist theory is an inadequate theoretical framework for analyzing world politics, and especially the rapid changes since the Cold War's end as well as the expanded practice of **multilateralism** and the activities of the UN and other IGOs. One major alternative is **liberalism**.[4]

Liberals regard states as important actors, but they place importance on a variety of other actors in the international system, including IGOs, NGOs, **multinational corporations (MNCs)**, and even individuals. States, in their view, are pluralistic, not unitary, actors. Moral and ethical principles, power relations, and bargaining among different domestic and transnational groups and changing international conditions shape states' interests and actions. There is no single definition of national interest; rather, states vary in their goals, and their interests change. Liberal theorists characterize the international system as an interdependent one in which there is both cooperation and conflict and where actors' mutual interests tend to increase over time. States' power matters, but it is exercised within a framework of international rules and institutions that help to make cooperation possible.

Neoliberal institutionalists have provided a somewhat different explanation for why cooperation occurs. For classical liberals, cooperation emerges from establishing and reforming institutions that permit cooperative interactions and prohibit coercive actions. For neoliberal institutionalists, cooperation emerges when actors have continuous interactions with each other. Institutions help prevent cheating; they reduce transaction and opportunity costs for those who seek gains from cooperation within them. Institutions are essential; they build upon common interests. They help to shape state's interests and state preferences. IGOs such as the United Nations make a difference in world politics by altering state preferences and establishing rules that constrain states. They are not merely pawns of the dominant powers but actually modify state behavior by creating habits of cooperation and serving as arenas for negotiation and policy coordination.

For some liberal theorists, the growth of multilateralism, IGOs, and international law is indicative of a nascent international society in which actors consent to common rules and institutions and recognize common interests as well as a common identity or sense of "we-ness." Within this emerging society, international institutions are changing the way states and other actors interact with each other. Many scholars argue that the growing role of nongovernmental actors represents an emerging global civil society.[5]

A third and relatively recent approach to international relations is **constructivism**, which has become important for studying various aspects of global governance, particularly the role of norms and institutions. Constructivism has several variants, and questions have arisen about whether it is a theory of politics. Yet it offers a valuable way of studying how shared beliefs, rules, organizations, and cultural practices shape the behavior of states and other actors as well as their identities and interests. Among the key norms affecting state behavior in constructivists' view is multilateralism. Several studies have examined the impact of norms and principled beliefs on international outcomes such as the evolution of the international human rights **regime**, bans on certain types of weapons, and humanitarian intervention in which the UN and other IGOs have played a role. They have found that international organizations can be not only "teachers" but also "creators" of norms; as such, they can socialize states into accepting certain political goals and values.[6]

Constructivists tend to see IGOs as actors that can have independent effects on international relations and as arenas in which discussions, persuasion, education, and argument take place that influence government leaders', businesspeople's, and NGO activists' understandings of their interests and of the world in which they live. The consequences are not always positive, however, because IGOs can also stimulate conflicts, their actions may not necessarily be in the interests of their member states, and IGO bureaucracies such as the UN Secretariat may develop agendas of their own, be dysfunctional, lack accountability, tolerate inefficient practices, and compete for turf, budgets, and staff.[7]

Realism, liberalism, and constructivism, then, are different "lenses" through which scholars view world politics and the United Nations.

Dilemmas the UN Faces in the 21st Century

No matter which theory one finds most valuable, understanding the role of the UN in the twenty-first century requires the exploration of three dilemmas.

Dilemma 1: Needs for Governance Versus the UN's Weaknesses

The United Nations has faced increasing demands that it provide peacekeeping and peacebuilding operations, initiate international regulation to halt environmental degradation and alleviate poverty and inequality in the world, promote greater human economic and social well-being, provide humanitarian relief to victims of natural disasters and violence, and protect human rights for various groups. These are demands for global governance—not world government—demands for rules, norms, and organizational structures to manage transboundary and interdependence problems that states acting alone cannot solve, such as terrorism, crime, drugs, environmental degradation, pandemics, and human rights violations.[8]

These governance demands test the capacity and the willingness of states to commit themselves to international cooperation and the capacity of the UN and other international organizations to function effectively. Can they meet these new demands without simply adding more programs? How can the initiatives be funded? Can the UN be more effective in coordinating the related activities of various institutions, states, and NGOs? Can it improve its own management and personnel practices? Can it adapt to deal with the changing nature of conflicts and persistent poverty and inequality? The most important issues concerning the global economy are discussed and decided outside the UN system. The UN Charter's provisions are designed for interstate conflicts, yet most post–Cold War conflicts have been intrastate civil wars. The UN's membership has grown from 50 to 193 states. The Security Council was structured to reflect power realities in 1945, not the twenty-first century.

Clearly, the UN needs to reform to increase its capacity to meet new demands, to mobilize resources, to reflect the changing distribution of power and authority in the twenty-first century, and to strengthen its links with nonstate actors. One of the UN's strengths to date has been its flexibility in response to new issues and a membership more than three times the size of the original membership. Its weaknesses are the rigidity of its central structures, its slowness to accommodate nonstate actors and the changing realities of geopolitics, and the continuing inability of member states to agree about major reforms. It has also been weakened by states' failure to meet their commitments for funding and their reluctance to empower the UN Secretariat too much. Yet the current demands for global governance require the commitment of states and enhanced institutional capacity in the UN; they therefore also require that states give up more of their sovereignty. This leads to the second dilemma.

Dilemma 2: Sovereignty Versus Challenges to Sovereignty

The longstanding principles of state sovereignty and nonintervention in states' domestic affairs are affirmed in the UN Charter, yet sovereignty has eroded on many fronts and is continually challenged in this era of globalization by issues and problems that cross states' borders and that states cannot solve alone. Historically, sovereignty empowered each state to govern all matters within its territorial jurisdiction. **Nonintervention** is the related principle that obliges other states and international organizations not to intervene in matters within the internal or domestic jurisdiction of a sovereign state. Global telecommunications, including the Internet, and economic interdependencies such as global financial markets, international human rights norms, international election monitoring, and environmental regulation are among the many developments that infringe on states' sovereignty and traditional areas of domestic jurisdiction. The growing activities of IGOs and NGOs have eroded the centrality of states as the primary actors in world politics. For example, Amnesty International (AI) and the International Commission of Jurists have been key actors in promoting human rights, sometimes exerting more influence than states themselves. Multinational corporations with operations in several countries and industry groups such as oil, steel, textiles, automobiles, and shipping are important players in trade and climate change negotiations, some having more resources than some states. Partnerships between the UN and private sector, including multinational corporations, have become increasingly important for a variety of governance challenges. The Global Compact initiated by UN Secretary-General Kofi Annan in 1999 was a step in this direction.

How is sovereignty challenged by these developments? Global telecommunications and particularly the Internet as well as heightened economic interdependence have diminished the control that governments can exercise over the information their citizens receive, the value of their money, financial transactions, and the health of their countries' economies. NGOs can influence legislators and government officials both from within countries and from outside through transnational networks and access to the media.

International norms and rules, such as those on trade, the seas, intellectual property rights, ozone-depleting chlorofluorocarbons (CFCs), and women's rights, have been established through UN-sponsored negotiations. They set standards for states and relevant industries as well as for consumers and citizens. When states themselves accept commitments to uphold these standards (by signing and ratifying international treaties and conventions), they are simultaneously exercising their sovereignty (the commitment they make) and accepting a diminution of that sovereignty (the agreement to international standards that will then be open to international monitoring). Climate change poses particularly daunting challenges for both global governance and state sovereignty.

Although multilateral institutions in theory take actions that constitute intervention in states' domestic affairs only with their consent, there is now a growing body of precedent for **humanitarian intervention**, which has emerged as a new norm of **responsibility to protect (R2P)** to justify international actions to alleviate human suffering during violent conflicts without the consent of the "host" country. It was first invoked to provide food relief and reestablish civil order in Somalia in 1993–1994, then to justify the bombing of Yugoslavia and Kosovo by the North Atlantic Treaty Organization (NATO) in 1999, and to call for international action against genocide in the Darfur region of Sudan in 2005–2006. The 2005 World Summit endorsed the R2P norm, but many states, particularly developing countries, feared its consequences for the norms of nonintervention and sovereignty. ...

Despite these apparent limitations on states' sovereignty, the reality remains that "the capacity to mobilize the resources necessary to tackle global problems also remains vested in states, therefore effectively incapacitating many international institutions."[9] That includes the United Nations. Thus, the dilemma associated with state sovereignty links also to the third dilemma: the need for leadership.

Dilemma 3: The Need for Leadership

World politics in the twenty-first century was marked initially by the dominance of the United States as the sole superpower and a diffusion of power among many other states, the European Union (EU), and a wide variety of nonstate actors that exercise influence in different ways. As noted above, however, even before the end of the first decade, it was apparent that the rise of emerging nations such as Brazil, India, and China as well as constraints on the United States were leading to shifting patterns of power and leadership. Yet traditional measures of power in international politics do not necessarily dictate who will provide leadership or be influential within the UN.

Multilateral institutions such as the UN create opportunities for small and middle powers as well as for NGOs, groups of states, and IGOs' executive heads to exercise initiative and leadership. UN secretaries-general, in fact, have often been important figures in the international arena depending on their personality and willingness to take initiatives such as mediating conflicts or proposing responses to international problems that may or may not prove acceptable to member states. Both Boutros Boutros-Ghali and Kofi Annan are noted, for example, for their leadership both within and outside the UN. Prominent individuals, such as former Australian prime minister Gareth Evans and Mohamed Sahnoun of Algeria, who chaired the independent International Commission on Intervention and State Sovereignty that in 2001 proposed the new norm of responsibility to protect as an obligation of states, can exercise leadership through technical expertise and diplomatic skill. Middle powers such as Australia, Canada, Brazil, and India have been influential in international trade negotiations on agricultural issues, as they have long been in peacekeeping and development. Canada provided leadership for the effort in the late 1990s to ban antipersonnel land mines, while Norway led a similar effort on cluster munitions that culminated in a treaty in 2008. Brazil, Japan, and India led the effort in 2005 to secure Security Council reform.

NGOs can also provide leadership along with states, UN secretaries-general, and other prominent individuals. The success of both the land-mine and cluster-munitions efforts owed much to the leadership of coalitions of NGOs. The Intergovernmental Panel on Climate Change (IPCC) has been a lead actor in international efforts since the late 1980s to analyze data on climate and to promote efforts to address the problem.

Still, states matter, and leadership from major powers with resources and influence matters. Hence, the dilemma. With the demise of the Soviet Union in 1991, the United States became the sole remaining superpower—the only state with intervention capabilities and interests in many parts of the globe. US economic, military, technological, and other resources still vastly exceed those of all other countries, notwithstanding China's rapid economic growth and emergence as a major economic power. The US gross domestic product is more than two and a half times that of China, whose GDP surpassed Japan's in 2010, and the American military expenditure is almost half that of the entire world. Power disparity such as this may still make the United States "bound to lead," but the style of leadership required in a world marked by multilateralism is not one of unilateral action but one geared to building coalitions and consensus and achieving active consultation and cooperation.

Furthermore, dominance tends to inspire resistance. A dominant power can rely on its sheer weight to play hardball and get its way—up to a point. The prolonged insurgency and failures in Iraq following US military intervention in 2003 demonstrated the limits of hard power. Leadership (and inspiring follower-ship) depends on soft power's inspiration and cultivation. In the late 1990s, US opposition to the creation of the International Criminal Court, the convention banning antipersonnel land mines, the Comprehensive Test Ban Treaty, and the Kyoto Protocol on Climate Change signaled a "go-it-alone" pattern that continued in the early years of the twenty-first century with the Bush administration's opposition to international treaties and invasion of Iraq.[10] This made many countries less willing to accept US dominance.[11] It also fueled anti-Americanism in many parts of the world.[12] Consequently, the United States lost a good deal of its soft power and ability to lead. President Obama has rectified some of that and been more inclined to forge international consensus, limiting US interventions, mindful also of the constraints of the US budget deficit and military commitments. In any case, the history of US engagement with the UN is one of "mixed messages" and considerable variation. ... Congress blocked full payment of US dues to the UN from the mid-1980s until 2000, and with the huge budget deficit, as well as Republican majority in the House of Representatives following the 2010 midterm elections, US payments to the UN are targeted for cuts again.

In a world of emerging powers, the likelihood that the United States can lead, even when it chooses to, is inevitably diminished. Yet those rising powers may not be willing or able to assume leadership either.

Notes

1. Inis L. Claude Jr., *The Changing United Nations* (New York: Random House, 1965), 32.

2. Christopher S. Wren, "Annan Says All Nations Must Cooperate," *New York Times,* September 6, 2000.

3. See, for example, Hans Morgenthau, *Politics Among Nations,* 4th ed. (New York: Alfred A. Knopf, 1967); and John J. Mearsheimer, "The False Promise of International Institutions," *International Security* 13, no. 3 (1994–1995): 5–49.

4. See, for example, Michael W. Doyle, "Liberalism and World Politics," *American Political Science Review* 80, no. 4 (December 1986): 1151–1169; Hedley Bull, *The Anarchical Society: A Study of Order in World Politics* (New York: Columbia University Press, 1977); Robert O. Keohane and Joseph S. Nye, *Power and Interdependence,* 3rd ed. (New York: Longman, 2001); and Robert O. Keohane and Lisa L. Martin, "The Promise of Institutionalist Theory," *International Security* 20, no. 1 (1995): 39–51.

5. See, for example, Ronnie Lipschutz, "Reconstructing World Politics: The Emergence of Global Civil Society," *Millennium: Journal of International Studies* 21, no. 3 (1992): 398–399; and Craig Warkentin, *Reshaping World Politics: NGOs, the Internet, and Global Civil Society* (Lanham, MD: Rowman and Littlefield, 2001).

6. See, for example, John Gerard Ruggie, "Multilateralism: The Anatomy of an Institution," in *Multilateralism Matters: The Theory and Praxis of an Institutional Form,* ed. John Gerard Ruggie (New York: Columbia University Press, 1993), 3–47; Martha Finnemore, *National Interests in International Society* (Ithaca: Cornell University Press, 1996); and Martha Finnemore and Kathryn Sikkink, "Taking Stock: The Constructivist Research Program in International Relations and Comparative Politics," *Annual Review of Political Science* 4 (2001): 391–416.

7. Michael Barnett and Martha Finnemore, *Rules for the World: International Organizations in Global Politics* (Ithaca: Cornell University Press, 2004).

8. Margaret P. Karns and Karen A. Mingst, *International Organizations: The Politics and Processes of Global Governance,* 2nd ed. (Boulder: Lynne Rienner, 2009).

9. Thomas G. Weiss and Ramesh Thakur, *Global Governance and the UN: An Unfinished Journey* (Bloomington: Indiana University Press, 2010).

10. Stewart Patrick and Shepard Forman, eds., *Multilateralism and U.S. Foreign Policy: Ambivalent Engagement* (Boulder: Lynne Rienner, 2002).

11. David M. Malone and Yuen Foong Khong, eds., *Unilateralism and U.S. Foreign Policy: International Perspectives* (Boulder: Lynne Rienner, 2003).

12. Joseph S. Nye Jr., *Bound to Lead: The Changing Nature of American Power* (New York: Basic Books, 1990); Joseph S. Nye, *The Paradox of American Power: Why the World's Only Superpower Can't Go It Alone* (Oxford: Oxford University Press, 2002).

Introduction

by John McCormick and Jonathan Olsen

*We cannot aim at anything less than the union of Europe as a whole,
and we look forward with confidence to the day when that union will be
achieved.*

—WINSTON CHURCHILL, THE HAGUE CONGRESS, MAY 1948

*That such an unnecessary and irrational project as building a European
superstate was ever embarked on will seem in future years to be perhaps
the greatest folly of the modern era.*

—MARGARET THATCHER, *STATECRAFT:
STRATEGIES FOR A CHANGING WORLD*, 2003

The European Union is the world's wealthiest capitalist marketplace, the world's biggest trading power, and—along with the United States—one of the two most influential political actors in the world. Its emergence has changed the character and definition of Europe, helped bring to the region the longest uninterrupted spell of general peace in its recorded history, and altered the balance of global power by helping Europeans reassert themselves on the world stage. By building a single market and developing common policies in a wide range of different areas, Europeans have come to relate to each other differently and have set aside many of their traditional differences in the interests of cooperation. The EU has brought fundamental changes to the way Europe functions, the way it is seen by others, and the way others—most notably the United States—work with Europe.

And yet the European project has raised many doubts and attracted many critics, even more so in the wake of a severe debt crisis that is testing the staying power of the euro, the EU's common currency. Some question the wisdom of European states transferring authority to a joint system of governance that is often criticized for its elitism and its lack of accountability and transparency. Others debate whether the

EU works as efficiently as it might and whether it has outgrown itself. It is often faulted for its inability to reach common agreement on critical foreign and security policy issues and to match its economic and political power with military power.

Skeptics have routinely drawn attention to the EU's economic difficulties (such as sluggish economic growth and pockets of high unemployment), to its mixed record on dealing with ethnic and religious diversity, and to worries about demographic trends as birthrates decline and Europeans become older. For journalists and academics it has become almost de rigueur to talk and write of the crises in European governance, to point with alarm and foreboding at the latest example of a failure by European leaders to agree, and to question the long-term viability of the EU. Indeed, in the light of recent economic problems, some have even begun to doubt whether the European project will survive or whether the EU can truly be considered a world powerhouse.

In a recent editorial in the *New York Times*, Timothy Garton Ash argued that to include the EU with the United States and China in a "global Big Three" would be to invite laughter from elites in Beijing, Washington, or other world capitals. For Garton Ash, the crisis in the eurozone had demonstrated that the "five great drivers of European unification"—the legacy of "never again" left behind by World War II; the Soviet threat; the determination of Germany, as Europe's economic powerhouse, to sacrifice its own interests for those of "Europe"; the desire of Eastern European countries to belong to a common Europe; and the assumption that the EU would mean a continuous rise in living standards—have been exhausted. If the EU is really going to play the role it sees itself as playing, Garton Ash concludes, then it will have to pursue a course of more thoroughgoing integration, with a common identity and more comprehensive and muscular policies, from the social and economic spheres to—most especially—foreign affairs.[1]

Meanwhile, many Europeans are puzzled and uncertain about how the EU functions and what difference it makes to their lives. Americans are even more puzzled; many are—or at least have been, until recently—only vaguely aware of its existence and do not yet fully understand what difference it has made to Europe or to transatlantic relations. American political leaders are more attuned to its implications, as are corporate and financial leaders who have had to learn to deal as much with a twenty-eight-member regional grouping as with each of the individual states in the EU; even American tourists have noticed a difference as they use the euro in place of many different national currencies. But doubts remain about the bigger picture and about what difference the EU has made. To complicate matters, there is no agreement on just how we should define and understand the EU. It is not a European superstate, and suggestions that it might one day become a United States of Europe are greeted with a volatile mixture of enthusiasm and hostility.

The origins of the EU, and the motives behind European integration, are relatively clear. Frustrated and appalled by war and conflict, many Europeans argued over the centuries in favor of setting aside national differences in the collective interest. The first serious thoughts about a peaceful and voluntary union came after the horrors of World War I, but the concept matured following the devastation of World War II, when the most serious Europeanists spoke of replacing national governments with a European federation. They dreamed of integrating European economies and removing controls on the movement of people, money, goods, and services; they were driven by the desire to promote peace and to build a single European market that could compete with the United States.

The first tangible step came in April 1951 with the signing of the Treaty of Paris, which created the European Coal and Steel Community (ECSC), set up at least in part to prove a point about the feasibility and benefits of regional integration. Progress in the 1950s and 1960s was modest, but then the European Economic Community (EEC) was launched, membership began to expand, the goals of integration became more ambitious, and we now have today's European Union: an entity that has its own institutions and body of laws, twenty-eight member states and more than 500 million residents, a common currency used by more than half its members, and increasing agreement on a wide range of common policy areas. The Cold War-era political and economic divisions between Western and Eastern Europe have almost disappeared, and it is now less realistic to think of European states in isolation than as partners in an ever-changing European Union. The fudge-word *integration* is used more often than *unification*

Map 2.2.1. The European Union

to describe what has been happening, but those who champion the EU suggest that political union of some kind is almost inevitable. It may not be a United States of Europe, and it may turn out to be a loose association in which more power rests with the member states, but they find it hard to imagine a future in which European political union is not a reality.

Like it or not, the EU cannot be ignored, and the need to better understand how it works and what difference it makes becomes more evident by the day. Hence this book, written mainly for students in courses on European politics in the United States and Canada. In three parts it introduces the EU, goes through the steps in its development, explains how it works, and provides an overview of its policy activities.

Part 1 (Chapters 1–4) provides context by first surveying the most important theories and concepts of regional integration and then showing how and why the EU has evolved. Giving the background on the earliest ideas about European unification sets the scene for the creation of the ECSC, whose founding members were France, West Germany, Italy, Belgium, the Netherlands, and Luxembourg. This was followed in 1957 by the signing of the two Treaties of Rome, which created the EEC and the European Atomic Energy Community (Euratom). With the same six members as the ECSC, the EEC set out to build an integrated multinational economy among its members, to achieve a customs union, to encourage free trade, and to harmonize standards, laws, and prices among its members. It witnessed greater productivity, channeled new investment into industry and agriculture, and became more competitive in the world market.

By the late 1960s, the EEC had all the trappings of a new level of European government, based mainly in Brussels, the capital of Belgium. Analysts refused to describe it as a full-blown political system, but it had its own executive and bureaucracy (the European Commission), its own protolegislature (the European Parliament), its own judiciary (the Court of Justice), and its own legal system. Over time, the word *Economic* was dropped from the name, giving way to the European Community (EC). Its successes drew new members, starting with Britain, Denmark, and Ireland in 1973, and moving on to Greece, Portugal, and Spain in the 1980s, East Germany joining via German unification, and Austria, Finland, and Sweden joining in the 1990s. The most recent round of enlargement came in 2004–07 with the addition of twelve mainly Eastern European member states, including Hungary, Poland, and the three former Soviet Baltic states, and Croatia became the EU's newest member in 2013. The character and reach of integration have been changed along the way with revisions to the founding treaties:

- In 1987 the Single European Act (SEA) led to the elimination of almost all remaining barriers to the movement of people, money, goods, and services among the twelve member states.
- In 1993 the Maastricht Treaty on European Union committed the EC to the creation of a single currency, a common citizenship, and a common foreign and security policy, and gave new powers over law and policy to the EC institutions. It also made the EC part of a broader new entity called the European Union.
- In 1998 and 2003 the treaties of Amsterdam and Nice built on these changes, fine-tuned the powers of the institutions, and helped prepare the EU for new members from Eastern Europe.

- An attempt was made in 2002–04 to provide focus and permanence by replacing the accumulated treaties with a European constitution. But the finished product was lengthy, detailed, and controversial, and it had to be ratified by every EU member state before it could come into force. When French and Dutch voters turned it down in 2005, there was another brief "crisis" before European leaders reached agreement in 2007 to draw up a new treaty based on much of the content of the failed constitution.
- The resulting Treaty of Lisbon fundamentally reformed several of the EU's institutions and attempted to give more coherence to the Union's policies, even while avoiding the language and trappings of a constitution that had been unpopular with many EU citizens.

The European Union today is the largest economic bloc in the world, accounting for one-fourth of global gross domestic product (GDP) and about 20 percent of global trade. It has replaced many of its national currencies with a new single currency, the euro, which has taken its place alongside the U.S. dollar and the Japanese yen as one of the world's primary currencies (its recent problems notwithstanding). There is now virtually unlimited free movement of people, money, goods, and services among most of its member states. The EU has its own flag (a circle of twelve gold stars on a blue background) and its own anthem (the "Ode to Joy" from Beethoven's Ninth Symphony); national passports have been replaced with a uniform EU passport, and in many ways Brussels has become the new capital of Europe.

Part 2 (Chapters 5–10) looks at the European institutions, explaining how they work and how they relate to each other. Their powers and authority have grown steadily since the 1950s, although their work is often misunderstood by Europeans, and analysts continue to disagree over their character and significance. There are five main institutions:

- *The European Commission.* Based in Brussels, this is the executive and administrative branch of the EU, responsible for developing new EU laws and policies and for overseeing their implementation.
- *The Council of the EU.* Also based in Brussels, this is the major decision-making body of the EU, made up of government ministers from each of the member states. Working with the European Parliament, the Council makes the votes that turn Commission proposals into European law.
- *The European Parliament.* Divided among Strasbourg, Luxembourg, and Brussels, the members of the European Parliament are directly elected to five-year terms by the voters of the member states. Although it cannot introduce proposals for new laws, Parliament can discuss Commission proposals, and it has equal powers with the Council of Ministers over adoption.
- *The European Court of Justice.* Based in Luxembourg, the Court interprets national and EU law and helps build a common body of law that is uniformly applied throughout the member states. It bases its decisions on the treaties, which in some respects function as a constitution of the EU.
- *The European Council.* This is less an institution than a forum, consisting of the political leaders of the member states. They meet at least four times per year to make broad decisions on policy, the details of which are worked out by the Commission and the Council of the EU.

Table 2.2.1. The EU in Figures

	Area (Thousand Square Miles)	Population (Millions)	Gross Domestic Product ($ Billion)	Per Capita Gross National Income ($)
Germany	137	82.3	3,571	43,980
France	212	62.8	2,773	42,420
United Kingdom	94	62.0	2,432	37,780
Italy	116	60.5	2,195	35,330
Spain	195	46.0	1,491	30,990
Netherlands	16	16.6	836	49,730
Sweden	174	9.4	538	53,230
Poland	121	38.3	514	12,480
Belgium	12	10.7	512	46,160
Austria	32	8.4	418	48,300
Denmark	17	5.5	333	60,390
Greece	51	11.4	299	25,030
Finland	130	5.4	266	48,420
Portugal	36	10.7	238	21,250
Ireland	27	4.5	217	38,580
Czech Republic	30	10.5	215	18,520
Romania	92	21.5	180	7,910
Hungary	36	10.0	140	12,730
Slovakia	19	5.5	96	16,070
Croatia	21	4.4	64	13,850
Luxembourg	1	0.5	59	78,130
Bulgaria	43	7.5	54	6,550
Slovenia	8	2.0	50	23,610
Lithuania	25	3.3	43	12,280
Latvia	25	2.3	28	12,350
Cyprus	4	1.1	25	29,450
Estonia	17	1.3	22	15,200
Malta	0.1	0.4	9	18,620
TOTAL	**1,691**	**504.8**	**17,616**	**33,982**
United States	3,718	310.4	15,094	48,450
China	3,705	1,341.0	7,298	4,930
Japan	146	126.5	5,867	45,180
Brazil	3,286	195.0	2,477	10,720
Russia	6,593	143.0	1,858	10,400
India	1,269	1,225.0	1,848	1,410
Canada	3,852	34.0	1,736	45,560
World	**57,309**	**6,894.6**	**69,971**	**9,488**

Source: Population figures for 2010 from the UN Population Division, http://www.un.org/esa/population. Economic figures for 2011 from the World Bank, 2012, http://data.worldbank.org. Eurozone states indicated in boldface.

Part 3 (Chapters 11–16) focuses on the policies pursued by the European Union, looking at what integration has meant for the member states and for Europeans themselves. Covering economic, monetary, agricultural, cohesion, environmental, social, foreign, and security policies, this section examines the EU policy-making process, identifies the key influences on that process, and looks at its consequences and implications. The final chapter focuses on relations between the EU and the United States, which have blown hot and cold over the years.

Because European integration continues to be a work in progress, with a final destination that remains unclear, the relative balance of power among national governments and EU institutions is still evolving. That balance will continue to change as more countries join the EU and as integration reaches further into the lives of Europeans. All of this raises the key question: Why should Americans care about the EU? More specifically: What does it matter on this side of the Atlantic, and what effect will these changes have on our lives?

The most immediate implications are economic. Through most of the Cold War, the U.S. had it relatively good: it was the world's biggest national economy and national exporter, it had the world's strongest and most respected currency, its corporations dominated the international marketplace and sold their products and services all over the world, and it led the world in the development of new technology. But much has changed in recent decades with the rise of competition first from Japan, then from Europe, and increasingly from China and India. The U.S. still has the world's biggest national economy, but the combined European market is nearly 20 percent bigger, and its population is nearly two-thirds bigger. European corporations are becoming bigger, more numerous, and more competitive; and the EU long ago displaced the U.S. as the world's biggest exporter and importer. And as one of the world's economic powers, naturally the EU's economic problems also have global economic significance.

All of this also applies to the bilateral relationship between the U.S. and EU. The U.S. does about one-fifth of its merchandise trade with the EU, which is the source of about two-thirds of all the foreign direct investment in the United States and Canada, most of it coming from Britain, the Netherlands, and Germany. Subsidiaries of European companies employ several million Americans—more than the affiliates of all other countries combined—and account for about 15 percent of all manufacturing jobs in the United States and Canada. U.S. corporations, meanwhile, have made their biggest overseas investments in the EU. We often see and hear worried analyses in North America about the rise of China, but while the volume of Chinese imports to the U.S. is certainly catching up with that from the EU, Europe is still by far the most important economic partner of the United States.

The rise of the EU also has important political implications for North America. During the Cold War the most critical political relationship in the world was that between the United States and the Soviet Union—much else that happened in the world was determined by the attempts of the two adversaries to outwit and outmaneuver one another. With the collapse of the USSR and the end of the Cold War, it became usual to see the United States described as the world's last remaining superpower, and even perhaps as a hyperpower. But while the United States is unmatched in the size, reach, and firepower of its military, globalization has helped make political and economic relationships more important than investments in the ability to wage war. The U.S. spends almost as much on defense every year as the rest of the world combined, but this has not guaranteed its security, and in the view of many critics has actually made both the U.S. and the world less safe.

Meanwhile, the political influence of the EU has grown. Its economic might cannot be ignored, its policy positions are often less controversial than many of those taken by the United States (particularly toward the Middle East), and while the U.S. is associated (not always fairly) with hard power (coercion, threats, and the use of military force), the EU is associated with soft power (diplomacy, economic opportunity, and negotiation). The contrast is clear in the records of the U.S. and the EU on the promotion of democracy. Recent American leaders have made much of the importance of spreading democracy, but they have invested more time and money in using military means to achieve their objectives. Meanwhile, the promise of access to the European marketplace or even—for the select few—of membership in the European Union has arguably had a greater effect on promoting lasting democratic change and economic development, at least for Europe's closest neighbors. It was reasoning such as this that was behind the award to the European Union in 2012 of the Nobel Prize for Peace.

Just in the past few years, the relative roles of the United States and the European Union in the international system have been transformed. During the Cold War, Western Europe relied on the United States for security guarantees and economic investment. The two partners gave the impression that they saw eye to eye and made many public statements of solidarity. But behind the scenes there were tensions and crises as they disagreed over policy and over how to deal with the Soviet threat. Since the end of the Cold War, the disagreements have spilled into the open. The two are now economic competitors, Europeans are less willing to accede to U.S. policy leadership, and the two have become increasingly aware of what divides them. They differ not just over the use of military power but on how to deal with many international problems (including terrorism, climate change, nuclear proliferation, and the Arab Israeli problem) and on a wide range of social values and norms. The result has been the emergence of two models of government, two sets of opinions about how the world works, and two sets of possible responses to pressing international concerns.

For all these reasons, we cannot ignore the European Union, nor can we understand the world today without understanding how the EU has altered the balance of global power. Not everyone is convinced that European integration is a good idea or that the EU has been able to fully capitalize on its assets and resources, but—like it or not—the changes it has wrought cannot be undone. The pace of global political and economic change is accelerating, and the results of the European experiment have fundamentally changed the way in which the world functions and the place of the United States in the international system.

Note

1. Timothy Garton Ash, "Can Europe Survive the Rise of the Rest?," *New York Times*, September 2, 2012, B5.

Human Security

Security, especially collective security, has always been a central preoccupation of politics. In the mid-1990s, however, the concept of *human* security shifted that focus from state sovereignty and borders to the safety of people and communities. The notion of human security was initially developed by a high-level commission that was created after the Secretary General of the United Nations called for a world "free from want" and "free from fear." They were building on the Four Freedoms outlined by President Franklin D. Roosevelt in 1941. The concept was then introduced to the public in the 1994 Human Development Report, which listed seven core elements of human security: economic, health, personal, political, food, environmental, and community.

The concept of human security poses three main challenges to the way political scientists thought about security. First, the idea challenged the existing state-based conceptualization of security in international relations to the way political scientists thought about security. Human security proponents questioned the goal of security: is it truly the territorial integrity of a state or is it the well-being of its people? Second, human security poses an *ethical* challenge to traditional international relations because whereas traditional political science approaches strive for objectivity, this approach makes judgments. It is a normative framework explicitly concerned with how things ought to be, not just how they are. This represents a departure from traditional academic reasoning. From an ethical perspective, the security claims of the state derive their values from meeting the needs of the individuals who comprise the state. (Tadbaksh and Chenoy 2007). Third, human security poses a challenge to the political perspective of realism. Human security turns the focus from state to individual security, thereby rejecting the realist view that sovereign states are the fundamental units of politics. The concept of human security presupposes that global stability depends on the well being of individuals.

Context played an important role. At a practical level, states are unable to protect their citizens from the cross-border threats in a globalized world. The waves of decolonization that followed the Cold War gave rise to the emergence of weak and unstable states. Elites misused power and citizens suffered from a basic lack of human services and human rights abuses—violating what they had presumably pledged their allegiance to a state for. This development created a complex set of needs and risks that a human security approach is designed to address. Another change was that with the end of the bipolar world dominated by the United States and the Soviet Union, the most prevalent types of conflict also changed. The proportion of conflicts taking place within state borders is now greater than the conflicts between states,[1] a development that the UN was not initially designed to address.

There are also technological factors that change the nature of conflict and therefore security. For most of human history, weapons relied on the brute strength of the operator. Today, arms are so light that children can use them as easily and effectively as adults. Rifles, grenades, light machine guns, and land mines are all portable. This is part of the changing landscape of conflict. A once sacrosanct distinction between combatants and civilians has become virtually impossible to uphold. Civilians have always suffered in war, but in many present-day conflicts they are the primary target. Warfare has taken on new and hybrid patterns of violence. All these developments contributed to a reevaluation of the concept of security.

---

1 Our World in Data, https://ourworldindata.org/civil-wars.

Advocates of human security suggest the approach provides a framework for dealing with the true complexity of contemporary security threats. And the human security framework takes advantage of a wide range of organizations, some of them discussed in this chapter, that provide opportunities for solving problems in a more integrated, less compartmentalized manner.

The Aims of Human Security

The concept of human security seeks to identify threats, avoid them when possible, and mitigate the effects when they occur, making it prevention oriented (Image 2.3). Prevention stands on two building blocks: protection and empowerment. The Commission on Human Security (CHS) defines protection as the "strategies, set up by states, international agencies, NGOs and the private sector, [to] shield people from menaces (Commission on Human Security: 2003: 10). Protection is sometimes called a "top-down" approach because it appreciates that many of the threats people face are beyond their control. Human security works around this tendency by aiming to protect people in a more systematic and less state-dependent way. But this top-down approach would be incomplete without a "bottom-up" approach to complement it. As the Commission on Human Security sees it, empowerment means advancing the capabilities of individuals and communities to find their own solutions by making informed choices and acting on their own behalf. The field of human security therefore aims to be people centered, empowering individuals from the bottom up. It envisions a world in which "people can exercise choices safely and freely" (Human Development Report 1994: 23).

Image 2.3. Possible Types of Human Security Threats

Type of Security	Examples of Main Threats
Economic security	Persistent poverty, unemployment
Food security	Hunger, famine
Health security	Deadly infectious diseases, unsafe food, malnutrition, lack of access to basic health care
Environmental security	Environmental degradation, resources depletion, natural disasters, pollution
Personal security	Physical violence, crime, terrorism, domestic violence, child labor
Community security	Inter-ethnic, religious and other identity-based tensions
Political security	Political repression, human rights abuses

How might one begin to compare human security across regions or assess a single country's progress over time? A Human Security Index was put into practice in 2008. Look at the index to see how a country that you are interested in is ranked. Human security is implemented in a number of ways. Foremost among them is the Human Security Unit of the United Nations Office for the Coordination of Humanitarian Affairs. The Unit works to disseminate lessons learned about human security and create practical tools for professionals.

Limitations

Human Security is sometimes referred to as paradigm shift. Thomas Kuhn (1962) popularized this term to describe how knowledge revolutions are characterize by the rise of ideas that challenge, defeat, and replace the previously accepted dogma. Despite the claims that human security represents a paradigm shift, it is still unclear if the concept can act as a guide or framework for policymaking on the part of governments, or research on the part of academics. The term is both expansive and vague. Can one concept serve as an umbrella for discussing deforestation and mental health? Roland Paris argues that a major weakness of the concept is that it has never been clearly defined. He states, "Human security is like 'sustainable development'—everyone is for it but few people have a clear idea of what it means" (2001: 88). If human security is safety from chronic threats such as hunger, political oppression, and disease as well as sudden or acute disruptions to daily life, then virtually anything and everything can be seen as a threat to human security.

The vagueness is, however, by design. Supporters of the concept have an interest in keeping the concept expansive. Paris argues that "the idea of human security is the glue that holds together a jumbled coalition of middle power states, development agencies and NGOs—all of which seek to shift attention and resources away from conventional security issues and toward goals that have traditionally fallen under the rubric of international development" (2001: 89). In other words, the term is designed to bring funds to causes.

This is not necessarily a bad feature. The concept of human security motivated the signing of the Anti-personal Landmines Convention and the International Criminal Court (ICC), both notable achievements. The point made by Paris and others who bring a critical perspective is that these accomplishments notwithstanding, the concept should be viewed more as a rallying cry than a viable framework of analysis (2001: 89).

International Criminal Court

The International Criminal Court (ICC) is a permanent tribunal to prosecute individuals for a set of specific abuses: genocide, crimes against humanity, war crimes, and the crime of aggression. The establishment of the Court marks the first time in history when states agreed to accept the jurisdiction of a permanent international court. To be clear, the ICC does not take the place of national courts. According to the Rome Statute that brought the Court into being, every state retains is obligation to use its criminal jurisdiction. The role of the ICC is to intervene when a state is unable or unwilling to carry out an investigation and prosecute perpetrators of serious crimes. As such, it is termed a court of "last resort."

The ICC is the product of decades of work that began with the Nuremburg Trials and progressed through the temporary international tribunals in places such as Rwanda and the former Yugoslavia. The main goal in establishing the Court has been to end impunity for the perpetrators of mass atrocities discussed in more detail in the next chapter.[2]

The ICC can be distinguished from the International Court of Justice (ICJ) that is one of six UN organs. First, whereas the ICJ settles disputes between UN member states as the judicial branch of the UN, the ICC is designed to prosecute individuals. Second, whereas the ICJ is part of the UN, the ICC is not part of the UN, though it has a close relationship with the UN because the UN Security Council can refer situations to it. Finally, the jurisdiction of the ICJ is wider: it has jurisdiction over all 193 UN member states. The ICC, in contrast, has jurisdiction only over its member states, which number 124 currently. A number of countries where mass atrocities are a serious issue have abstained from joining, limiting the power of the Court. Neither the United States nor Russia has ratified the Rome Statute.

One thing the ICJ and ICC have in common is a lack of enforcement units. The ICC relies on the law enforcement forces of states to arrest suspects and bring them to trial. In practice, states have been reluctant to facilitate the work of the ICC in this way unless it is in their direct self-interest to do so.

References

Clausewitz, Carl von. Michael Howard and Peter Paret, eds. and trans. (1989) [1832]. *On War.* Princeton, NJ: Princeton University Press.

Commission on Human Security. 2003. Human Security Now: Protecting and Empowering People [online: ReliefWeb] https://reliefweb.int/report/world/human-security-now-protecting-and-empowering-people accessed July 3, 2018

Evans, Peter B. 2009. "The Eclipse of the Nation-State? Reflections on Stateness in an Era of Globalization." In Lawrence Mayer, Dennis Patterson, and Frank Thames (eds.), *Contending Perspectives in Comparative Politics.* Washington, DC: CQ Press, 245–260.

Hirst, Paul, and Grahame Thompson. 1999. *Globalization in Question: The International Economy and the Possibilities for Governance.* Cambridge: Polity Press.

Hirst, Paul and Grahame Thompson. 1995. "Globalization and the future of the nation state," Economy and Society 24 (3): 408.

Hobbes, Thomas. 2012. "Leviathan." In *The Clarendon Edition of the Works of Thomas Hobbes*, Vols. 3–5. Oxford: Clarendon.

Human Development Report. 1994 United Nations Development Program.

Kacowicz, Arie M., and Mor Mitrani. 2016. "Why Don't We Have Coherent Theories of International Relations about Globalization?" *Global Governance* 22 (2): 189–208.

Kuhn, Thomas. 1962. *The Structure of Scientific Revolutions.* Chicago: University of Chicago Press

Levitsky, Melvyn. 2018. Guest Lecture for International Studies 101, February, 2018.

Paris, Roland. 2001. "Human Security—Paradigm Shift or Hot Air?" *International Security* 26 (2): 87–102.

---

2   International Criminal Court https://www.icc-cpi.int/about

Reich, Robert. 2014. "The New Tribalism and the Decline of the Nation-State," robertreich.org

Rodrik, Dani. 2009. "Sense and Nonsense in the Globalization Debate." In Lawrence Mayer, Dennis Patterson, and Frank Thames (es.), *Contending Perspectives in Comparative Politics.* Washington, DC: CQ Press, 261–269.

Staab, Andreas. 2013. *The European Union Explained: Institutions, Actors, Global Impact.* Bloomington: Indiana University Press.

Seymour, Michel. 2014. *The Fate of the Nation-State.* Online.

Tadbakhsh, Shahrbanou, and Anuradha M Chenoy. 2007. *Human Security: Concepts and Implications.* New York: Routledge.

Image Credits

CHAPTER THREE

Human Rights and Humanitarianism

Chapter Two considered how the territorially-based Westphalian system has been a durable way of organizing politics since the mid-seventeenth century. This is a system in which each state is responsible for the safety and welfare of its citizens. States, however, often fall short of this task. Human rights and humanitarianism arose as a response to this conundrum. The first main topic to be explored in this chapter is the concept of human rights and the institutions responsible for protecting them. The second main topic concerns the strengths of humanitarian action and the challenges it faces. Given the number and the seriousness of crises today, a crucial question for nation-states and the international community is when to intervene.

This chapter picks up a theme from Chapters One and Two, which is the importance of the individual. Most of the rights in the Universal Declaration of Human Rights (UDHR), and the two international treaties or "covenants" that followed are considered individual rights.[1] In many ways, then, human rights represent a way of asserting the moral primacy of the individual. As noted in Chapter One, in the contemporary era of globalization, technological innovations are quite literally in the hands of individuals. The individual is also at the center of the conceptual and legal framework of human rights—one of the most impressive developments of the twentieth century. We will return to the topic of human rights in Chapter Five because the evolving human rights regime exerted a considerable influence on the project of human development.

What are Human Rights?

Human rights are the rights one has by virtue of being human. The concept of human rights recognizes the inherent dignity of every person. In theory, there are three primary characteristics associated with the "human" component of human rights. First, all humans possess these rights *equally* because one either is or is not a human being. Second, these rights are inalienable. They can't be taken away because regardless of how bad one's behavior might be, one cannot stop being human. Third, they are universal, held by all human beings, regardless of any characteristic, including race, religion, gender, ethnicity, and national origin.

---

1 http://www.un.org/en/universal-declaration-human-rights/

Human rights are categorized by philosophers as negative rights. A negative right is a right to be *not* subjected to an action (e.g., torture) on the part of someone else. Negative rights require others to abstain from action. Positive rights, by contrast, are those rights that impose an obligation on others: they require others to provide a good or a service. One may immediately surmise why framing human rights as negative was more widely accepted Positive rights are more complicated to justify and costly to implement.

How Did the Idea of Human Rights Originate?

Scholars take two main approaches to describing the evolution of human rights. The extended or comprehensive view traces human rights to the values embedded in world religions and recognizes developments that occurred even before rights were referred to as "human rights." A more concise view, by contrast, focuses on the time when the words "human rights" were defined and codified in the post-World War II period.

In the historical view, religion provides an excellent starting point for thinking about human rights because the world's religions place a high value on honoring and protecting the dignity and worth of human life. Many religions also espouse helping strangers, the core of humanitarianism. For example, the story of the good Samaritan is an important parable in the Christian Bible. Islam requires alms or *zakat* of its followers. *Zakat* is one of the Five Pillars of Islam and consists of an obligation to share wealth for those who have reached a sufficient amount of savings, referred to as *Nisaab*. The amount of *zakat* paid to the poor and the needy is 2.5 percent of *Nisaab*. The Hebrew Bible also teaches that one must aid people in need. In Judaism, material support for the needy is called tzedakah. It is not charity per se but a part of "righteous behavior" and social justice. Of course, religions have also supported violence and repression at some point in their history, making the relationship between religion and human rights a complex one.

In the extended view of the origin of human rights, the signing of Magna Carta marks a turning point. Signed in 1215, the Magna Carta established (among other things) that everyone, including the king, is subject to the law. An important next step was taken when Hugo Grotius, a Dutch politician and jurist, defined "natural rights" as something that people have separate from God's will. This was a novel idea for the seventeenth century. A great problem of political philosophy had been the question of the basis of the state's right to power. Grotius challenged the traditional answer, a combination of "God" and "might makes right." He suggested that people should be able to use their rights independently of the church as part of a contractual foundation for social life. Grotius and his successors wanted to emphasize the entitlements that belong to the person who has rights. This emphasis paved the way to making a distinction between rights and duties (Miller 2014). Grotius thought the right to life, body, freedom, and honor were the basic natural rights. Lynn Hunt suggests that he may have been concerned about human slavery (Hunt 2007: 119). John Locke took a slightly different view. He saw "Life, Liberty, and Estate" as natural rights, placing an emphasis on property rather than on slavery. In the long view, human rights gained greater specificity in Renaissance Europe as the religious conservatism and the feudal authoritarianism that had characterized the Middle Ages was replaced with a different set of values. The philosophical discussion of rights resonated in a secularizing European society that was interested in alternatives to religious faith as a basis for social life.

The term "natural rights" warrants more explanation. Philosophers and political scientists distinguish natural and legal rights. Natural rights are those rights that are not contingent on the laws, customs, or beliefs of any particular society or government, making them universal and inalienable. In contrast, legal rights are the rights a person gains as a result of inclusion in a specific legal system. But there is more to human rights than natural rights. Theorists of human rights construed them as more practical than natural rights. Natural rights are basically hypothetical rights—the rights one has before institutions are created. In contrast, human rights are designed to serve as a guide for state laws, and protect the values a society deems important.

The comprehensive view of the origins of human rights continues with the American and French Revolutions. Thomas Jefferson utilized the writings of seventeenth- and eighteenth-century European philosophers when he penned the 1776 Virginia Declaration of Rights. The Virginia Declaration articulated what were described as "fundamental rights and freedoms." The document translated ideas that circulated primarily in the realm of philosophy into something tangible. The Declaration asserted that King George III had sufficiently violated the rights of the colonists that it warranted creating a new and separate government. The growing conviction that the legitimacy of a government rests on its ability to guarantee the human rights of its citizens was a crucial step in the evolution of human rights.

The Declaration of the Rights of Man and of the Citizen that emerged from the French Revolution was also influenced by Enlightenment political philosophy. Whereas Americans wanted to create a separate and independent government, France emphasized fairness and equality. The document declared the natural, inalienable, and sacred rights of man to be the foundation of any and all governments. One of the things that was most remarkable about the document is that unlike the Virginia Declaration, it never mentions king, nobility, or church (Hunt 2007: 132). The French saw rights as coming from secular sources, a significant departure from previous doctrine. The drafters' (the Marquis de Lafayette, Thomas Jefferson, and Honoré Mirabeau) claim that the document pertains to all men and all citizens, not just French people, was controversial and provoked debate.

In the comprehensive view of the emergence of human rights, the movement for the abolition of torture as a form of punishment, and the abolition of slavery are based on the notion of human dignity and therefore part of the story of human rights. Judicially sanctioned torture to extract confessions and to punish crimes were common in sixteenth, seventeenth, and eighteenth-century Europe and the American colonies. Hunt argues the pain that was caused was seen as having a higher religious and political purpose. Physical punishment was used to restore the moral, political, and religious order (Hunt 94). The use of torture was halted because this framework was gradually replaced by one in which individuals "owned" their own bodies and recognized that other people had sentiments and sensations just as they did (Hunt 2007: 112).

Human Rights Developments Post-World War II

In the concise view of the development of human rights, what receives attention is the dramatic up-surge in a remarkably short period of time of a set of laws, institutions to implement those laws, and literally thousands of NGOs to monitor the protection of human rights. This perspective recognizes the aforementioned developments as significant, but argues they can be bracketed out of a history of human rights. Rather, the concise story focuses on the *institutionalization* of human rights *as* human rights that takes place after World War II. The development of a human rights regime has been called a human rights "revolution" because of the depth and speed with which the idea flowed around the world. Cmiel claims that few political agendas have seen such a dramatic growth (Cmiel 2012: 27).

In the concise view, it would be difficult to overstate the influence of World War II. Though precise numbers will never be known, the estimate is 70 million casualties.[2] The destruction inspired new determination to identify a commonly agreed upon set of principles that could provide a basis for peace. The newly created United Nations therefore called for a commission to draft an international bill of rights that would meet this need.

Success was unlikely. First, the prospect of concretizing human rights raised philosophical quandaries. Second, there were political challenges to face. An "iron curtain" was surrounding the Soviet Union and the strategic arms race was escalating. Conflict in Palestine was taking place over the new state of Israel, and violence was erupting within colonial empires as peoples demanded their rights to self-determination. How was a commission going to bring all of the countries of the United Nations into agreement?

The task of bringing scholars, policy makers, and human rights practitioners together fell to Eleanor Roosevelt as the chair of the newly created Human Rights Commission. She used diplomacy and deter-mination to move the draft document forward when members of the commission could not agree. Once the text of the document was complete, the second phase was to obtain political agreement from all UN member states. As Waltz points out a process that the United States hoped would be completed in a matter of days took two months because the language in the Articles needed to be refined on a line-by-line basis in the General Assembly (2008: 21)

In this volume, Claude Welch provides an excellent overview of the Universal Declaration of Human Rights (UDHR) (Welch 2008). He argues the Declaration is among the most important documents of the twentieth century. Welch views the declaration favorably because it articulates the basic value that "All humans are born free and equal in dignity and rights." He also offers a positive assessment because of the impressive array of treaties, which are enforceable, that followed. It took decades, but in the 1970s, the International Bill of Rights come to fruition. The International Bill of Rights consists of the Universal Declaration and two "covenants" or treaties: the International Covenant on Economic, Social and Cultural Rights and the International Covenant on Civil and Political Rights (Image 3.1). You may wonder why two covenants followed in quick succession instead of one. The answer is that having two covenants, each devoted to a different set of rights, maximized the number of signatories by allowing countries to commit to protecting some, but not necessarily all rights.

---

2   http://www.pwencycl.kgbudge.com/C/a/Casualties.htm

Image 3.1. International Bill of Rights

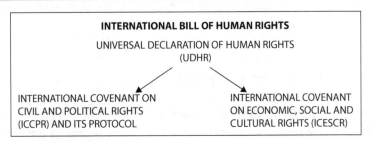

INTERNATIONAL BILL OF HUMAN RIGHTS

UNIVERSAL DECLARATION OF HUMAN RIGHTS
(UDHR)

INTERNATIONAL COVENANT ON
CIVIL AND POLITICAL RIGHTS
(ICCPR) AND ITS PROTOCOL

INTERNATIONAL COVENANT
ON ECONOMIC, SOCIAL AND
CULTURAL RIGHTS (ICESCR)

Generations of Rights

Human rights are sometimes organized into "generations." The distinction between generations was initially made by Karel Vasak in a speech he made as the director of the Division of Human Rights and Peace at the United National Educational, Scientific and Cultural Organization (UNESCO). To his way of thinking, the first generation is focused on liberty in relation to state power, the second generation emphasizes equality, and the third generation rights are focused on solidarity. The resemblance to the French "Liberté, Égalité, et Fraternité" is immediately apparent (Zehra and Arat 2006: 34).

All of these rights find expression in the UDHR. First-generation rights are the civil and political rights that enable one to participate in political life. These rights have to do with claims that could be potentially made against the state. They include rights to physical protection against torture and inhumane treatment, and the civil rights to vote and be free of arbitrary arrest. They also include "liberties" such as freedom of thought, assembly, and voluntary association. First-generation rights can be found in Articles 3–21 of the UDHR and are fully elaborated and made law in the International Covenant on Civil and Political Rights (ICCPR).

Second-generation rights are socioeconomic in nature. They provide norms about the meeting of material needs such as work, fair wages, and an adequate standard of living as well as the goods that are prerequisite to political participation and the meeting social needs. Shelter, health care, and education are considered second-generation rights. These rights constitute duties of a government. They can be found in Articles 22–27 of the UDHR and are elaborated in the International Covenant on Economic, Social, and Cultural Rights.

Third-generation rights are more collective in nature. These are the rights that groups hold in relation to the state in which they live. The right to a clean environment, the right to economic development, and the right to self-determination (e.g., indigenous groups) are examples of third-generation rights. While third-generation rights can be found in international treaties, there is significant disagreement regarding the best method to protect them. Countries that place a high value on the collective find that the UDHR neglects the importance of group rights. Their interlocutors contend that group rights are best served by better defense of individual human rights (Le 2016: 204).

Most scholars would agree that the three "generations" of rights are only theoretically distinct. In practice, the generations of human rights complement one another. Privileging one to the detriment of another is likely to be damaging to a country's ability to protect human rights. For example, to prioritize civil and political rights and ignore socioeconomic rights could potentially create disadvantaged groups, a highly undesirable outcome. Similarly, the provision of socioeconomic rights without civil and political rights is likely to lead to political disenfranchisement and dissent. Thus, human rights are conceptually distinct but indivisible in practice.

Perspectives on Human Rights

Although it is possible to say there has been a human rights "revolution," the international human rights regime is still contested. One major criticism is that although the means to promote, implement, and enforce rights exist, political will is still lacking. Another important criticism is that universal rights are not universal, but culture-specific: they are Western in origin and designed to serve Western purposes.

Lack of Political Will

Critics of the mechanisms in place to implement and enforce human rights point to the genocide in Rwanda in 1994, the ethnic cleansing that took place in Srebrenica in 1995, and the use of torture by the United States in its "war on terror." It would be hard to say it is a question of time before the protection of rights becomes more robust because there are more recent examples as well. The refugee crises of the Rohingya people in Myanmar, and the famine and cholera outbreak among the people of Yemen demonstrate that the international political will to intervene on behalf of human rights may be lacking. The Rohingya people have faced ethnic cleansing for decades, and their situation became dramatically worse in October 2017 when more than 600,000 fled violence and arrived in Bangladesh.[3] The lack of action makes sense according to the realist view already familiar to readers of this volume. If states are fundamentally self-interested actors that behave in a way that maximizes their power and chances of survival, states will intervene to protect human rights only when it is in their interest to do so. In this volume, Posner argues that when it is not in a state's interest to intervene on behalf of human rights, human rights issues will be ignored. The vague way in which rights have been articulated, and the weakness of enforcement mechanisms, gives states considerable policy leeway to do this.

Cultural Relativism

Staunch cultural relativists argue that the only valid basis for human rights is culture. Norms and values vary across cultures, suggesting that the rights in the UDHR can't simply be assumed to be universally applicable. A subset of the rights in the UDHR (such as the right to private ownership of the industrial capacity, age at marriage, or the types of marriage that are permissible) are at odds with traditional practices in some societies (Le 2016: 204). For example, in some places, families have rights to use but not own land because it is communally owned. Therefore, the institutionalization of human rights in state laws is subject to legitimate variation (Donnelly 2003). Although certain values, such as the right to life, are embedded in all societies, the list of such rights is not as long as the rights in the UDHR (Donnelly 2003).

The argument that human rights must accord with a culture to be valid has been countered in a number of ways. One point often raised is that the process of creating the UDHR was international and participatory: from the membership of the Commission to the debates in the General Assembly,

3   https://www.cnn.com/2017/11/12/asia/rohingya-crisis-timeline/index.html

all UN member states had a say in the document that emerged. The point is not a strong one, however, because the individuals who were involved in the writing of the UDHR were Western-educated elites who did not necessarily represent the concerns of ordinary citizens of the societies they represented (Le 2016). A better point on this score is that the growing number of national laws that incorporate human rights demonstrates that human rights are relevant to large numbers of people globally. Donnelly therefore suggests one think about human rights as having *instrumental value*: He writes that "to the extent that we can assess their merits empirically. I contend that for most of the goals of non-Western countries, as defined by these countries themselves, human rights are as effective as, or more effective than, either traditional approaches or modern strategies not based on human rights" (2003: 85).

The argument that human rights make sense in cultural contexts leads to a related criticism, that of Western imperialism. Critics in China, Iran, Syria, and Malaysia have criticized the recent emphasis on gender equality and acceptance of homosexuality in particular. They suggest that efforts to implement these rights are an example of Western cultural imperialism. While this criticism has merit, it must also be put in historical perspective. In the 1950s, human rights were enthusiastically embraced in some of the same countries now issuing "cultural" critiques. Countries that were advocating for self-determination found human rights legitimized their struggle in the context of decolonization. It was only later that rejecting the UDHR became a way to signal criticism of the political systems of the wealthy Western and industrialized nations.

Flows

A productive way to think about human rights is in terms of the flow of a powerful idea. The Universal Declaration of Human Rights influenced many national, regional, and international articulations of rights. New constitutions incorporated its language. Judicial opinions, court cases, and postwar bilateral treaties all began referring to the UDHR in their reasoning. In the years that followed the Declaration, the UN strengthened the concept of human rights with binding treaties or covenants and limited enforcement mechanisms such as the International Criminal Court.

The existence of regional regimes demonstrates the global nature of this flow. The structures of regional regimes mirror that of the international regime. Regional regimes are typically constituted by a convention or charter, a council, a committee, and a court with varying kinds and degrees of jurisdiction.

Europe

The Council of Europe initiated the first and in some ways the most powerful regional regime. The European Convention for the Protection of Human Rights (ECHR) came into force in 1953. The Convention sets out the human rights norms for the countries that belong to the Council of Europe, an entity that is actually separate from the European Union. Whereas the European Union has 28 members, the Council of Europe has 47. The Convention was initially proposed by Winston Churchill and is explicitly based on the UDHR.

The Convention also created the European Court of Human Rights. The primary purpose of the court is to ensure the enforcement of the ECHR. The court is notable for being the first court to accept cases brought by *individuals* in addition to states. Not every complaint is admissible, however. The Court has strict standards that must first be met and the waiting time for a case to be heard may be considerable. Only individuals who have been unable to remedy their claim through their national legal system may petition the Court. The judgments of the European Court of Human Rights are executed by the Committee of Ministers of the Council of Europe. This body is made up of the Ministers of Foreign Affairs of member states.

The Inter-American System

The Latin American states used the European model to establish the Inter-American Court of Human Rights. This court is notable because it sought to remedy the lack of enforcement mechanisms in the largely declaratory American Declaration of the Rights and Duties of Man signed in 1948. The Inter-American Court of Human Rights is located in San Jose, Costa Rica and is known for denouncing atrocities and violations of human rights on the part of the region's authoritarian governments. It operates under the American Convention on Human Rights that was adopted in 1969 and came into force in 1978. Because it was signed in San Jose, Costa Rica, this Convention is sometimes called the Pact of San Jose. Not every country in the Americas ratified the Convention, however. To date, twenty-five American nations have ratified or adhered to the Convention. The Inter-American Commission on Human Rights, an autonomous organ of the Organization of American States (OAS), oversees the implementation of human rights in the region. Both the Commission and the OAS are headquartered in Washington, DC. The Commission is a proactive entity that carries out site visits to investigate specific abuses and observes the general human rights situation in particular countries. The concept of human rights played an important role in ending military dictatorships in Latin America and the human rights situation in Latin America has improved over the last three decades.

Middle East

The topic of human rights in the Middle East is an especially complex one because of disagreement about whether the international human rights articulated in the UDHR are compatible with Islam. Some argue that human rights norms are against Shari'ah law. Others emphasize that Shari'ah law contains principles such as the protection of human life and dignity and good governance, and there is no inherent contradiction.[4] As early as 1968, the League of Arab States established a Permanent Arab Commission on Human Rights. Its activities have been limited, however, to discussion of the human rights situation in Israeli-occupied territories. The Arab Charter on Human Rights that entered into force in 2008 demonstrated an interest in defining and tailoring human rights for Arab nations. The Charter was openly criticized by the United Nations Commissioner for Human Rights at the time.

---

4   http://www.e-ir.info/2011/03/30/human-rights-in-the-middle-east-questions-of-compatibility-and-conflict/

The Commissioner issued a statement that the death penalty for children and the paucity of rights of women and noncitizens are problematic aspects of the Charter.[5]

The Arab League has been planning for an Arab Court for Human Rights for some time. In 2014, the League approved the Statute of the Arab Court of Human Rights (ACtHR) completing a two decade process. The goal was to establish mechanisms to protect human rights that would be similar to those in Europe and the Americas. The Court is unlikely to be able to hold leaders or governments accountable, however, because only states, not individuals or NGOs, can file complaints.

In spite of slow progress setting up human rights institutions, many commentators argue the idea of human rights has disseminated to the Middle East. Concern about human rights were especially visible during the uprisings known as the Arab Spring, although each country has a unique story. Recent changes to law in Saudi Arabia are another sign that the idea of human rights has spread. In Saudi Arabia, women's rights have been extended recently to voting and driving. The status of human rights in the Middle East therefore presents a complex picture that defies simple stereotypes.

Africa

The African system is the most recently established of the regional human rights regimes. The continent's main human rights instrument is the African Charter on Human and Peoples' Rights. It came into effect in 1986. Drafted in Banjul, Gambia, the agreement is informally referred to as the "Banjul Declaration." There are some important innovations in Africa such as an emphasis on collective and people's rights. The Charter also includes individual *duties*. Individual duties were too contested to be included in the UDHR. The Charter created an African Commission. In practice, its activities have been limited by a lack of resources and the requirement of complete confidentiality until an investigation is concluded.

The African Court of Justice and Human Rights was founded in 2004. It represents a merger of the African Court on Human and Peoples' Rights, and the Court of Justice of the African Union. In 2017, the African Union expanded the jurisdiction of this Court, creating a structure that is parallel to the International Criminal Court (ICC). The functions of the ICC and the African Court overlap because both try mass atrocities. The African Court of Justice and Human Rights, however, gives heads of state immunity from prosecution. Eliminating the immunity from prosecution was one of the principle aims of the ICC. How their work will be coordinated is an unanswered question at this time.

Southeast Asia

In 2012, the Association of Southeast Asian Nations (ASEAN) adopted an ASEAN Human Rights Declaration (AHRD). Just as other regional regimes encompass only a subset of the potential member states, ASEAN is constituted by ten—not all—Asian nations. The ASEAN Intergovernmental Commission of Human Rights (AICHR) oversees the implementation of human rights in the ten countries.

---

5   https://news.un.org/en/story/2008/01/247292-arab-rights-charter-deviates-international-standards-says-un-official

The implementation of human rights by ASEAN nations is complicated because the members of the very important Commission are appointed by state authorities. This puts the appointees in the difficult position of balancing the interests of the government, the individual rights of the people, and job security.[6] There are two other signals that acceptance of human rights is limited. The first is that ASEAN nations maintain a tradition of not intervening or criticizing one another's internal affairs A second sign is the Declaration itself. The Declaration does not cover human rights of LGBTQ individuals. The Declaration has therefore been criticized for not protecting rights to sexual orientation and gender identity. In its current state of activity, the AICHR is best viewed as a body for promoting human rights, rather than implementing or enforcing them.

Humanitarian Action

Humanitarian action aims to alleviate suffering and save lives. Many would say this is part of what defines the human species. What this means concretely is the provision of emergency food, water, shelter, and medical care. Under international humanitarian law, these activities are supposed to be without political, religious, or other agendas.

The International Committee for the Red Cross (ICRC) provided greater specificity to this definition by emphasizing three criteria: neutrality, impartiality, and independence. This is considered an ideal or "gold standard" of humanitarian action. Though these three qualities may sound very similar, the distinctions are important. Neutrality means that if a party is endeavoring to save lives in a conflict zone, it refrains from taking a political side. Impartiality means that aid workers provide assistance without regard to the identity of the person; his or her dignity as a human comes first. Independence means humanitarian organizations like the ICRC must strive to make decisions independently of the political influences from funders, and avoid becoming implementers of government policies and priorities.

The ICRC is an especially significant and in some ways unique organization in the field of humanitarian action. In addition to the operational work helping the victims of disasters, the organization has been instrumental in developing and promoting international humanitarian law. The ICRC was founded in 1863 by Swiss citizen Henry Dunant. Dunant's contribution was surprisingly random and yet enormously consequential. While on a business trip, he happened on the carnage resulting from the Battle of Solferino. He witnessed how soldiers were treated as dispensable and allowed to die terrible deaths. Civilians near the battle helped, but their efforts were vastly out of proportion with the needs. Dunant advocated for the creation of relief societies that would work separately from armed forces' medical services to alleviate suffering and save lives. The idea was that humanitarian work in times of conflict will be most successful when there are guarantees that it is independent of the warring parties. This idea was formally recognized in the first Geneva Convention, which assigns the ICRC a special role in promoting and strengthening humanitarian law (Image 3.3).

One of Dunant's contemporaries, Florence Nightingale, had a very different idea. She thought that creating independent organizations to care for the sick and wounded would take too much responsibility away

---

6   https://thediplomat.com/2018/01/is-promoting-human-rights-in-asean-an-impossible-task/

from state militaries. Freed of some of the cost and responsibility for medical care, states might be more inclined to keep fighting. Her idea was that the medical departments of state militaries should remain accountable. When put to the test of acceptance on the part of government leaders, European authorities embraced Dunant's ideas. The first Geneva Convention was a direct outgrowth of Henry Dunant's work.

Geneva Conventions

The Geneva Conventions are a series of international treaties that were concluded between 1864 and 1949. The four Conventions are considered the foundation of International Humanitarian Law. They define acceptable humanitarian treatment and set the standards for international law pertaining specifically to situations of armed conflict. The Conventions have been subject to a continual process of refinement to bring them into alignment with changing practices of war. For example, the 1864 Convention was amended and extended in 1906 by the second Geneva

Image 3.2. Henry Dunant

Convention which added maritime warfare. Similarly, the third Geneva Convention of 1929, required that prisoners of war be treated humanely. After World War II, when belligerents did not observe the principles of earlier conventions, a conference was held to revise and approve four conventions:

- The Convention for the Amelioration of the Condition of the Wounded and Sick in Armed Forces in the Field
- The Convention for the Amelioration of the Condition of the Wounded, Sick and Shipwrecked Members of Armed Forces at Sea
- The Convention Relative to the Treatment of Prisoners of War
- The Convention Relative to the Protection of Civilian Persons in Time of War.[7]

Challenges to Humanitarian Action

Acting to alleviate suffering and save lives faces many challenges. Two primary difficulties are accessing the population in need and, when people leave their country of origin, sharing the responsibility for care.

Access

Helping people in their country of origin is complicated by the traditional Westphalian notion of sovereignty. States are reluctant to intervene in one another's affairs, or allow other states to intervene in

---

7   https://www.icrc.org/en/war-and-law/treaties-customary-law/geneva-conventions

their affairs. Countries with significant humanitarian needs sometimes invoke sovereignty as a reason to reject assistance and large numbers of lives may be lost. This has been the case even when the humanitarian needs arise from events like natural disasters that are no fault of the state authorities.

Ongoing violence in the region in need creates additional access problems. Humanitarians therefore make a distinction between emergencies that arise from natural disasters and those that are human-caused. So-called "complex emergencies" arise from a combination of factors that include a breakdown of state structures or the questioned legitimacy of the authorities.

A common response to the access challenge posed by complex emergencies is the militarization of aid. Militarization resolves some access problems by making it possible to work in insecure environments. Military cover enables humanitarians to set up tents or distribute food while conflict continues. The risk associated with militarization is legitimate confusion about the distinction between aid workers and the military. A humanitarian worker's best defense is his or her clear and unambiguous identity as a person who is neutral, impartial, and independent. This confusion has led to attacks on humanitarian aid workers. To make matters more complicated, military operations have often been referred to by government authorities and news media as humanitarian ones.

A second response to the challenge of access is the creation of a safe zone within a contested one—a humanitarian "corridor." For example, access was a challenge during the wars in the former Yugoslavia, where aid organizations had to negotiate access to civilians with Serb militants intent on carrying out ethnic cleansing. During the siege of Sarajevo, the UN was able to negotiate corridors, but the militants took a large proportion of the aid flowing in and distributed it according to their own needs. The humanitarian dilemma was whether to carry out an evacuation or not. If the UN refugee agency, mandated to protect refugees, chose evacuation, it would be helping to create a refugee flow, possibly even assisting with the objective of ethnic cleansing. On the other hand, providing aid to the people where they were already living might temporarily prolong their lives, but it was unlikely to achieve a durable solution for those involved.

There are more recent examples as well. In the context of the war in Syria, Russia proposed a humanitarian corridor out of Aleppo. This 2016 idea was deeply flawed because it forced the people living in Aleppo to choose between remaining in a besieged area under artillery fire, and fleeing, basically, into the arms of aggressors.

In today's world, the majority of humanitarian needs stem from complex emergencies, making humanitarian needs difficult to meet.

Image 3.3. Conflict Arising from Humanitarian Needs

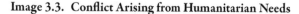

Refugees

A very different set of challenges confronts the international community when people leave their country of origin. After World War II, there were some 60 million people displaced within Europe. The 1951 Convention Relating to the Status of Refugees offered the first internationally agreed upon and formal definition of what it means to be a refugee. A primary distinction was made between those who have a legitimate fear of persecution and those who chose to leave to improve their lives. The inability, due to the fear, to avail themselves of the protection of their country means the responsibility for refugee legal protection is an international one.

The 1951 Convention on the Status of Refugees established international agreement on basic principles for the refugees displaced within Europe by World War II. The most important principle it enshrines is that countries must not return a migrant to a place where he or she fears persecution. This has been so widely accepted and practiced that it is considered customary law. A 1967 Protocol lifted the time and place restrictions to address the growing numbers of refugees and migrants as a result of decolonization. Still, there were no solid international guidelines for how to equitably share responsibility at an international level.

Responsibility Sharing

The ability to share responsibility has been tested recently. In 2015, more than one million migrants and refugees crossed into Europe.8 The European Union had been preparing for such refugee surges by creating legislation meant to direct and control the flow of asylum seekers within its borders. The legislation is called the Dublin Regulations, and the first agreement was signed in 1990. While the regulations are complex, the core idea is that the European Union member state where the migrant first arrives is responsible for adjudicating his or her claim. If the asylum seeker makes a second claim in a different European country, he or she is to be sent back to the state of entry—the seeker may not restart the process in another jurisdiction while awaiting a decision.

The Dublin Regulations have been revised and updated over time. Nevertheless, they proved insufficient to deal adequately with the refugee flows to Europe in 2015. Dublin meshed poorly with European geography and history because those who received the most migrants were also the least financially able to cope with the asylum determination process. The crux of the European refugee crisis is therefore a responsibility-sharing crisis.

The inequity between the resources of the various member states and their reception capacities relative to the number of irregular migrants presents complex issues that the European Union was unable to resolve definitively. A partial measure currently in place is an agreement to send some of the refugees to Turkey. Turkey agreed to accept asylum seekers in exchange for payment and a resumption of their European Union accession process, as well as visa privileges for Turkish citizens. Critics of the arrangement question its legality.

The magnitude of the responsibility-sharing challenge is especially clear in the ranking of countries that host the most refugees. Ten countries host 60 percent of the world's refugees, and none of them

---

8   http://ec.europa.eu/echo/node/4115

are in Europe. These statistics demonstrate concretely how geography and policy exert a shaping force on the selection of durable solutions when refugees present challenges to responsibility sharing.

The notion of what constitutes a durable solution warrants further explanation. Intergovernmental organizations concerned with recognized refugees place a priority on finding long-term solutions for refugees. The United Nations High Commissioner for Refugees recognizes three solutions as durable, where durable is defined as options that provide refugees with an opportunity to rebuild their lives. The first and in many aspects most desirable solution is *voluntary repatriation*. Repatriation restores and protects the right to live in the country of one's nationality. But this is not always possible. Refugees are to return only when they can be assured a life in dignity and safety. A second durable solution is *local integration*. Local integration refers to situations in which refugees are welcomed in the country to which they initially fled, and in which they have access to the economic, legal, and social structures that enable them to rebuild their lives. A primary advantage of this solution is that when refugees stay within their region, they are likely to acculturate more easily than if they move farther from their country of origin. The third durable solution is *third country resettlement*. This is the most costly and the least utilized. According to UNHCR, only about 1 percent of the world's refugees are resettled to third countries.[9]

Responsibility to Protect

The humanitarian landscape is very different than when Dunant and Nightingale debated how best to care for the war wounded. Now that armed factions do not always make a distinction between civilian and combatant, there are serious questions about whether the ideal is even possible to achieve. To deal with this situation and encompass growing appreciation for human rights, humanitarian practitioners and policy makers outlined a new norm to guide decision making. This new norm reframed the notion of sovereignty studied in the preceding chapter. Sovereignty is best understood not as a right enjoyed by states, they argued, but as a responsibility that states have toward citizens.

The doctrine of Responsibility to Protect, or R2P, has three main "pillars" or conceptual cores. The first is that a state has a responsibility to protect its population from "mass atrocities" (see explanation below). The second pillar is that the international community has a responsibility to assist states in fulfilling these obligations. Crises may be averted with preventive activities. The third pillar is that if a state fails, and if peaceful measures such as negotiation fail, the international community has the responsibility to intervene. The Responsibility to Protect is a norm, not a law. It can only provide guidance on how and when to intervene. Criteria used to invoke R2P are:

1. Just Cause—does the situation involve mass atrocities?
2. Right Intention—is the primary intention to alleviate suffering or are there ulterior economic and political motives?
3. Final Resort—have other measures been taken into account and deemed unlikely to succeed (whether tried or not). Is military action the only route to success?
4. Legitimate authority—rests with the UN Security Council.

---

9   http://www.unhcr.org/en-us/resettlement.html

5. Proportional Means—the minimum intervention sufficient to make change
6. Reasonable Prospect—of doing more good than harm. How likely is it to succeed?

Mass Atrocities

Mass atrocity is an umbrella term that encompasses genocide, ethnic cleansing, crimes against humanity, and war crimes. These terms are sometimes used interchangeably but each has a specific meaning. *Crimes against humanity* refers to acts that are part of a systematic attack directed at a civilian population. Although military personnel may also be victims, the primary target is the civilian population. *Ethnic cleansing* is the forced removal of ethnic or racial groups from a particular area. Typically, this is carried out by a more powerful group with the aim of making the place where they live more homogeneous. Ethnic cleansing may include deportation, murder, and forced migration. *War crimes* are grave breaches of the Geneva Convention of 1949 consisting of acts committed against persons and property protected by the Geneva Conventions. Examples include willful killing, torture and inhumane treatment, intentionally causing suffering, destroying property not justified by military necessity, etc.[10]. Finally, *genocide* refers to acts carried out with the intent to destroy a group in whole or in part. To be considered genocide, the entire group does not have to perish. For an act to be considered genocide, people have been targeted because of their membership in a group, and the intent is to destroy the group.

The responsibility to protect provides an optional decision-making framework. Its chief strength is that it creates new guidelines for using tools that already exist, such as the UN Charter, but have been used inconsistently. The unrepresentative nature of the Security Council and the ever-present possibility of a Great Power veto make the Security Council a clumsy and imperfect mechanism for deciding when and how to intervene. Specifically, chapter VII of the Charter of the United Nations gives the United Nations Security Council the authority to intervene to maintain international peace and security. According to the Charter, each of the five Permanent Members States (China, France, Russian Federation, United Kingdom and United States) has the right to veto a resolution. (To pass, a Security Council resolution must have a total of at least nine members, and be without a veto of any of the five members.) The voting rules mean that the Permanent Five members have inordinate power to approve or decline an intervention. This raises the possibility that an intervention that enjoys broad consensus will be ruled out owing to the priorities of one or more of the Permanent Members. There is no guarantee that a Security Council decision involves a genuinely collective assessment. In sum, while acting to save lives and reduce suffering may at first seem uncontroversial, the specific manner in which humanitarian action takes place is highly contentious.

Perspectives on Humanitarianism

Perspectives on when and where it is advisable to intervene are shaped by geography, history, wealth, and power. Countries in the developing world have noticed humanitarian intervention can lead to a long-term engagement, becoming a form of governance. Although some would call this international administration (Ayoob 2004), others would call it humanitarian imperialism (Bricmont 2006).

---

10   http://www.un.org/en/genocideprevention/war-crimes.html

Colonialism provides a useful starting point to understand this. Postcolonial states are reluctant to cede authority to outsiders when it is perceived to threaten their hard-won sovereign status. Humanitarian assistance that includes policy advice is experienced as a continuation of the subjugation these countries experienced as colonies . Under colonialism, European notions and standards were used to assess colonies without appreciation of their unique history. Similarly, humanitarian intervention is accompanied by a spoken or unspoken judgement of existing governance. Many governments are reluctant to expose themselves to scrutiny.

Reservations about allowing humanitarian intervention revolve around questions of who has the legitimate authority to decide a course of action, what action is to be taken, and where the agents carrying out the intervention come from. All too often, Security Council resolutions appear to be motivated more by geostrategic alliances that than humanitarian need. The deepening crisis in Yemen in 2018 is a good example: U.K. and U.S. interests in Saudi Arabia are likely to have forestalled the international community from sanctioning the Saudi-led coalition that created the conditions for widespread famine and the spread of cholera.[11]

Countries in the developing world do not have a single perspective on humanitarian action within their borders. Postcolonial countries in sub-Saharan Africa are typically more receptive to intervention than postcolonial states in Asia and Latin America (Ayoob 2004). African states often understand weak governance to be the primary cause for crises, making international intervention more welcome (Ayoob 2004). In West and Central Africa in particular, countries have called for assistance in ending violence and disorder. And sub-Saharan African countries like Rwanda have noted that they have been neglected by the Security Council and have not received the support or resources to prevent mass atrocities.

The area where the selectivity and the double standards associated with humanitarian intervention are most contested is the Middle East (Ayoob 2004). The inability of the Security Council to be more effective in this region has made acts of intervention suspect. Acts that circumvent the Security Council undermine trust. For example, during the Kosovo war, NATO decided to act without Security Council approval and launched a bombing campaign that ended the war. This made countries even more wary of the motives behind international humanitarian intervention.

Asian countries such as China and India have sufficiently robust state structures that they neither want nor need the governance that accompanies humanitarian action. The Chinese perspective is perhaps the starkest. Chinese leaders have argued that humanitarianism and intervention are so incommensurable that the term humanitarian intervention is an oxymoron (International Commission on Intervention and State Sovereignty 2001). They see the practice of humanitarian intervention in the world today as seriously challenging the working of international law and negatively affecting international relations. They disagree that human rights violations justify disregarding a country's sovereignty. China's rival India has taken the same view.

One can analyze the merits of humanitarian intervention in concert with the advisability of international administration and judge individual cases accordingly. When nation-states are weak, corrupt, or have limited resources, international organizations can help. The next chapters will explore this reality from the perspective of global health and environment and human development.

---

11   https://www.washingtonpost.com/world/national-security/yemen-is-a-humanitarian-nightmare-but-the-us-is-resisting-calls-to-end-its-role-in-the-war/2018/03/19/5c8c3bd2-294b-11e8-bc72-077aa4dab9ef_story.html?utm_term=.6bf193a1b81f

References

Ayoob, Mohammed. 2004. "Third World Perspectives in Humanitarian Intervention." *Global Governance: A Review of Multi-lateralism and International Organizations,* Vol. 10(1): 99–118.

Bricmont, Jean. 2006. *Humanitarian Imperialism.* New York: Monthly Review Press.

Cmiel, Kenneth. 2012. "The Recent History of Human Rights." In Akira Iriye, Petra Goedde, and William Hitchcock (eds.), *The Human Rights Revolution.* Oxford: Oxford University Press, 27–51.

Donnelly, Jack. 2003. *Universal Human Rights in Theory and Practice* (2nd ed.). Ithaca, NY and London: Cornell University Press.

Hunt, Lynn. 2007. *Inventing Human Rights: A History.* New York: W. W. Norton and Co.

Iriye, Akira, Petra Goedde, and William Hitchcock, eds. 2012. *The Human Rights Revolution.* New York: Oxford University Press.

International Commission on Intervention and State Sovereignty. 2001. The Responsibility to Protect: Research, Bibliography, and Background." Ottawa: International Development Research Center, 392.

Le, Nhina. 2016. "Are Human Rights Universal or Culturally Relative?" *Peace Review: A Journal of Social Justice* 28 (2): 203–211.

Miller, Jon. 2014. "Hugo Grotius." In Edward N. Zalta (ed.), *The Stanford Encyclopedia of Philosophy,* https://plato.stanford.edu/archives/spr2014/entries/grotius/.

Waltz, Susan. 2008. "Who Wrote the Universal Declaration of Human Rights?" "The Universal Declaratkion of Human Rights at Sixty" U.S. Department of State E Journal Vol. 13 No. 11, November 2008, 19–23.

Zehra, F., and Kabasakai Arat. 2006. *Human Rights Worldwide: A Reference Handbook.* Santa Barbara, CA: ABC-CLIO.

Readings

Claude Welch provides an excellent overview of the significance of the Universal Declaration of Human Rights (UDHR). He argues the declaration is among the most important documents of the twentieth century. Welch views the declaration favorably because it articulates the basic value that "All humans are born free and equal in dignity and rights." He also offers a positive assessment because of the impressive array of treaties, which are enforceable, that followed. Though the UDHR is a remarkable achievement, it is not an enforceable treaty. Therefore, its accomplishments are constrained by many factors. (Welch, Claude. 2008. "The Universal Declaration of Human Rights at Sixty" *U.S. Department of State E Journal* Vol. 13 No. 11, November 2008, 3–7.)

The current **UN Secretary General's António Guterres'** speech to the General Assembly on taking office offers an important window on the mood in the General Assembly today. This speech by Guterres is not a scholarly argument in favor of intervention or against it. Rather, his is primarily a moral appeal for the international community to step up to the challenge of preventing crises wherever they may be occurring, or at the very least speak out against them. Guterres, as a spokesperson for refugees and other marginalized groups, takes the position that well-reasoned humanitarian intervention is not a form of imperialism, as some have charged, but a moral imperative. Further, he has specific ideas about how the UN "family of agencies" could be changed to make it more responsive. (Guterres, Antonio. 2012. Secretary

General designate Antonio Guterres' remarks to the General Assembly on taking the oath of office. https://www.un.org/sg/en/content/sg/speeches/2016-12-12/secretary-general-designate-ant%C3%B3nio-guterres-oath-office-speech.)

In "Who Wrote the Universal Declaration of Human Rights" **Susan Waltz** tells the engaging story of how the UDHR came into existence, in spite of the odds. The article familiarizes readers with some of the influential personalities behind the drafting of the document.

In "The Twilight of Human Rights Law" **Eric Posner** takes a very different view than either Welch or Guterres (this volume). Posner argues that human rights law is simply failing to accomplish its objectives. He acknowledges that the world might be a freer place than it was fifty years ago, but asks the provocative question (and one worthy of debate) whether that is due to the expansion of a human rights regime or other forces such as the end of the Cold War and impressive economic growth. (Posner, Eric A. 2014. *The Twilight of Human Rights Law*, Cambridge and Oxford, UK: Oxford University Press.)

In "The Dilemma of Humanitarian Intervention" **Jayshree Bajoria** gives a basic overview of what is at stake in humanitarian intervention. She provides a "tour" of the major international agreements that are intended to govern decisions about whether or not to intervene, including the "Responsibility to Protect." She calls particular attention to the way that humanitarian intervention has, in the past, been used as a means to accomplish regime change. (Bajoria, Jayshree. 2013. "The Dilemma of Humanitarian Intervention." *Council on Foreign Relations Backgrounder*, http://www.cfr.org/humanitarian-intervention/dilemma-humanitarian-intervention/p16524.)

Online Resources

Universal Declaration of Human Rights (UNDR). United Nations. 1948. http://www.un.org/en/universal-declaration-human-rights/.

Image Credits

Image 3.1: Source: http://hrlibrary.umn.edu/edumat/hreduseries/hereandnow/Part-1/from-concept.htm.
Image 3.2: Source: https://commons.wikimedia.org/wiki/File:Henry_Dunant-young.jpg.

The Universal Declaration of Human Rights at Sixty

by Claude Welch

Courtesy Franklin D. Roosevelt Presidential Library

Eleanor Roosevelt with the Universal Declaration of Human Rights.

Claude Welch is SUNY Distinguished Service Professor and professor of political science at the State University of New York at Buffalo. He has published 14 books and close to 40 chapters and academic articles in fields including human rights, African politics, and the roles of armed forces in political affairs. In 2006, he received the first-ever Lifetime Achievement Award given by the financial services firm TIAA-CREF and the SUNY Research Foundation.

Claude Welch, "The Universal Declaration of Human Rights at Sixty," *Celebrating 60 Years of Human Rights*, ed. Jonathan Margolis, pp. 3–7. 2008.

December 10, 2008, marks an important anniversary: It is 60 years since the United Nations General Assembly ratified the Universal Declaration of Human Rights and opened a new era of international history. Why the UDHR matters, how it came into existence, what it says, and the results it produced are the focus of this article.

Why the Universal Declaration Matters

© KEYSTONE/Sandro Campardo

A delegate at work during the 2007 session of the U.N. Human Rights Council.

The Universal Declaration is among the most important documents of the 20th century. It has been translated into 337 different languages. It has become a touchstone for actions by governments, individuals, and nongovernmental groups. It has been ratified by every country in the world. Practically no other international instrument can claim this honor. In short, the UDHR has acquired a moral and political significance matched by few documents.

The Universal Declaration provides both a guide to present action and an evolving set of ideas for future implementation at the national level. Increasingly, the UDHR's principles have been embodied in what states do, and it serves as the foundation for the International Bill of Rights and of several other crucial human rights agreements. And, not least, the Universal Declaration has proven a remarkably flexible foundation for a continued broadening and deepening of the very concept of human rights. How many treaties can claim such honors?

The UDHR was one response to the horrendous destruction of peoples, lands, and infrastructure during the Second World War. Almost all of Europe had been shattered by conflict. Much of Asia also had been wracked by war. Vast reconstruction was necessary so people could return to "normalcy." And with the war's end, nationalist reactions against foreign rule and demands for independence suggested that the new, postwar world would not necessarily be free from conflict. In short, a new beginning was essential. The Universal Declaration of Human Rights resulted directly from this yearning for a new global set of rules.

How the Universal Declaration Came into Being

Every country in the world had been touched directly or indirectly by World War II. Seventy million people perished. Planning for a future international organization to succeed the League of Nations started during the war. In the spring of 1945, 50 governments and hundreds of nongovernmental organizations met in San Francisco. The states hammered out the "constitution" of a new United Nations. The resulting "charter" embodied both "official" and "unofficial" ideas.

The Preamble to the United Nations Charter includes these famous words:

> We the peoples of the United Nations determined ... **to reaffirm faith in fundamental human rights,** in the dignity and worth of the human person, in the equal rights of men and women and of nations large and small, ...

Much thought, time, and energy went into determining the United Nations' structure. Many readers will recognize and understand the respective roles and powers of the General Assembly (where all 192 U.N. members sit) and of the Security Council (10 elected and five permanent members). Far less known, however, are parts of the United Nations devoted exclusively to human rights.

The U.N. Charter called for a commission on human rights. Eleanor Roosevelt, widow of U.S. President Franklin Delano Roosevelt, chaired it. With the help of the United Nations Educational, Scientific, and Cultural Organization, the new Commission on Human Rights studied how different cultures, nations, and philosophers viewed human rights. These multiple perspectives deepened the commission's understanding and improved its work.

In September 1948 the commission sent its draft to the U.N. General Assembly. Lengthy debates clarified the draft language and built increasing consensus. Discussion and approval took two full years, including 81 meetings, 168 amendments to the draft text, and nearly 1,400 votes. The climax came on December 10, 1948. The General Assembly adopted the Universal Declaration without a single dissenting vote, although eight states abstained. This was a remarkable conclusion to an extraordinary process.

What the UDHR Says

The Universal Declaration of Human Rights sets forth a number of objectives, some to be achieved immediately, others as rapidly as feasible. The UDHR also provided the foundation for a series of other international agreements, both global and regional. Finally, the UDHR inspired people around the world to claim their rights, not simply accept the diktat of others.

The UDHR provides "a common standard of achievement for all peoples and all nations." Every "individual and every organ of society" shall promote "respect for these rights and freedoms ... by progressive measures ..." The goal was "to secure their universal and effective recognition and observance."

Underlying the entire Declaration is a basic value. "All human beings are born free and equal in dignity and rights," Article 1 states. This assertion ran in the face of centuries of practice and widespread beliefs. The Universal Declaration could not by itself reverse or transform popular attitudes. Nonetheless, it pointed in a crucial direction.

Perhaps most important, the clarity and directness of its language inspired millions. An increasing number of translations and conscious efforts to spread the UDHR's message popularized its principles. Men and women everywhere recognized that they enjoyed rights that no government should take away.

Drafters of the UDHR consciously drew upon several legal and philosophical traditions. Many of its 30 articles deal with civil and political rights, which protect individuals from government and from state-condoned private abuses. Others discuss freedoms common to each individual, such as the right to free expression. Still others set forth economic, social, and cultural rights, such as access to education and the right to work.

Results of the Universal Declaration

© AP Images/Manish Swarup

The Dalai Lama addresses a Human Rights Day ceremony in New Delhi, India, in 2003.

Even more significant than the Universal Declaration's inspirational language have been its results. In international law, several major treaties, ratified by more than 100 countries, trace their origins to the UDHR. They include, in chronological order:

- The International Convention on the Elimination of Racial Discrimination (1965);
- The International Covenant on Economic, Social, and Cultural Rights (1966);
- The International Covenant on Civil and Political Rights (1966);
- The Convention on the Elimination of All Forms of Discrimination Against Women (1979);
- The Convention Against Torture and Other Cruel, Inhuman, or Degrading Treatment or Punishment (1984);
- The Convention on the Rights of the Child (1989).

When a country ratifies an international agreement, it assumes a legal obligation. Citizens of states signing on to the UDHR and its progeny thus possess rights they may not have fully enjoyed earlier because their government has acknowledged and pledged to respect those rights. Signatories to many human rights treaties must prepare and submit regular reports on their citizens' freedoms. All these reports go to U.N. specialists who study them carefully and recommend where changes are needed.

Citizens groups increasingly provide their own reports, with additional details. Thus, one of the hopes of the drafters of the Universal Declaration has been increasingly met: People have a voice in their own destiny.

Still other international agreements have stemmed from the Universal Declaration:

- Prosecution of indicted war criminals by the International Criminal Court, functioning as of 2002;
- The "responsibility to protect," as approved by the General Assembly in 2005, which places a moral obligation on countries to help states wracked by widespread disturbances or civil wars;
- An August 2006 agreement on a draft convention on the rights of the disabled;
- Adoption of a Universal Declaration of Indigenous Rights by the United Nations in September 2007;
- Reducing or eliminating the death penalty in much of Europe and elsewhere;
- Giving more attention to how transnational corporations affect human rights where they operate.

These developments required significant discussion. Nearly 20 years passed between adoption of the Universal Declaration and the "entry into force"—in other words, full acceptance into international law—of the two international covenants described above. Twenty-five years of discussion preceded General Assembly acceptance of the Universal Declaration of Indigenous Rights. On the other hand, agreement about establishing the International Criminal Court came within four years, and the convention on children's rights in less than a year. The picture is thus mixed.

What Steps Lie Ahead?

For six decades, the Universal Declaration of Human Rights has proven its durability. Yet debates remain.

Cultural distinctiveness continues to arouse discussion about universality, the "U" in UDHR. Although the Universal Declaration's principles have been reaffirmed time after time, some assert that cultures or regions differ so much that no real global standards can exist.

A second area of controversy swirls around the rights of persons belonging to ethnic groups and national minorities. As individuals, they cannot be discriminated against because of their backgrounds. However, long-term economic or political disadvantages, deeply engrained social attitudes, and the like *against the groups to which they belong* raise profound questions. Do groups per se have rights?

Additional uncertainty exists with respect to internally displaced persons. They are individuals who cannot live in their usual homes because of conflict, but have not crossed an international border. Internally displaced persons (known as IDPs) confront horrendous, dangerous living conditions. They also exist in a legal no-man's-land. Had they left their own countries, they would have enjoyed international legal protection. Having remained at home or near home, they continue to be liable to many problems.

© Peter Turnley/CORBIS

A German youth waves victoriously from the top of the Berlin Wall in November 1989.

A fourth area of controversy centers on how best to settle large-scale civil conflicts. Should the international community intervene for humanitarian reasons? Should peace and reconciliation committees or similar groups to establish the "truth" be set up"? Should negotiations be encouraged between opposing groups by promising amnesty to those accused of war crimes? Or would justice be served better by trying to arrest and try them in the International Criminal Court? How far do the obligations of the "right to protect" extend? Who should take responsibility for any coercive intervention?

Still another area of concern involves apologies and reparations for previous human rights injustices. Earlier violence against large numbers of people of other nationalities can—and does—sour relations between and among governments and their populations. Hence, this whole area is fraught with political difficulties, irrespective of its importance for human rights generally.

Truth commissions and truth and reconciliation groups provide an additional dimension, showing the evolution and growth of human rights. They investigate previous abuses. Their establishment suggests that previous "human wrongs" cannot be hidden forever.

Serious economic issues undercut how much—and indeed whether—individuals can enjoy full human rights. If human rights "begin with breakfast," persons must have reasonable chances for employment and schooling. They must be able to break out of the trap of poverty and avoid the debilitating impact of malnutrition and endemic disease. The Universal Declaration speaks about these concerns in general terms. However, serious problems remain in light of economic inequalities within and between nations. Wasteful or corrupt practices by government officials reduce what is available for other needs.

Finally, and in many ways most significant, the Universal Declaration of Human Rights cannot be enforced by "traditional" means of coercion. The United Nations has no armed forces of

The first meeting of the committee that drafted the Universal Declaration.

its own, but must obtain parts of other states' militaries for help. The U.N. agencies directly concerned with human rights, such as the Geneva-based Office of the High Commissioner for Human Rights, receive little funding.

Looking back to 1948, however, progress has been remarkable. A visionary document has become a living reality. The Universal Declaration should be celebrated for its firm foundation and flexible structure. December 10, 2008, should be celebrated around the world.

The opinions expressed in this article do not necessarily reflect the views or policies of the U.S. government.

Who Wrote the Universal Declaration of Human Rights?

by Susan Waltz

Charles Malik (Lebanon), Eleanor Roosevelt (United States), and René Cassin (France) were instrumental in crafting the UDHR.

Susan Waltz, a specialist in human rights and international affairs, is professor of public policy at the Gerald R. Ford School of Public Policy, the University of Michigan. She is the author of Human Rights and Reform: Changing the Face of North African Politics (1995), and she has recently published a series of articles on the historical origins of international human rights instruments and the political processes that produced them. From 1993 to 1999, Waltz served on Amnesty International's International Executive Committee, and from 2000 to 2008 she was a member of the American Friends Service Committee national board.

Susan Waltz, Selection from: *Who Wrote the Universal Declaration?*, pp. 19–23. 2008.

Eleanor Roosevelt's name is commonly associated with the Universal Declaration of Human Rights, and for good reason. The widow of U.S. President Franklin Delano Roosevelt served as chair of the U.N. Human Rights Commission from 1946 to 1951, and she brought to that role the respect and affection of people all around the world. In the difficult political environment of the late 1940s—with an emerging Cold War and mounting opposition to colonial rule—Mrs. Roosevelt's political acumen, diplomatic skills, and steadfast determination were crucial for the success of efforts to secure a human rights declaration.

While her role proved a vital one, Eleanor Roosevelt was not in any sense the author of the UDHR. She supplied neither the text nor the substantive ideas that shaped the UDHR. How, then, did this important document come into being? While Mrs. Roosevelt and a number of draftsmen played significant roles, the historical record discloses that the Universal Declaration reflects the contributions of diplomats from many nations and represents a true international consensus and a real commitment—even if only partially fulfilled—to expand and secure the rights of individuals everywhere.

In the most literal sense, credit for proposing a bill of human rights to the United Nations belongs to Ricardo Alfaro, former president of Panama. As Panama's representative to the United Nations' inaugural meeting in 1945, Alfaro brought with him a draft bill of international rights and formally proposed that it be incorporated into the U.N. Charter. Civic groups around the world, legal professionals, and public intellectuals such as British writer H.G. Wells had been advocating an international proclamation of rights for several years, and Alfaro had worked with the American Law Institute (a group of judges, lawyers, and law teachers that drafts "model" laws—templates from which legislatures can craft simpler, more easily understood statutes) to produce the draft he carried. Diplomats assembled that May in San Francisco were not prepared to adopt anything as specific as Alfaro's proposal, but they did decide to establish a Commission on Human Rights, and they agreed informally that among the commission's first tasks would be to develop an international bill of human rights.

The next months were spent setting up the bodies envisioned by the U.N. Charter and appointing staff to work with them. Canadian law professor John Humphrey was asked to head up a small Division of Human Rights at the U.N. Secretariat, and a preparatory committee appointed by the U.N.'s new Economic and Social Council gave shape to the U.N. Human Rights Commission. By January 1947, 18 member states had been chosen and the commission set to work.

Seeking a Common Approach

Drafting, however, turned out to be a protracted affair. The initial intention was to have the commission's three officers prepare a draft for discussion, but that plan proved unworkable. When Eleanor Roosevelt invited Commission Vice Chairman Zhang Pengjun (also known as P.C. Chang) and Rapporteur Charles Habib Malik (Lebanon) to work on the draft at her New York apartment, the two men spent the afternoon locked in philosophical argument. One a proponent of natural rights philosophy and the other a Confucianist, the commission's two towering intellects were unable to agree on a common approach, leaving Roosevelt and Humphrey despairing in the wings.

The impasse between Zhang and Malik had important consequences for the ultimate shape of the Universal Declaration. A high-phrased, philosophical approach to the Declaration was abandoned in favor of a pragmatic, negotiated text, and the task of preparing the draft was transferred to the U.N. Secretariat. John Humphrey—a practically minded legal scholar—was charged with producing a "documented outline" for the Declaration. At the same time, the commission's internal drafting group was expanded to include representatives from five more states, a recognition of the inherent difficulties in crafting a text acceptable to all.

It did not take Humphrey long to produce a text because he already had at hand an impressive array of documents. Included among them were drafts and proposals submitted by numerous countries and nongovernmental associations, as well as the constitutions of all U.N. member states. Borrowing freely from these documents, Humphrey produced the first

An early draft of the Universal Declaration of Human Rights.

and basic draft of the UDHR. Over the next 15 months, this text was worked and reworked. French legal scholar René Cassin was asked to rearrange the articles and provide a preamble to frame them, and the drafting committee subsequently discussed and edited every line.

If the main task in 1947 was to develop and hone the text, the challenge in 1948 was to secure political agreement from all the U.N. member states. When the U.N. General Assembly convened in late September 1948, U.S. State Department officials hoped that deliberations over the Declaration would not last more than a few days. Those hopes were quickly dashed. The General Assembly's Third Committee (covering social, humanitarian, and cultural affairs) was charged with reviewing the document before it was considered in the plenary session, and Charles Malik was elected to preside over the hearings. Malik recognized that broad participation was necessary to build consensus and to foster among member states a shared sense of political ownership. He therefore resisted efforts to rush the process. "Matters must be allowed to mature slowly, free from sharp corners," he counseled.

After opening statements from more than 40 countries, Malik proceeded to lead an article-by-article scrutiny of the text. In daily sessions over a period of two months, delegates considered scores of written amendments (the great majority submitted by Cuba, the Soviet Union, Panama, Lebanon, France, and Egypt). Each amendment was debated, some extensively, and each article of the draft Declaration was put to a separate vote. The debate on Article 1 alone spanned six days, and though Malik eventually bought a stopwatch to ensure that speakers did not exceed time limits, the official record of the Third Committee's painstaking deliberations fill some 900 printed pages.

© AP Images.

A Pakistani woman at a Lahore rally marking World Human Rights Day. Her poster reads, "Women's rights are human rights."

When the Third Committee finally completed its work in early December of 1948, it referred the Declaration to the plenary session of the General Assembly for one more article-by-article review. The General Assembly's historic vote on the final text took place shortly after midnight on December 10, the date now celebrated as Human Rights Day. Twenty-three of the 30 articles were accepted unanimously, and while South Africa, Saudi Arabia, and the Soviet bloc abstained on the final vote, 48 states cast affirmative votes. No state opposed.

Negotiating a Text

For many years, the detailed history of this elaborate process lay forgotten or obscured, and in the absence of nuanced understanding, many unwarranted assumptions were made. With the benefit of recent research, we now recognize that world powers were not the moving force behind the UDHR, the document did not have a single author, and its text was shaped by diplomats and civil servants rather than philosophers. Not only was each element scrutinized, but every article was modified over the course of the Declaration's two-year incubation: The resulting text bears the stamp of many individuals representing many countries.

The story behind that text may surprise some readers today. The most ardent champions of socio-economic rights, for example, came from Latin America (rather than Soviet bloc countries, as often

© AP Images

Children participate in a Human Rights Day rally in Calcutta, India

supposed). The Soviet bloc delegations resisted encroachments on sovereignty but tenaciously pressed the issue of nondiscrimination, and it is thanks in large part to their persistence that every article of the Declaration applies to everyone. Egypt is responsible for the strong statement of universality at the opening of the Declaration, its delegate having pushed to make the Declaration's provisions applicable "both among peoples of the Member States and among peoples of territories under their jurisdiction."

Anticipating concerns of our own times, delegates from India, the Dominican Republic, and Denmark fought to have rights expressed in gender-neutral language and for explicit recognition of the rights of women. The delegate from Poland called attention to the issue of human trafficking, and the draft was amended to prohibit slavery "in all its forms." A young woman delegate from Pakistan, herself raised in purdah (the custom of keeping women fully covered with clothing and apart from the rest of society), spoke out strongly against child marriage. And evoking the abuses—and worse—of the Nazi regime in Germany, the Philippine delegate argued forcefully against weakening the Declaration's prohibition of torture by referring to local cultural customs. Diluting the ban, he cautioned, could provide cover for those who cloak their abhorrent practices in cultural justification.

The record leaves no doubt that the diplomats charged with preparing the Universal Declaration embraced their task and were fully aware of its potential significance. They frequently reminded each other of the need to find language acceptable to all, so that the document's legitimacy would not be questioned. The strength of their commitment, however, was not sufficient to bridge all divisions and to correct every flaw.

© AP Images/Eugene Hoshiko

Masked human rights protestors in Cebu, Philippines, on Human Rights Day, December 10, 2006.

Differences over the importance of sovereignty, the status of socioeconomic rights, and the ultimate question of implementation lurked just beneath the surface of many discussions, at various times threatening the whole enterprise. The eruption of war in the Middle East, South Asia, and elsewhere, and the plight of the resulting refugees, underscored the salience of human rights considerations—but also reminded delegates that rhetorical commitments unmatched by action would be futile. Some have numbered among the Declaration's weaknesses its emphasis on rights and its relegation of companion duties to one of the final articles, where it risks appearing as an afterthought. As it happens, this placement was due to a last-minute change proposed by the Chinese delegate. John Humphrey saw this as a lapse, as no one had been more attentive than Zhang Pengjun to the need to balance rights with duties.

Time pressures may also have been responsible for the diplomatic failure that resulted in the Saudi Arabian abstention in the final vote on the UDHR. Citing the historical crusades and more recent proselytizing by missionaries, the Saudi delegate objected to the phrase "freedom to change religion" and withheld support from the Declaration. The fact that a few years later, in the context of negotiating a legally binding treaty, the same Saudi representative agreed to the somewhat more nuanced phrase "freedom to adopt a religion" suggests that greater diplomatic effort in 1948 might have secured the Saudi vote and eliminated one source of cultural ambivalence about the Declaration. Finally, the Declaration's failure explicitly to address minority rights may have owed to the tensions brewing between the Soviet Union and Yugoslavia. The Soviets rarely bypassed an opportunity to expose heinous racial practices and inequities in the United States, but they were unwilling to push the principle of nondiscrimination when its application came closer to home. Notably, and regrettably, many delegations focused more intently on the failings of their political adversaries than on practices in their own country, a tendency as evident among small states as among their more powerful counterparts.

The Tasks Ahead

Such political considerations inevitably slowed the work of the Human Rights Commission, which had set out in 1946 to develop a binding legal instrument and an implementation mechanism alongside the Declaration. Completing those additional tasks ultimately required 18 more years. In the interim, U.N. member states reluctantly agreed to create two treaties rather than one, separating civil and political rights from social, cultural, and economic rights, each with its own implementation machinery. By the time the two treaties (or covenants) were ready for approval, the U.N. membership had grown to more than 100 states and political dynamics had changed. In the early years of these negotiations, as many as half of member states had advocated strong enforcement mechanisms, but by the mid-1960s, rising concerns about intervention and sovereignty instead often took precedence. Proposals to permit individual and NGO complaints, authorize U.N. investigations, or refer issues to the International Court of Justice were all abandoned. Instead, two standing committees, or "treaty bodies," were established to monitor human rights performance through periodic reports submitted by the states that ratified the covenants.

To anyone who tracked the full 20-year negotiation process, the disparity between early aspirations and eventual results was abundantly evident. An optional protocol attached to the covenant on civil and political rights did create an opportunity for states to provide a complaint mechanism for their citizens, but this was not the robust enforcement machinery many had envisioned at the outset. The UDHR project did not fulfill optimists' dreams, but it has exceeded the expectations of the pessimists. When the texts of the two covenants were forwarded to the General Assembly in 1966, the votes were unanimous. This time no state abstained or opposed.

U.N. member states have since reaffirmed their commitment to the Universal Declaration at a 1993 world conference on human rights, and more than 150 countries have ratified the two covenants. Collectively, these three documents—the Universal Declaration of Human Rights, the International Covenant on Civil and Political Rights, and the International Covenant on Social, Economic, and Cultural Rights—are informally called the International Bill of Rights. Together, they form the bedrock of international human rights law.

The History of International Human Rights Law

by Eric Posner

Prehistory—Before World War II

The animating idea behind human rights is the moral obligation not to harm strangers, and possibly the moral obligation to help them if they are in need. Most human groups—families, clans, tribes, nations, states—impose obligations on their members not to harm and, in most cases, to provide aid to, each other. These obligations are often strict, like the parents' obligation to care for their children, or the child's obligation to honor the parent. States may obligate citizens to fight and die for the sake of their co-nationals. These types of obligations stop at the border of the group. In Talmudic law, Jews may not lend at interest to other Jews, but may lend at interest to Gentiles. And, indeed, some groups do not forbid their members to harm strangers; it may be permissible to cheat, or rob, or even slaughter them. And even when constraints are imposed on the mistreatment of strangers, this is often pursuant to strategic imperatives, like the need to avoid war.

But there always coexisted with these basic moral structures a recognition of the common humanity of strangers, an acknowledgment that their well-being is entitled to consideration of some sort. In ancient literature, authors recognized people from other tribes or cultures as human beings, with similar wants and needs, and the capacity to suffer. The *Iliad* reaches its climax when Achilles permits King Priam to reclaim the corpse of his son, Hector, and give him proper burial rites. Perhaps some level of empathy for other human beings generally—not just members of the family or tribe or nation—is built into our biological makeup, or is learned by ordinary people as a matter of course. Tribes attack each other, but they also trade with each other, and intermarry, and these interactions would have made possible a sense that we owe obligations to others by virtue of their humanity (and so still excluding animals), even if those obligations are weaker than the obligations we owe to people in our family, tribe, or clan.

These ideas can be found in one form or another throughout recorded history, including in the major religions, and especially Christianity, with its radical notion that all humans are equal in the eyes of God. Anyone who harms another human being offends God; in this way, strangers may become an object of moral concern. Morality becomes universal in the sense that it applies to all human beings rather than to one's community or group alone.

Modern human rights thinking nonetheless did not develop until the Enlightenment in the eighteenth century. The historian Lynn Hunt argues that human rights evolved as a result of the expansion of literacy and reading, which exposed people to other human beings outside their immediate social, national, and kin groups, enabling them to learn that strangers are just like them.[4] This enhanced people's empathy for strangers and hence their receptiveness to the idea of human rights—that all human beings owe a moral obligation to all other human beings to respect their legitimate interests. Perhaps she is right, but the evidence that reading literature enhances people's capacity for empathy is weak.

A more plausible explanation for the development of theories of human rights in the Enlightenment is that Enlightenment thinkers believed that they needed to systematize moral thinking so as to defend themselves from the claim that secularization bred immorality. Seeking to throw off the influence of religion and irrational tradition, they needed to show that morality would persist in their absence, and they did so by locating the source of morality in human nature. If morality is a matter of human nature, then it is shared by all human beings.

It was a short step from there to the idea of human rights. Legal rights were well understood at the time. A legal right entitled a person to do something; if someone else tried to stop him, then the first person could seek aid from the government. Thus, a person who has an ownership right in land can seek aid from the government against trespassers and poachers. Enlightenment thinkers argued that just as people had rights against other people's interference with their property and lives, they also had rights against *government's* interference with their property and lives. What exactly these rights were and how one could vindicate them were complicated questions, but there was agreement that such rights existed, and that these rights were human rights. By virtue of a person's humanity, the government may not do certain things to him, like take his property without compensation, force him to quarter soldiers, or torture and kill him or his family.

The two major political documents that embodied these views were the U.S. Declaration of Independence, and the French Declaration of the Rights of Man. Both documents explained why the people could overthrow their government—because the government had violated their rights. (At the time, people often used the term "natural rights" rather than "human rights," but the terms meant the same thing.) The people could set up their own governments, and these governments would be required to comply with human rights.

But it was soon recognized that the political value of human rights was limited by a significant problem: the very idea that rights are universal conflicted with the imperative of building a nation. This is why human rights were a more powerful revolutionary idea than constitutional idea, mainly cited to explain why a government or foreign occupier was illegitimate, and not used to organize domestic constitutional arrangements. In the United States, human rights were domesticated as constitutional rights, which would for the most part protect Americans only, not foreigners (except those who came to settle in the United States). In France, human rights collapsed with Napoleon's dictatorship and the restoration of monarchy, after which, as in the United States, those rights took the form of constitutional protections for Frenchmen rather than universal imperatives applicable to all human beings.

Democratic impulses in Europe throughout the nineteenth century were closely allied with nationalism, which afforded the best hope for political organization on a large enough scale to provide for defense and domestic order. Great Britain provided a model. People possessed rights, but they were rights sanctified by history and tradition. Parliament respected the rights of Englishmen because of tradition, or because Englishmen demanded those rights, not because Englishmen are human beings. Other European countries that moved toward democracy or constitutional monarchy also recognized the rights of subjects or citizens because doing so brought political peace. The idea of human rights, that is, as rights enjoyed by all human beings irrespective of nationality, played a very small role, if any, in these developments.

This is not to say that people stopped taking an empathic interest in the well-being of foreigners. As I noted earlier, this seems like a basic stance of people, who are capable of feeling sympathy for "strangers" who are not a part of their community. People would thus feel distress when disasters struck foreigners, like the Lisbon earthquake of 1755. A deep popular revulsion toward slavery emerged in Great Britain in the nineteenth century, and it was revulsion toward slavery wherever it existed, anywhere in the world, rather than only slavery on British soil. Motivated by, or at least intertwined with, their religious convictions, the British pressured their government to ban the international slave trade. Parliament passed a law prohibiting the trade in 1807. Over the following decades, Britain successfully pressured Portugal, Spain, France, and Brazil to limit or end their participation in the slave trade. The United Kingdom was able to do this because of its dominance of the seas and its global commercial and political power.

Even imperialism, whose purpose was mainly economic and strategic, needed to be given a humanitarian gloss. Empires claimed to bring the benefits of religion and civilization to the natives. Where the reality diverged too far from the official story, scandals often ensued. Eventually, the imperial powers were forced to publicly rationalize colonization as a temporary expedient, justified only until domestic populations could govern themselves, and no longer. When those populations finally repudiated their imperial masters, imperialism became impossible to sustain as a moral matter.

The nineteenth century also witnessed a series of what we could today call "humanitarian interventions," military actions taken to rescue civilians in foreign countries who were being massacred by their governments or not protected by their governments from atrocities committed by armed groups. Britain, Russia, and France intervened repeatedly in the Balkans to protect Christians from being massacred by mobs or Ottoman troops. These actions often had a strategic role and were rarely perfectly humanitarian—the British were more concerned about Christians being massacred by Ottoman Turks than the other way around, or, for that matter, Christians being massacred by Christians. Nevertheless, actions such as these reflected at least some influence of the humanitarian impulse to help other human beings who were in need regardless of their group membership.

Countries also criticized each other. Western countries criticized Russia for tolerating pogroms that victimized Jews. The persecution of German Jews by the Nazis met with widespread condemnation elsewhere in Europe and North America. After Kristallnacht in 1938, leading figures and media around the world heaped scorn on Germany, accusing the Nazis of "barbarism" and "savagery."

By the eve of World War II, the international moral-legal system had the following characteristics. There was a strong idea, going back to the Peace of Westphalia of 1648, that states were "sovereign," which meant that governments mostly had a free hand to treat their populations however they wanted. This idea had been invoked by governments for centuries, and was based on the hard-won, pragmatic truth that when countries reserve the right to intervene in each other's affairs in order to protect subject populations, warfare is a common outcome. It also played well with the nationalist thinking of the nineteenth century.

But there was also a rough idea that all governments *should* treat their populations humanely, simply by virtue of the fact that their populations consisted of human beings. One could criticize foreign governments for massacring their own citizens, or allowing pogroms, or failing to alleviate famines, or tolerating slavery. In limited cases, especially when the foreign country was weak, or depended on foreign trade, or did not live up to what Europeans regarded as the standard of civilization, a powerful country might use commercial or military force to punish despots and dictators who mistreated their populations. But this was a weak idea, and not embodied in international law as it was then understood.

The Universal Declaration

During World War II, some of the allies, notably the United States and the United Kingdom, justified their war aims in more general terms than self-defense. They sought to repudiate fascism and perhaps any sort of authoritarianism, arguing that governments should be obliged to respect basic civil and political rights and to provide for basic needs. While these general aims received enthusiastic support from political elites in many countries, especially once the war ended, there was, from the start, considerable disagreement about what they would mean in practice. Many allied governments committed atrocities during the war but did not regard themselves (unlike Germany) as having violated international law, and virtually all governments abused citizens in ways that at least echoed Nazi ideas or practices—Jim Crow in the United States, political repression in the colonies of the United Kingdom, and all kinds of repression and misery in the Soviet Union, to name a few.

But these disagreements were swept under the rug at the start, and the United Nations charter provided in a few ambiguous phrases ("reaffirm faith in fundamental human rights" in the Preamble and "assisting in the realization of human rights" in Article 13) that its members would work to advance human rights. A few years later, the General Assembly approved a Universal Declaration of Human Rights. The Universal Declaration provided a long list of rights, most of which are the familiar "negative" or "political" rights that are listed in the U.S. Constitution, or that have been constructed by American courts over the years. The Universal Declaration was not dictated by the United States, however. It reflected the contributions of many different countries, and included rights that were not central to the American national constitutional tradition. Some of those rights were what philosophers call "positive" or "social" rights, including the right to work, which received a boost from Franklin Roosevelt's "Four Freedoms" speech, but more directly reflected currents in political thought in European and other countries. Table 3.4.1 lists some of the important rights in the Universal Declaration.

Table 3.3.1. Selected Provisions of the Universal Declaration of Human Rights

Article	Rights Recognized
Article 3	To life, liberty, and security of person.
Article 5	Not to be subjected to torture or to cruel, inhuman, or degrading treatment or punishment.
Article 10	To a fair and public hearing by an independent and impartial tribunal, in the determination of his rights and obligations and of any criminal charge against him.
Article 17	1. To own property alone as well as in association with others. 2. Not to be arbitrarily deprived of one's property.
Article 18	To freedom of thought, conscience, and religion.
Article 23	1. To work, to free choice of employment, to just and favorable conditions of work, and to protection against unemployment. 2. To equal pay for equal work. 3. To just and favorable remuneration ensuring for himself and his family an existence worthy of human dignity, and supplemented, if necessary, by other means of social protection. 4. To form and to join trade unions for the protection of his interests.
Article 24	To rest and leisure, including reasonable limitation of working hours and periodic holidays with pay.
Article 25	To a standard of living adequate for the health and well-being of himself and of his family, including food, clothing, housing, and medical care and necessary social services, and the right to security in the event of unemployment, sickness, disability, widowhood, old age, or other lack of livelihood in circumstances beyond his control.
Article 27	1. Freely to participate in the cultural life of the community, to enjoy the arts, and to share in scientific advancement and its benefits. 2. To the protection of the moral and material interests resulting from any scientific, literary, or artistic production of which he is the author.

The Universal Declaration was not a treaty in the formal sense: no one at the time believed that it created obligations legally binding on nations. It was not ratified by nations but approved by the General Assembly, and the UN Charter did not give the General Assembly the power to make international law. Moreover, the rights were described in vague, aspirational terms.

This did not auger well for the project of mandating the protection of human rights. Not even the liberal democracies were ready to commit themselves to binding legal obligations. The United States did not commit itself to eliminating Jim Crow, and Great Britain and France did not commit themselves to liberating the subject populations in their colonies. Several authoritarian states—including the Soviet Union, Yugoslavia, Poland, Czechoslovakia, and Saudi Arabia—refused to vote in favor of the Universal Declaration and instead abstained. The words in the Universal Declaration may have been stirring, but no one believed at the time that they portended a major change in the way international relations would be conducted, nor did they capture the imagination of voters, politicians, intellectuals, leaders of political movements, or anyone else who might have exerted political pressure on governments.

The Cold War Era

Part of the problem was that a disagreement opened up early on between the United States (as leader of the Western countries) and the Soviet Union (along with its satellites) about the content of human rights. The Americans argued that human rights consisted of political rights—the rights to vote, to speak freely, not to be arbitrarily detained, to practice a religion of one's choice, and the like. These rights were, not coincidentally, the rights in the U.S. Constitution. The Soviets argued that human rights consisted of social or economic rights—the rights to work, to health care, and to education. Although Stalin's 1936 constitution contained political as well as economic rights, it was plain to everyone by the 1940s that political rights did not exist in the Soviet Union. The Soviets thus argued that human rights consisted of rights associated with work and well-being, and did not include political rights. The Soviets maintained that those rights could be satisfied only by communism; capitalism, they insisted, led to poverty, unemployment, and inequality.

Human rights became yoked to the ideological conflict between the United States and the Soviet Union. And although the language of human rights was used from time to time, everyone understood that the debate was really about the market versus state planning; about democracy versus "dictatorship of the proletariat" or what could most charitably be called rule by a self-perpetuating elite; about God versus atheism. As was so often the case during the Cold War, the conflict was zero-sum. Either you supported political rights (that is, liberal democracy) or you supported economic rights (that is, socialism). The one major human rights treaty the two countries could agree to—the Genocide Convention of 1951, which prohibited countries from engaging in genocides—hardly showed that they shared much common ground. Negotiations to convert the Universal Declaration into a binding treaty were split into two tracks, and it would take another 18 years for the United Nations to adopt a political rights treaty and an economics right treaty, and another decade after that for the treaties to go into force. The result was the International Covenant on Civil and Political Rights (ICCPR) and the International Covenant on Economic, Social, and Cultural Rights (ICESCR), which finally took effect in 1976.

Meanwhile, the United States and the Soviet Union moved toward détente, and in 1975 signed the Helsinki Accords, under which the United States recognized the Soviet Union's control over Eastern Europe, in return for, among other things, Soviet agreement to respect human rights, which led the Soviet Union to ratify the ICCPR in 1976. Dissident groups throughout the Soviet sphere of influence formed Helsinki Watch committees, which reported on human rights violations and pressured Eastern Bloc governments to respect human rights.

In his important book *The Last Utopia*, Samuel Moyn argues that international human rights law did not begin to exercise influence until the mid-1970s, and there is a lot of evidence to support his position if one looks at human rights as a sociological rather than legal phenomenon. Legally, the modern era of human rights began with the Universal Declaration and the recognition that individuals, rather than merely states, possess rights under international law, and thus are entitled to legal protection from abuses by their own governments. Before then, abused populations could appeal to a foreign government for aid, but no one would have said that their appeal was grounded in violations of individual rights.

As Moyn explains, this idea did not become a major force in international relations until the 1970s. It was then that the Helsinki process began; it was a few years later that President Carter announced that human rights would be central to American foreign policy. Congress passed a law in 1977 that conditioned certain types of aid on compliance with human rights norms and required the State Department to issue reports on foreign countries' compliance with those norms. The Helsinki process itself was ambiguous from a human rights perspective, for while the Soviets were forced to agree to respect human rights (mainly at the insistence of the Europeans, not the Americans), it was also widely understood that the West was recognizing Soviet control of Eastern Europe—which meant those countries were condemned to lack democracy and self-determination.

Carter's emphasis on human rights seems to have been a reaction to Vietnam and the gruesome real-politik of the Nixon/Kissinger era, but Carter himself was unable to maintain a consistent line on human rights. Human-rights violating allies like Iran and Saudi Arabia were just too important for American security, and seen as an important counterweight to Soviet influence, so Carter could not consistently follow through on his rhetoric by threatening to withhold diplomatic support or economic resources from some of the worst violators of human rights.

Still, something changed with Carter. The frequency with which U.S. presidents invoked human rights spiked during the Carter administration, and while subsequent presidents did not emphasize human rights quite as much as Carter did, Carter did effect a lasting change in presidential rhetoric. Carter's five successors—Republicans and Democrats alike—have invoked the term "human rights" far more frequently than any president before Carter. It is not that presidents became more idealistic—Wilson and FDR frequently used idealistic rhetoric. Rather, it is that presidents starting with Carter increasingly began to express their idealistic goals (or to conceal their strategic goals) in the idiom of human rights.

Meanwhile, although Soviet influence was expanding in Africa, Asia, and South America, the ideological basis of Soviet power was beginning to lose its appeal. In the 1970s and 1980s, it became clear that the Soviet system stood not only for political repression (which had been known at least since the 1950s) but also for the failure to deliver economic prosperity. Thus, President Reagan, while not emphasizing human rights as much as President Carter did, nonetheless used them as a cudgel against the Soviets, complaining about their treatment of political dissidents and religious minorities.

The collapse of the Soviet Union was not caused by its human rights violations, or by domestic opposition fueled by those violations. The decline in the price of oil played a much greater role. But with the collapse of the Soviet Union, the major ideological alternative to liberal democracy was gone, and so was the only country that could prevent the United States from imposing its values (for good or ill) on foreign countries.

Three more human rights conventions came into force during this period: the Convention on the Elimination of All Forms of Discrimination Against Women (1979); the Convention Against Torture and Other Cruel, Inhuman or Degrading Treatment or Punishment (1984); and the Convention on the Rights of the Child (1989). With the collapse of communism and the spread of liberal democracy, states joined these and the other human rights treaties in increasing numbers. The most recent treaty is the Convention on the Rights of Persons with Disabilities (2008). Figure 3.4.1, below, tells the story.

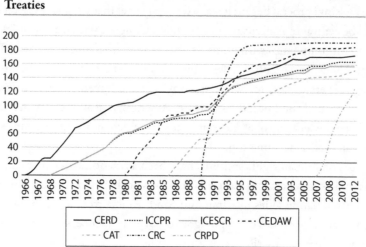

Figure 3.3.1. Growth of Membership in Seven Major Human Rights Treaties

States increasingly appear to regard ratification of the latest human rights treaty—with a few exceptions—as all but compulsory.

It is commonly believed that the West initiated the human rights treaties, and the developing world either followed or resisted. This simplifies a complex story. The general idea of human rights treaties originated in the West, and the rights themselves had been heavily institutionalized in certain Western countries for many years. But many treaties, while heavily influenced by Western norms, were actually initiated by groups in developing countries who hoped to improve rights in those countries and sought outside support. The ICESCR, as we saw, was an effort by the Soviet Union to provide an alternative model to Western-style political rights. But there are other examples as well. The Convention on the Elimination of All Forms of Discrimination Against Women was drafted in response to a UN resolution introduced in 1963 by 22 developing and Eastern European countries. The Convention on the Rights of the Child was initially proposed by Poland and other Soviet bloc countries. And while the Convention on the Rights of Persons with Disabilities can be traced back to a proposal made by Sweden and Italy in 1987, Mexico, Jordan, South Africa, and many other developing countries played a prominent role in its negotiation—while the major Western countries had to be dragged along.

The Modern Era

By the 1990s, it was possible to argue that there really was an international human rights "regime," in the sense that there was something like a consensus among nations that all countries must respect human rights, despite considerable disagreement as to what this meant. Not all countries had ratified all the treaties; but most countries had ratified most of the treaties. (Today, each of the six major human rights treaties has been ratified by more than 150 countries, and some treaties—including the ICCPR and the Rights of the Child Convention—have been ratified by nearly all countries.) Nor was there agreement about all the rights and what they meant, but most countries seemed to agree about many of the rights.

Some legal theorists began talking about a global constitution or international bill of rights—higher law that superseded domestic law and other forms of international law, and that states could not withdraw from. Others argued that human rights had entered customary international law, a body of law that was thought to bind states even though it was not embodied in treaties, because states gave their implicit (or explicit) consent to particular norms. On this view, norms in treaties reflected customary international law and hence bound even states that had not ratified those treaties.

However, this view emerged at the same time that events made a mockery of it. One was the horrifying genocide in Rwanda, where in a matter of months in 1994, members of the Hutu majority slaughtered more than 800,000 members of the Tutsi minority along with their Hutu supporters. Other countries stood by when they could have intervened and stopped it. The other event was the civil war in Yugoslavia, which featured significant civilian massacres as well as other atrocities. The civil war was not worse than other civil wars that had taken place in Asia, Latin America, and Africa during the Cold War and after, but it struck a nerve because it took place in Europe. Foreign countries did intervene, albeit slowly.

Human rights supporters could take comfort in the fact that, while the United Nations responded slowly, it set up international tribunals to try the worst perpetrators of atrocities in Rwanda and the former Yugoslavia. These criminal trials revived the idea, which had been defunct since the Nuremberg and Tokyo trials after World War II, that individuals could commit international crimes by engaging in human rights violations that exceeded an ambiguous threshold of atrocity. The tribunals were not entirely successful. They were enormously expensive, and resources were only enough to try a small handful of the perpetrators. Some of the doctrines that they developed to facilitate conviction were criticized for relying on guilt by association, and all factions believed that the tribunals were biased against them. A new controversy has recently erupted over whether the Yugoslavia tribunal is cutting back on criminal liability.

Unhappiness with the tribunals led to the establishment of the International Criminal Court in 1998, which gained general jurisdiction over all international crimes committed in a member country or by a national of a member country. But the ICC has experienced significant growing pains since it began operations in 2002. It has tried very few people, and it has taken jurisdiction only over African countries, which has led to accusations of bias even though several of those countries sought ICC intervention.

More to the point, human rights law never became a consistent factor in U.S. foreign policy. The United States continued to tolerate human rights violations by important allies. No president after Carter made human rights as central to his foreign policy rhetoric as Carter did. Still, the 1990s were the high-water mark for human rights. With the collapse of the Soviet Union, economic and social rights lost their stigmatizing association with communism and entered the constitutional law of many Western countries, with the result that all major issues of public policy were increasingly seen as shaped by human rights. Human rights played an increasingly important role in the European Union, although the focus there was always on internal consolidation. Members of the European Union respected human rights as a matter of domestic constitutional law, but they also recognized an increasing role for human rights in

European law, and insisted that countries that sought to join the EU in order to obtain the economic benefits of being part of the union be required to respect human rights as well. At the same time, the EU has never put significant resources into advancing human rights outside of Europe. The activity of NGOs devoted to advancing human rights as they defined them also increased during this period. And many countries that emerged from under the Soviet yoke adopted Western constitutional systems—even Russia itself made halting movements in that direction.

Then came September 11, 2001. America's recourse to torture was a significant challenge to the human rights regime. Human rights advocates tried to attribute it to a wayward Republican administration, but the fact is that many Americans supported the use of torture. Most polls of Americans between 2001 and 2009 found that a substantial portion of the population (between 15 percent and 54 percent) was in favor of torture. Governments of other countries, including traditional liberal countries like those of Western Europe, were complicit in U.S. torture. In February of 2013, the Open Society Justice Initiative released a report accusing 54 countries, including major European countries like Germany and the United Kingdom, of participating in the torture and abuse of detainees in the U.S. extraordinary rendition program. The detention center at Guantanamo Bay also posed a challenge to the spirit of the human rights treaties, although indefinite detentions and military tribunals pose a closer legal question than torture does. As long as the conflict with Al Qaeda could be classified as a "war" (a controversial but not clearly wrong view), then those institutions could be justified under the laws of war. Torture, however, could not be justified under the laws of war or human rights law.

What was striking and awkward for human rights supporters is that the United States was a traditional leader in human rights, and one of only a few countries that has used its power and resources to advance human rights in other nations. Moreover, the prohibition on torture is at the core of the human rights regime; if that right is less than absolute, then surely the other rights are as well. Many commentators, foreign governments, and NGOs criticized the United States for engaging in torture, and the U.S. government eventually backed down. It remains unclear, however, why it backed down, and whether or not it was influenced by this criticism.

Moreover, many countries remain hostile to human rights. Foremost among them is China, the most dynamic country in the world, which is on the cusp of superpower status. China has worked quietly but assiduously behind the scenes to weaken international human rights institutions and, more noisily, to reject international criticism of the political repression of its citizens. It has offered diplomatic and economic support to human-rights violators like Sudan, which Western countries have tried to isolate. Along with Russia, it has used its veto in the Security Council to limit Western efforts to advance human rights through economic pressure and military intervention. And it has joined with numerous other countries hostile to human rights—major emerging powers like Vietnam, and Islamic countries that fear Western secularization—to deny many of the core values that human rights are supposed to protect.

This raises the question of how much human rights *law* has actually influenced the behavior of countries. In one view, the answer is quite a bit. As I have described, most countries have ratified the majority of the most important human rights treaties. Today, when governments criticize each other, they frequently invoke the language of human rights. NGOs that advocate human rights have proliferated; Amnesty International and Human Rights Watch are just the most prominent of hundreds of organizations. The media discuss their reports. Numerous UN organizations monitor human rights, and there are regional courts that enforce human rights law, most notably the European Court of Human Rights. Law schools teach human rights law. There is even private litigation in America based on international human rights violations. None of this was true 50 years ago.

And yet there is a nagging question as to whether all of this activity has actually improved people's lives. It turns out that this question is hard to answer. In a very rough sense, the world is a freer place than it was 50 years ago, but is it freer because of the human rights treaties or because of other events—such as economic growth or the collapse of communism? In Chapter 4, I will discuss the evidence that human rights treaties have improved respect for human rights in detail, but the bottom line for present purposes is that if they have, the effect has been small; plus, as I will explain, it is hard to rule out offsetting factors that have negated any existing positive effects.

Notes

1. Joseph Raz, Human Rights Without Foundations 321, in The Philosophy of International Law (Samantha Besson & John Tasioulas eds., Oxford Univ. Press 2010).

2. David L. Cingranelli & David L. Richards, The Cingranelli and Richards (CIRI) Human Rights Data Project, 32 Hum. Rts. Q. 401 (2010); the data are available at http://humanrightsdata.blogspot.com/.

3. Arch Puddington, Freedom in the World 2013: Democratic Breakthroughs in the Balance, at 4 http://www.freedomhouse.org/sites/default/files/FIW%202013%20Booklet_o.pdf. Freedom House is associated with conservative figures in the American political establishment, and therefore its scoring is sometimes treated as suspect.

4. Lynn A. Hunt, Inventing Human Rights: A History (W. W. Norton & Co. 2007).

Remarks to the General Assembly

by António Guterres

Thank you very much for all your kind words. I am deeply honoured by the trust and confidence Member States have placed in me, and determined to be guided by the purposes and principles of the Charter.

First of all, I would like to pay tribute to Secretary-General Ban Ki-moon. Secretary-General, your principled leadership has helped to chart the future of the United Nations—through the 2030 Agenda for Sustainable Development; through your commitment to peace and security; through your initiative to put human rights at the heart of our work. Under your direction, the world committed to the historic Paris Agreement on climate change—and ratified it in record time. I strongly believe this momentum is unstoppable. Dear Secretary-General Ban Ki-moon, it is an honour to follow in your steps, defending the same values that unite us. Thank you very much.

> In the end, it comes down to values, as was said so many times today. We want the world our children inherit to be defined by the values enshrined in the UN Charter: peace, justice, respect, human rights, tolerance and solidarity.

Twenty-one years ago, when I took the oath of office to become Prime Minister of Portugal, the world was riding a wave of optimism. The cold war had ended, and some described that as the end of history. They believed we would live in a peaceful, stable world with economic growth and prosperity for all. But, the end of the cold war wasn't the end of history. On the contrary, history had simply been frozen in some places. When the old order melted away, history came back with a vengeance.

Hidden contradictions and tensions resurfaced. New wars multiplied and old ones reignited. Lack of clarity in power relations led progressively to greater unpredictability and impunity. Conflicts have become more complex—and interlinked—than ever before. They produce horrific violations of international humanitarian law and human rights abuses. People have been forced to flee their homes on a scale unseen in decades. And a new threat has emerged—global terrorism. Megatrends—including climate change, population growth, rapid urbanization, food insecurity and water scarcity—have increased competition for resources and heightened tensions and instability.

At the same time, the last 20 years have seen extraordinary technological progress. The global economy has grown; basic social indicators have improved. The proportion of people living in absolute poverty has fallen dramatically. But, globalization and technological progress have also contributed to growing inequalities. A lot of people have been left behind, even including in developed countries where millions of old jobs have disappeared and new ones are out of reach for many. In many parts, youth unemployment has exploded. And globalization has also broadened the reach of organized crime and trafficking.

All this has deepened the divide between people and political establishments. In some countries, we have seen growing instability, social unrest—even violence and conflict. A little bit everywhere, voters now tend to reject the status quo, and whatever Government proposal is put to a referendum. Many have lost confidence not only in their Governments, but in global institutions—including the United Nations.

Fear is driving the decisions of many people around the world. We must understand their anxieties and meet their needs, without losing sight of our universal values. It is time to reconstruct relations between people and leaders—national and international; time for leaders to listen and show that they care, about their own people and about the global stability and solidarity on which we all depend. And it is time for the United Nations to do the same: to recognize its shortcomings and to reform the way it works. This Organization is the cornerstone of multilateralism, and has contributed to decades of relative peace. But, the challenges are now surpassing our ability to respond. The United Nations must be ready to change.

Our most serious shortcoming—and here I refer to the entire international community—is our inability to prevent crises. The United Nations was born from war. Today, we must be here for peace.

La prévention exige que nous nous attaquions aux causes profondes à travers les trois piliers des Nations Unies: la paix et la sécurité, le développement durable et les droits humains. Cela doit être la priorité dans tout ce que nous faisons.

La prévention exige que nous soutenions plus les pays dans leurs efforts pour renforcer leurs institutions et rendre leurs sociétés plus résilientes.

Il s'agit aussi de rétablir les droits humains comme une valeur fondamentale qui doit être défendue en tant que telle, et non à des fins politiques autres. Tous, y compris les minorités de tout genre, doivent pouvoir jouir de l'ensemble des droits humains—civils, politiques, économiques, sociaux et culturels—sans aucune discrimination.

Protéger et autonomiser les femmes et les filles est primordial. L'égalité des genres est essentielle au développement, et le rôle clé qu'elle joue dans la consolidation et le maintien de la paix devient de plus en plus indéniable.

La prévention n'est pas un concept nouveau: c'est ce que les fondateurs des Nations Unies nous ont demandé de faire et elle constitue le meilleur moyen de sauver des vies et d'alléger la souffrance humaine.

Mais lorsque la prévention échoue, nous devons redoubler d'efforts pour régler les conflits.

Des crises les plus aïgues, en Syrie, au Yémen, au Soudan du Sud et ailleurs, aux disputes de longue date, y compris le conflit israélo-palestinien, il nous faut davantage de médiation, d'arbitrage et de diplomatie créative.

Je suis prêt à m'engager personnellement à travers mes bons offices dans la résolution des conflits mais lorsque cela constitue une plus-value, tout en reconnaissant le rôle de premier plan des États Membres.

L'échelle des défis auxquels nous sommes confrontés nous contraint à travailler de concert, pour réformer les Nations Unies de manière approfondie et continue. Je souhaiterais esquisser ici trois priorités stratégiques de cette réforme: dans notre travail en faveur de la paix; notre appui au développement durable; et notre gestion interne.

Les femmes et les hommes travaillant dans les opérations de maintien de la paix des Nations Unies nous apportent une contribution héroïque au péril de leurs vies. Toutefois, ils se voient souvent confier la tâche de maintenir une paix qui n'existe pas. Nous devons donc nous entendre sur ce que recoupe le travail de maintien de la paix, afin de jeter les bases d'une réforme urgente.

Nous devons créer un fil conducteur pour la paix qui relie la prévention et la résolution des conflits, le maintien et la consolidation de la paix, et le développement. Nous devons nous appuyer sur les conclusions des trois récents rapports, ainsi que les résolutions parallèles de l'Assemblée générale et du Conseil de sécurité. Le moment est venu pour nous tous, inspirés par le nouveau concept de pérennisation de la paix, de nous engager dans une réforme globale de la stratégie, des opérations et des structures des Nations Unies visant la paix et la sécurité.

Cette réforme doit également inclure un examen de notre travail dans le domaine de la lutte anti-terroriste, et un meilleur mécanisme de coordination entre les 38 entités des Nations Unies qui sont concernées.

The United Nations system has not yet done enough to prevent and respond to the appalling crimes of sexual violence and exploitation committed under the UN flag against those we are supposed to protect. I will work closely with Member States on structural, legal and operational measures to make the zero-tolerance policy for which Secretary-General Ban Ki-moon has fought so hard a reality. We must ensure transparency and accountability and offer protection and effective remedies to the victims.

The second key element of the reform agenda concerns the United Nations support to Member States in achieving the Sustainable Development Goals and the objectives of the Paris Agreement, an expression of global solidarity, with their promise to leave no one behind. To do this, we will reposition development at the centre of our work, and engage in a comprehensive reform of the United Nations development system, at Headquarters and country levels. This must involve leadership, coordination, delivery and accountability. We will build on the outcome of the recent discussions among Member States.

We must also bring the humanitarian and development spheres closer together from the very beginning of a crisis to support affected communities, address structural and economic impacts and help prevent a new spiral of fragility and instability. Humanitarian response, sustainable development and sustaining peace are three sides of the same triangle.

This approach relates to the new way of working agreed at the World Humanitarian Summit. To achieve this, we need more accountability, on the level of each individual agency carrying out its mandate, but also its contribution to the work of the United Nations system and of the system as a whole. A strong culture of accountability also requires effective and independent evaluation mechanisms.

The third key area is management reform. We will build on existing efforts and implement the recent initiatives that were approved. But, looking at United Nations staff and budgetary rules and regulations, one might think that some of them were designed to prevent, rather than enable, the effective delivery of our mandates.

We need to create a consensus around simplification, decentralization and flexibility. It benefits no one if it takes nine months to deploy a staff member to the field. The United Nations needs to be nimble, efficient and effective. It must focus more on delivery and less on process; more on people and less on bureaucracy. A culture of accountability also requires strong performance management and effective protection for whistle-blowers.

And it is not enough just to do better. We must be able to communicate better about what we do, in ways that everybody understands. We need a substantial reform of our communications strategy, upgrading our tools and platforms to reach people around the world.

Finally, management reform must ensure we reach gender parity sooner rather than later. The initial target for the equal representation of women and men among United Nations staff was the year 2000. Sixteen years later, we are far from that goal. I pledge to respect gender parity from the start in all my appointments to the Senior Management Group and the Chief Executives Board.

By the end of my mandate, we should reach full gender parity at the Under-Secretary-General and Assistant Secretary-General levels, including special representatives and special envoys. We need a clear road map with benchmarks and time frames to achieve parity across the system, well before the target year of 2030. And the same concern applies to regional diversity.

Finally, any investment in a stronger United Nations must take staff into account. I look forward to working once again alongside over 85,000 men and women carrying out our mandate in 180 countries across the globe. Many of them work in difficult and sometimes dangerous circumstances. With their professionalism, expertise and dedication, they are the United Nations' most important resource, a resource that has to be cared for, developed and used efficiently, and whose voice needs to be heard.

We live in a complex world. The United Nations cannot succeed alone. Partnership must continue to be at the heart of our strategy. We should have the humility to acknowledge the essential role of other actors while maintaining full awareness of our unique convening power.

Our humanitarian and development efforts would be insignificant without the active involvement of Member States and the contributions of civil society, international financial institutions, private investors and even financial markets. Several mediation efforts and peace operations would not be possible without the engagement of regional organizations, particularly the African Union, our most relevant international regional partner, both in peace and security and in development.

Recientemente hemos puesto en marcha diferentes iniciativas importantes junto con nuestros socios. Nos corresponde ahora llevarlas a buen término antes de iniciar otras nuevas.

Pero en nuestra estrategia hay un vacío: el labor con los jóvenes. Durante demasiado tiempo, los jóvenes se han visto excluidos de la toma de decisiones que afectan a su futuro.

Debemos aprovechar la labor realizada en el pasado con el apoyo de los Estados Miembros, el Enviado para la Juventud y la sociedad civil. Pero esta no puede ser una iniciativa donde los ancianos sean quienes hablen de las nuevas generaciones. Las Naciones Unidas deben empoderar a los jóvenes y aumentar su participación en la sociedad y su acceso a la educación, la formación y el empleo.

Today's paradox is that, despite greater connectivity, societies are becoming more fragmented. More and more people live within their own bubbles, unable to appreciate their links with the whole human family. In the end, it comes down to values, as was said so many times today. We want the world our children inherit to be defined by the values enshrined in the United Nations Charter: peace, justice, respect, human rights, tolerance and solidarity. All major religions embrace these principles, and we strive to reflect them in our daily lives.

But, the threats to these values are most often based on fear. Our duty to the peoples we serve is to work together to move from fear of each other, to trust in each other. Trust in the values that bind us and trust in the institutions that serve and protect us.

My contribution to the United Nations will be aimed at inspiring that trust, as I do my best to serve our common humanity. Thank you very much.

The Dilemma of Humanitarian Intervention

by Jayshree Bajoria and Robert McMahon

Introduction

The crackdown by Libyan leader Muammar al-Qaddafi on mass anti-regime protests in early 2011 resulted in strong condemnation by the international community. In a historic move, the UN Security Council invoked the principle of "responsibility to protect" and adopted **Resolution 1973**, endorsing a no-fly zone over Libya and authorizing member states to "take all necessary measures" to protect civilians under attack from Qaddafi's government. As a result, some Western countries, including the United States, began air strikes over Libya, which spurred a debate on whether forced intervention was warranted. Countries like Russia, China, Brazil, and India abstained from voting on the UN resolution, spotlighting the sensitive nature of the issue. Some states in Asia and Africa, especially former colonies, have long seen intervention of any kind as a threat to their sovereignty. This was evident in the divide that followed a **devastating cyclone** in Myanmar in May 2008. There have been some instances in the recent past where countries have opened up to outside aid in the aftermath of natural disasters, but sovereignty remains a sticking point.

Responsibility vs. Sovereignty

The United Nations, formed in the aftermath of World War II to promote peace and stability, recognizes the importance of sovereignty, especially for newly independent nations or those seeking independence from colonizers. The **UN Charter** says: "Nothing contained in the present Charter shall authorize the United Nations to intervene in matters which are essentially within the domestic jurisdiction of any state." The principle does not rule out the application of enforcement measures in case of a threat to peace, a breach of peace, or acts of aggression on the part of the state. The **Genocide Convention** of 1948 also overrode the nonintervention principle to lay down the commitment of the world community to prevent and punish. Yet inaction in response to the Rwanda genocide in 1994 and failure to halt the 1995 Srebrenica massacre in Bosnia highlight the complexities of international responses to crimes against humanity.

> *"R2P is not solely about military intervention but, if it is to have any meaning at all, must include that option as a last resort."*
>
> —Ramesh Thakur

In 2000, the Canadian government and several other actors announced the establishment of the **International Commission on Intervention and State Sovereignty (ICISS)** to address the challenge of the international community's responsibility to act in the face of the gravest of human rights violations while respecting the sovereignty of states. It sought to bridge these two concepts with the 2001 Responsibility to Protect (R2P) **report (PDF)**. A year later, the co-chairs of the commission, Gareth Evans of the International Crisis Group and Algerian diplomat Mohamed Sahnoun, wrote in *Foreign Affairs:* "If the international community is to respond to this challenge, the whole debate must be turned on its head. The **issue must be reframed** not as an argument about the 'right to intervene' but about the 'responsibility to protect.'"

The commission included environmental or natural disasters as possible events after which the international community could intervene if the state failed in its responsibility to protect its population. But in 2005, when the responsibility to protect doctrine was incorporated into a **UN outcome document**, environmental disasters had been dropped as a reason for intervention. The document did say it was every state's responsibility to protect its citizens from "genocide, war crimes, ethnic cleansing, and crimes against humanity." If a state fails to do so, the document says, it then becomes the responsibility of the international community to protect that state's population in accordance with **Chapter VII of the UN Charter**. Chapter VII includes use of military force by the international community if peaceful measures prove inadequate. The UN outcome document was unanimously adopted by all member states but is not legally binding.

The doctrine was hailed by international affairs specialists as a new dawn for peace and security. In a 2007 Council Special Report, former CFR Senior Fellow Lee Feinstein wrote that the adoption of R2P was a watershed, "**marking the end** of a 350-year period in which the inviolability of borders and the monopoly of force within one's own borders were sovereignty's formal hallmarks." He says the doctrine's adoption begins to resolve the historic tension between human rights and states' rights in favor of the individual.

Failure to Address Humanitarian Intervention

Following Myanmar's cyclone in May 2008, some experts say the spirit of the R2P doctrine, if not its letter, was tested. The country's regime was incapable of providing relief to millions of affected citizens and it refused to let in international aid and aid workers for several days. French Foreign Minister Bernard

Kouchner suggested the United Nations invoke the R2P doctrine as the basis for a resolution to allow the delivery of international aid even without the junta's permission. But the French proposal faced opposition from Security Council members Russia, China, and South Africa. China's UN ambassador, Liu Zhenmin, argued it was **not an issue** for the Security Council. "The current issue of Myanmar is a natural disaster," and the situation should not be politicized, he said. Experts warned that Southeast Asian nations and India might also take exception to intervention in Myanmar.

In identifying one possible case for the application of military force, the 2001 R2P report had included "overwhelming natural or environmental catastrophes, where the state concerned is either unwilling or unable to cope, or call for assistance, and significant loss of life is occurring or threatened." But Ramesh Thakur, one of the original R2P commissioners, says politically, "we cannot ignore the **significance of the exclusion** of natural and environmental disasters between 2001 and 2005." To attempt to reintroduce it today, he writes, "would strengthen suspicion of western motivations and reinforce cynicism of western tactics." Former U.S. Secretary of State Madeleine K. Albright writes in a *New York Times* oped that the "notion of **national sovereignty as sacred** has gained ground after the U.S. invasion of Iraq." And despite recent efforts to enshrine the doctrine of a 'responsibility to protect' in international law, the concept of humanitarian intervention has lost momentum," she says.

Though sovereignty concerns linger, especially in Asia, some instances in the recent past have suggested countries in the region might be warming to humanitarian aid intervention.

Proponents of the doctrine say another way to raise pressure for action in Myanmar is to focus on rebuilding the country. Those who helped write the 2001 report emphasized that R2P embraced not just the "responsibility to react" but the "responsibility to prevent" and the "responsibility to rebuild" as well. Evans and Sahnoun argued in *Foreign Affairs*: "Both of these dimensions have been much neglected in the traditional humanitarian-intervention debate. Bringing them back to center stage should help make the concept of reaction itself more palatable." The 2005 UN document also emphasized prevention. It noted: "We also intend to commit ourselves, as necessary and appropriate, to helping States build capacity to protect their populations . . . and to assisting those which are under stress before crises and conflicts break out."

But David Rieff, a journalist who specializes in humanitarian issues, writes in the New York Times Magazine: "Use any euphemism you wish, but in the end these **interventions have to be about regime change** if they are to have any chance of accomplishing their stated goal." In the wake of the 2011 crisis in Libya following calls for regime change, Thakur also argued: "R2P is not solely about military intervention but, if it is to have any meaning at all, must include that option **as a last resort (*Ottawa Citizen*).**"

A Positive Shift?

The doctrine was most notably applied to mediate Kenya's post-election violence in 2008, which Thakur refers to as the "**only successful R2P marker to date**" (*TOI*). Following the mass atrocity crimes as a result of a highly disputed election in Kenya, the international community rapidly responded to apply political and diplomatic pressure to stop violence and encourage a political solution which resulted in a coalition government. Before being invoked explicitly in 2011 in reference to the situation in Libya, the Security Council also invoked the R2P doctrine for first time in its 2006 **Resolution on Darfur**.

Though sovereignty concerns linger, especially in Asia, some instances in the recent past have suggested countries in the region might be warming to humanitarian aid intervention. In the 2004 Indian Ocean tsunami, one of the worst-hit areas was Indonesia's Aceh Province, where the government had been fighting a secessionist movement for more than four decades. The province, under martial law, was off-limits for most international human rights groups, aid organizations, and reporters. But after initial hesitation, the Indonesian government allowed international aid in what **Elizabeth Ferris** and **Lex Rieffel** of the Brookings Institution call "one of the **largest disaster recovery** and reconstruction efforts in modern times, as well as the peace agreement, which led to the election of a former secessionist leader as governor of the province."

Similarly, after a powerful 2005 earthquake rocked the long-disputed Kashmir region dividing India and Pakistan, the Pakistani government decided to give access to international relief agencies. Moreover, it accepted food and relief aid from neighboring India, with which it has fought three wars over Kashmir. The move was significant enough for regional experts to ask if this could **lead to peace**. More recently, an earthquake in China's Sichuan Province in May 2008 led Beijing to make unprecedented moves to open up. The Chinese government, which in the past has spurned foreign aid, accepted international aid publicly, opened a hotline for the U.S. military to have increased communication with its Chinese counterparts, and eased media restrictions.

> "Humanitarian/military intervention outside of a UN Security Council mandate remains a very highly contested area of international law."
>
> —Matthew Waxman, CFR

India, by contrast, refused international aid both after the 2004 tsunami and after the 2005 earthquake in Kashmir. Experts say isolationist governments spurn assistance because they seek to retain complete control over their populations, but other countries may reject foreign aid as a matter of international prestige. Pratap Bhanu Mehta, director of the New-Delhi based Center for Policy Research, saw India's decision to refuse aid after the 2005 earthquake as a reflection of its desire to be seen as an **emerging global power** (*NYT*).

A Worrying Future

Several experts saw the situation in Libya as a test case for the Security Council and its implementation of the R2P doctrine. "The **international military intervention** (*SMH*) in Libya is not about bombing for democracy or Muammar Qaddafi's head," says Evans, a principal author of the R2P concept. "Legally, morally, politically, and militarily, it has only one justification: protecting the country's people." R2P proponents also point to regional backing for the no-fly zone from organizations such as the Arab League, the Gulf Cooperation Council, and the Organization of the Islamic Conference, stressing its international legitimacy.

But others recommend caution, saying that without sufficient military commitment, the intervention would do more harm than good. "The trouble is, although we are prepared to 'do something' and pull out the most impressive kit in the U.S. toolbox—military power—we aren't actually willing to get involved at the **level required to win (ForeignPolicy)**," writes CFR's Micah Zenko.

Beyond the operational and political, military intervention also involves legal issues, says CFR's Matthew Waxman. "Humanitarian/military intervention outside of a UN Security Council mandate remains a very **highly contested area of international law**," he says. And Russia and China have historically been reluctant to support any form of intervention. Besides their longstanding noninterference policy in the internal affairs of other countries, they are "particularly worried that it could create a precedent for the international community to have a say in how they treat their own, sometimes restive, minority populations," says **Stewart M. Patrick**, CFR senior fellow and director of the program on international institutions and global governance.

The willingness to use armed force is also inevitably influenced not only by the desperation of the affected population but also by geopolitical factors, including the relevance of the country to the world community, regional stability, and the attitudes of other major players, say experts.

The choice over humanitarian intervention remains equally difficult. At present the world community has limited options for responding to humanitarian crises. UN General Assembly **Resolution 46/182** formed guiding principles for the international community's response to humanitarian disasters and was central to the establishment of the office of the UN emergency relief coordinator and the development of the **Inter-Agency Standing Committee**.

But the General Assembly resolution reiterates that "the sovereignty, territorial integrity, and national unity of States must be fully respected in accordance with the Charter of the United Nations," which makes it difficult to operate in situations where the affected country denies access. In such cases, the role of regional actors and neighbors becomes critical. The **Association of Southeast Asian Nations** played a very active role in changing the minds of Myanmar's regime to let in international aid after the initial refusal, experts say. But "if our methods short of armed force have no impact and we are not willing to threaten to use military action, there are no good options," says Patrick.

At the same time, Patrick says, forced humanitarian intervention is a difficult choice to make. "The crime that the government is guilty of may be a crime of omission rather than commission, so that the level of culpability appears to be less than a government actively making war against its people, for instance in the case of a genocide," says Patrick.

CHAPTER FOUR

Global Health and Environment

Global Health

The Hippocratic Oath requires a new physician to swear by the healing gods to adhere to ethical standards.[1] The text is ascribed to Hippocrates, who lived in the 5th century B.C.E, but authorship has never been firmly established for the document. Although it was written in antiquity, its principles still guide the ideal conduct of physicians: according to NOVA, the administration of a modernized version of the oath has risen from 24 percent in 1928 to almost 100 percent today. In 2017, the World Medical Association updated a successor to the Hippocratic Oath in the form of the Declaration of Geneva. Although intended to be global, the Declaration has an uneven uptake; in some countries it is legally binding, and in others it is modified or not used at all.[2] The Hippocratic Oath and the Declaration of Geneva may continue to inspire physicians, but they are not well-suited for a globalized world.[3] Physicians no longer have total control over patient–physician relations. How will they maintain patient privacy when both national and international health care organizations demand health care information? Are physicians morally obligated to treat diseases with the virulence of Ebola? If a country lacks the medical resources to care for its population, which doctors from which countries are responsible for coming to these patients' aid? The field of global health has developed in part in answer to these questions.

Global Health is defined as "collaborative transnational research and action for promoting health for all" (Beaglehole and Bonita 2010: np). Although international health is sometimes used as a synonym for global health, it is important to make some distinctions. The field of global health is particularly interested in the health issues that are shared across national borders. International health focuses on health issues in low-income countries. Because health issues often exceed the capacity of a single country to resolve alone, the field of global health takes a collaborative approach

1 http://www.pbs.org/wgbh/nova/body/hippocratic-oath-today.html
2 https://www.bioedge.org/bioethics/new-hippocratic-oath-for-doctors-approved/12496
3 http://www.pbs.org/wgbh/nova/body/hippocratic-oath-today.html

whenever possible. In recognizing disparities, global health places an emphasis on both improving health and achieving health equity for all people (Koplan et al. 2009: np).

This topic is connected to previous chapters: to understand health and respond to health issues, it is necessary to take into account globalization (the topic of the first chapter), international relations (a topic in the second chapter), economic development (the topic of the next chapter), on top of progress in medicine. Expanding the frame of reference beyond the science in general or medicine in particular paves the way to understanding the biological, behavioral, economic, social, and political determinants of health as a complex whole.

Burdens of disease are unevenly distributed globally. Epidemiologists[4] have observed that with an increase in wealth, mortality and disease patterns make a corresponding shift. "Lifestyle" diseases that result from poor exercise and food choices gradually replace pandemics and infectious disease as the main causes of death. Therefore, while people in more developed, wealthier nations are more likely to die of conditions such as heart disease, people in less developed parts of the world are more likely to die from the spread of viruses and bacteria. Socioeconomic improvement can have a great impact on population health (Delaet and Delaet 2012: 30). This does not necessarily protect people in less wealthy countries from acquiring lifestyle conditions such as obesity, heart disease, and so forth. These, diseases are being globalized, leading to new burdens of disease around the world. These global inequalities, and strategies for reducing them, will be explored here, and in the next chapter.

Flows

In the field of global health, flows of people, practices, pathogens, knowledge, and technology are all important. Globalization has long been accompanied by the spread of disease. The diffusion of pathogens that accompanied European expansion in the fifteenth century had an enormous impact on the demographic composition of the New World. When Columbus landed on American shores he did not just help bring the Old World and the New World into contact; he also brought disease. In fact, in Crosby's view, the worst enemy of the indigenous peoples was not European power or practices, but the invisible killers—smallpox, diphtheria, and influenza—that they carried (Crosby 1972: 31). Scholars estimate that 80 to 100 million Native Americans—an estimated 90 percent of the Native American population—died because of the diseases brought by the early settlers. To be clear, it is not only the travel of humans that caused the epidemics. Rather, sedentary and agriculture-based communities also create powerful vectors of disease when cattle, poultry, rodents, and insects live in close proximity. Trading ships brought pathogen-carrying rodents, mosquitoes, and fleas. The dissemination of disease was therefore probably the earliest and most significant negative outcome of globalization.

---

4 Epidemiologists are public health professionals who investigate patterns and causes of disease and injury in humans. They seek to reduce the risk and occurrence of negative health outcomes through research, community education, and health policy. United States Department of Labor Bureau of Labor Statistics http://www.bls.gov/ooh/life-physical-and-social-science/epidemiologists.htm

A good example of how the spread of disease reconfigures politics and economies is the Black Death. The first known case of the disease was in China in 1331. From there, it reached Crimea by means of Italian merchant ships and within two years had moved to Constantinople. From there, it went to major ports in Europe, and spread rapidly. Some accounts suggest that as high as 60 percent of the population of Europe, about 50 million people, died as a result (Benedictow 2004: 393). The process of recovery changed Europe. For example, the shortage of labor inspired the creation of more efficient production methods and labor-saving devices. The death of so many people translated into greater per capita wealth—and spending power for survivors. Their spending flowed around the globe, and when the coins ran short, there was a new search for precious metals. Disease led, indirectly, to development (Image 4.1).

The fact that infectious diseases are both treatable and preventable has motivated professionals to strengthen international institutions and governance. The first rules to cooperate on health were formulated in the 1850s, but never had a serious impact on the power or authority of states. That began to change with the outbreak of severe acute respiratory syndrome (SARS) virus. In the face of SARS, the global health infrastructure initiated the first-ever globalized response to a disease. At this time, the World Health Organization took the lead in creating an inspection regime and a travel advisory system.

Networked cooperation among health professionals has led to the successful control of diseases that could have been much more damaging. Over time, the global response to the flow of disease has become much more sophisticated. In Chapter Two, the ways in which cooperation can be challenging for the international state system, even on matters of common concern, were considered. Some

Image 4.1. Spread of Black Death

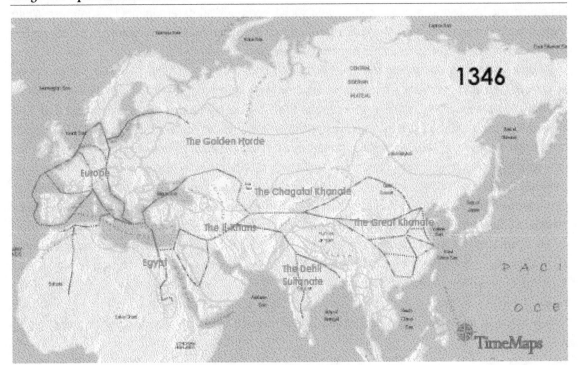

practitioners argue that cooperation on health issues is especially significant because it can serve as a model and training ground for international cooperation on issues that are more contentious (Long 2011). Global health provides an opportunity to study how actors can cooperate to achieve mutual goals by bringing together the health agencies of nation-states, large intergovernmental organizations, NGOs, and for-profit firms.

An example of how cooperation on issues of health may provide a template for other forms of cooperation is avian influenza. When avian influenza, or "bird flu," was identified, health officials in the Middle East, Israel, Palestine, and Jordan worked together closely to prevent further transmission. The cooperation continued even during outbreaks of violence in the region in 2006 and 2009 (Long 2011). Regional initiatives such as this one show that the challenges of interstate cooperation are surmountable in some, if not all, areas of activity.

Thus while globalization facilitates the rapid spread of disease and harmful lifestyles, it can also disseminate knowledge, build systems for sharing effective treatment, and combat inequities.

Perspectives on Health

There are two main perspectives on the treatment of disease that one may contrast: the biomedical model and the biosocial model. The biomedical approach is most interested in identifying the individuals who are at risk, reducing their risk, and when illness occurs, treating their disease. The biosocial model (called the social epidemiological approach in the reading in this chapter) is interested in the full spectrum of potential determinants contributing to health outcomes. The interplay of individual biological and behavioral, as well as economic, social, and political determinants is of interest. While the biomedical and the biosocial models take very different approaches to health and disease, the approaches are not antithetical but rather complementary.

Another way to understand perspectives on health, and one that is useful for making comparisons across cultures, is to consider what kind of logic or logics are being used to formulate a response. Scientific logic is based on evidence. Other logics that have a bearing on decisions are legal logic and economic logic. Legal logic is concerned with liability in the event something goes wrong. "Informed consent" grew out of this approach. Practitioners must always weigh a course of action with respect for the legal logic that shapes the relationship between a service provider and a patient. Economic logic becomes a decision-making factor when assessing the costs and benefits associated with a course of treatment and has a powerful influence on health policy at the level of the nation-state. Ideally, policy makers use these logics together, and no single logic skews decision making.

Canadian health policy regarding the Inuit living in the Canadian Far North provides an example of how the logics sometimes conflict. In the 1970s, the Canadian health system (using economic and legal logic) stopped sending knowledgeable midwives to the North to facilitate Inuit births. They began a practice of evacuating Inuit women from their communities and placing them in hospitals farther south to give birth. Legal logic—preoccupied with reducing the risk of mortality—dominated the decision-making process. The policy caused more problems than it solved because it set to the side the scientific logic—epidemiological evidence (Daviss 1997: 445). Daviss argues that the policy failed to consider that when women were moved to hospitals in southern Canada, it would create new health problems for women who had to sit for weeks in southern cities waiting to go into labor with strange food, little exercise, and devoid of community, spiritual, and family support. It also disrupted families, and result in the loss of traditional medical knowledge (1997: 445). There were many cases in which mothers were emotionally traumatized by their experience, children left at home were neglected, and the work of the community was interrupted. A movement to allow the low-risk births to take place in the Inuit communities, using scientific logic in addition to the legal logic, led to dramatically improved maternal and infant health.

Intellectual Property Rights and Indigenous Peoples

Although the most common conception is that medical knowledge and expertise has flowed from relatively wealthy and developed western nations to less developed and wealthy regions, that conception is incomplete. The development of medicine and global health is not a one-way exchange. The majority of the world's medications have been developed from plants, and much of the information that has permitted these discoveries comes from indigenous knowledge (Smallman and Brown 2011: 249). Modern medicine continues to benefit from the heritage of indigenous knowledge even as the field of synthetic chemistry advances. There are important debates taking place about whether and how indigenous people could be compensated for their knowledge. Court cases aim to remedy the fact that indigenous people are rarely paid for their knowledge.

The notion of intellectual property rights is at the center of these debates. The intellectual property rights codified in national and international law are not easily reconcilable with the beliefs and values of indigenous peoples. Traditionally, indigenous people view nature and knowledge as goods that are not to be commodified (Sapp 2006). Indigenous people who adhere to traditional beliefs may be quite averse to the concept of knowledge as private property (Sapp 2006: 201). According to this thinking, knowledge is a public good. The research and development agenda of many pharmaceutical companies' has capitalized on the uncompensated use of indigenous peoples' knowledge of traditional natural remedies (Smallman and Brown 2011: 249).

Take the Hoodia plant. Pharmaceutical companies have taken a keen interest its effects. (Image 4.2). The San people of South Africa, commonly known as the Bushmen, discovered the hoodia plant can be made into an appetite suppressant and have used it for hundreds of years. Nevertheless, the South

Image 4.2. Hoodia Plant

African Council for Scientific Research (CSIR) was able to patent the hoodia plant, calling it P57 (Sapp 2006: 194) A British biotech company, Phytopharm, then entered into a licensing agreement with the Council to further commercialize P57, initially unbeknownst to the San. This proved to be highly lucrative for Phytopharm.

One of the barriers to compensating indigenous people is the patent law used by the World Trade Organization and many wealthy industrialized nations. Patent law excludes traditional knowledge from patent protection. First, this knowledge does not meet the novelty requirement that reflects a distinctly Western point of view privileging the new. As Sapp points out, by definition the traditional knowledge of indigenous people is not novel: indigenous people have been using various healing plants for centuries (Sapp 2006: 197). Second, products of nature are excluded. This means it is virtually impossible to patent indigenous medicinal knowledge. These are only two of the many permutations to the laws governing intellectual property rights.

Although existing intellectual property laws do not address the traditional knowledge very well, indigenous people have found ways to be compensated for their knowledge by entering into licensing and profit sharing agreements. In this particular case, the San brought a case against CSIR, and a benefit- sharing program was developed, in which the San will receive a percentage of royalties.

Readings

In "Key Concepts in Global Health" **Debra Delaet** and **David Delaet** provide a useful overview of the economic, social, and biologic determinants of health. These authors teach us the meaning of terms needed to be conversant in the field of public and global health. For example, the demographic and the epidemiological transitions are concepts that are especially needed because they provide a way to understand the relationship between socioeconomic gains and population health. This is foundational for appreciating the very real benefits to be gained from the human development project. Delaet, Debra and David Delaet. 2016. "Key Concepts in *Global Health" in Global Health in the 21st Century: The Globalization of Disease and Wellness*. New York: Routledge.

In the article "On the (f)utility of pain" **Scott Stonington** explores cross-cultural differences in attitudes about pain. He argues that a misguided conflation of pain with suffering may cause the misuse of medications for pain such as opiates. He uses ethnographic fieldwork in Thailand to contrast a culture in which a tolerable amount of pain is part of life, with the view that pain is by definition a form of suffering. His biosocial approach, which complements his biomedical knowledge, is crucial to uncover this insight. Stonington, Scott. 2015. "On the (f)luidity of pain," *Lancet* [2015] 385(9976): 1388–1389.

In "Whose Autonomy," Stonington argues that a biomedical approach leads us to see people as autonomous agents. A biosocial approach reveals that this view is far from universal. Logics other than the logic of individual decision making may be relevant and meaningful for making ethical choices. Using examples from both the United States and Thailand, Stonington shows that group harmony may be a priority for some families in both East and West. Stonington, Scott, 2014. "Whose Autonomy" in *JAMA* [2014] 312(11): 1099–1100.

Key Concepts in Global Health

by Debra DeLaet and David DeLaet

Introduction

This chapter introduces key concepts in global health. It provides an introduction to the determinants of health, including biological and behavioral factors as well as economic, social, and cultural determinants. It introduces the key indicators of health and provides an overview of commonly used measures of burden of disease. The chapter describes the relative burden of various diseases among different populations and in different geographic regions. Lastly, the chapter covers the concepts of demographic transition and epidemiological transition as they relate to the economic development of a population and the associated variations in the health status and age composition of that population.

Determinants of Health

In studying global and comparative population health, it is critical for students to first understand the key variables that contribute to the well-being of any individual, regardless of geographic location. As this chapter shows, the overall health status of an individual is determined by a complex interaction of both individual variables and social, cultural, and environmental factors.

Historically, the health sciences have focused on a **biomedical model of health**, which emphasizes individual-level determinants of health, including genetics, individual behaviors, and direct exposure to harmful particles and organisms.[1] However, marked population differences in health status between countries—for example, 2007 data reveal the average life expectancy at birth is 83 years in Japan versus 42 years in Afghanistan—clearly suggest that individual factors alone cannot explain health outcomes, thus dictating the need for a more complex model.[2] **Social epidemiology** emerged as a field in which scholars and practitioners attempt to explain factors external to the individual that contribute to health outcomes.[3] These factors include, but are not limited to, socioeconomic status, education, culture, the physical environment, and access to health care services. The purpose of this section is to review the major determinants of health. In doing so, the chapter demonstrates that a complex interplay of both individual and external variables provides the best explanation for most health outcomes.

Biological Determinants of Health

Genetic makeup is one innate factor that determines the health of an individual. Certain diseases occur only among individuals who inherit specific gene variants. For example, sickle cell anemia, a condition characterized by abnormally functioning red blood cells, manifests only when an individual inherits an abnormal gene from both parents. Though the severity of the disease may vary from one person to another, all individuals inheriting two abnormal gene variants will exhibit some features of the condition, while those with one or no abnormal gene variant will not develop the disease. More commonly, however, diseases with a genetic predisposition do not present in such an all-or-none fashion. Rather, the inheritance of gene variants places an individual at increased risk for a specific condition, but whether a susceptible person develops the disease depends on other factors. For example, although Type II diabetes mellitus has a substantial genetic

KEY CONCEPTS IN THE DETERMINANTS OF HEALTH

Biomedical Model of Health: a model of health that emphasizes individual-level determinants of health, including genetics, individual behaviors, and direct exposure to harmful particles and organisms.

Demographic Transition: the shift of a population from one of high levels of both fertility and mortality and a low rate of population growth to one of low levels of both fertility and mortality and a low rate of population growth.

Epidemiological Transition: a change in mortality and disease patterns whereby a society experiences a shift from a period of high and fluctuating mortality rates largely attributable to communicable diseases to a period of lower and more stable mortality rates primarily due to chronic, noncommunicable diseases.

Gender: social roles and categories associated with men and women that are based on culturally prevailing constructs of presumed "normal," "appropriate," or "ideal" behavior and identities of men (masculinity) and women (femininity).

Social Capital: a broad range of economic, cultural, and personal resources attained through the social relationships of individuals living and interacting together in communities.

Social Epidemiology: a field in which scholars and practitioners attempt to explain factors external to the individual, including socioeconomic status, levels of education, culture, and access to health care, that contribute to health outcomes.

component, whether a genetically susceptible individual develops the disease is also strongly influenced by factors such as obesity. Similarly, an individual's risk for cardiovascular disease is significantly increased if there is a family history of the disease, but other factors—such as smoking, age, biological sex, and the presence or absence of other medical conditions such as diabetes mellitus, hypercholesterolemia (high cholesterol), hypertension (high blood pressure), and obesity—contribute to the development of disease.[4]

Another innate determinant of health is biological sex. Social and cultural determinants of health often impact men and women differently. However, biological sex also contributes to the development of specific diseases. Certain cancers are possible in only one gender—ovarian and cervical cancer in women and prostate cancer in men. A perhaps less obvious example is the sex-specific risk of cardiovascular disease. Among individuals less than 60 years of age, men have a twofold risk of cardiovascular disease as compared with women, a disparity that decreases with age until the disease rate is equivalent between genders, by the eighth decade of life.[5]

Age is another biological variable that determines individual health. For example, children are much more likely to succumb to diarrheal illnesses, particularly in lesser developed countries where access to appropriate rehydration therapy may be limited.[6] Conversely, chronic illnesses such as osteoarthritis, hypertension, and Type II diabetes mellitus by their very nature cause increasing morbidity and mortality with the increasing age of an individual. As previously referenced, advancing age is also a risk factor for cardiovascular disease, with risk increasing after 45 years of age for men and 55 years of age for women.[7]

Behavioral Determinants of Health

The health of an individual is also determined by personal behaviors. Individual choices about whether to use seat belts, child restraints, or motorcycle helmets have obvious health implications. Sexual behaviors affect the likelihood of acquiring sexually transmitted diseases such as human immunodeficiency virus (HIV), viral hepatitis, syphilis, gonorrhea, and *Chlamydia*. Chronic alcohol abuse increases one's risk for developing liver disease. As a final example, physical inactivity and smoking can greatly increase an individual's risk of developing cardiovascular disease.[8]

Although personal behaviors have clear effects on health outcomes, it is important to note that political, social, and, in some instances, genetic variables shape individual behaviors with health consequences. In the case of motor vehicle safety, governmental policies and educational outreach can fundamentally shape individual behavior, leading to much-improved health outcomes. Similarly, education regarding safe sexual practices is critical in preventing sexually transmitted diseases. In the case of health risks associated with alcohol abuse, research suggests a strong genetic predisposition to alcoholism. Social factors can greatly influence one's physical activity level. Smoking behavior is influenced by socioeconomic status as well as by the behavior of others. Individuals of lower income and educational attainment are more likely to smoke, and it has also been demonstrated that children of smokers are more likely to smoke.[9] As these examples indicate, personal behaviors are not entirely "individualized." Rather, behavioral determinants of health are rooted in a social and political context.

In a similar vein, it is important to consider the manner in which individual behavior influences not only individual health outcomes but also population health outcomes. By adhering to safe motor vehicle practices, an individual impacts his or her own well-being as well as that of others. As another example, secondhand smoke exposure among children has been shown to increase the risk of sudden infant death syndrome, respiratory and middle ear infections, and more frequent and severe asthma attacks. The most intimately shared environment is that of the pregnant mother and the developing fetus, and thus the health status and behavioral choices of the mother obviously have a profound impact on the immediate and future health of the fetus. Smoking during pregnancy has been shown to increase the risk of a child being born prematurely and of small birth weight. Such birth outcomes not only affect early child health and development but may also increase the risk of adverse health outcomes as an adult, including an increased risk of cardiovascular disease.[10]

Economic, Social, and Political Determinants of Health

Social factors, including socioeconomic status, employment, and education, have a significant impact on health. Poverty greatly influences one's risk of developing specific diseases. As an example, transmission of HIV is much greater among individuals living in developing countries.[11] It has been shown that even in more developed countries, poverty is the single most important risk factor associated with HIV infection among heterosexuals living in urban settings.[12] Individuals of lower-income status are more likely to smoke, thus increasing their risk of conditions such as cancer and cardiovascular disease while posing a risk of secondhand smoke exposure to close contacts.

Another social factor that shapes health outcomes is the employment status of an individual. Employment obviously contributes directly to one's financial well-being, which itself has effects on health. Employment status often determines health insurance coverage in specific countries. Variables related to employment, occupation, and unpaid labor can have negative consequences on one's health, and certain occupations increase the risk of exposure to potential physical health hazards.

Work-related health risks are often unequally distributed according to **gender**. For example, in developing countries, women are often responsible for unpaid tasks of maintaining the home, such as providing water and fuel. These responsibilities have been shown to increase the risk of exposure to waterborne illnesses such as schistosomiasis as well as mosquito-borne illnesses such as malaria.[13] Cooking on open stoves in such settings also increases women's risk of burns and illnesses due to smoke pollution.[14] In more developed countries, women often constitute a higher percentage of the labor force in industries such as textiles and clothing manufacturing, and thus they also suffer higher rates of asthma and allergies due to exposure to dust in the workplace.[15] Conversely, men are more likely to suffer accidents in the workplace.[16] Further, men in developed countries report greater occupational exposure than women to noise, vibrations, extreme temperatures, chemicals, and physical stress and are thus more likely to suffer illnesses associated with such exposures.[17]

Employment can influence health outcomes in more subtle ways. For example, the Whitehall study in Britain demonstrated that, among British civil servants, employment grade was associated with adverse cardiovascular outcomes in a continuous and downward-sloping gradient.[18] In other words, individuals with a lower job rank were more likely to have cardiovascular disease; when comparing groups of workers across job rank categories, workers in the lower job rank category consistently had higher rates of heart disease than workers in the next highest ranking group. As the study was conducted among civil

UNDER THE MICROSCOPE
Determinants of Cardiovascular Disease

The likelihood that an individual will develop a specific disease state and the severity with which that disease will manifest in an individual are determined by many interdependent risk factors, risks often unevenly distributed by gender, race, and socioeconomic status. A review of the determinants of the development of cardiovascular disease illustrates the complex interplay among individual, behavioral, social, and political determinants of health.

An individual's likelihood of developing cardiovascular disease is influenced by biological factors such as genetic susceptibility and gender. Risk increases with advancing age. Interestingly, gender discrepancies noted among younger individuals are not seen when comparing elderly males and females. It has been suggested that individual biological risk of cardiovascular disease may be increased by prematurity and low birth weight, the risk of which is, in turn, impacted by maternal health status, behavior, and access to appropriate health care.

The development of cardiovascular disease is further influenced by individual behaviors such as level of physical activity and smoking, behaviors that are not only influenced by educational interventions but also often shaped by the behavior patterns of the members of one's family and community. Further, the community-level behavior patterns can be influenced by availability of green space, access to healthy foods, and perceived safety of the neighborhood—factors that are themselves shaped by complex economic and political determinants. As was shown in the previously discussed Whitehall study, even the employment grade of an individual can increase his or her risk of cardiovascular disease.

Additionally, whether one has access to affordable and appropriate health care can contribute not only to the development of disease but also to the severity of disease expression. As there are many underlying medical conditions that serve as risk factors for the development of cardiovascular disease (for example, hypertension, Type II diabetes mellitus, and hypercholesterolemia), consistent access to health care for individuals with these conditions is critical in the prevention of cardiovascular disease. Social and political factors also play an important role in shaping the risk of cardiovascular disease. For example, access to appropriate care for cardiovascular disease may be limited for both women and minority groups. Historically, even research studies of interventions for cardiovascular management have been biased against women and minority groups.

The example of cardiovascular disease clearly demonstrates the complicated interplay among individual, social, and political variables that determine the health of an individual in regard to a specific health condition.

servants, all of whom earned above living wage and had access to health care services, the implication is that psychosocial pathways contributed to this increased cardiovascular risk.

One's educational attainment also determines health outcomes in both direct and indirect ways. Directly, appropriate educational interventions can lead to the adoption of healthy lifestyle practices. As previously referenced, education regarding safe sexual practices has been shown to reduce the transmission of sexually transmitted diseases such as HIV/AIDS. Educational interventions also have been associated with decreased tobacco use among adolescents. Indirectly, higher educational attainment typically leads to better employment with associated higher income and social status. This, in turn, impacts health in ways previously described in this section.

One's physical environment also has clear implications for health. As an example, individuals living in developing countries have less consistent access to clean water supplies, with the resultant increased risk of waterborne illnesses. These populations also are at increased risk for respiratory illnesses associated with higher rates of indoor air pollution. Highlighting the fact that individual health determinants do not operate in isolation, young children in these populations are particularly vulnerable to these adverse health outcomes.[19] Studies have suggested that one's environment has an important effect on health outcomes in developed countries as well. As an example, one's risk of developing respiratory conditions such as asthma increases if there is early postnatal exposure to common allergens such as dust mites and cockroaches,[20] and asthma severity is often impacted by outdoor air pollution.[21]

One's local environment and community can affect health outcomes in other ways as well. In the past several decades, considerable research has been done on the concept of **social capital**. Social capital suggests that individuals gain access to a broader range of economic and cultural resources through the social relationships they create.[22] Studies have suggested that higher levels of individual-level social capital are associated with better self-rated health.[23] Conversely, it has been suggested that social mistrust is closely associated with higher rates of mortality and violent crime.[24] Other studies have highlighted the effect that neighborhoods have on disease states such as obesity, Type II diabetes mellitus, hypertension, and mental health disorders.[25] As one specific example, it has been shown that obesity is associated with poor access to healthy foods and neighborhood green space for exercise.[26]

Finally, governmental policies shape individual and population health outcomes in significant ways. National health policy may lead to more efficient and effective spending of health care dollars, resulting in a greater number of individuals having access to affordable health care services. Further, economic and taxation policies may contribute to more uniform distribution of national wealth, and educational policy may ensure better access to appropriate educational and vocational opportunities for individuals. In this way, public policy can result in better living conditions for a greater number of individuals in a given population. National and local legislation can also directly shape individual behaviors in a manner that results in better health outcomes. As previously mentioned, adoption of safe motor vehicle practices can be influenced by legislation. As an additional example, smoke-free air laws have been shown to reduce secondhand smoke exposure among nonsmoking youth.

Population Health Assessment

Whereas the prior section addressed the determinants of individual health, this section introduces concepts pertinent to **population health**. In order to evaluate the health status of populations, one must have an understanding of the key indicators of population health as well as measures commonly used to assess the burden that specific diseases place on a population. Additionally, knowledge of these concepts is critical to inform national, state, and local policy-setting in ways likely to improve the health of a specific population. To this end, this section provides definitions for commonly used indicators of population health and measures of disease burden. Additionally, the section provides an overview of global trends of comparative population health.

Key Indicators of Population Health

When assessing population health, it is imperative to have available a set of key indicators of health that can be consistently applied such that reliable comparisons might be made between various populations. These indicators should also be able to provide insight into variants of health by gender and age within and across populations.

KEY INDICATORS OF HEALTH

Adult Mortality Rate: the probability of dying between the ages of 15 and 60 years (per 1,000 population) per year among a hypothetical cohort of 100,000 people who would experience the age-specific mortality rate of the reporting year.

Health-Adjusted Life Expectancy (HALE): the average number of years that a person can expect to live in full health by taking into account the years the person is in less than full health due to disease and/or injury.

Infant Mortality Rate: the probability of a child born in a specific year or period dying before reaching the age of one, if subject to age-specific mortality rates of that period.

Life Expectancy at Birth: the average number of years that a newborn is expected to live if mortality patterns at the time of its birth were to prevail throughout the child's life.

Maternal Mortality Ratio: the annual number of female deaths from any cause related to or aggravated by pregnancy or its management (excluding accidental or incidental causes) during pregnancy and childbirth or within 42 days of termination of pregnancy, irrespective of the duration or site of the pregnancy, per 100,000 live births, for a specified year.

Mortality Rate: an estimate of the proportion of a population that dies during a specified period. The numerator is the number of persons dying during the period; the denominator is the total number of people in the population, usually estimated as the midyear population.

Neonatal Mortality Rate: the number of registered deaths in the neonatal period (the first 28 completed days of life) per 1,000 live births in a given year or period of time.

Under-Five Mortality Rate: the probability (expressed as a rate per 1,000 live births) of a child born in a specific year or period dying before reaching the age of five, if subject to age-specific mortality rates of that period.

The **mortality rate** is one of the most basic indicators used in studies of population health. Simply stated, a mortality rate is an estimate of the proportion of a population that dies during a specified period. A mortality rate can be determined for any population or subpopulation (for example, **adult mortality rate**) for any defined period of time, based on the specific health outcomes one wishes to assess. Another commonly employed health indicator is **life expectancy at birth**, defined as the average number of years that a newborn is expected to live if mortality patterns at the time of its birth were to prevail throughout the child's life. A similar health indicator is the **health-adjusted life expectancy (HALE)**, defined as the average number of years that a person can expect to live in full health by taking into account the years the person is in less than full health due to disease and/or injury.

Current estimates of these population health indicators for the six World Health Organization (WHO) global regions are presented in Table 4.1.1, along with the gross national income per capita of those regions. As the data demonstrate, poverty is associated with poorer health outcomes for each of these key health indicators. Also, it appears that these poorer health outcomes are particularly noteworthy for women and young children living in poverty, as evidenced by the somewhat greater disparity between higher-and lower-income regions for **maternal mortality ratio** and **neonatal, infant, and under-five mortality rates** as compared with the other key health indicators. The reasons for these contrasting health outcomes are likely multifactorial. An introduction to the factors that lead to disparate health outcomes was provided in the previous section on the determinants of health.

Table 4.1.1. Key Indicators of Population Health, by WHO Region, 2008

	Africa	Americas	Southeast Asia	Europe	Eastern Mediterranean	Western Pacific
Neonatal mortality rate (per 1,000 live births)	40	9	34	7	35	11
Infant mortality rate (per 1,000 live births)	85	15	48	12	57	18
Under-five mortality rate (per 1,000 live births)	142	18	63	14	78	21
Maternal mortality ratio[a] (per 100,000 live births)	900	99	450	27	420	82
Adult mortality rate (per 1,000 population)	392	126	218	149	203	113
Life expectancy at birth (years)	52	73	63	71	63	72
Health-adjusted life expectancy (HALE) at birth[b] (years)	45	67	57	67	56	67
Gross national income per capita (PPP int. $)	2,279	24,005	3,043	22,849	3,805	8,958

a. 2005 data
b. 2007 data

Source: World Health Organization, "Part II: Global Health Indicators," *World Health Statistics 2010*. Available online at: http://www.who.int/whosis/whostat/EN_WHS10_Part2.pdf.

Common Measures of Disease Burden

In evaluating population health, it is important to assess not only the health status of that population but also the diseases that most significantly contribute to mortality, morbidity, and disability for that population. To do so, one must be familiar with commonly used measures of **burden of disease**. This section introduces these measures and provides a brief overview of the categories of diseases. Additionally, this section highlights data on the global burden of disease.

Individual **mortality**, **morbidity**, and **disability** may occur due to injury or the presence of disease. Typically, diseases are broadly categorized as either communicable or noncommunicable. **Communicable diseases** are transmitted directly or indirectly from one individual to another via a microbial agent such as a virus, bacteria, parasite, or fungus. Key examples of a communicable disease include tuberculosis, malaria, and HIV. Conversely, **noncommunicable diseases**, such as Type II diabetes mellitus, occur in the absence of such infectious agents and are not transmissible between individuals. ...

Measures commonly used to describe disease burden include prevalence, incidence, and cause-specific mortality rates. **Prevalence** is defined as "the number of affected persons present in the population at a specific time divided by the number of persons in the population at that time."[27] Typically, this measure is applied as *point prevalence*, with the assessment made at one specific point in time rather than over a period of time. **Incidence** is "the number of new cases of a disease that occur during a specified period of time in a population at risk for developing the disease."[28] Whereas prevalence measures the current burden of disease in a population, incidence reflects the current risk of developing the disease in those not currently affected by the disease. These two measures are related in that, as disease incidence increases, so too does disease prevalence. Prevalence also increases with improvements in disease management that allow an individual to survive a specific illness for a greater duration of time. Conversely, prevalence decreases if individuals are cured of the illness or die. Population disease burden can also be assessed using **cause-specific mortality rates**, an estimate of the proportion of a population that dies

KEY HEALTH TERMS

Communicable Diseases: diseases that are transmitted directly or indirectly from one individual to another via a microbial agent such as a virus, bacteria, parasite, or fungus.

Disability: an impairment, activity limitation, or participation restriction.

Morbidity: the state of having a disease.

Mortality: a fatal outcome; death.

Noncommunicable Diseases: diseases that occur in the absence of infectious agents and are not transmissible between individuals.

Population Health: the health outcomes of a group of individuals, including the distribution of such outcomes within the group.

during a specified period as a result of a specific disease or injury. For example, the WHO routinely includes cause-specific mortality rates for tuberculosis, malaria, and HIV/AIDS in its updated global health reports.

These measures are useful in demonstrating how commonly a specific disease or injury occurs within a population as well as the contribution of that disease or injury to the overall mortality rate of a population. However, these are imperfect measures of disease burden in that they fail to capture the contribution of a specific disease or injury to morbidity and disability within a population.[29] Therefore, measures of population health have been developed that allow for the combined impact of death, disability, and morbidity to be considered simultaneously.[30] The most commonly used of these measures is the **disability-adjusted life year (DALY)**. The DALY is defined as the sum of years of potential life lost due to premature mortality and the years of productive life lost due to disability; in essence, it "measures the difference between a current situation and an ideal situation where everyone lives up to the age of standard life expectancy, and in perfect health."[31]

Applying this measure, the WHO periodically determines the leading causes of disease burden to global populations. The most recently published estimates for the ten leading causes of disease burden, stratified by country income, are presented in Table 4.1.2. As can be seen, communicable diseases contribute the majority of disease burden in low-income countries, whereas high-income countries are much more likely to suffer morbidity, disability, and mortality as a result of noncommunicable diseases. Disease burden in middle-income countries appears to more closely parallel that of high-income countries than low-income countries, with the exception that communicable diseases such as lower respiratory infections and HIV/AIDS are significant contributors to morbidity, disability, and mortality in middle-income countries. Careful inspection of the data in Table 4.1.2 provides further insights. For one, it can be seen that in low-income regions, considerable disease burden results from pregnancy- and birth-related disease and injury, again highlighting that women and young children living in poverty are particularly vulnerable

COMMON MEASURES OF DISEASE BURDEN

Burden of Disease: the impact of a health problem in a particular area (for example, at the country, region, or global level) or for a specific group (such as men and women or different ethnic groups), typically measured by morbidity, mortality, or a combination of both.

Cause-specific Mortality Rate: an estimate of the proportion of a population that dies during a specified period as a result of a specific disease or injury.

Disability-adjusted Life Years (DALYs): the sum of years of potential life lost due to premature mortality and the years of productive life lost due to disability.

Incidence: the number of new cases of a disease that occur during a specified period of time in a population at risk for developing the disease.

Prevalence: the number of affected persons present in the population at a specific time, divided by the number of persons in the population at that time.

Table 4.1.2. Leading Causes of Burden of Disease (DALYs), Countries Grouped by Income, 2004

Disease or Injury	DALYs (Millions)	Percentage of Total DALYs	Disease or Injury	DALYs (Millions)	Percentage of Total DALYs
World			**Low-Income Countries**		
Lower respiratory infections	94.5	6.2	Lower respiratory infections	76.9	9.3
Diarrheal diseases	72.8	4.8	Diarrheal diseases	59.2	7.2
Unipolar depressive disorders	65.5	4.3	HIV/AIDS	42.9	5.2
Ischemic heart disease	62.6	4.1	Malaria	32.8	4.0
HIV/AIDS	58.5	3.8	Prematurity and low birth weight	32.1	3.9
Cerebrovascular disease	46.6	3.1	Neonatal infections	31.4	3.8
Prematurity and low birth weight	44.3	2.9	Birth asphyxia and birth trauma	29.8	3.6
Birth asphyxia and birth trauma	41.7	2.7	Unipolar depressive disorders	26.5	3.2
Road traffic accidents	41.2	2.7	Ischemic heart disease	26.0	3.1
Neonatal infections	40.4	2.7	Tuberculosis	22.4	2.7
Middle-Income Countries			**High-Income Countries**		
Unipolar depressive disorders	29.0	5.1	Unipolar depressive disorders	10.0	8.2
Ischemic heart disease	28.9	5.0	Ischemic heart disease	7.7	6.3
Cerebrovascular disease	27.5	4.8	Cerebrovascular disease	4.8	3.9
Road traffic accidents	21.4	3.7	Alzheimer's and other dementias	4.4	3.6
Lower respiratory infections	16.3	2.8	Alcohol use disorders	4.2	3.4
Chronic obstructive lung disease	16.1	2.8	Hearing loss, adult onset	4.2	3.4
HIV/AIDS	15.0	2.6	Chronic obstructive lung disease	3.7	3.0
Alcohol use disorders	14.9	2.6	Diabetes mellitus	3.6	3.0
Refractive errors	13.7	2.4	Trachea, bronchus, lung cancers	3.6	3.0
Diarrheal diseases	13.1	2.3	Road traffic accidents	3.1	2.6

Source: Reproduced from the World Health Organization, *The Global Burden of Disease: 2004 Update.* Available online at: http://www.who.int/healthinfo/global_burden_disease/GBD_report_2004update_full.pdf.

to poor health outcomes. Additionally, the data demonstrate that with socioeconomic advances, populations are faced with increasing morbidity and mortality associated with advancing age, such as dementia and chronic illnesses such as ischemic heart disease, chronic obstructive lung disease, and cancers.

Demographic and Epidemiological Transitions

This chapter would be incomplete without a discussion of the two distinct yet closely related concepts of epidemiological transition and demographic transition. As described earlier in this chapter, individual health is determined by the interplay among individual, social, and political variables. Further, population health is closely linked with economic, social, and political determinants. The concepts of epidemiological transition and demographic transition serve as examples of how these variables interact to shape not only the health of populations but also population growth, as well as the relative burden of specific diseases within populations. This section provides a brief review of these two concepts and discusses the implications of these transitions for specific populations.

Epidemiological Transition

The concept of **epidemiological transition** was first described in 1971 by Abdel Omran as a transition of a population in which "a long shift occurs in mortality and disease patterns whereby pandemics of infection are gradually displaced by degenerative and man-made diseases as the chief form of morbidity and primary cause of death."[32] In essence, a population moves from a period when mortality rates are high and fluctuating, with death largely attributable to famine and infectious diseases, to a state of lower and more stable mortality rates, with morbidity and mortality largely due to chronic, noncommunicable diseases.

The determinants that influence this transition are complex. However, most research has suggested that cultural and socioeconomic factors leading to improvements in living conditions, nutrition, and hygiene have contributed most significantly to this transition, particularly for most Western populations that began this transition in the 19th century. Advances in public health and medicine, including improved public sanitation, immunizations, and development of therapies such as antibiotics, have played an additional role in populations undergoing this transition more recently.[33]

Most developed countries have undergone such a transition, with relatively low and more stable mortality rates and disease burden attributable most significantly to noncommunicable diseases. Conversely, many developing countries exhibit higher mortality rates with significant disease burden due to infectious diseases, suggesting the epidemiological transition has not yet been completed.

Demographic Transition

The **demographic transition** represents the shift of a population from one of high levels of fertility and mortality and a low rate of population growth to one of low levels of fertility and mortality and a low rate of population growth.[34] Socioeconomic, public health, and medical advances within a population result in decreased mortality rates for that population, particularly improving health outcomes for infants and young children. As depicted in Figure 4.1.1, the decline in mortality leads to a resultant increase in the population growth rate, particularly among younger members of the population. After some time, there is a subsequent decline in the fertility rate of the population, with a resultant slowing of population growth until there is again a zero, or sometimes negative, population growth rate.

Figure 4.1.1. The Demographic Transition

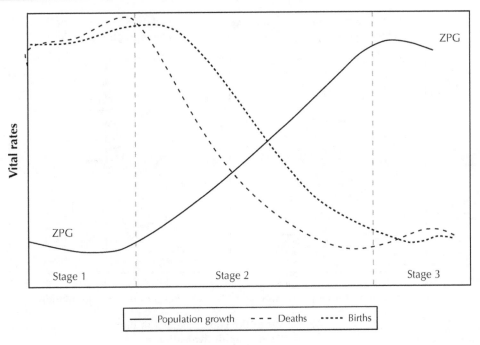

ZPG = zero population growth
Source: Adapted from the Australian Department of Families, Housing, Community Services and Indigenous Affairs, *Policy Research Paper No. 13*. Available online at: http://www.facs.gov.au/about/publicationsarticles/research/socialpolicy/Documents/prp13/sec1.htm.

The reasons for the decline in population fertility rates are unclear yet likely multifactorial. In part, this decline is presumably attributable to the fact that, with the realization of a greater likelihood of child survival to adulthood, there is an associated parental desire for fewer births with a greater financial investment in the health and education for each child.[35] Also, it is likely that, in addition to reducing infant and child mortality rates, the socioeconomic advances of a population also allow for greater educational and employment opportunities for women and, in turn, a desire for fewer children.[36] As many populations began the demographic transition in the late 18th and 19th centuries, the role of such medical advances as contraception in the decline in fertility rates is likely minimal, though access to contraceptives may play a greater role in populations more recently entering this transition period.[37]

As represented in Figure 4.1.2, the most notable result of this transition is ultimately a shift in the age composition of the involved population, represented by a greater ratio of older to younger members. In stage 1 of the demographic transition, populations experience high levels of fertility and mortality and a relatively low rate of population growth. In stage 2, high levels of fertility coupled with decreasing mortality rates lead to relatively high rates of population growth. Finally, in stage 3, populations experience low rates of population growth as fertility rates decline to match lower mortality rates.

Figure 4.1.2. Population Pyramids Representing the Stages of Demographic Transition

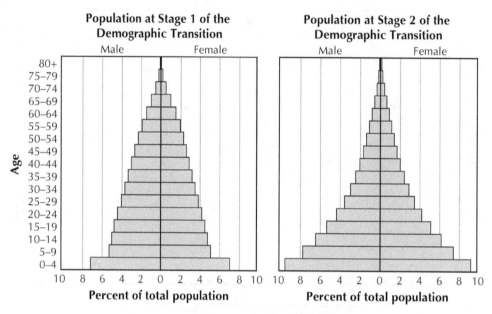

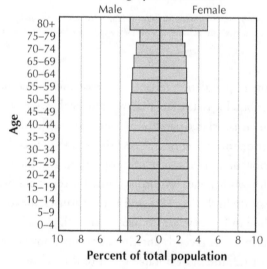

Source: Adapted from U.S. Census Bureau, "International Population Reports WP/02," *Global Population Profile: 2002* (Washington, DC: U.S. Government Printing Office, 2004). Available online at: http://www.census.gov/prod/2004pubs/wp-02.pdf.

Implications of the Demographic and Epidemiological Transitions

The demographic and epidemiological transitions have several key implications for population health. The socioeconomic gains of a society have considerable positive influence on population health, typically more so than advances in medicine. Investments made in improving living conditions, sanitation, nutrition, and hygiene lead to a decrease in infectious disease burden and, thus, reduced mortality of members of the population typically most vulnerable to infectious diseases, namely, infants and young children. As infant and child mortality falls, and prior to the anticipated subsequent decline in fertility rates, population growth, particularly among the young, necessitates further investments in resources to support the care and education of these younger members of the population. When fertility rates decline, population shifts ultimately lead to an aging population that will be faced with the morbidity associated with chronic, noncommunicable diseases. This shift tends to occur at the same time that fewer young adults are entering the workforce. Thus, governments facing these implications of the demographic transition are faced with the challenges of taking care of larger aging populations—for example, by funding pension plans and expanding health care—at the same time that their tax base may be decreasing due to a smaller workforce.

Conclusion

A wide variety of individual, social, and political variables shape human health across the globe. Notably, these variables do not operate in isolation. Rather, a complex interplay among personal behaviors, social environment, and public policy is responsible for variations in individual and population health outcomes. Poverty and levels of national economic development also are critical in determining the distribution of disease within particular countries and the overall health of a given population … . The epidemiological transition and the demographic transition demonstrate the ways in which improvements in the socioeconomic status of a population as well as advances in medicine affect not only the distribution of disease within particular countries but also the demographic composition of specific populations. In turn, the demography of a given population has important consequences for national health policies and health outcomes in specific countries. Thus, it is critical for students of global and comparative health to have a solid understanding of the determinants of health as well as the interrelated effects among them.

Web Resources

WHO The Determinants of Health: http://www.who.int/hia/evidence/doh/en/
WHO Global Burden of Disease: http://www.who.int/healthinfo/global_burden_disease/en/
WHO Statistical Information System: http://www.who.int/whosis/whostat/en/

Notes

1. Sridhar Venkatapuram, "Global Justice and the Social Determinants of Health," *Ethics & International Affairs* 24: 2 (Summer 2010): 119–130.

2. World Health Organization, *World Health Statistics 2009* (2009). Available online at: http://www.who.int/whosis/whostat/2009/en/index.html.

3. Venkatapuram: 119.

4. P.W. Wilson, "Established Risk Factors and Coronary Artery Disease: The Framingham Study," *American Journal of Hypertension* 7: 2 (1994): 7S–12S.

5. A. Blum and N. Blum, "Coronary Artery Disease: Are Men and Women Created Equal?" *Gender Medicine* 6: 3 (2009): 410–418.

6. C.G. Victora, J. Bryce, J.O. Fontaine, and R. Monasch, "Reducing Deaths from Diarrhoea Through Oral Rehydration Therapy," *Bulletin of the World Health Organization* 78: 10 (2000): 1246–1255.

7. Wilson: 7S–12S.

8. *Ibid.*

9. LaTisha Marshall, Michael Schooley, Heather Ryan, Patrick Cox, Alyssa Easton, Cheryl Healton, Kat Jackson, Kevin C. Davis, and Ghada Homsi, "Youth Tobacco Surveillance—United States, 2001–2002," *Morbidity and Mortality Surveillance Summaries* 55: SS-3 (2006): 1–56.

10. D.J. Barker, "Fetal Origins of Cardiovascular Disease," *British Medical Journal* 311: 6998 (1995): 171–174.

11. Joint United Nations Programme on HIV/AIDS, *UNAIDS Report on the Global AIDS Epidemic 2010*: 20–21. Available online at: http://www.unaids.org/globalreport/Global_report.htm.

12. U.S. Centers for Disease Control and Prevention, *New Study in Low-income Heterosexuals in America's Inner Cities Reveals High HIV Rates* (July 19, 2010). Available online at: http://www.cdc.gov/nchhstp/newsroom/povertyandhivpressrelease.html.

13. E.H. Michelson, "Adam's Rib Awry? Women and Schistosomiasis," *Social Science & Medicine* 37: 4 (1993): 493–501; S.B. Kendie, "Survey of Water Use Behaviour in Rural North Ghana," *Natural Resources Forum* 16 (1992): 126–131.

14. V.N. Mishra, M. Malhotra, and S. Gupta, "Chronic Respiratory Disorders in Females of Delhi," *Journal of the Indian Medical Association* 88: 3 (1990): 77–80.

15. European Agency for Safety and Health at Work, *Gender Issues in Safety and Health at Work: Summary of an Agency Report* (2003): 2. Available online at: http://osha.europa.eu/en/publications/factsheets/42/.

16. S. Islam, A.M. Velilla, E.J. Doyle, and A.M. Ducatman, "Gender Differences in Work-related Injury/Illness: Analysis of Workers Compensation Claims," *American Journal of Industrial Medicine* 39: 1 (2001): 84–91.

17. World Health Organization, *Gender, Health, and Work* (2004): 3. Available online at: http://www.who.int/gender/other_health/Gender,HealthandWorklast.pdf.

18. M.G. Marmot, G.D. Smith, S. Stansfeld, C. Patel, F. North, J. Head, I. White, E. Brunner, and A. Feeney, "Health Inequalities Among British Civil Servants: The Whitehall II Study," *Lancet* 337: 8754 (1991): 1387–1393.

19. World Health Organization, *Healthy Environments for Children—Initiating an Alliance for Action* (2002): 11. Available online at: http://whqlibdoc.who.int/hq/2002/WHO_SDE_PHE_02.06.pdf.

20. S.H. Arshad, "Does Exposure to Indoor Allergens Contribute to the Development of Asthma and Allergy?" *Current Allergy and Asthma Reports* 10: 1 (2010): 49–55.

21. P.T. Nastos, A.G. Paliatsos, M.B. Anthracopoulos, E.S. Roma, and K.N. Priftis, "Outdoor Particulate Matter and Childhood Asthma Admissions in Athens, Greece: A Time-series Study," *Environmental Health* 9: 7 (2010): 45–53.

22. Alejandro Portes, "Social Capital: Its Origins and Applications in Modern Sociology," *Annual Review of Sociology* 24 (1998): 1–24.

23. Richard Rose, "How Much Does Social Capital Add to Individual Health? A Survey of Russians," *Social Science and Medicine* 51: 9 (2000): 1421–1435.

24. Richard G. Wilkinson, Ichiro Kawachi, and Bruce P. Kennedy, "Mortality, the Social Environment, Crime and Violence," *Sociology of Health & Illness* 20: 5 (1998): 578–597.

25. Ana V. Diez Roux and Christina Mair, "Neighborhoods and Health," *Annals of the New York Academy of Sciences* 1186 (February 2010): 125–145.

26. *Ibid.*

27. Leon Gordis, "Measuring the Occurrence of Disease," in *Epidemiology* (Philadelphia: W.B. Saunders Company, 1996): 32.

28. *Ibid.*: 31.

29. Marthe R. Gold, David Stevenson, and Dennis G. Fryback, "HALYs and QALYs and DALYs, Oh My: Similarities and Differences in Summary Measures of Population Health," *Annual Review of Public Health* 23 (May 2002): 115–134.

30. *Ibid.*

31. World Health Organization, "Part 4, Burden of Disease: DALYs," *The Global Burden of Disease 2004 Update* (2004). Available online at: http://www.who.int/healthinfo/global_burden_disease/GBD_report_2004update_part4.pdf.

32. Abdel R. Omran, "The Epidemiologic Transition: A Theory of the Epidemiology of Population Change," *Millbank Quarterly* 83: 4 (2005): 736–737.

33. *Ibid.*

34. U.S. Census Bureau, "International Population Reports WP/02," *Global Population Profile: 2002* (Washington, DC: U.S. Government Printing Office, 2004). Available online at: http://www.census.gov/prod/2004pubs/wp-02.pdf.

35. Ronald Lee, "The Demographic Transition: Three Centuries of Fundamental Change," *Journal of Economic Perspectives* 17: 4 (2003): 167–190.

36. *Ibid.*

37. *Ibid.*

On the (F)utility of Pain

by Scott Stonington

Some time ago during my medical internship in Boston, MA, USA, I took care of a 74-year-old man, Daniel, with bone metastases from prostate cancer. His son had brought him to the emergency department for pain control. On arrival, Daniel told me that he was in pain and admitted that he was not taking his full pain regimen. His son said, "my father is just being stoic". Daniel's response was: "son, there are worse things than pain". This remark struck me, mostly because many of the patients I had seen over the years had seemed to feel that there was nothing worse than pain. When I asked what he meant, Daniel clarified: "I want to be here for this", he said with a sweep of his hand around the room, "even for the pain. Not really being here would make me suffer."

I had been taught in my medical training to think of patients like Daniel as stoic and to push back against this trait. In caring for Daniel, this impulse was strong: I was uncomfortable seeing him in pain, and I found myself formulating persuasions—"pain may disrupt your experience more than opiates", or "bone metastases are a different kind of pain, you're going to need help". But alongside this impulse, my training as an anthropologist alerted me to something in Daniel's explanation: he had separated the concepts of pain and suffering in a way that was unusual in western biomedical contexts.

There is another trope that physicians encounter in pain medicine: the so-called drug-seeking patient, who seems intent upon acquiring opiates at all costs. There is an informal sense among practitioners that many patients on opiates can fall into either the "stoic" or "drug-seeking" category, and we spend much time encouraging the former towards treatment and steering the latter away from it. Yet Daniel's claim about the difference between pain and suffering, as well as the existence of something "worse than pain", casts some light onto these poles of judgment about how people relate to pain.

Before examining Daniel's story further, I turn to another place for guidance: my longitudinal ethnographic fieldwork on palliative care and pain management in northern Thailand, where a conceptual division between pain and suffering is in many ways more explicit than in western countries. When I began my fieldwork, my initial instinct was to ask about the adequacy of treatment, because in many low-income countries pain relief is often not available. The response from Thai physicians was often a shrug, and the phrase, "the patient is enduring it well (*thon dai*)". When I pressed one clinician further about a patient who seemed to be in ongoing pain, he exclaimed: "You Americans are so concerned with comfort! Don't you think anything should be difficult? This patient is dying." When I asked the patient about this, she explained: "Pain is necessary. It is a reality one needs to face. Running away from it is what leads to suffering." At the time, this notion was unfamiliar to me, and I began to turn my ethnographic inquiry toward it. From listening to Thai patients and physicians, I encountered two explanations about pain: one based on a worldview in which the idea of *kam* (karma) is important, and another based on a difference between pain and suffering.

I spent some time with Mahu, a patient dying of metastatic rectal cancer with extensive local invasion. When I asked how he dealt with his illness, he said, "Ah, it is easy. My disease is a *chao kam nāi wēn*." I leave these words in Thai since they require a brief cultural tour to translate. *Kam* is the concept that all actions have consequences, whether metaphysical, moral, or practical; *wēn* means both "duty" and "fate", and when combined with the word *kam*, implies that one has a duty in the present that is the result of a past action; *chao nāi* means "authority" or "master", something that reigns over someone. Combined, these terms refer to an entity from the past that has returned to exact a toll in payment for a past action. Mahu explained further to me: "My whole life, I was a buffalo farmer. I leashed buffaloes with rings through their noses. Last week, when I went into the hospital, I had a nasal cannula ... when they put it in, it made me sneeze and cough just like the buffaloes. I also had a nasogastric tube, and when I turned my head, it pulled on me just like I pulled on buffaloes." Another patient, Mali, talked about her pancreatic tumour in a similar way: "My tumour is here because it thinks that I harmed it in the past. It is also suffering, so I cannot be angry at it. That would harm it more, and make it grow and gnaw at me like an angry little dog. So I am present to the tumour and send it loving kindness (*mētta*) and ask its forgiveness. As soon as I do this, I relax and stop suffering." To Daniel, Mali's and Mahu's emphasis on past actions would surely have seemed strange. But their distinction between pain and suffering might have appealed to him, as would their point that being present to the pain was a way to suffer less from it. Suffering and pain were not the same.

Interestingly, among the physicians I met during my fieldwork, the distinction between pain and suffering was understood in relation to a different conception of addiction: rather than linking addiction to the pharmacological properties of opiates, people seemed to link it to pain relief itself. One Thai physician, Dr Lek, told me: "The global medical trend is to rate pain on a scale, and treat until it is gone. Recently, we do this more here, but I don't think it fits. If a patient has 0/10 or 3/10 as a goal, it is already a problem, already addiction. Pain is part of all things. Wanting 0/10 means looking outside oneself to escape reality. The mind is already addicted, before ever taking anything. But one shouldn't have 10/10 pain, either—that is too much for the mind! Maybe the goal should be 5/10."

When I heard this explanation, I thought about my oath as a physician to relieve suffering, an oath that still guides my every moment in clinical practice. My initial instinct was to reject Dr Lek's explanation as a lack of compassion for his patients' suffering. But he hadn't used the word suffering (*khwām thuk thōramān*) as the thing that must be accepted; he had used pain (*khwām chep pūat*). When I asked Dr Lek about this, he gave a common Buddhist scriptural response about the need to accept the painful reality of existence enough to be present to it, and thus to avoid suffering from it. "If there is too much pain", he explained, "then we cannot focus at all. But if we want there to be no pain, we suffer endlessly trying to make it disappear, to achieve the impossible. That is addiction. And it is not limited to patients. We doctors are uncomfortable seeing pain, and want 0/10 for our patients. We are part of it."

In western biomedicine, physicians learn that the "stoic" patient and the "drug-seeker" are separate tropes, that the desire to relieve pain is different from what makes us addicted. In my residency, I was trained to think of Daniel's pain as different from that of a "drug-seeking" patient because of the aetiology of his illness. Daniel had cancer, whereas so-called drug-seeking patients often live with some kind of chronic pain. But in my discussions with Dr Lek, I encountered a view in which such a distinction was dissolved. He told me that "The connection between escape and suffering is not just with chronic pain: cancer patients suffer as much as anyone from trying to escape reality. In cancer, the suffering may be overshadowed by the course of illness, but it is there."

Such conceptions of pain made me reflect on the expectations of both physicians and patients about pain management in western environments. Treatment of pain is a major problem around the world. In some low-income countries that lack pain medications altogether, patients die in devastating pain. The provision of pain treatment in such contexts is a clear moral imperative. But in many high-income countries, the situation is different. Has the pendulum of pain management swung too far towards opiate administration? During the 1990s and 2000s there was a move to consider pain the "fifth vital sign", and to overcome so-called opiophobia by measuring pain on a scale, with a goal of 0–3/10 pain or 80–100% relief. One result has been an increase in both prescription and nonprescription opiate use. But when I think about Mahu, Mali, or Daniel, for whom trying to achieve a 0–3/10 pain score would itself cause suffering, I wonder about the merit of this conceptual approach. Yet it also does not make sense to leave people in severe pain, which Dr Lek explained as "too much" for the mind. Is there a "middle path" between these two poles?

The views I listened to during my research in Thailand suggest a possible answer to this question: perhaps it is the misguided conflation of pain and suffering that is causing some of the current problems in pain management. This takes the addiction debate away from "opiate-seeking" patients or from the properties of opiates themselves, putting the problem instead into the realm of "being human", to use Dr Lek's words about the tendency to confuse pain and suffering. This includes practitioners who want a quick fix for the pain of those sitting in front of them.

For my part when caring for Daniel, I spent more time rallying him to pain treatment than understanding the meaning of pain in his world. In retrospect, I wish that I had (at least partly) set aside advocating deliverance and sat down to be present to him and see where his suffering lay. Since then, I have changed my approach to pain management. I no longer ask

The Tightrope Walker (1904) by Everett Shinn

Private Collection/Photo © Christie's Images/Bridgeman Images

"Is this patient in pain?" Instead, I ask "How do I relieve this person's suffering?" For some patients in severe pain, opiates are of clear benefit. But other patients have the impossible hope that opiates will obliterate rather than reduce their pain, a hope which might make them suffer more as they seek a pain-free existence. I now begin every conversation about pain management by acknowledging the reality of an individual's pain, expressing an alliance to reduce his or her suffering, and then discussing how relieving suffering may not always be the same thing as relieving pain.

Scott D Stonington

Internal Medicine, Brigham and Women's Hospital and Global Health and Social Medicine, Harvard Medical School, Boston, MA 02115, USA scott.stonington@stanfordalumni.org

Further reading

Bennett DS, Carr DB. Opiophobia as a barrier to the treatment of pain. *J Pain Palliat Care Pharmacother* 2002; 16: 105–09

Krakauer EL. Just palliative care: responding responsibly to the suffering of the poor. *J Pain Symptom Manage* 2008; 36: 505–12

Lembke A. Why doctors prescribe opioids to known opioid abusers. *N Engl J Med* 2012; 367: 1580–81

Livingston J. Improvising medicine: an African oncology ward in an emerging cancer epidemic. Durham, NC: Duke University Press, 2012

Stonington SD. Facing death, gazing inward: end-of-life and the transformation of clinical subjectivity in Thailand. *Cult Med Psychiatry* 2011; 35: 113–33

Whose Autonomy?

by Scott Stonington

Department of Global Health and Social Medicine, Brigham and Women's Hospital, Harvard Medical School, Boston, Massachusetts.
Corresponding Author: Scott D. Stonington, MD, PhD (scott.stonington@stanfordalumni.org).
Section Editor: Roxanne K. Young, Associate Senior Editor.

During my medical residency, I took care of a 64-year-old man, Ian (a pseudonym, as are all names in this essay). He had come to the emergency department for an exacerbation of his chronic obstructive pulmonary disease. He also had rheumatoid arthritis, and before I could take a history, his wife Sarah pulled me aside to say that he was in increasing pain from his arthritis. He never missed a dose of methotrexate, but refused to take nonsteroidal anti-inflammatory drugs. I asked if there was some ill effect from them, but she said, "No, it is just part of his self-image to be tough and not treat his pain. But he needs treatment, whether he will say so or not." When I saw Ian, it was clear that he was in pain, and I inquired about his opposition to NSAIDs, expecting some adverse effect or fear of harm. But he simply said, "I don't need them. My wife is just putting you up to this." Sarah responded, "Ian, you're being ridiculous. You're in pain!" He rolled his eyes and said, "Fine, just this once, for *her*," and acquiesced to a one-time dose. To me this seemed like progress, but in subsequent encounters when I met with Ian alone, he resisted any suggestion of a more stable regimen.

I found myself uncomfortable in these interactions. Initially, I shared with a co-resident that I was caught in "family dynamics." But on further reflection, I realized that it was more than this: it was a tension between autonomy and paternalism, between following my patient's wishes and convincing him of what his wife and I thought best. It called to mind my anthropological fieldwork on end-of-life care in Northern Thailand, where I came to understand exactly how deeply bio-medicine had taught me to view the world with an autonomy lens, and how problematic that lens could become in the midst of families and other social roles. This insight was the product of "rationality ethnography," designed to systematically analyze conceptual differences in logic and decision making.[1,2]

Early in my fieldwork in Northern Thailand, a friend, a Thai nursing student, told me about a patient she had just cared for, an elderly man with colorectal cancer who had developed abdominal pain at home. He did not want to come into the hospital, instead saying, "I am fine. Don't worry about me. I have had a good life and am reconciled to this." But his son said, "No way. We're taking you to the hospital, and we will do everything that medicine has to offer." At the hospital, the old man said often, "I want to go home. I don't need any of this treatment." But his son always told the physicians, "We are treating until the very end." One day, the old man's heart faltered, and the medical staff gave him cardiopulmonary resuscitation. He regained consciousness and requested to go home. They decided instead to continue with the plan to take him to surgery to debulk his tumor in preparation for chemotherapy. After surgery, his heart arrested again, and he received another round of CPR. He spent several days on mechanical ventilation in the intensive care unit. His physicians then informed the son that his father had little chance of recovery, that it was time to take him home to die, to assure that his spirit separate from the body in a metaphysically beneficial place.[2]

After my friend relayed this story, I was deeply perplexed. "This man clearly expressed his wishes," I said, "and everyone went against what he wanted."

She rolled her eyes at me. "You think so like a foreigner! The role [sūan] of a father is to say 'Don't worry about me, I am fine, I am ready for whatever comes.' And the role of a son is to say 'We're doing everything until the end.' They both do the right thing, and they both get merit [bun]."

She was right about my thinking like a foreigner—her logic was unfamiliar to me. And explaining it requires a brief tour of terms. "Merit"(bun) is a metaphysical principle based on the law of karma (kam), the concept that all actions have consequences. Positive actions generate positive consequences, known as "merit" (bun). Merit can be made, destroyed, and transferred, part of a moral and metaphysical economy. The word "role" or "part" (sūan) invokes a play—not to imply falseness, but to imply instead that there is a script, with each family member following his or her part in the play. Even though there is conflict, each individual is playing his part well, thus accruing "merit" (bun). In other words, the old man and son in my friend's case were each "doing the right thing." If, in contrast, the father had said, "Yes, please take me to the hospital," it would have shown that he was clinging to life, willing to burden his family with his own selfish interests. Likewise, if the son had said, "Okay, Father, we'll stay at home," it would have shown a lack of caring, an unwillingness to pay back the debt that he owed his father for parentage and a life of caregiving.

My friend's story produced in me a wave of cultural dizziness. How can one respect the rights of patients, when part of the "right thing to do" in a family system is to go against one another's wishes and to have one's explicit wishes transgressed? I had encountered some of this in studying "role theory" in the social sciences, but the concept of role was conspicuously absent in the autonomy-dominant bioethics I had learned in my medical training. Medical care in Western countries has needed to find an ethical system able to appear universal enough to deal with a diversity of beliefs and cultures, and the approach to this diversity has been to rely ever-increasingly on individual rights and autonomy, so much that autonomy has come to seem universal. Edmund Pellegrino, after years of research on cultural differences in bioethics, was still driven to claim:

Autonomy is still a valid and universal principle because it is based on what it is to be human. The patient must decide how much autonomy he or she wishes to exercise, and this amount can vary from culture to culture.

It seems probable that the democratic ideals that lie behind the contemporary North American concept of autonomy will spread and that something close to it will be the choice of many individuals in other countries.[3]

In opposition to this, some scholars have countered that individual autonomy does not apply to some societies, including "East Asian" societies, which instead function on a principle of "family determination," with "family harmony" allowing distribution of decision making between patients and their family members.[4] Ian, who acquiesced to treatment only because it was partly *for* his wife, hints that this phenomenon may be less of an "East Asian" reality and may instead be an axis of family dynamics for all families to a greater or lesser extent everywhere. Scholars advocating "family determination" would argue that perhaps we need to hold less tightly to individual autonomy and think more about how families make decisions as a whole.

But the story of the old man in Northern Thailand also unsettles this idea of "family harmony." What if disagreement, rather than harmony, is part of a family's script? Love, care, and ethical decisions may not always be achieved through harmony. In my friend's story, parts of the "roles" of the old man and his son were to disagree until the very end without ever reaching an explicit agreement on how to proceed. This was the "right thing to do" for both of them.

This is a challenging concept. It is even more challenging to decide what to do with it. If the individual may not always be the unit of autonomy, and group autonomy may not always manifest as harmony, doesn't that put us on a slippery slope? Why stop at the family? One could easily talk about patients' many roles—relative to friends or physicians, governments, or religious institutions[1]—each playing a rightful "role" in contradicting patients' expressed wishes. Aren't these precisely the power relationships that medical ethicists have worked so hard to break, using autonomy as a concept?

One need not reject autonomy completely to benefit from understanding its limitations. How might a respect for family roles help patient care without sliding into right-defying paternalism? Because of my fieldwork, and driven by this simple question, I began to explore the way that Ian's and Sarah's family roles were put together. I asked Ian about Sarah's insistence on treating his pain. He said, "She thinks I'm trying to be tough, that I'm putting on an act, and that she needs to take care of me in spite of myself." When I asked Sarah, she explained, "He is prideful. He can't feel like he's the one asking for help." Similar to the old man in Thailand, it was Ian's role not to need care and Sarah's role to care for him in spite of this. Whenever I framed pain treatment as the best thing for him, he put up a wall; it was only when the treatment was framed as a reluctant acquiescence to her wishes that he would receive it. Ultimately, we agreed on a stable pain regimen for Ian "to satisfy his wife," but we settled on lower doses than I would likely have used for others with the same disease, and he seemed satisfied with this arrangement. Ian's treatment plan was not a product of his individual autonomy; it was a hybrid that satisfied both his and Sarah's family roles. It was also not straightforward "family harmony," since Ian and Sarah needed precisely to remain in conflict, in tension, over the management of his suffering. This tension preserved their places in their family system. It was only seeing the family as the patient, rife with its autonomy-violating internal role dynamics, that I was able to achieve a sustainable care plan for Ian's pain.

Conflict of Interest Disclosures: The author has completed and submitted the ICMJE Form for the Disclosure of Potential Conflicts of Interest and none were reported.

Notes

1. Stonington S. Facing death, gazing inward: end-of-life and the transformation of clinical subjectivity in Thailand. *Cult Med Psychiatry*. 2011; 35(2):113–133.

2. Stonington SD. On ethical locations: the good death in Thailand, where ethics sit in places. *Soc Sci Med*. 2012;75(5):836–844.

3. Pellegrino ED. Is truth telling to the patient a cultural artifact? *JAMA*. 1992;268(13):1734–1735.

4. Fan R. Self-determination vs. family-determination: two incommensurable principles of autonomy: a report from East Asia. *Bioethics*. 1997; 11(3–4):309–322.

Global Environment

A Material World

In this text, the flows of cultural products (Chapter One), power (Chapter Two), ideas (Chapter Three), and pathogens (this chapter) have been explored. The focus of this section is the flow of oil, considered the world's most important commodity (Wenar 2016: x). Humans have used petroleum for millennia. People in what is now China were the first to use the substance, in an unrefined state, as fuel (Rapp 1985: 237). The first known oil wells were drilled in China beginning around AD 347 (Rapp 1985: 237). The centrality of oil to the global economy, however, is relatively recent. The Industrial Revolution increased demand for energy, but this was met by sources like coal and whale oil until it was discovered that kerosene could be extracted from oil and used as a heating and lighting fuel. The demand for crude oil then rose, making it the most valuable resource of all (Halliday 2012: 279).

The metaphor of flows used throughout this text is particularly apt for the world's energy supplies. The supply of oil, coal, and other nonrenewable resources is integral to development (the topic of the next chapter); a reason for geopolitical conflict; and the source of carbon emissions that are contributing to climate change. Oil and gas are responsible for massive destruction to the environment, destruction that often disregards national borders. Although the precise supply chains of petroleum are not public, flow is so central to the petroleum industry that it categorizes its operation into upstream, midstream, and downstream.

Petroleum is central to the global economy because of the sheer diversity of purposes it has been put to. It fuels the cars on the roads, the trucks that transport products, and the asphalt underneath them. It heats buildings and schools. Petroleum products provide the nitrogen added to fertilizers used to boost agricultural yields. Plastic is a petroleum-based product that pervades the global economy in the form of packaging, toys, furniture, and car parts. Petroleum is also used in the manufacture of clothing, perfume, vitamins, and many other products. Thus, even with the advent of electric cars and alternative energy sources, petroleum remains central to the global economy.

Because the resource is nonrenewable, there are serious concerns that the supply will run out. Hubbert's "Peak Oil" theory suggested that oil depletion would lead to the failure of markets (Hirsch, Bezdek and Wendling 2005). This theory became the center of an academic community, and later a movement with its own website. Peak Oil theory postulates that when the extraction of oil reaches a maximum, it will begin an irreversible decline. Hubbert (1962) projected that the peak would be reached for the United States in 1970 but this obviously proved inaccurate. Importantly, new discoveries of reserves forestall reaching a peak indefinitely, and demand may decrease with a turn to other, more sustainable, energy sources.

Given how vital energy is to the economy, it is not surprising that the purchase and sale of oil is a source of international tensions. After all, the countries that need to use the most oil to keep their economies functioning are not the same countries that produce the most oil. At the center of the world's oil economy is OPEC, the Organization of Oil Exporting Countries. The organization was formed

Image 4.3. Crude Oil

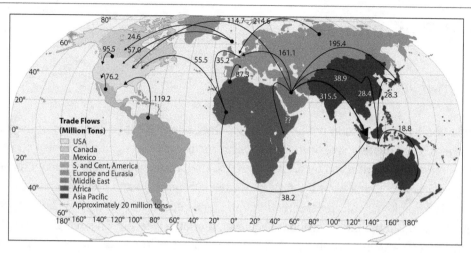

by Iran, Iraq, Kuwait, Saudi Arabia, and Venezuela in 1962, to be joined by ten other nations later. According to the organization's website, the mission of OPEC is "to coordinate and unify the petroleum policies of its Member Countries and ensure the stabilization of oil markets in order to secure an efficient, economic, and regular supply of petroleum to consumers, a steady income to producers, and a fair return on capital for those investing in the petroleum industry."[5] When prices for oil begin to decline, the member countries reduce supply by curtailing production. This has the effect of increasing demand and the price of oil. This practice has proven highly contentious. Non-OPEC countries resent the wealth and power the cartel brings to its members.[6,]

This was not always the case. The tables were turned prior to the organization's creation. In the first half of the twentieth century, multinational corporations located in the United States and Europe, sometimes called the Seven Sisters, dominated the petroleum industry. Less developed countries were expected to allow these companies to explore, extract, and profit on their territories. OPEC member nations saw this as a form of exploitation and sought to limit the power of the multinational corporations. The organization's Declaratory Statement emphasizes "the inalienable right of all countries to exercise permanent sovereignty over their natural resources in the interest of their national development."[7] They pointed out that oil companies' behavior displaced populations, and led to the loss of flora and fauna. The waste dumped in water sources contaminated food supplies, such as fish, and led to health problems.

OPEC and non-OPEC countries have contrasting visions of how best to organize the petroleum industry. Gulf States have traditionally adhered to a model in which oil extraction is state-controlled.

---

5   http://www.opec.org/opec_web/en/about_us/23.htm

6   OPEC countries produce 44 percent of the world's crude oil and about 20 percent of the world's natural gas supply (https://www.statista.com/topics/1830/opec/).

7   http://www.opec.org/opec_web/en/about_us/24.htm

This entails nationalizing the petroleum industry and assigning state governments the job of managing these resources. Proponents of this model argue this leads to better funding of social support and public goods because funds flow to the government from the oil industry. To support their approach, OPEC countries point to places like Nigeria that have experienced negative side effects as a result of having oil developed by multinationals.

Critics of the OPEC approach point out that it functions like a monopoly and that countries that adopt this model are less likely to be democratic. For the most part, non-OPEC countries tend to support a neoliberal model in which private companies acting in their own interest are thought to produce oil efficiently and at the lowest cost to all through free enterprise, open markets, and competition.

Oil and Power

The flow of energy around the world is one component of geopolitical stability. Oil has figured as both the goal and the fuel for waging many of the twentieth-century wars. Oil was an element in World War II (1939–1945), the USA–Japan conflict (1941–1945); the Nigerian Civil War (1967–1970); the Iran–Iraq War (1980–1988); the Gulf War (1990–1991); and many other conflicts.

Petroleum becomes a source of conflict in at least three ways. First, disputed border zones and international waters that contain oil reserves become worth fighting over, whether or not they are habitable. The South China Sea is an example of one such area. Second, oil becomes a factor in what could be called dynastic struggles: whoever controls the government controls the oil and an immense fortune. It is in the interest of anyone excluded from power to gain control. This scenario sometimes leads to terrorism and coups d'état. Nigeria and Saudi Arabia provide examples here. Third, oil becomes a factor in ethnic and sectarian disputes when the revenue flows to government officials. Members of minority groups will find an incentive to fight for a greater share, up to and including establishing a separate state. The Kurdish region of Iraq and the southern part of Sudan are examples of this type of conflict over oil.

Political scientists and development specialists have called the dynamics surrounding oil a "resource curse." According to Paul Collier (2007), extracting resources often leads to competition over those resources and fuels corruption. Countries that are rich in natural resources but lack strong governance do not always distribute the wealth to citizens. The mix of competition and corruption can spiral into outright conflict. Wealth gained from natural resources can also perpetuate an existing conflict by funding ongoing fighting. An abundant natural resource may also lead a government to rely on one industry, neglecting the development of other sectors of its economy. Reliance on extractive resources, Collier tells us, correlates with more frequent and longer civil wars. Chechnya, Sudan, and Syria are among the examples that could be cited. Although correlation is not necessarily causation, the "Freedom in the World" index provides some support for this theory. Countries are rated by the NGO Freedom House on the extent to which they secure civil liberties and political rights. Only roughly a sixth of the world's oil is in countries assessed "free" (Wenar 2012: xv).

Resources can present a curse, but they can also benefit a country. The key is effective policy making. A great deal depends on the quality of government institutions, and the amount of funds devoted to investment.

Perspectives on the Paris Agreement

The exploitation of common resources, sometimes called "The Tragedy of the Commons," has long plagued the relationship between humans and the environment. Whether or not you agree that the problem is a "tragedy," the term coined by Garret Hardin, establishing a more equitable and sustainable use of common resources is one of the most urgent problems facing the world. There are a several perspectives, not necessarily mutually exclusive, on the best way to address environmental challenges.

One is a call to conscience. The Paris Climate Agreement is significant in this regard. In 2015, representatives of 196 countries negotiated an agreement that aims to keep climate change below 2 degrees Celsius.[8] The agreement is designed to accommodate widely differing needs and capacities: it allows each country to set its own targets. A second notable feature is that wealthy industrialized countries reaffirmed their commitment to finance climate change adaptation and mitigation in less industrialized and developed countries. This takes into account the issue of justice: the already developed nations are primarily responsible for the rise in greenhouse gasses in the atmosphere (Image 4.4). Finally, almost fifty countries made the radical commitment to use only renewable energy by 2050.[9] The Paris Agreement has been championed as charting a new course in the global response to climate change. [10]

Image 4.4. Greenhouse Effect

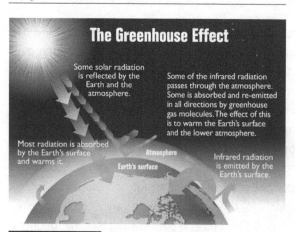

Calls to conscience work best when accompanied by strong governance. The Kyoto Protocol, a part of the United Nations Framework Convention on Climate Change, set binding targets for reducing the emission of harmful greenhouse gasses. The Protocol offered market-based mechanisms, such as emissions trading, to help countries reach these binding targets.[11] The Kyoto Protocol ran into problems, however, because the largest emitters, namely the United States, China, and India, are not parties to the treaty.[12] The governance of climate change mitigation and adaptation is an enormous challenge

8   https://unfccc.int/process-and-meetings/the-paris-agreement/the-paris-agreement
9   http://unfccc.int/paris_agreement/items/9444.php
10   https://unfccc.int/process-and-meetings/the-paris-agreement/the-paris-agreement
11   https://unfccc.int/process/the-kyoto-protocol/mechanisms
12   https://harvardmagazine.com/2002/11/problems-with-the-protoc.html

that requires the governments of states to bring their laws regulating multiple economic sectors into alignment with global priorities.

Some argue that allowing markets instead of governments to deal with climate change is more effective. In a peer-reviewed article published in *Global Policy*, Lomborg (2015) argues that the climate impact of all Paris Agreement promises is miniscule. Even if every nation fulfills every commitment, the temperature reduction will be only 0.048 degree Celsius or 0.086 degree Fahrenheit. He also lays out this argument at his website with the subtitle "Get the facts straight." In his 2001 book *The Skeptical Environmentalist: Measuring the Real State of the World* (2001), Lomborg took the climate-skeptic stance that the environment is actually improving, and mainstream media accounts regarding pollution, biodiversity, and the greenhouse effect are inflated. Since then, Lomborg has agreed climate is an important global issue. Still, he objects to approaching climate through either the call to conscience (Paris Accords) or coercion (Kyoto Protocol). He suggests the technological innovation called for in both the call to conscience and the governance approach is better achieved through privatization. Privatization advocates like Lomborg favor less government regulation accompanied by a free market economy and private ownership of industry. Habitats will thrive under private ownership, they argue, because it will be in the interest of the parties who own the habitats to preserve species and environments. Similarly, the incentive to develop new and more cost-effective sources of energy will be high for the owners and shareholders that stand to profit.

Climate is a an especially complicated issue because changes touch on many aspects of economic development. Critics of contemporary environmental movements take the stance that advocates have failed to adequately weigh the economic repercussions of what they propose. The predominant narrative needs to take the concerns of low-income people into greater account. A central concern is that changes proposed by the environmental movement could adversely affect jobs in the economies of the countries making changes. The rebuttal to this argument is that the needs of the planet as a whole cannot ethically be compromised to meet the needs of a specific demographic that can be assisted in other, more environmentally conscious, ways.

The Story of Ozone

Comparing the contemporary response to anthropogenic climate change with the international response to the ozone hole provides additional insight into why climate change is a divisive issue. In 1984, scientists discovered a thinning in the ozone layer above Antarctica. By 1986 NASA scientists were able to use satellite data to present a dramatic picture (Image 4.5).

The thinning in the atmosphere was associated with the presence of chlorofluorocarbons (CFCs) in the earth's atmosphere. CFCs are natural compounds typically used in refrigerants and aerosol propellants. Scientists hypothesized that these molecules were stable enough to remain in the atmosphere and deplete the fragile ozone layer beginning in the early 1970s. This idea met with considerable skepticism until the NASA photographs provided colorful visual representation in a time lapse format.

Image 4.5. Earth's Ozone Layer

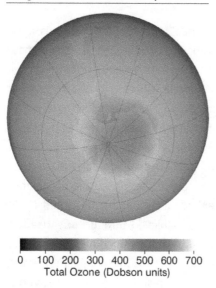

0   100 200 300 400 500 600 700
Total Ozone (Dobson units)

The images of what was happening at the South Pole proved to be very persuasive.

Negotiations among governments yielded the Montreal Protocol on Substances that Deplete the Ozone Layer.[13] The Protocol entered into force in 1989, only fourteen years from the initial understanding that human choices were part of the problem to the negotiation of the treaty. This is exceptionally rapid when compared to the process of addressing anthropogenic climate change. The Montreal Protocol was the first treaty to address an environmental problem at an international, regulatory level. It may surprise you to know that the treaty also considered national differences in responsibility and financial accountability. Why was the Montreal Protocol effective?

One of the factors believed to contribute to its success was that the problem was so visible, making it tangible for large numbers of people in a way that climate change is not tangible. The public was convinced of imminent risk. A second factor is that a feasible solution existed: phase out the production and consumption of ozone-depleting substances. Climate is considerably more multifaceted. Third, the same people bearing the costs and inconvenience of the phase-out would experience the benefits. In contrast, people who make sacrifices to address climate change aren't the direct beneficiaries, which is primarily future generations.

Image 4.6. Climate Change Indicators

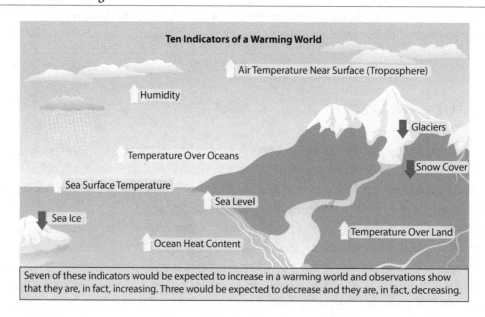

Ten Indicators of a Warming World

Air Temperature Near Surface (Troposphere)

Humidity

Glaciers

Temperature Over Oceans

Snow Cover

Sea Surface Temperature

Sea Level

Sea Ice

Temperature Over Land

Ocean Heat Content

Seven of these indicators would be expected to increase in a warming world and observations show that they are, in fact, increasing. Three would be expected to decrease and they are, in fact, decreasing.

---

13   http://ozone.unep.org/en/treaties-and-decisions/montreal-protocol-substances-deplete-ozone-layer

Environment Readings

In "Governing the Global Environment" **Regina Axelrod** and **Stacy Vandeveer** describe how a system of global environmental governance came into being. They demonstrate how international relations theories of realism, liberalism, and constructivism can be used to illuminate some of the international political dynamics surrounding climate change. (*The Global Environment: Institutions, Law, and Policy.* Los Angeles: CQ Press, 1–10.)

In "Bjorn Lomborg: The Dissenting Climate Change Voice Who Changed His Tune," **Juliette Jowit** gives readers a tour of writings by the controversial climate skeptic.

The Global Environment: Institutions, Law and Policy

by Regina Axelrod and Stacy Vandeveer

H umans change their environments. Environmental change is driven by the things we eat, build, make, buy, and throw away—and by the decisions we make as citizens and voters. Over the past few decades we have acquired the power to change the planet's climate. The early twenty-first century finds the Earth's physical and biological systems under unprecedented strain. The growing human population exceeds seven billion, and the global economy has grown to more than $70 trillion annually. The United Nations estimates that one-third of the world's people live in countries with moderate to high shortages of fresh water. Many of the world's largest cities are choked by pollution. As carbon dioxide and other greenhouse gases build in the atmosphere, the average surface temperature of the Earth has reached the highest level ever recorded, measured on an annual basis, as glaciers and polar ice recede. The biological diversity of the planet is also under heavy stress. Scientists believe that a mass extinction of plants and animals is under way and predict that a quarter of all species could be pushed to extinction by 2050 as a consequence of global warming alone. Without question, human impacts on the biosphere will remain one of the most critical issues of the century.

Scientists and conservationists have recognized the threats to the Earth's flora and fauna, water systems, and atmosphere for more than a century, but only in the past four decades have nations begun to address these issues on a global scale. The 1972 United Nations Conference on the Human Environment (UNCHE) in Stockholm, Sweden, attended by 113 states, marked the beginning of organized international efforts to devise a comprehensive agenda to safeguard the environment while also promoting economic development. Although no binding treaties were adopted at Stockholm, the conference established the United Nations Environment Programme (UNEP), creating a permanent forum for monitoring global environmental trends, convening international meetings and conferences, and negotiating international agreements. Among UNEP's most important achievements are the 1985 Vienna Convention for the Protection of the Ozone Layer and the binding 1987 Montreal Protocol on Substances That Deplete the Ozone Layer.[1] In 1987 the World Commission on Environment and Development (WCED, also known as the Brundtland Commission for its chair, former Norwegian prime minister Gro Harlem

Brundtland) issued its historic report *Our Common Future*, which called for a new era of "sustainable development."[2] To begin implementing this strategy, the United Nations Conference on Environment and Development (UNCED), known as the Earth Summit, was convened in Rio de Janeiro, Brazil, in June 1992. The conference produced major international treaties on climate change and biodiversity, two declarations of principle, and a lengthy action program (Agenda 21) for implementing sustainable development around the world. Ten years later, in August 2002, 191 nations attended the World Summit on Sustainable Development (WSSD) in Johannesburg, South Africa, to reassess and renew commitments to sustainable development.[3] Another ten years found public, private, and civil society actors returning to Rio for the United Nations Conference on Sustainable Development, or Rio+20.

As a result of such diplomatic achievements and the politics, policy making, and activism that surround them, a system for global environmental governance now exists. This system consists of states and hundreds of intergovernmental organizations such as the United Nations and UNEP (and dozens of issue-specific organizations set up by treaty) and thousands of nongovernmental organizations (NGOs) ... , a framework of international environmental law based on several hundred multilateral treaties and agreements ... , and a diverse host of complex international cooperation regimes and other governance arrangements ... .

Hundreds of bilateral and regional treaties and organizations, such as those involving the United Nations Regional Seas Programme and the European Union ... , deal with dozens of transboundary and shared resource issues. By one count, 1,190 multilateral international agreements (MEAs) and more than 1,500 bilateral environmental agreements are currently in effect.[4] Some date back to the nineteenth century, while some were created as recently as 2013, when the Minamata Convention on Mercury was signed in Japan.

Particularly since the 1990s, a host of nongovernmental organizations, including international environmental interest groups, scientific bodies, business and trade associations, women's groups, and indigenous peoples' organizations, have also come to play an important role in international environmental governance ... . Environmental activists and NGOs (small and large) can now be found all around the globe, engaged in politics and social action and organizing from neighborhoods and local communities to national and global politics.[5] These organizations participate in international negotiations, help to monitor treaty compliance, and often play leading roles in implementing policies. At the 2002 Johannesburg summit, more than twenty thousand individuals registered as participants, and countless others attended the parallel Global People's Forum and summit of indigenous peoples.[6] The increased access to and transparency of international environmental governance is one of the most remarkable achievements of the emerging global environmental governance system.

Despite these strides, there is a growing perception that the current international governance system remains weak and ineffective.[7] Many international environmental institutions lack adequate funding and effective enforcement mechanisms. Because no world government or global sovereign political authority exists, international agencies often work at cross-purposes and rely on individual states to carry out their policies. States are reluctant to relinquish their sovereignty and their right to pursue their own national interests. Consequently, many trends and patterns of global environmental degradation have not been reversed, leaving us on a path toward devastating ecological crises unless global institutions are strengthened and public, private-sector, and civil society actors—and individual citizens and consumers—take on far more responsibility for environmental governance.

The role of the United States in international environmental diplomacy has been especially disappointing in recent years. Although the Clinton administration signed the 1997 Kyoto Protocol, which set targets and timetables for reducing greenhouse gas emissions that cause global warming, neither this treaty nor others, such as the Convention on Biological Diversity, the Basel Convention on the trade in hazardous wastes, and agreements covering biosafety and a host of transboundary air pollutants, have been ratified by the U.S. Senate. President George W. Bush repudiated the Kyoto Protocol in 2001 and showed little interest in other multilateral environmental agreements and institutions. U.S. support for many international environmental programs has declined over time. This indifference often results in deep divisions between the United States and both the European Union and the developing nations of the global South ... .[8] Yet even here the picture is more complex than it might seem at first glance. Although the U.S. federal government largely abandoned environmental policy development in the early years of this century, many U.S. states and cities continued to make policy in response to international environmental challenges. Many states, for example, enacted policies to combat climate change and expand renewable energy generation even when the federal government was opposed to doing so.[9] In 2009, the Obama administration arrived in Washington, D.C., pledging to return to domestic environmental policy making and to steer the United States toward reengagement in global environmental cooperation (and in other areas of multilateral politics). Such changes take time and require the support of Congress and the American people. Congress has repeatedly opposed environmental initiatives—ignoring calls to act to reduce greenhouse gas emissions, to set clear regulations for hydraulic fracturing (fracking) and natural gas extraction, and to enact serious energy efficiency regulation—and has struggled to sustain even modest support for renewable energy generation. While a reelected President Obama pledged to lead on climate change and other environmental issues in both domestic and global politics, his administration's ability to do so remains constrained by congressional inaction and opposition. In 2013, attempting to circumvent congressional hostility toward climate policy, President Obama initiated a series of executive actions and EPA-driven regulatory processes, engendering ongoing opposition.

This book presents an overview of the development of international environmental institutions, laws, and policies and attempts to assess their adequacy. The authors analyze developments since World War II, with an emphasis on trends since the 1992 Earth Summit in Rio. They share both an optimism that people and nations can work together to address global problems and growing concern and pessimism about trends in both global environmental degradation and governance in the past two decades. They also take a longer view in evaluating emerging environmental regimes, because global cooperation is difficult to establish and sustain. Most of the contributors to this volume argue that there are important lessons to learn and reasons for hope. They caution, however, that more serious attention to global environmental governance is required of citizens and governments alike if disturbing and dangerous trends are to be reversed.

The past forty-plus years have seen dramatic and often surprising political and economic changes from which this volume seeks to learn. In addition to the large global summits on the environment and sustainable human development, the past twenty-five years witnessed developments such as the end of apartheid in South Africa, the collapse of Soviet-style communism in Eastern Europe and across the Soviet Union, a host of other transitions to democratic rule in Latin America and elsewhere, and the recent dramatic social and political changes across parts of North Africa and the Middle East. These changes brought unprecedented growth in the number of democracies in the world. The same era witnessed deepening European integration and expansion of the European Union from twelve countries to twenty-eight member states (with more applicants negotiating entry). China, India, Brazil, and a few other developing countries have roared into the global economy, reshaping aspects of their domestic politics, international relations, and global resource and environmental trends. These developments can both affect and inspire global environmental governance. For example, many of these political and economic changes help drive ever-increasing use of the Earth's resources (along with the seemingly never-ending growth in North American-style consumption). Yet if Europeans can overcome generations of war to build a unified Europe and citizens living under nondemocratic governments can demand their democratic and basic human rights and replace dictators with elected officials, then it may be possible for humankind to reverse global environmental degradation and build effective global environmental governance institutions to engender sustainable development around the globe.

The next two sections of this chapter provide a brief overview of the theoretical context for studying international environmental governance. The first of these summarizes the most important perspectives from international relations theory relevant to the emergence of international environmental institutions and law. The second discusses the concept of sustainable development, which became the dominant ideological framework for global environmental policies in the 1990s. The third section below outlines the organization and contents of the book, briefly discussing each of the three parts: (I) international environmental actors and institutions; (II) big players in global environmental policy making; and (III) cases, controversies, and challenges in global environmental governance. A short conclusion summarizes some of the themes of the book.

International Relations, Regimes, and Governance

International politics and governance institutions associated with environmental and sustainable development issues have produced a large and growing body of social science research and analysis.[10] Similarly, a large body of international relations theory is applicable to the development of international environmental institutions and agreements ... .[11] The study of international relations has traditionally been dominated by two broad theoretical schools: realism and liberalism. "Realists" view the world as an anarchic collection of sovereign nation-states, each of which is a unitary actor in pursuing its unique national interests. These interests are largely defined in terms of relative power and security compared with other states. In this perspective, nation-states do not cooperate with one another unless it is clearly in their self-interest to do so, and cooperative behavior will continue only as long as the parties perceive this condition to be met. International laws and institutions are thus essentially instruments for promoting or defending national interests and have little or no independent effect on the behavior of nations. Indeed, such laws and institutions can usually function only if strong or hegemonic states maintain them and enforce their decisions against weaker members or other states. The potential for international cooperation is therefore quite limited, and international laws and institutions are likely to be fragile and impermanent.[12]

This anarchic, state-centered perspective has been increasingly challenged in recent decades by a variety of "liberals," "neoliberals," and "liberal institutionalists." While most of these theorists concede that states are the primary actors on the international level, they hold that the traditional view of state sovereignty and unitary interest cannot explain the steady growth of international cooperation or the persistence of many specialized international institutions in the contemporary world. Although there are many strands of thinking, most liberal theorists hold that states are interdependent and, in fact, have many common interests that lead them to cooperate; moreover, they believe that international institutions not only serve these common interests but also create further incentives for cooperation.[13] In other words, institutions matter, and they influence the preferences and behavior of states by allowing states to improve collective welfare outcomes by cooperating. Whereas realists focus on *relative* status gains (especially regarding military security), liberals tend to emphasize *absolute* benefits (especially mutual economic gains) made possible by international agreements and institutions that solve collective action problems.

Over the past generation, a third, broad theoretical perspective has joined realism and liberalism in the pantheon of common theoretical approaches to understanding global environmental politics: constructivism.[14] Constructivism focuses attention on the influence of ideas, collective values, identities, and norms in international politics. The name given to this perspective refers to the argument that social reality is "constructed" through social interaction—that humans, collectively, construct the world in which they live through their identities and debates about values and norms (about what is justified or appropriate). Because of constructivism's attention to the influence of ideas and values, some international relations theorists view it as the contemporary variant of idealism.[15] For constructivists, international cooperation is more than mere ad hoc coalitions or a reflection of shared interests. It reflects who the participants are (or believe they are), and it can shape how they see themselves over time and what they view as appropriate. In other words, cooperation has the potential to be transformative in constructivism. For example, political scientist Peter Haas argues that a constructivist understanding of the effectiveness or impacts of conferences like the global environmental and sustainable development summits in 1972, 1992, 2002, and 2012 focuses more on how such meetings shape actor understandings, raise awareness, and bring political actors to agreement on norms, values, and ideas (on which they may act later).[16]

In other words, global environmental politics both reveals and shapes emerging, collectively held consensus positions and norms—about policies, problems, and how we understand the global environment and our place in it (and the place of international politics). For example, constructivists might examine scientific and policy debates around climate change to understand how some actors reach consensus or agreement while others continue to question widely held views or understandings. They might also explore the role and use of language and discourse in such debates.

Building on these three approaches to international relations theory during the past two decades, many environmental policy scholars have turned to the concept of regimes. International environmental regimes are composed of the international treaties and agreements, intergovernmental organizations, binding and nonbinding norms and principles, relevant national and local government institutions, and associated nongovernmental and private institutions that define and implement policies in different issue areas, such as climate change, maritime oil pollution, and endangered species protection. In Chapter 4 of this volume, David Leonard Downie explains regime theory in more detail and discusses many prominent examples of international environmental regimes. Drawing on other strands of international relations theory and systems theory, he also analyzes the obstacles to effective international cooperation. His chapter thus reveals the real difficulties of achieving effective international environmental policies.

Some theorists are more optimistic about the potential for a global governance system comprising an increasingly dense and interactive network of international regimes.[17] "Governance" in this sense does not presuppose a central government; rather, that coordination of action can occur through many different institutions, including private social and economic systems and nongovernmental organizations, as well as a variety of governmental institutions at different levels. This concept often presupposes some kind of global "civil society" or decentralized network of autonomous social institutions that represent citizens and organized interests and engage in cooperative actions to achieve broad goals such as sustainable development. Increased communication and exchange of information among individuals and groups around the world through the Internet and other means can magnify the impact of such civic action to the point where common ideas and values begin to influence the actions of governments from the bottom up.[18] Recent work within the "governance turn" in global environmental politics scholarship has begun to catalog and analyze large numbers of transnational or regional governance initiatives—or experiments—around the world involving complex sets of public, private, and civil society actors and a diverse set of institutionalized relationships and environmental goals.[19]

This brief discussion highlights the fact that whatever one's basic theoretical perspective, the development of international environmental cooperation has become one of the most fruitful and dynamic fields of international relations. Although there is no consensus among scholars on the nature of the world system or the autonomy and durability of current international environmental institutions, laws, and policies, it is undeniable that the global environment has become a principal concern of political actors as well as scholars around the world. From this broader vantage point, the halting and confused human response to gathering evidence of potential ecological catastrophe may be less discouraging than short-term observations suggest.

Sustainable Development

Cutting across theoretical disputes are the realities of world economic and social development. Environmental threats are the products not only of individual actions; they are also deeply embedded in our cultural, economic, political, and social systems. Perhaps the most obvious realities are that these systems are highly fragmented and differentiated and that global economic development is grossly uneven. The gap between the world's richer and poorer states is enormous and growing. So, for example, while gross domestic product per capita in the United States is more than $46,000, about a billion people, concentrated mostly in the world's fifty poorest countries, live on less than one dollar per day. These differences among nations at various stages and levels of development have profound implications for the global environment. Recognized since the Stockholm Conference is the fact that the needs and agendas of developed nations ("the North") are often fundamentally different from those of developing countries ("the South"); thus it is difficult to reach consensus on international policies that benefit all parties ... . Essentially, while the North gives substantial political attention to environmental issues that threaten ecological stability, the South has placed greater emphasis on immediate needs for economic growth to raise standards of living. Indeed, developing countries at the Stockholm Conference feared that environmental protection was a plot by the North to limit their development—a concern that still echoes through all international negotiations.[20]

The North-South division raises fundamental issues of international equity.[21] Developing countries (rightly) argue that the developed countries have benefited from environmental exploitation in the past and are responsible for most of the worlds pollution and resource depletion, including that leading to ozone depletion and climate change. Thus, the argument goes, it should be primarily their responsibility to deal with these problems. Furthermore, developing countries are not willing to foreclose opportunities for economic growth that would permanently lock them into poverty and dependence while the peoples of the North engage in profligate consumption. Representatives of developing countries (organized as the Group of 77 in the United Nations since 1964 but now actually including more than 130 states) thus usually condition their willingness to participate in international environmental treaties and agreements on concessions from the North, such as guarantees of special funding and transfer of technologies to enable them to reduce their impact on the environment while increasing economic growth.

Another fundamental dimension of global environmental protection concerns intertemporal, or intergenerational, equity. That is, policies must consider the needs of both the present generation and the future. Edith Brown Weiss defines three essential principles: (1) each generation should be required to conserve the diversity of the resource base so that it does not unduly restrict the options available to future generations; (2) each generation should maintain the planet's overall quality so that it is bequeathed in no worse condition than it was received; and (3) members of every generation should have comparable rights of access to the legacy of past generations and should conserve this access for future generations.[22] The third principle implies a degree of intragenerational equity as a condition for intergenerational equity; that is, no group should either be denied a right to present environmental resources or be asked to bear a disproportionate share of environmental burdens (a principle often referred to as *environmental justice*).

The concept of sustainable development was born of these concerns. First set out by Dennis Pirages in 1977 in *The Sustainable Society* and in *World Conservation Strategy,* published by the International Union for Conservation of Nature (IUCN) with the World Wildlife Fund (WWF, now the World Wide Fund for Nature) and UNEP in 1980, the concept was popularized in the Brundtland Commission report of 1987. The famous definition of sustainable development comes from this report: "Sustainable development is development that meets the needs of the present without compromising the ability of future generations to meet their own needs." This is followed immediately by the explication of two key concepts embedded within the definition: "the concept of 'needs,' in particular the essential needs of the world's poor, to which overriding priority should be given"; and "the idea of limitations imposed by the state of technology and social organization on the environment's ability to meet present and future needs."[23]

Several elements in this definition are critical for an understanding of sustainable development. First, the concept clearly represents an attempt to bridge the concerns and interests of developed and developing nations, but it applies to both. That is, both the wealthiest and the less developed countries will need to change their production and consumption patterns. Second, it attempts to reconcile economic growth and environmental protection, not view them as trade-offs. Third, the concept is strongly anthropocentric. It starts from the premise that human needs must be met before a state can address environmental problems. Thus improvement in the living conditions in poor countries, and especially those of women and marginal social and economic groups, is an essential precondition for ecological preservation. Fourth, the limits to growth are not ultimately physical or biological but social and technological; it is assumed that environmental problems can be solved. Finally, the concept is extremely general, lacking specific content on how sustainable development is to be attained or who is responsible for achieving it. This vagueness is deliberate: it allows the idea to be adopted by virtually everyone as a way of bringing people together to seek common ground. In this formulation it is clearly a political and social construct, not a scientific concept or blueprint.[24]

Sustainability is now a ubiquitous term used by governments, the business sector, NGOs, and international organizations. It has become difficult to assess sustainability paradigms or initiatives and to separate serious and potentially transformative ones from "greenwashing" in which the term is used as meaningless jargon for corporate branding.[25] Whatever the conceptual and ideological differences below the surface, there have been numerous attempts to translate sustainable development into policy initiatives. The most important political effort to do so occurred at the UN Conference on Environment and Development in 1992 in Rio de Janeiro. UNCED produced both a general declaration of principles (the Rio Declaration on Environment and Development) and Agenda 21, a massive effort to define strategies and policies for implementing sustainable development. Governments pledged to formulate sustainable development plans and programs, and the Commission on Sustainable Development was established by the UN General Assembly to monitor these commitments. Many regional, national, and local organizations have adopted the principles and goals of sustainable development since 1992. Organizations such as UNEP, the IUCN-World Conservation Union, the World Bank, the Organization for Economic Cooperation and Development, and the U.S. National Academy of Sciences have also been actively working to identify specific empirical "indicators" for measuring progress toward sustainable development.[26]

Despite such efforts, there is a general sense of disappointment, if not despair, regarding implementation of Agenda 21 in the twenty years since the Rio summit. For example, international aid flows for sustainable development have failed to come close to the levels considered necessary; indeed, official development assistance has *declined* in absolute terms.[27] A sense of pessimism pervaded both the 2002 World Summit on Sustainable Development in Johannesburg and Rio+20 in 2012. The WSSD attempted to focus on implementing existing obligations rather than on launching new programs, although some new policy goals, financial commitments, and public-private partnerships were agreed upon. Like most global summits, Rio+20 produced debate about its value, accomplishments, and underlying values and assumptions.[28] At best, one can characterize its accomplishments as modest and its results as mixed. Little sign of the political will and urgency suggested by environmental trends and environmental science was on evidence in the actual commitments made by states. Nothing illustrates this more than the disappointing outcomes of ongoing global climate change cooperation efforts such as the Kyoto Protocol, which expired in 2012 with no serious global agreements to replace it as global greenhouse emissions of all kinds continue to rise.

Notes

1. See especially Richard Elliot Benedick, *Ozone Diplomacy: New Directions in Safeguarding the Planet,* enlarged ed. (Cambridge, MA: Harvard University Press, 1998); Edward A. Parson, *Protecting the Ozone Layer: Science and Strategy* (Oxford: Oxford University Press, 2003). See also Chapters 4 and 5 in this volume.

2. World Commission on Environment and Development, *Our Common Future* (New York: Oxford University Press, 1987).

3. On UNCED and WSSD, see Philip Shabecoff, *A New Name for Peace: International Environmentalism, Sustainable Development, and Democracy* (Hanover, NH: University Press of New England, 1996); James Gustave Speth, "Perspectives on the Johannesburg Summit," *Environment* 45, no. 1 (January–February 2003): 24–29.

4. Ronald B. Mitchell, International Environmental Agreements (IEA) Database Project, Version 2013.2, accessed July 2013, http://iea.uoregon.edu/page.php?file=home.htm.

5. Paul F. Steinberg and Stacy D. VanDeveer, *Comparative Environmental Politics: Theory, Practice, and Prospects* (Cambridge: MIT Press, 2012).

6. United Nations Development Programme, *World Resources 2002–2004: Decisions for the Earth—Balance, Voice, and Power* (Washington, DC: World Resources Institute, 2003), 140–141.

7. Ibid., 138–139; James Gustave Speth, *Red Sky at Morning: America and the Crisis of the Global Environment* (New Haven, CT: Yale University Press, 2004), esp. chap. 5, "Anatomy of Failure"; Hilary French, *Vanishing Borders: Protecting the Planet in the Age of Globalization* (New York: W. W. Norton, 2000); Ronnie D. Lipschutz, *Global Environmental Politics: Power, Perspectives, and Practice* (Washington, DC: CQ Press, 2004).

8. See also Miranda A. Schreurs, Henrik Selin, and Stacy D. VanDeveer, eds., *Transatlantic Environment and Energy Politics: Comparative and International Perspectives* (Farnham, UK: Ashgate, 2009); Norman J. Vig and Michael G. Faure, eds., *Green Giants? Environmental Policies of the United States and the European Union* (Cambridge: MIT Press, 2004).

9. See Henrik Selin and Stacy D. VanDeveer, eds., *Changing Climates in North American Politics: Institutions, Policymaking, and Multilevel Governance* (Cambridge: MIT Press, 2009).

10. The quarterly journal *Global Environmental Politics* is the premier example among many such periodicals as well as many university press and commercial books published each year.

11. Kate O'Neill, *The Environment and International Relations* (New York: Cambridge University Press, 2009); Steinberg and VanDeveer, *Comparative Environmental Politics.*

12. See John J. Mearsheimer, "The False Promise of International Institutions," *International Security* 19 (1995): 5–49. Classic realist texts include Hans J. Morgenthau, *Politics among Nations: The Struggle for Power and Peace,* 5th ed. (New York; Knopf, 1978); Kenneth N. Waltz, *Theory of International Politics* (New York: Random House, 1979).

13. For a standard text, see Robert O. Keohane and Joseph S. Nye Jr., *Power and Interdependence: World Politics in Transition* (Boston: Little, Brown, 1977).

14. O'Neill, *The Environment and International Relations;* Kate O'Neill, Joerg Balsiger, and Stacy VanDeveer, "Actors, Norms and Impact," *Annual Review of Political Science* 7 (2004): 149–175.

15. Jack Snyder, "One World, Rival Theories," *Foreign Policy*, November/December 2004, 52–62.

16. Peter Haas, "UN Conferences and the Constructivist Governance of the Environment," *Global Governance* 8 (2002): 73–91.

17. Oran R. Young, ed., *Global Governance: Drawing Insights from the Environmental Experience* (Cambridge: MIT Press, 1997); Paul F. Diehl, ed., *The Politics of Global Governance* (Boulder, CO: Lynne Rienner, 1997); Deborah D. Avant, Martha Finnemore, and Susan K. Sell, eds., *Who Governs the Globe?* (Cambridge: Cambridge University Press, 2010).

18. See, for example, Ronnie D. Lipschutz with Judith Mayer, *Global Civil Society and Global Environmental Governance* (Albany: State University of New York Press, 1996); Margaret E. Keck and Kathryn Sikkink, *Activists beyond Borders: Advocacy Networks in International Politics* (Ithaca, NY: Cornell University Press, 1998); Lipschutz, *Global Environmental Politics.*

19. Mathew J. Hoffmann, *Climate Governance at the Crossroads: Experimenting with a Global Response after Kyoto* (New York: Oxford University Press, 2011); Harriet Bulkeley, Liliana Andonova, Michele Betsill, Daniel Compagnon, Thomas Hale, Mathew Hoffmann, Peter Newell, Matthew Paterson, Charles Roger, and Stacy D. VanDeveer, *Transnational Climate Change Governance* (Cambridge: Cambridge University Press, 2014); Philip Andrews-Speed, Raimund Bleischwitz, Tim Boersma, Corey Johnson, Geoffrey Kemp, and Stacy D. VanDeveer, *The Global Resource Nexus: The Struggles for Land, Energy, Food, Water, and Minerals* (Washington, DC: Transatlantic Academy, 2012).

20. On the conflict preceding the Stockholm Conference, see Lynton K. Caldwell, *International Environmental Policy,* 3rd ed. (Durham, NC: Duke University Press, 1996), 57–62.

21. See, for example, John Lemons and Donald A. Brown, eds., *Sustainable Development: Science, Ethics, and Public Policy* (Dordrecht, Netherlands: Kluwer Academic Publishers, 1995); Ian H. Rowlands, "International Fairness and Justice in Addressing Global Climate Change," *Environmental Politics* 6 (Autumn 1997): 1–30; Keekok Lee, Alan Holland, and Desmond McNeill, eds., *Global Sustainable Development in the 21st Century* (Edinburgh: Edinburgh University Press, 2000).

22. Edith Brown Weiss, "The Emerging Structure of International Environmental Law," in *The Global Environment: Institutions, Law, and Policy,* ed. Norman J. Vig and Regina S. Axelrod (Washington, DC: CQ Press, 1999), 106–107. For a full discussion, see Edith Brown Weiss, *In Fairness to Future Generations: International Law, Common Patrimony, and Intergenerational Equity* (Dobbs Ferry, NY: Transnational Publishers, 1989).

23. WCED, *Our Common Future,* 43.

24. For an excellent collection of essays on this topic, see Susan Baker, Maria Kousis, Dick Richardson, and Stephen Young, eds., *The Politics of Sustainable Development* (London: Routledge, 1997). See also Thomas M. Parris, "Toward a Sustainability Transition: The International Consensus," *Environment* 45, no. 1 (January–February 2003): 12–22; John C. Dernbach, ed., *Stumbling toward Sustainability* (Washington, DC: Environmental Law Institute, 2002).

25. Peter Dauvergne and Jane Lister, *Eco-Business: A Big-Brand Takeover of Sustainability* (Cambridge: MIT Press, 2013).

26. Some of these are discussed in Leslie Paul Thiele, *Sustainability* (London: Polity, 2013); Thaddeus C. Trzyna, *A Sustainable World: Defining and Measuring Sustainable Development* (Sacramento: California Institute of Public Affairs, 1995); and Simon Bell and Stephen Morse, *Measuring Sustainability: Learning from Doing* (London: Earthscan, 2003). See also Joy E. Hecht, "Sustainability Indicators on the Web," *Environment* 45, no. 1 (January–February 2003): 3–4.

27. Paul G. Harris, *International Equity and Global Environmental Politics: Power and Principles of U.S. Foreign Policy* (Aldershot, UK: Ashgate, 2001); Paul G. Harris, "International Development Assistance and Burden Sharing," in Vig and Faure, *Green Giants?*, 252–275; Adil Najam, Janice M. Poling, Naoyuki Yamagishi, Daniel G. Straub, Jillian Sarno, Sara M. DeRitter, and Eonjeong M. Kim, "From Rio to Johannesburg: Progress and Prospects," *Environment* 44, no. 7 (September 2002): 26–38.

28. For nice summaries of such debates, see Maria Ivanova, "The Contested Legacy of Rio+20," *Global Environmental Politics* 13, no. 4 (2013): 1–11; Steven Bernstein, "Rio+20: Sustainable Development in a Time of Multilateral Decline," *Global Environmental Politics* 13, no. 4 (2013): 12–21.

Bjørn Lomborg: The Dissenting Climate Change Voice Who Changed His Tune

by Juliette Jowit

With his new book, Danish scientist Bjørn Lomborg has become an unlikely advocate for huge investment in fighting global warming. But his answers are unlikely to satisfy all climate change campaigners.

Few statisticians can have inspired more passion than Bjørn Lomborg, the Danish academic who became famous as the author of the controversial (some would say contrarian) Skeptical Environmentalist, which set him up as perhaps the world's best-known critic of the dominant scientific view of global warming and the ensuing climate change.

Lomborg's prolific output has been almost matched by books rubbishing his work: critics have described him as selective, unprofessional and confused. Rajendra Pachauri, chairman of the UN's climate change panel, has compared him to Adolf Hitler—for the statistical crime of treating human beings too much like numbers.

Meanwhile, Time Magazine declared Lomborg one of the 100 most influential people in the world in 2004. The respected Cambridge University Press (CUP) has published many of his books in the UK and the US, and the award-winning documentary maker Ondi Timoner and X-Men films producer, Ralph Winter, are about to release a film of his 2007 book Cool It (which carries the subtitle: the first optimistic film about global warming).

The Danish Committee on Scientific Dishonesty once declared Lomborg guilty of exactly that, but a government review later cleared him.

Lomborg's latest book, published by CUP next month, is likely to reignite these passions, because it appears to contradict so much of what he has said before and because he is straying into newly controversial territory. He is advocating that much more attention and money be lavished on climate engineering methods, such as whitening clouds so that they reflect back more of the sun's heat.

Heat is something he is resigned to. When he gives talks, he says, he often meets "people who come up and say: 'I thought I'd hate you.'"

But Lomborg's record on climate change is more nuanced than the stereotype suggests. From the beginning, he has said global warming is happening and is largely caused by humans. However, he has been consistently critical of what he sees as exaggeration of how much this matters, and of policies to tackle the problem. These would achieve too little and cost too much, he argues, meaning the money would be better spent on, say, reducing malaria and HIV/Aids, or extending clean water and sanitation.

In an example of the approach that enraged Pachauri, Lomborg argues in Cool It that predicted temperature rises could save more than 1.3 million lives a year. This, he says, is because many more people would be spared early cold-related deaths than would be at risk from heat-related respiratory fatalities. (Other academics reject his figures.) Lomborg concludes that because of imbalances in where deaths occur, the proposed extension of the Kyoto protocol to cut carbon emissions would "save 4,000 people annually in the developing world [but] end up sacrificing more than a trillion dollars and 80,000 people annually."

Given this background, the title of Lomborg's new book immediately indicates a change of emphasis. It is called Smart Solutions to Climate Change: Comparing Costs and Benefits. This impression is reinforced by comments in the introduction that climate change is "undoubtedly one of the chief concerns facing the world" and "a challenge that humanity must confront".

Later in the book, reflecting on analysis by five economists of eight types of solution, he estimates that spending $100bn (£65bn) a year "could essentially resolve the climate change problem by the end of this century".

He finishes: "If we care about the environment and about leaving this planet and its inhabitants with the best possible future, we actually have only one option: we all need to start seriously focusing, right now, on the most effective ways to fix global warming."

Speaking to the Guardian about climate engineering as a back-up plan, he raises the possibility of "something really bad lurking around the corner": the small-chance, big-consequence outcome his previous work appeared to dismiss.

Not unexpectedly, however, Lomborg denies performing a U-turn. He reiterates that he has never denied anthropogenic global warming, and insists that he long ago accepted the cost of damage would be between 2% and 3% of world wealth by the end of this century. This estimate is the same, he says, as that quoted by Lord Stern, whose report for the British government argued that the world should spend 1–2% of gross domestic product on tackling climate change to avoid future damage.

The Stern report estimated that damage at 5–20% of GDP, however, not 2–3%. The difference, according to Lomborg, is that the two use a different "discount factor". This is the method by which economists recalculate the value today of money spent or saved in the future—or, to put it another way, the value today of this generation's grandchildren's lives. Neither is measurably "right", he says: they are judgments, albeit ones with a profound impact on subsequent analysis of the costs and benefits of spending money now to stop climate change.

Lomborg says false views of his position are held mostly by people who have never read his work. He says: "I keep trying to fight this, mainly because people often hear what I say through others." These intermediaries are often hostile critics, he adds.

Another cause of misunderstandings could be the difference between the content and the tone of his work. In it, brief statements about the unarguable fact of man-made global warming are accompanied by long arguments about how greenhouse gas emissions, the main man-made cause, and temperatures have been higher in the (very distant) past, and by claims that impacts such as rising sea levels and the threat to polar bears have been distorted.

Meanwhile, some statements appear to contradict each other directly. In the space of four pages of Cool It, he writes that "climate change will not cause massive disruptions or huge death tolls", that "the general and long-term impact will be predominantly negative", and that it is "obvious that there are many other and more pressing issues".

"The point I've always been making," he explains now, "is, it's not the end of the world. That is why we should be measuring up to what everybody else says, which is we should be spending our money well."

This detailed analysis by economists of how best to spend money to help the world's people was first reported in his book Global Crises, Global Solutions in 2004. It has now been institutionalised in the Copenhagen Consensus Centre, of which Lomborg is the director, and is the model for the latest book on climate "solutions".

This result is where Lomborg is most vulnerable to allegations of a volte-face on the need to take action on climate change and the value of doing so. But he says circumstances have changed. The first Copenhagen Consensus considered only the predominant idea of cutting carbon emissions through a cap or tax. When the exercise was repeated in 2008, however, the team examined new ideas. Lomborg says he then challenged himself and selected economists to look at eight different "solutions" (comprising 15 policy suggestions). These included boosting R&D in technology, cleaning up soot and methane, which also contribute significantly to global warming, planting more trees, and climate engineering. Critics may argue he should have carried out this study before rubbishing climate policies.

As a result, he is still deeply critical of the dominant, cutting-carbon approach, which four of the five economists who were asked to rank the options put at the bottom of their lists. Only Nancy Stokey, of the University of Chicago, ranked lower- and mid-level carbon taxes more highly, around the middle of her list. Instead, the book suggests the best policies would be investment in clean technology research and development, and more climate engineering development work. He suggests this could be funded by a $7-a-tonne tax on carbon emissions, which he says would raise $250bn a year. Of this, $100bn could be spent on clean-tech R&D, about $1bn on climate engineering, $50bn on adapting to changes (building sea defences, for example), and the remaining $99bn or so on "getting virtually everybody on the planet healthcare, basic education, clean drinking water, and so on. It seems a pretty good deal," he says.

Lomborg is not alone in finding fault with the Kyoto process, which many variously agree has been too slow to deliver, too vulnerable to unkept promises, and unrealistic in restraining the aspirations of developing countries. Critics add that it has proved to be a clumsy, ineffective way of delivering necessary investment in energy efficiency and clean electricity, and has resulted in often unnecessarily expensive policies. For most policy areas, such as crime, says Lomborg: "We say to people, what are the smartest ways to deal with this?" Curiously, with climate change, they say there's a right solution: that's cutting carbon."

The "biggest bang for the buck" Copenhagen Consensus approach is instinctively commonsense. But it is flawed, say critics, because it relies too heavily on the huge assumptions needed to convert human wellbeing and suffering into numbers (such as the discount rates) and excludes many factors that have simply never been quantified, such as the predicted total loss of coral reefs and other impacts of rapid ocean acidification.

Professor Katherine Richardson, a marine biology expert and vice-dean of science at the University of Copenhagen, says: "A lot hinges on whether you think that societal decision should be made by economists alone. [For example] I can think of much cheaper ways of taking care of our elderly in society than building expensive and modern nursing homes. In reality, we get very little return for that investment."

Many climate change scientists also fear huge disruption caused by changing tack will delay political action on avoiding the worst of the problem for a dangerously long time.

Lomborg's aggressively sceptical reputation will no doubt win few such people over, although he says he has no regrets about how he has conducted the debate. "Fundamentally," he says, "it would have been better if Pachauri or Stern were to make this argument. This isn't about ownership of the idea, but it's an idea we need to listen to if we want to get the climate fixed."

Research and Development

Research and development can mitigate the challenges associated with reliance on fossil fuels. The amount of money invested in research on sources of renewable energy has soared over the last decade (Temple 2016). As a result, sustainable energy is likely to become increasingly efficient and affordable.

One of the possibilities intriguing scientists as a way to replace gasoline as a transportation fuel is artificial photosynthesis. Artificial photosynthesis would mimic nature's ability to convert sunlight, carbon dioxide, and water into fuel. "Bionic" leaves could conceivably capture 10 percent of the energy in sunlight, a rate that is ten times better than that of the plants on earth (Reuell 2016).

New ways to manage the carbon dioxide resulting from the burning of fossil fuels could be developed in your lifetime. Scientists are exploring the possibility of carbon storage. In Iceland, companies are experimenting with injecting carbon dioxide and water underground. This combination is transformed into stone when it reacts with volcanic basalt rock (Matter et al. 2016).

The technology behind offshore wind farms may be refined and their use expanded. Offshore wind-farms use cables to transmit energy captured from wind to the energy grid on land. The wind offshore tends to travel more quickly than on land, yielding large returns when it comes to energy. This is only a sample of the ideas that will change humans' consumption of energy and relationship to the planet.

References

Beaglehole, Robert, and Ruth Bonita. 2010. "What Is Global Health?" *Global Health Action* 3: 10:340/gha. v3i0.5142.

Benedictow, Ole J. 2004. *The Black Death 1346–1353: The Complete History.* Woodbridge, CT: Boydell.

Collier, Paul. 2007. *The Bottom Billion: Why the Poorest Countries Are Failing and What Can Be Done About It.* Oxford: Oxford University Press.

Crosby, Alfred. 1972. *The Columbian Exchange: Biological and Cultural Consequences of 1492*. Westport, CT: Greenwood.

Daviss, Betty Anne. 1997. "Heeding Warnings from the Canary, the Whale and the Inuit: A Framework for Analyzing Competing Types of Knowledge about Childbirth." In Robbie E. Davis-Floyd (ed.), *Childbirth and Authoritative Knowledge: Cross-Cultural Perspectives*. Berkeley: University of California Press, 441–473.

Delaet, Debra and David Delaet. 2016. "Key Concepts in Global Health" in *Global Health in the 21st Century: The Globalization of Disease and Wellness*. New York: Routledge.

Halliday, Fred. 2012. *The Middle East in International Relations*. Cambridge: Cambridge University Press.

Hirsch, Robert, Roger Bezdek, and Robert Wendling. 2005. "Peaking of World Oil Production: Impacts, Mitigation, and Risk Management." Washington, DC: U.S. Department of Energy [updated 2016].

Hubbert, M. King. 1962. "Energy Resources." National Academy of Sciences Publication 1000-D. Washington, DC: National Academy of Sciences.

Koplan, J. P., T. C. Bond, M. H. Merson, K. S. Reddy, M. H. Rodriguez, and N. K. Sewankambo. 2009. "Towards a Common Definition of Global Health." *Lancet* 373(9679): 1993–1995.

Long, William. 2011. *Pandemics and Peace*. Washington, DC: United States Institute for Peace.

Lomborg, Bjorn. 2001. *The Skeptical Environmentalist: Measuring the Real State of the World*. Cambridge: Cambridge University Press.

Lomborg, Bjorn. 2015. "Impact of Current Climate Proposals." *Global Policy* 7 (1): 109–118.

Matter, Juerg, Martin Stute, Sandra Snaebjornsdottir, Eric Oelkers, Sigurdur Gislason, and Edda Aradotti. 2016. "Rapid Carbon Mineralization for Permanent Disposal of Anthropogenic Carbon Dioxide Emissions." *Science* 352 (6291): 1312–1314. http://science.sciencemag.org/content/352/6291/1312

Rapp, George. 1985. *Archaeomineralogy*. New York: Springer Science+Business Media, 237.

Reuell, Peter. 2016. "Bionic Leaf Turns Sunlight into Liquid Fuel." *The Harvard Gazette*, June 3, 2016. https://news.harvard.edu/gazette/story/2016/06/bionic-leaf-turns-sunlight-into-liquid-fuel/

Sapp, Heather. 2006. "Monopolizing Medicinal Methods: The Debate Over Patent Rights for Indigenous Peoples." *Temple Journal of Science, Technology and Environmental Law* 25 (2): 191–212.

Smallman, Shawn, and Kimberley Brown. 2011. *Introduction to International and Global Studies*. Chapel Hill: University of North Carolina Press.

Temple, James. 2016. "The Biggest Clean Energy Advances in 2016." https://www.technologyreview.com/s/603275/the-biggest-clean-energy-advances-in-2016/

Wenar, Leif. 2016. *Blood Oil: Tyrants, Violence, and the Rules That Run the World*. New York and Oxford: Oxford University Press.

Image Credits

CHAPTER FIVE

Human Development

Poverty has been accepted as inevitable for most of human history. Since the Industrial Revolution and advances made in methods of agriculture, however, the proportion of people in the world who are living in absolute poverty has been declining. Technological innovation means poverty in general and hunger in particular are questions of resource distribution. The field of human development explores how best to address allocation.

The idea that aid should flow from wealthier and developed nations to less developed nations has some of its roots in the Cold War between the United States and the Soviet Union. A first step was taken with the Truman Doctrine. Concern that Greece and Turkey could be attracted into the communist bloc, Truman requested Congress to authorize assistance for these economically struggling nations. Shortly after, Secretary of State George C. Marshall advocated a similar approach to Western Europe. The Marshall Plan that emerged had multiple motivations: fighting postwar poverty and hunger, stimulating the American economy, and protecting countries from the spread of communism were at the top of the list.

Subsequently, both the United States and the Soviet Union used aid as a way to secure the loyalty of less developed countries in Latin America, Asia, and Africa. Bilateral aid was also extended from European countries to colonies that were gaining independence based on historic relationships and strategic considerations. A new multilateral phase began in the 1960s. The International Development Association was set up under the leadership of the World Bank. The objective of the aid was to overcome the lack of domestic resources by raising the rates of investment. This model came under question when research suggested there was no conclusive evidence that aid contributed to growth on a sustainable basis (Browne1997). By the 2000s, development aid was reframed as a moral commitment and banks and development agencies had more experience and more models to work with. Recognition spread that ready-made solutions to development problems often fail. More attention is now devoted to what a struggling nation may do for itself.

The study of human development has its disciplinary home in the field of economics. According to the American Economic Association, economics is the study of scarcity, the study of how people use resources and respond to incentives, or the study of decision making.[1] The discipline of economics

---

1   https://www.aeaweb.org/resources/students/what-is-economics

studies, models, and makes projections about flows of wealth. According to dominant economic theories, rational actors seek to maximize utility by evaluating costs and benefits. The underlying assumption is that humans have unlimited desires, limited resources, and act in inherently self-interested ways. These assumptions are a matter of debate, and those who adhere to them note their utility for developing workable models at a statistical level. Economics is often divided into two subfields. Whereas microeconomics is interested in individual decision making, macroeconomics is more interested in the economy as a whole. Thus the "unit of analysis" in economics can be individual actors, corporations, institutions, or states.

One of the first things students may notice when reading about development is a multitude of categories: in order to discuss development, scholars and policymakers categorize nation-states based on their level of development. The World Bank and the UN use four variously defined categories. These categories provide a way to track the development progress of a country and to make comparisons across countries. The algorithms used to determine how a country ranks are continually being discussed, debated, and refined.

Economic growth increases the potential to reduce poverty, but indicators of wealth such as Gross Domestic Product (GDP) don't provide enough information about quality of life or allocation of resources within a nation. A crucial distinction in this chapter is therefore between *economic* development and *human* development. While the former term refers to advances in material wealth and focuses on economic growth, human development is assessed by examining variables that provide information about health, education, and life expectancy. Human development can include any activity that improves lives. As a way to enhance people's ability to live long and creative lives, human development is closely tied to political freedoms, human rights, and human security.

Flows: Capital, Goods, Services, and Ideas

Human development is fostered by the flow of capital, goods, and services around the globe. By some accounts, the process of integrating local and regional economies into a global one began with the Silk Roads that linked the Roman Empire, the Parthian Empire, and the Han Dynasty in commerce. The Silk Road, or more accurately, Silk Routes, comprised of a large network of land and sea routes. The routes were given their name from the Chinese silk trade, but so much more than silk was traded. People came to depend on the myriad products including paper, gunpowder, spices, tea, horses and camels, gold and silver, textiles and dyes, salt, medicines, and glassware that became available. Of course, human capital —slaves—was also widely exchanged. The networks were active from when the Han opened trade with the west in about 130 BCE to when the Ottoman Empire ended trade with the West and shut down the routes in 1453 (Mark 2018: n.p.).

The closure of the Silk Routes inspired the Age of Discovery. European navigators embarked to find new sea routes to reach the products that had previously moved through the Silk Routes. Historians trace the origins of the modern capitalist economy to this European expansion. Merchants were especially important to this process because they acted outside of traditional feudal relationships and made wider economic connections possible. An especially important driver of this expansion was a hunger for the spices that had previously been traded along the

Silk Routes. The Dutch East India Company was created to facilitate the trade of spices and other goods. In addition to being one of the largest European trading companies, it was the first joint stock enterprise to be owned by investors—the first example of private corporate actors becoming involved in global trade (Balaam and Dillman 2011). This was an age of mercantilism, defined as the pursuit of profit by selling goods at advantageous prices (creating and maintaining export outlets) while simultaneously protecting domestic markets by making foreign goods more expensive. The trade in manufactured goods resulted in European countries' the accumulation of national wealth and power.

British colonialism and expansionism played an especially important role in the integration of the increasingly global economy. At the same time, it facilitated the creation of massive disparities in wealth between the colonizers and the colonized. British colonialism is of particular interest because Great Britain was a hub for the Industrial Revolution, and therefore had both the resources and the rationale for colonial expansion. British political and military power propelled the creation of a vast colonial empire in which raw materials from the colonies fed factories in Great Britain. These enterprises produced products for sale both domestically and abroad. Britain had the added advantage of serving as a financial center. The system was based on gold and supported by the pound sterling, the British currency.

Mercantilism was a form of protectionism that was hotly contested. In the late 1700s, Adam Smith and David Ricardo argued that free and open markets are a better means to reach economic prosperity than government regulation (Smith 1934). Ricardo is credited with the idea that free trade would promote efficiency by encouraging countries to specialize in producing and exporting the goods for which they had a "*comparative advantage*." Ricardo maintained that if countries export those goods they can produce at a lower cost, and import the items that other countries produce more cheaply, everyone will benefit.

This brief discussion demonstrates the global economy is shaped as much by politics as economics. Economic globalization reached a peak before the World War I when both trade and immigration were high. The global economy contracted appreciably following World War I when governments' instituted trade barriers that limited commercial interactions. Combined with currency instabilities, this lead to the Great Depression. These experiences gave government authorities and academics added appreciation of the importance of international economic cooperation. In the post-World War II era, dramatic strides were made to create institutions that could facilitate international cooperation on issues of not only peace, but prosperity.

Human Development

The conventional definition of development as economic growth was based on the assumption that when an economy grows, everyone benefits and countries' trajectory of growth is usually upward. One does not have to venture into the developing world to appreciate that economic growth is a necessary but not sufficient component for reducing poverty. Many urban areas in the United States display a pattern of fabulous wealth next to abject poverty.

Image 5.1. Human Development Index

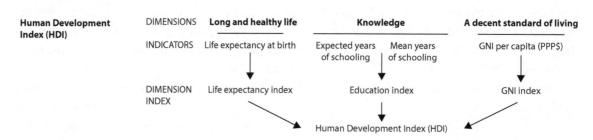

The first Human Development Report in 1990, opened with the innovative and refreshing premise that "People are the real wealth of a nation." The report turned the idea of development upside down: economic growth was not the goal but rather improvements in health and well-being. The focus shifted from maximizing income to expanding capabilities, and from prioritizing growth to enlarging freedoms. Based on theorizing that had been going on in both academic and policy circles, the report argued, "People are the real wealth of a nation."[2] New definitions required new ways of measuring progress. The Human Development Index (HDI) measures human development using three overarching metrics. A "decent standard of living" is measured by Gross National Income per capita. A "long and healthy life" is measured by life expectancy at birth, and "knowledge" is measured by mean years of schooling and expected years of schooling.

Key thinkers behind the 1990 Human Development Report include Mahbub ul Haq who was responsible for arguing that the ultimate goal of human development is to enable people to have more choices. Amartya Sen was another influential thinker and was awarded the 1998 Nobel Prize in Economics for his intellectual contribution. He argued that development instigated from the top down will tend to infringe on human rights. His alternative is to treat development as "capacity" and development as "freedom" (Sen 1999). Sen's model emphasizes "functionings" (states of well-being and the activities that go into them), "capabilities" (the substantive freedoms a person uses to live a life of his or her choosing), and "agency" (the ability to pursue the goals that one values) (Sen 1999: 87). The Human Development Index changed the way development is measured.

Another important step was taken in 2000, when the United Nations Development Program put forward the United Nations Millennium Declaration. The Declaration articulated eight goals to be achieved by 2015. The goals, often referred to as the MDGs, were to eradicate extreme poverty; achieve universal primary education; promote gender equality and empower women; reduce child mortality; improve maternal health; combat HIV/AIDS, malaria, and other diseases; ensure environmental sustainability; and create a global partnership for development. These goals reflected international priorities at the time. The MDGs were designed with measurable targets and defined indicators for tracking progress. There was also agreement that the states that have achieved the goals have an obligation to help those who have not.

Many, but not all, of the goals were reached. It is important to avoid conflating correlation with causation, however. The fact that goals were reached does not necessarily mean that it is the UN

---

2   http://hdr.undp.org/en/reports/global/hdr1990

Image 5.2. Sustainable Development Goals

millennium initiative that is responsible. Some of the changes could have taken place without the goals in place. Development is complex enough that there is no scientific way to isolate whether the UN development programs are responsible.

In 2015, the UN agreed on a new set of goals, referred to as the Sustainable Development Goals (SDGs). The new set of goals encompasses a wider range of issues and offers some improvements on the MDGs. For example, the negotiation process for achieving the goals was more egalitarian, including a more representative group of people from both the developed and less developed world. And for the first time, high-income countries were assigned goals in acknowledgment of the fact that improvements are needed in highly developed nations as well as those struggling with poverty and underdevelopment. With the developed world included, the SDGs rightly aim to identify barriers to sustainable development by addressing indefensible consumption patterns and environmental degradation, which the MDGs overlooked. Values such as "equity," and "empowerment" are an explicit part of the calculus. The expanded agenda has the notable drawback that it introduces significant complexity and difficult trade-offs. Action to meet one target (e.g., to reduce hunger through increasing agricultural land use) could have unintended consequences for other targets (e.g., loss of biodiversity, or unsustainable water use). Thus, development strategies will need to be carefully coordinated.

Many of the countries that were once considered underdeveloped or developing have moved into very different categories. Terms readers may encounter in this regard are the "Asian Tigers" of Singapore, Taiwan, South Korea, and Hong Kong. There is also a category called "BRICS" that was defined largely based on the countries' growth potential: Brazil, Russia, India, China, and South Africa. Together, they account for half of the world's population. There are some predictions that by 2050 these economies will dominate the global economy.

Perspectives on Human Development

The project of human development has been criticized from two important angles. The first set of criticisms is methodological and revolves around the way that human development is being measured. In general, these critics hold that the HDI uses suboptimal variables and that it does not reflect the idea of human development accurately. For example, Sagar and Najam (1998) contend that the HDI presents a "distorted" image of the world. Others assert that the HDI presents an oversimplified account that should be questioned because it relies on low-quality data (Kovacevic 2010). As a result of these limitations, the harshest critics take the view that the HDI does not offer much more information than GDP.

A second set of criticisms is substantive and has to do with the outcomes of the development project itself. While development was envisioned as a project that would make the world a better place, the way it has been carried out has not always been successful. Ernesto Sirolli [Ted Talk video] argues that the chief problem with the project of human development is the knowledge, expertise, and goals of locals are not sufficiently taken into account.[3] He makes reference to the book *Dead Aid*, in which Dambisa Moyo challenges the most basic assumptions that have informed development projects. She argues that the billions of dollars that have flowed into African nations kept the nations in a state of dependency (Moyo 2009).

The concept of "post-development" advances just such a critical perspective on development. Arturo Escobar first developed this idea, emphasizing that the idea that the less developed world is "poor" was manufactured by the West after it became rich (Escobar 1995). He maintains that many of the countries now categorized as less developed did not consider themselves to be lacking or underdeveloped until the United States and European countries managed to spread a narrative about their own affluence and superiority. Escobar's core thesis is that development as conceived by contemporary intergovernmental organizations is an attempt to spread a specific ideology. He claims that with development funds came foreign norms and values that were imposed on people who, for political and economic reasons touched upon above, were not in a good position to refuse. Western prosperity and well-being became the measure of success, but these measures fit comfortably only in a consumption and consumer-oriented culture. He contends that a better approach is to take into careful account the full spectrum of goals and priorities when considering development.

Escobar expands his argument by demonstrating how the discourse on development is best understood as a form of *orientalism* (2005: 11). To explain, orientalism is a term introduced by Edward Said to describe how wealthy Western countries developed a pattern of viewing societies unlike theirs as lacking civilization. Since the publication of Edward Said's *Orientalism* in 1978, the term "orientalism"

---

3   https://www.youtube.com/watch?v=SpIxZiBpGU0&list=PLaCqVS0ceWqYR_ugpQfIeWivsWUBJD0jM

has been used to describe any generally patronizing attitude toward Middle Eastern, Asian, and North African societies (Mamdani 2004). Said illustrated how Western countries treat societies in the Middle East, Asia, and North Africa as static and undeveloped, regardless of their economic development or cultural achievements. The outcome is an inherently negative objectification. "Oriental" culture becomes an exoticized object of scrutiny. This is accompanied by treating "Western" society as better: it is perceived as more developed, more rational, more disciplined, and more productive. In this artificial dichotomy, the Orient is supposedly characterized by qualities such as laziness and excess hedonism (Mamdani 2004).

From the perspective of post-development (Rahnema and Bawtree 1997), the higher goals of the human development project are consistently undermined. Escobar suggests it is unrealistic to assume there is a desire to change according to the traditional growth model; some countries, such as Cuba and Bhutan, have rejected this path altogether. Other countries have alternative visions of prosperity. If development professionals use a technical vocabulary to articulate the same traditional notion that Europe and the United States are more advanced, they can hardly accomplish what the project of human development set out to do.

References

Balaam, David, and Bradford Dillman. 2011. *Introduction to International Political Economy*. Boston: Longman.

Browne, Stephen. 1997. "The Rise and Fall of Development Aid." World Institute for Development Economics and Research United Nations University Working Paper No. 143.

Escobar, Arturo. 2005. Encountering Development: The Making and Unmaking of the Third World. Princeton, New Jersey: Princeton University Press.

Kovacevic, Milorad. 2010. "Review of HDI Critiques and Potential Improvements." Human Development Research Paper 2010/33. United Nations Development Fund.

Mark, Joshua. 2018. "Silk Road," Ancient History Encyclopedia May 1, 2018 https://www.ancient.eu/Silk_Road/ accessed July 7, 2018.

Mamdani, Mahmood. 2004. *Good Muslim, Bad Muslim: America, the Cold War, and the Roots of Terrorism,* New York: Pantheon, 32.

Moyo, Dambisa. 2009. *Dead Aid: Why Aid Is Not Working and How There Is a Better Way for Africa.* New York: Macmillan.

Rahnema, Majid and Victoria Bawtree. The Post-Development Reader. Chicago: University of Chicago Press.

Sagar, Ambuj D., and Adil Najam. 1998. "The Human Development Index: A Critical Review." *Ecological Economics* 25 (3): 249–264.

Sen, Amartya. 1999. *Development as Freedom.* New York: Anchor Books.

Smith, Adam. 1934. *The Wealth of Nations.* London, England: Dent; New York: Dutton.

Readings

In "Underdevelopment and Diversity in the Global South," **Andy Baker** offers conceptual tools for understanding both the similarities and differences among countries in the global South. He provides a definition of what is meant by the phrase "less developed country" and, in alignment with the comparative interdisciplinary approach of international studies, explore the economic, social, and political aspects of underdevelopment. In this reading, you will find an important discussion of the causes of poverty, as well as explanations of important terms such as Gross Domestic Product (GDP). Baker, Andy. 2014. "Introduction: Underdevelopment and Diversity in the Global South" in Shaping the Developing World: The West, the South and the Natural World. Thousand Oaks California: Sage CQ Press.

Kennedy Odede offers a very personal perspective on the same underdevelopment discussed by Baker. Odede has a Kenyan perspective on "slum tourism," a practice in which people from the developed world see—and try to understand—poverty firsthand. His observations add valuable perspective to academic readings such as the chapter by Baker. Odede questions whether slum tourism truly promotes greater social awareness or begins to address poverty. In his experience, it turns poverty into entertainment. Odede, Kennedy. 2010. "Slumdog Tourism" The New York Times, August 9, 2010. Odede, Kennedy. 2010. "Slumdog Tourism." *New York Times*, August 10 [online], http://www.nytimes.com/2010/08/10/opinion/10odede.html.

In "The Danger of a Single Story," **Chimamanda Ngozi Adichie** explores how it is one often comes to have a single story about countries other than one's own. She writes from the perspective of a Nigerian with a middle-class childhood. In her view, stereotypes are easy to fall into, but undermine the ability to understand. Adiche, Chimamanda Ngozi. 2009. "The Danger of a Single Story" TedGlobal 2009. https://www.ted.com/talks/chimamanda_adichie_the_danger_of_a_single_story/transcript?language=en.

Image Credits

Image 5.1: Source: http://hdr.undp.org/en/content/human-development-index-hdi.
Image 5.2: Source: https://commons.wikimedia.org/wiki/File:Sustainable_Development_Goals.jpg.

Introduction: Underdevelopment and Diversity in the Global South

by Andy Baker

Nathalie of the Democratic Republic of Congo. Nathalie is an eight-year-old girl residing in the world's poorest country, the Democratic Republic of Congo. She lives in a remote rural village in the eastern province of South Kivu. Nathalie has five siblings, and another died in childbirth. Tragically, her mother also died during this stillborn birth. For the most part, Nathalie is now being raised by her aunts and a grandmother. Her family and fellow villagers grow their own food and thus have a precarious food supply. Nathalie, in particular, is malnourished. She is listless and undersized—given her height and weight, she would be mistaken for a six-year-old if in the United States.

Nathalie goes to school in a small building with forty-six other children and one teacher. In a few years, Nathalie's schooling will be done. Few girls are expected to be educated past thirteen, the age at which many of their fathers arrange for them to be married. She is absent from school quite frequently. Twice a week she misses school to walk four miles round-trip to fetch clean drinking water. (Although she struggles to carry and balance three gallons of water on her head, Nathalie's brothers stay in school and are not expected to perform this task.) Nathalie also misses school quite frequently due to illness. She sleeps with her siblings under a mosquito net given to her family by a foreign humanitarian group, but every year Nathalie still suffers a few bouts of malaria sickness—chills, fever, vomiting, and headache. Even when in school, malnourishment complicates her ability to pay attention. Despite the schooling, Nathalie cannot read a simple text.

Nathalie's province has been troubled by war for years. Marauding bands of rebels, some of them from neighboring Rwanda, are known to sweep through the provinces' villages, stealing supplies, ransacking homes, and raping women and girls. Nathalie's village has been spared from the violence, yet she knows about the potential threat from adult villagers. They are debating whether to abandon the village and move to a refugee camp that would be a twelve-hour walk through thick forest and over muddy roads. The prospect terrifies Nathalie, as she has never been more than ten miles from her village. Despite the ongoing violence and potential threat in the province, Nathalie has never seen a Congolese soldier or police officer.

Priya of India. Dharavi, a neighborhood in the city of Mumbai (India), is considered by some to be Asia's largest slum. About the size of a large U.S. college campus, Dharavi has 1 million residents. Many of the homes in Dharavi are small wooden shacks with dirt floors that become muddy, like the unpaved streets outside, during the heavy rains of the summer monsoon. Few have toilets, so public restrooms are shared by hundreds of families. To avoid the wait at these latrines, some neighbors put their waste in a bag that is then hurled onto the street or nearby creek—so-called flying toilets. The neighborhood is seen by many as unsafe, and few parents allow their children to go outside after dark.

Priya is a twenty-eight-year-old Dalit woman who moved to Dharavi from a small rural village when she was six. Her parents had just died and her new caretakers, her aunt and uncle, moved with her to the city in search of better economic opportunities. Priya dropped out of school to marry around the age of sixteen and has since birthed three daughters. She works as a maid for a middle-class family and gets paid in cash the equivalent of US$22 per month. Her husband works a steadier manufacturing job, earning US$54 per month, but every day he endures an hour-long commute on crowded trains. Once off the train, he has to compete with hundreds of other commuters to hail an auto rickshaw to carry him the last two kilometers. On these combined wages, Priya's family rarely lacks for food, although their diet is not incredibly diverse or rich in protein. Still, their income is not always sufficient to cover other expenses for items such as medicine, the family cell phone, train tickets, and entertainment for the girls. To supplement, Priya occasionally borrows money at about 15 percent monthly interest from a grocer who owns a small store down the street, and she remains indebted to him. She also keeps some extra savings in a bag under her bed, holding it for health emergencies or her daughters' weddings.

Priya's house contains two rooms—one bedroom for Priya, her husband, and oldest daughter; and a second multipurpose room with a stove, dining table, TV, and couches where everyone else sleeps. This includes an unrelated single man who pays them US$11 per month in rent. The home does have electricity, but it draws from an illegal hookup that is potentially unsafe and not monitored by the utility company. Although Priya's home is meager, she is concerned about losing it. The Mumbai municipal government, which Priya voted against in the last election, would like to develop the area with modern housing, infrastructure, and amenities. If this development project occurs, a family like Priya's, which simply built its home without first securing ownership of the land beneath it, might have to leave Dharavi without receiving any compensation for its lost residence. While the government promises to give each dispossessed family a small flat (about 300 square feet) in the redeveloped neighborhood, Priya is doubtful. Without proof of ownership, there are no guarantees, and with no real sense of their future in Dharavi, Priya's family is hesitant to ever improve their home.

Cheng of China. With a sense of foreboding, Cheng looks over his sixteen-year-old son's shoulder as he works on the family computer. His son is filling out applications for admission to some of the top universities in China. He is a talented student who attends an elite private prep school, but Cheng silently worries about his son's chances for admission. A year earlier, Cheng became an unlikely environmental activist and critic of local officials in the Chinese Communist Party. He thinks that, in having doing so, he may have derailed his son's educational aspirations. Cheng fears that the government could covertly keep the boy out of top schools.

Cheng's entry into Chinese politics was sudden and unexpected. After all, he is a forty-two-year-old computer engineer whose salary affords his three-person family an apartment in a luxury high-rise complex, a car, a flat-screen television, a personal computer, and other modern amenities. Such comforts are not usually a recipe for political dissidence, but Cheng became a vocal critic of the ruling party when its environmental policy hit home. Cheng lives on the outskirts of the city of Wuxi near the shores of Lake Tai, long known as a haven for fishermen and, because of its natural beauty, tourists. Lake Tai in recent decades has become a hotbed of manufacturing activity. Local political officials encouraged industry as a means to raise the region's gross domestic product, and it dramatically boosted their tax revenues and the region's economic living standards. However, the boom around Lake Tai came with a dramatic cost, one that spurred Cheng's political activity: environmental degradation. Lake Tai is now heavily polluted. The thousands of chemical factories on its shores dump toxic industrial waste into its waters. Most fish and many other aquatic species have died off along with the lake's attraction to potential tourists. Most notoriously, the lake periodically experiences algal blooms, or overgrowths of toxic algae that literally turn the lake a fluorescent green color and emit a noxious odor that can be detected up to one mile away.

During one algal bloom, Wuxi's tap water turned yellowish-green and became undrinkable. Residents who showered in it smelled for the rest of the day. Cheng and other citizens queued for hours at shopping malls to buy bottled drinking water, which quickly became very expensive and was ultimately rationed by store owners. At nearly the same time, Cheng's mother died from cancer, a condition he suspected was caused by toxins in the city's water, food, and air. In response to both incidents, Cheng decided to organize small meetings with family and friends and even one street protest against pollution. He also investigated nearby factories to determine who was dumping waste, informing local political officials of his findings in the hopes that they might shut down or at least enforce regulations against polluting factories. His complaints were ignored and, in actuality, he has been followed and verbally intimidated by police. Cheng has kept his job, but he fears for his son's academic future.

Defining the Developing World

What do an African peasant girl, an Indian maid, and a Chinese software engineer have in common?[1] At first glance, seemingly very little. Nathalie and Priya are poor, yet Cheng leads a comfortable middle-class lifestyle. Nathalie is often hungry, but Priya and Cheng are not. Cheng resides in an authoritarian country, Priya lives in a democracy, and Nathalie lives in a place where the government has virtually no presence at all. Nathalie is rural, Priya is urban, and Cheng is suburban. Their very different life experiences would seem to undermine any attempt to lump them or the countries in which they live together, and yet Nathalie, Priya, and Cheng are united in the fact they are all residents of the developing world. Not all of them are poor themselves, but their lives are shaped by the fact that they live in a less developed country.

Naming the Developing World

A developing or **less developed country** (LDC) is one in which a large share of the population cannot meet or experiences great difficulties in meeting basic material needs such as housing, food, water, health care, education, electricity, transport, communications, and physical security For a society, the state of experiencing these deprivations is called **underdevelopment**, and the gradual process of shedding them is called development. Less developed countries are different from developed countries like the United States, since U.S. citizens have a relatively high average income and are largely able to meet basic needs. In sum, whether or not a country is defined as less developed depends on material factors of an economic and social nature.

The use of these terms and classification scheme is not always straightforward. The term "developing country" itself is imperfect because, as a descriptor, it is often inaccurate. Many poor countries are not developing. For example, Nathalie's DR Congo has become less prosperous, not more so, over the last fifty years. The notion of a less developed country is thus more accurate because it does not imply economic progress, yet even this seemingly innocuous term has its critics. In particular, the word "developed" offends some who see it as betraying a sense that rich countries and their peoples are more evolved, perfected, and superior to underdeveloped ones.

Other commonly used labels for poor countries also have shortcomings. Two are "global South" or just "the South." These terms make use of the geographical fact that the wealthiest countries are in the northern hemisphere with poorer countries to their south: Latin America is to the south of the United States, Africa and the Middle East are south of Europe, and the poorer regions of Asia are south of industrialized Russia. Like the others, these terms are imperfect. For example, wealthy Australia and New Zealand are among the southernmost countries of the world. Moreover, these terms obfuscate the classification issue by using a locational label for what is an economically and socially defined category of countries.

Another term frequently used is "Third World." French anthropologist Alfred Sauvy coined the term in 1952 to give identity to the many countries that, during the Cold War, were not formally allied with either the wealthy capitalist First World countries of the West (meaning the U.S. and Western Europe) or the Second World communist countries of the East. Thus, at its inception, the term Third World had a political and not an economic or social meaning. However, since the world's nonaligned countries also tended to be non-industrialized, the term eventually took on the economic meaning that has stuck to this day Few users of the term today realize that some of today's so-called Third World nations, most notably China, were not originally classified as such. Because of this inaccuracy, along with the fact that many dislike the term because it implicitly ranks the quality of countries on a scale from one to three, "Third World" is largely avoided in this textbook. In the end, although each of the terms has its flaws and slightly divergent connotations, this textbook uses "less developed countries," "LDCs," "developing countries," "underdeveloped countries," "global South," and "South" interchangeably.

Delineating the Developing World

The map inside this book's front cover identifies the world's developing countries. Those classified as something other than less developed are shaded in gray. LDCs are colored by the five geographical regions that comprise the developing world: East Asia and the Pacific, Latin America and the Caribbean, the Middle East and North Africa, South Asia, and sub-Saharan Africa. To provide a point of contrast, information for the traditionally defined developed countries will often be described and summarized as the "High-income OECD" category. (The Organisation for Economic Co-operation and Development, or OECD, is an international organization that has included only rich countries since its inception in 1961.)[2] As is clear from the map, the vast majority of countries are less developed, and in fact about 80 percent of humanity resides in an LDC. Underdevelopment is thus much more prevalent than prosperity as a context of the human experience.

Furthermore, a large minority of humans are themselves impoverished. Many experts treat US$2 per day as the global poverty line, and anyone below US$1.25 per day is classified as extremely poor. In 2008, about 2.5 billion people, or 35 percent of the world's population, were below the poverty line, and 18 percent of humanity, or about 1.2 billion people, were below the extreme poverty line. As a region, South Asia has the largest number of these global poor, although sub-Saharan Africa stands as the world region with the highest share of its population below the extreme poverty line. Table 5.1.1 summarizes some of these economic and poverty statistics for each of the six world regions.[3]

The simple label "less developed" disguises a vast array of prosperity levels throughout the developing world. To better illustrate this diversity, Map 5.1.1 places LDCs into one of three categories based on the average economic living standards of their populations. The four categories are delineated by levels of gross national income (GNI) per capita. GNI per capita, along with the closely related gross domestic product (GDP) per-capita statistic, is the most commonly used measure of a country's overall economic prosperity (See Understanding Indicators: Measuring Prosperity with Gross Domestic Product.) For a given country, it can be thought of as the average citizen's income. According to the World Bank, low-income countries have an annual GNI per capita of US$995 or less. At this cutoff, the average citizen has an income of about US$3 per day Lower-middle-income countries have average incomes between US$996 and US$3,945, or about US$3 and US$10 per day, respectively. Upper- middle-income countries are between US$3,946 and US$12,195. In contrast, high-income or developed countries are those with an average annual income greater than US$12,196. Map 5.1.1 makes it clear that less developed countries

Table 5.1.1. Poverty and Income Statistics in Six World Regions

Region	Average Income	Percentage and Number Living in Poverty	Percentage and Number Living in Extreme Poverty
East Asia and the Pacific	US$2,720	33 percent (640 million)	14 percent (240 million)
Latin America and the Caribbean	**US$6,860**	**12 percent (68 million)**	**6 percent (34 million)**
Middle East and North Africa	US$3,380	14 percent (45 million)	3 percent (10 million)
South Asia	**US$964**	**71 percent (1.1 billion)**	**36 percent (575 million)**
Sub-Saharan Africa	US$1,100	69 percent (560 million)	48 percent (390 million)
High-Income OECD	**US$40,000**	**<1 percent**	**<1 percent**

Source: Compiled from World Development Indicators, 2008, http://data.worldbank.org/data-catalog/world-development-indicators.

Notes: Average income is GNI per capita, Atlas method. Percentage and number living in poverty are those < US$2 per day. Percentage and number living in extreme poverty reflects those < US$1.25 per day.

Map 5.1.1. Developing Countries by Average Economic Living Standards

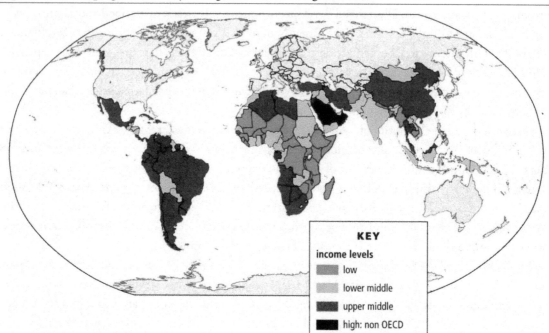

Source: Modified by author from data at the World Bank, World Development Indicators, http://data.worldbank.org/data-catalog/world-development-indicators.

span everything from the many low-income countries of sub-Saharan Africa to numerous upper-middle income countries scattered throughout all five regions.

As indicated by these maps, this textbook does not include the countries of the former Soviet Union among its contents. These former members of the Second World have economic and social characteristics that are distinct from the traditionally defined less developed countries. In particular, they became independent countries in 1991 (much more recently than virtually all LDCs), with higher levels of industrialization, equality, educational attainment, and life expectancy than standard LDCs. To be sure, many still have major pockets of poverty and social underdevelopment, giving them some shared characteristics with less developed countries. On most grounds, however, they are treated as a case apart. Throughout the book, readers will find data on LDCs and developed countries contrasted in tables and figures. In some figures, case study countries and some developed countries are labeled to make comparisons easier. A list of these country code labels is in the books Appendix.

Economic, Social, and Political Characteristics

Given its diversity, the developing world defies simple summary. Few individuals in the developing world actually match the horrific images—such as the naked, starving child with the bloated belly or the illiterate child soldier—that are often seen in Western media and characterize many Westerners' notions of life in the developing world. Still, there are certain economic, social, and political commonalities that characterize most developing countries and that distinguish them from developed ones. [...]

Economic Characteristics

To say that LDCs tend to have relatively high rates of poverty or low per-capita GDPs is merely a starting point in describing their economies and economic characteristics. Another defining economic feature of the developing world is low productivity In any given day, a typical person in the developing world produces fewer goods and services of value than does an average person in the developed world. Indeed, asking why a country is poor is nearly equivalent to asking why it is not productive: "Prosperity is the increase in the amount of goods and services you can earn with the same amount of work."[4] This is why gross domestic *product* is such a popular proxy for prosperity.

It is important to point out that, in describing people in the developing world as less productive, they are not being characterized as inherently lazy or deficient. It is not personal ability or effort but people's surroundings—the general characteristics of the economies in which they live—that largely determine how productive and thus how wealthy they are. The importance of economic context is most evident in the fact that, worldwide, a person's country of residence is more than three times as important for determining their income than are all of their individual characteristics, including innate ability and effort.[5] Rich countries have the technologies and institutions in place that make their citizens' efforts highly productive. For example, most of the things that make successful U.S. engineers rich are well beyond their making: the schools they attended, the banks that gave them loans for their education, the companies that hired them, the many customers rich enough to afford their services, the roads they use to get to work, the computer and telecommunications technologies they use at their work, the police force and legal system that protect their ownership of their earnings and home, and so on. In contrast, Nathalie and her family from this chapter's opening stories remain poor because, despite working hard to grow food and collect water, they toil in a context that does not provide them with these things. They lack modem farming equipment, roads and security to transport crops to markets, good schools, banks from which to borrow, a pool of well-off potential customers, and, of particular import to Nathalie's productivity, a clean water tap nearby

Another feature of economies in the developing world is poor **infrastructure**, a term that refers to the facilities that make economic activity and economic exchange possible. Infrastructure is generally divided into four sectors: transport, communications, energy, and water. Roads, telephones, electricity, and indoor plumbing are all examples of infrastructure. The opening vignettes to this chapter provide numerous examples of poor infrastructure in the developing world. Priya's husband wriggles onto a crowded train every morning and often cannot hail a rickshaw to complete his journey Priya lives on muddy streets, has no toilet, and must use an illegal electricity hookup. Throughout India, only two-thirds of the population even has access to electricity Nathalie lives far from any paved roads and has never seen a telephone. In her country, there are less than 2,000 miles of paved roads, and less than 20 percent of the population has a telephone.[6] Cheng is deeply affected by the polluted drinking water in his city, and China has some of world's most polluted freshwater sources.

As another economic characteristic, a large portion of economic activity in LDCs is concentrated in the primary sector, which is largely comprised of farming activities, and in unskilled labor. Less than 5 percent of the workforce in developed countries is in agriculture, yet in LDCs the amount is typically far greater than this. The vast majority of Nathalie's compatriots reside, like her, in rural areas and farm small plots of land for survival. The same applies to more than 40 percent of the Chinese and Indian populations. For those who do not work in agriculture, unskilled labor in the secondary (manufacturing) or tertiary (services) sectors is likely. As a maid, Priya provides manual labor in the services sector and her husband, as a factory worker, in the secondary sector. Skill-oriented jobs and economic activities that require a high degree of specialization and education are rarer in LDCs than in developed countries.

Finally, less developed economies have large informal sectors. The informal sector is comprised of economic activity that occurs outside the monitoring and legal purview of the government. Between 30 percent and 60 percent of all economic activity in most LDCs takes place in the informal sector.

MEASURING PROSPERITY WITH GROSS DOMESTIC PRODUCT
Understanding INDICATORS

A set of indicators all closely related to **gross domestic product (GDP)** contains the most widely used and recognized yardsticks of a country's prosperity. This includes the GNI per-capita figures used by the World Bank to classify countries into the groups reported in Map 5.1.1. Roughly speaking, a country's GDP for a given year is the total value added in the production of goods and services by all residents of that country, and the value of a good or service is determined by its price in the local currency. (GNI differs only in that it also includes income earned by citizens from assets or jobs they have abroad.) Dividing the total GDP by population size yields the GDP per-capita measure, which is the total value produced by the average citizen in the relevant year. GDP per capita is the most widely used measure of a country's average level of material well-being. Scholars convert GDP per-capita figures that are denominated in local currency to U.S. dollars (using the prevailing exchange rate) to make international comparisons of well-being more straightforward. In turn, a final adjustment that facilitates crossnational comparison of these dollar amounts is the purchasing power parity (PPP) fix. A dollar goes farther in a country with a low cost of living, so, to better measure its average level of material prosperity, its raw GDP per capita figures can be adjusted upward to reflect the greater purchasing power of a dollar in its economy. In the end, of the various indicators within the GDP family, the GDP per capita at PPP measure allows for the most informative crossnational comparisons of citizens' well-being and will be frequently used in this book.

All that said, the heavy reliance on GDP-related measures to gauge human well-being has generated a number of criticisms. First, GDP equates the value of an economic activity or product to its price and thus does not accurately gauge its worth to quality of life. GDP excludes the many activities that contribute to a sense of fulfillment and purpose but that have no market price: volunteer activity, time spent with one's family, leisure activities, physical and mental wellness, intellectual fulfillment, political freedoms, happiness, cultural belonging, social connectedness, natural beauty, clean air, personal efficacy, and so on. Meanwhile, GDP gives value to many things that do not enhance quality of life. For example, traffic jams (which increase the demand for gasoline), rising crime (which raises demand for lawyers and security personnel), threats to national security (military hardware), natural disasters (construction materials and services), unnecessary medical procedures (health equipment and doctors), and environmental catastrophes (cleanup services) all boost GDP.

Second, GDP overlooks the sustainability of production. For instance, politicians incentivized to grow short-term GDP figures have repeatedly created bubble economies driven by unsustainable debt that eventually implode in recession or depression. Similarly, it ignores what is destroyed in the production process. GDP makes no accounting for the depletion of natural resources used in production or for their availability to future generations. Environmental damage, greenhouse gas emissions (unless they are priced), and deaths caused by modern technologies are unaccounted for. As one example, the conversion of tropical rain forest to agricultural land by felling trees boosts a country's GDP since it makes the land more economically productive, yet this has devastating consequences for the local and global environment

Finally, GDP per capita is indifferent to equality—that is, how dispersed the gains from production are around the average income. Decreases in inequality do not register as higher GDP, and GDP figures grow even when much of the newfound wealth accrues to the wealthy. Subsequent chapters in this book will introduce inequality measures and raise alternatives to GDP.

Despite its shortcomings, why is GDP per capita so widely used as a measure of prosperity?

What might be some better ways to measure human wellbeing than GDP?

In developed countries, where this percentage ranges from the single digits to the teens, governments register, regulate, and tax most businesses, workers, and major assets. In doing so, governments can provide a variety of benefits and services to citizens. Priya's story provides three examples of informality and its costs. First, she is paid at her maid job in cash, or under the table. This means that she receives none of the side benefits, such as an eventual retirement pension or unemployment insurance, that are typically offered workers in developed countries. Also, since her workplace is unregulated, there are no safety standards or rules against her dismissal in the event of illness or pregnancy. In India, an estimated 80 percent of nonagricultural jobs are informal.[7] Second, Priya's ownership of her home is neither recognized nor protected by the government. She thus has no means to protect this asset from theft, damage, or expropriation by other citizens or by the government itself. Third, Priya relies on informal channels to manage her cash flow. Priya stashes money in her house, making it susceptible to loss, theft, and depreciation through inflation. She also borrows from a nearby storekeeper at a very high interest rate. In India, less than 10 percent of the poor have formal bank accounts, and the average annual interest rates they pay on loans are more than five times the rates on offer in the developed world.[8]

Table 5.1.2. Economic Characteristics in Six World Regions

Region	Paved Roads (As a percentage of all roads)	Share of Labor Force Working in Agriculture	Size of the Informal Sector (As a percentage of total economy)
East Asia and the Pacific	30.7 percent	39.6 percent	32.3 percent
Latin America and the Caribbean	**22.5 percent**	**14.3 percent**	**41.2 percent**
Middle East and North Africa	75.2 percent	27.2 percent	28.0 percent
South Asia	**53.9 percent**	**53.5 percent**	**33.2 percent**
Sub-Saharan Africa	18.8 percent	65.0 percent	40.8 percent
High-Income OECD	**79.7 percent**	**3.3 percent**	**3.3 percent**

Sources: Data on paved roads and labor force compiled from World Development Indicators, 2004–2009, http://data. worldbank.org/data-catalog/world-development-indicators; informal sector from Friedrich Schneider, Andreas Buehn, and Claudio E. Montenegro, "Shadow Economies All over the World," *World Bank Policy Research Working Paper*, no. 5326 (2010).

Table 5.1.2 illustrates some of these features of less developed economies by summarizing information by world region about infrastructure (paved roads as a percentage of all roads), the primary sector (share of labor force working in agriculture), and informality (share of economic activity that is informal).

Social Characteristics

Underdevelopment is more than just an economic characteristic. Social underdevelopment is also a common feature in the global South. A society with poor social development fails to deliver educational and health amenities to large shares of its population. The systematic exclusion and disempowerment of major groups is also an aspect of social underdevelopment.

In the area of health, LDCs fall short of developed countries on a long list of indicators. Life expectancies are shorter, as deaths from diseases that are easily curable or preventable in the West are more common. Recall that both Nathalie and Priya had parents who died at a relatively young age. Moreover, Nathalie herself contracts malaria a few times year, a disease that children in the West almost never get. All told, average life expectancy is only in the high forties in DR Congo and the midsixties in India. Infant mortality rates are also higher. Again, the tragedy of Nathalie's sibling, who died at birth, attests to this. Nearly one in six children die before their fifth birthday in the DR Congo, and in India the figure is one in seventeen. Furthermore, nearly one woman in twenty dies in childbirth in the DR Congo. Even in China, where average life expectancies and infant mortality rates are closer to Western standards, the poor quality of the environment poses an ongoing health threat.

Moreover, in LDCs, levels of educational attainment and the quality of schooling tend to be lower, while literacy rates are often higher. Nathalie has little hope of being educated past primary school. What she is able to attain is of low quality, as she is in a classroom with more than forty children and can herself barely read. In DR Congo, only about one half of children complete primary education, and a third of adults are illiterate. Similarly, Priya did not complete secondary school in India, where only a minority of people do so. The same is true in China, Cheng's advanced degree notwithstanding.[9]

Table 5.1.3. Social Characteristics in Six World Regions

Region	Infant Mortality Rate	Rural Population with Improved Sanitation	Urban Population with Improved Sanitation	Female Literacy Rate	Male Literacy Rate
East Asia and the Pacific	17.0	57 percent	76 percent	91 percent	97 percent
Latin America and the Caribbean	**16.2**	**59 percent**	**84 percent**	**91 percent**	**92 percent**
Middle East and North Africa	26.1	59 percent	80 percent	68 percent	84 percent
South Asia	**48.3**	**28 percent**	**59 percent**	**50 percent**	**73 percent**
Sub-Saharan Africa	69.4	23 percent	42 percent	55 percent	72 percent
High-Income OECD	**4.6**	**99 percent**	**99 percent**	**100 percent**	**100 percent**

Source: Compiled from World Development Indicators, 2010, http://data.worldbank.org/data-catalog/world-development-indicators.

Notes: Infant mortality rate is death per 1,000 live births.

Social exclusion based on group status is also a common characteristic of underdevelopment in LDCs. Various forms of gender discrimination are particularly pernicious in many parts of the global South. Nathalie, not her brothers, is expected to fetch water and miss school because of it. She will also have a limited say over who her eventual marriage partner is. Cheng's only child is a son in a country where many parents strongly prefer sons to daughters and are willing to have sex-selective abortions to achieve this goal. Moreover, rural dwellers also tend to suffer higher degrees of exclusion than city dwellers in LDCs. Worldwide, about 75 percent of those living in extreme poverty are residents of rural areas, even though less than 60 percent of LDC residents are rural.[10] Health and educational services, as well as infrastructure, are much less likely to reach rural areas than urban ones. Although urban slums such as Priya's Dharavi are often portrayed as the context for developing world poverty, Nathalie's rural reality is a much more common setting for the global poor.

Table 5.1.3 illustrates some of the social deficits that exist between rich and less developed countries. It reports regional averages for indicators of health (infant mortality), the social exclusion of rural populations (rural/urban gap in access to sanitation facilities), and gender discrimination (female/male gap in literacy).

Political Characteristics

Providing broad characterizations of the political systems of the less developed world is more difficult than describing its economic and social characteristics. After all, the very term "less developed" refers to an economic and social state of being, not a political one. Still, there are some tendencies that make political systems in LDCs different on average from those in developed countries. The most important is that **political regimes**—that is, the set of rules that shape how a society is governed—tend to be more authoritarian and less democratic than regimes in developed countries. The developed countries of Europe and North America are democracies with free and fair elections, alternations in power among competing political parties, and legal protections of basic civil rights and liberties. In contrast, many of the top political leaders throughout the developing world are not selected through free and fair elections, nor do they uphold and respect their citizens' fundamental civil and political rights. All told, only about forty percent of LDCs are democracies, and virtually all of the political systems of the Middle East, as well as many in Africa and Asia, are authoritarian, including Cheng's China. Even in the LDCs where democracy does prevail, such as Priya's India, it is likely the case that the country became a democracy only in recent decades. By comparison, most Western countries have been democracies for nearly a century or more.

LDCs also experience more political instability than developed countries. Political instability exists when there is high uncertainty about the future existence of the current political regime. Wholesale changes in the political regime happen with some frequency in the developing world. Events that fall slightly short of this—widespread protest, political assassinations, terrorism, armed insurgencies, frequent turnover of the chief executive, failed efforts to change the government through illegal means (*coup d'état* attempts)—but that nonetheless indicate that the existing regime is under threat are also more prevalent in the developing world. The violence propagated by the armed bands in Nathalie's DR Congo is one indicator of political instability. By contrast, in the democracies of the developed world, alternations in power occur through election-based competition, and regime change and political violence are rare.

Another feature of LDC political systems is that they tend to have lower state capacity. State capacity is the degree to which a state is able to successfully and efficiently carry out its designated responsibilities and provide high-quality public goods and services. For example, many governments in LDCs are entirely ineffective at providing a safe environment for their citizens to live in. Recall that Nathalie has never seen a police officer or Congolese army soldier, despite the fact that she lives in a war-stricken province. Priya worries about safety because her city is deficient in preventing crime and lacks a legal system that can prosecute criminals. At the extreme, low state capacity can manifest as complete state failure, in which a state has no presence or ability to govern at all in most of its territory.

Finally, the vast majority of today's LDCs are former colonies. Colonialism is the governing of a territory by individuals and institutions from outside the territory, with the colony being the territory that is governed by foreigners. In the early 1500s, Spain and Portugal colonized much of Central and South America, commencing a five-hundred-year era of Western imperialism during which European powers took and held much of the non-Western world as their colonial possessions. Great Britain, France and the Netherlands were the other major Western colonizers during this era. Most of Africa, Asia, and the Western Hemisphere fell under Western colonial rule at various points during the era, which did not completely end until the decolonization of Africa in the 1960s and 1970s. For example, parts of Priya's India were colonized by various European powers—Netherlands, Denmark, France, Portugal, Great Britain—in the sixteenth and seventeenth centuries, and colonial rule of the entire Indian subcontinent was centralized under the British in the nineteenth century until Indian independence in 1947. Nathalie's DR Congo was colonized by King Leopold II of Belgium and then Belgium itself starting in the late 1800s, and European powers occupied many of the cities in Cheng's China during the nineteenth century.

Table 5.1.4. Political Characteristics in Six World Regions

Region	Democratic Countries	Failed and Successful Coups Since 1946	Average Government Effectiveness Score*
East Asia and the Pacific	8 (of 16)	57	−.02
Latin America and the Caribbean	**19 (of 24)**	**130**	**−.06**
Middle East and North Africa	2 (of 18)	68	−.42
South Asia	**3 (of 7)**	**29**	**−.23**
Sub-Saharan Africa	19 (of 48)	226	−.82
High-Income OECD	**30 (of 30)**	**13**	**1.33**

Sources: Data on countries that are democratic is compiled from Polity IV Project: Political Regime Characteristics and Transitions, 1800–2010, www.systemicpeace.org/polity/polity4.htm; failed and successful coups, Monty Marshall and Donna Ramsey Marshall, "Coup D'État Events 1946–2011," Center for System Peace, http://www.systemicpeace.org/inscr/CSPoupsCodebook2011.pdf; government effectiveness, World Governance Indicators, 2011, http://info.worldbank.org/governance/wgi/index.asp.

2.5 is least effective and +2.5 is most effective

Table 5.1.4 illustrates a number of these political features by contrasting regional averages on three political indicators: regime type (percentage of countries that are democracies), political instability (number of failed and successful coups), and state capacity (government effectiveness score assigned by the World Bank).

A Brief History of Economic Development

When looking at all of human history, the existence of less developed parts of the world is actually a rather recent occurrence, since modern economic growth and a set of more developed countries emerged just 250 years ago. A brief overview of this history helps put modern development and underdevelopment into context.

The Pre-Industrial Eras

Homo sapiens as a species has existed in its modern physiological form for about 200,000 years. For the first 190,000 (or 95 percent) of those years, humans lived as hunter-gatherers in small bands of a dozen to a few dozen people. Hunter-gatherers lived by foraging for edible plants, hunting live animals, and nomadically moving from place to place when food sources in one area became exhausted. The distribution of well-being across the human population was extremely equitable, as most food findings were shared within bands and there were no technologies or assets such as machinery or homes to make some bands wealthier than others.

Around 10,000 years ago, a variety of **agricultural revolutions**, defined as the invention and dissemination of farming, occurred in different pockets of the world and ushered in the Neolithic Era. The domestication of plants and animals enabled humans to exert greater control over the production of food. This increased food yields dramatically and freed up a minority of individuals in each society to take up professions—such as priest, merchant, engineer, inventor, soldier, politician, or artist—that did not directly involve food production. Farming also tied people to particular plots of land, removing the need for nomadism and leading to sedentary societies. The first civilizations (Sumerian, Egyptian, Indus Valley) were stable settlements whose emergence was made possible by the agricultural revolution. The emergence of new specializations and the associated division of labor, along with variations in productivity across different farmers, introduced wealth inequalities into the human experience.

After the agricultural revolution spread to most human societies, economic experience remained defined by and fixed to agriculture for millennia. Up until the late 1700s, the vast majority of individuals worldwide were small-time farmers. Many were peasants engaged strictly in subsistence agriculture, growing themselves what they and their families ate and rarely, if ever, having a surplus to sell to others. Even in the most advanced civilizations of the 1700s, such as those of Europe and China, nonfarmers comprised at most 20 percent of the population. Average living standards, especially in comparison to modern ones, were very low. Famine was common, and even in times of plenty most people ate a nutrition-poor and undiversified diet. Most humans died of highly curable (by today's standards) infectious diseases or malnutrition in their thirties. Housing was primitive, with entire families sharing sleeping quarters and often, if fortunate enough to not sleep on a dirt floor, a single bed. Cities did not have underground sewage and indoor plumbing, so human waste ran everywhere in urban centers. Neither people nor information moved faster than horses could carry them, and individuals rarely travelled from their city or town. By the early 1700s, the ratio of average income in the world's richest societies to the world's poorest was a modest three to one.[11] In a sense, everyone yet no one lived in the developing world. In other words, all humans lived in poor societies, yet because there was no developed world to speak of, there was no *less* developed world to speak of.

The Industrial Revolution

These conditions began to change very gradually in a few societies with the advent of the **Industrial Revolution** in the late eighteenth century. The Industrial Revolution ushered in a new stage in economic history, the era of "modern economic growth," which has only been in existence for the last 0.1 percent of human history. This was not the first time that human economic activity grew more productive, but it was the first time that growth was so rapid and sustained. To illustrate, world GDP growth between 1500 and 1820 was .04 percent per year, but from 1820 to 1992 it was 1.21 percent per year.[12] Beginning first in Great Britain and then spreading to other parts of Western Europe and the United States, the Industrial Revolution rose out of a variety of inventions and small improvements to existing technologies that replaced human and animal labor with inanimate machine power. In other words, vast improvements in economic productivity were driven by the improvement and rapid accumulation of **physical capital**, the machines and factories that can be used to produce goods and services. Engines driven by steam and fossil fuels powered machines that could carry out menial tasks and create consumer products such as cotton clothing in a fraction of the time that it had taken previously. The advent of telegraph and railroad technology dramatically increased the speed of transport. Incremental technological advances in farming, such as better plows, seeding tools, and fertilizers, boosted annual crop yields and created surpluses that farmers could sell to others. These advances also freed up former farmers to move to cities and work in manufacturing or service jobs that were wholly unrelated to food production. Improvements in medical knowledge and the increasing availability of education for the masses led to dramatic improvements in **human capital**—the skill, knowledge, and health of the labor force.

Thus began a long and steady economic divergence between the West and the rest of the world. This divergence created the gap, still in existence today, between the rich countries that initially adopted the technologies and organizational features of the Industrial Revolution and the less developed countries that did not until much later. Figure 5.1.1 depicts an example of this divergence by showing the trend between 1800 and 1950 in GDP per capita of one of these early Western developers: the United States.[13] Its trend is shown in comparison to GDP per-capita trends in the three countries that were the subject of this chapter's opening vignettes: China, DR Congo, and India. The figure depicts quite clearly the

Figure 5.1.1 The Economic Divergence between the West and the Global South, 1800–1950

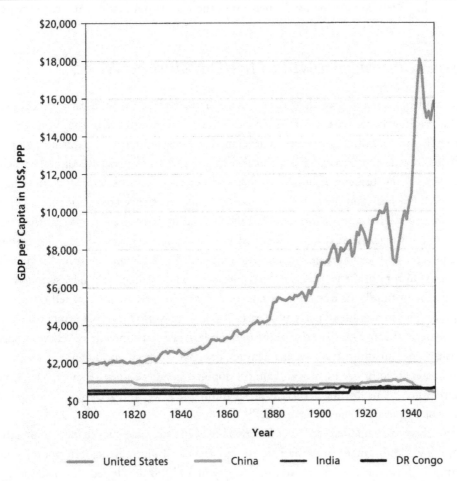

Source: Data compiled from Gapminder, www.gapminder.org/.

severity of the divergence. The United States did have a tiny head start as of 1800, but by any modern standards it was a poor country, with roughly the GDP per capita that African countries Cameroon or Senegal have today. A US$1,000 gap between the United States and China in 1800 grew into a $6,000 one by 1900, and by 1950 it was a US$15,000 gap. The United States, along with a small number of other Western countries, left the rest of the world behind between 1800 and 1950. In doing so, the West created not just the developed world but a lagging less developed world. During these 150 years, the ratio of incomes in the richest to poorest countries had grown from about three to one to about forty to one.

This bifurcation between a wealthy developed world and a set of relatively poor less developed countries and colonies persisted until the 1950s. To be sure, some industrialization and catching up did occur among non-Western nations before then. After 1870, Eastern Europe (including Russia/Soviet Union), parts of Latin America (Argentina, Brazil, and Mexico), parts of the Middle East, and Japan began developing a manufacturing base. Given their late starts, however, they still lagged well behind Western living standards in 1950, with average incomes typically less than US$2,500 per year. Economically speaking, it is only a slight oversimplification to say that the world featured two camps in 1950: a wealthy West comprising just 20 percent of the world's population, and the very poor rest of the world.

Modern Economic Growth in the Developing World

After 1950, modern economic growth finally occurred in many of the countries that had been left behind by the Industrial Revolution. Many have grown as fast as or even faster than the West during this era, complicating the simple distinction between developed and developing world. This wave of progress has been much more widespread in its geographical scope than the Industrial Revolution, reaching most of the non-Western 80 percent of humanity that had been left behind. Countries throughout Latin America, the Middle East, Southeast Asia, and East Asia have experienced dramatic increases in GDP per capita and average livelihoods. Most began the 1950s mired in desperate poverty, yet the vast majority of countries in these regions today have developed at least a minimal industrial base, lowered their rates of extreme poverty, and seen average incomes rise well past US$2,500 per person. As one scholar puts it, "Never in the history of the world have the incomes of so many people risen by so much over such a prolonged period of time."[14] The fraction of humanity living in extreme poverty fell from well over 50 percent in the 1950s to around 18 percent by early 2013,[15] and world GDP per capita rose from US$21 13 in 1950 to over US$10,000.[16] The size of the middle class, defined as people who have enough income to meet basic needs and afford at least some luxuries, has risen in every world region. By some measures, it has more than tripled in size in Asia and almost doubled in Africa since 1990.[17] Today, according to public health expert Hans Rosling, "There is no such thing as a 'we' and a 'they,' with a gap in between. The majority of people are living in the middle."[18]

To be sure, this wave of modern economic growth has been extremely uneven in its timing throughout the developing world. It ranges from the East Asian "Tigers" of Hong Kong, Singapore, South Korea, and Taiwan, which skyrocketed from extreme poverty in 1950 to developed world status by 1980, to

Figure 5.1.2. Average Incomes in Six Countries, 1950–2009

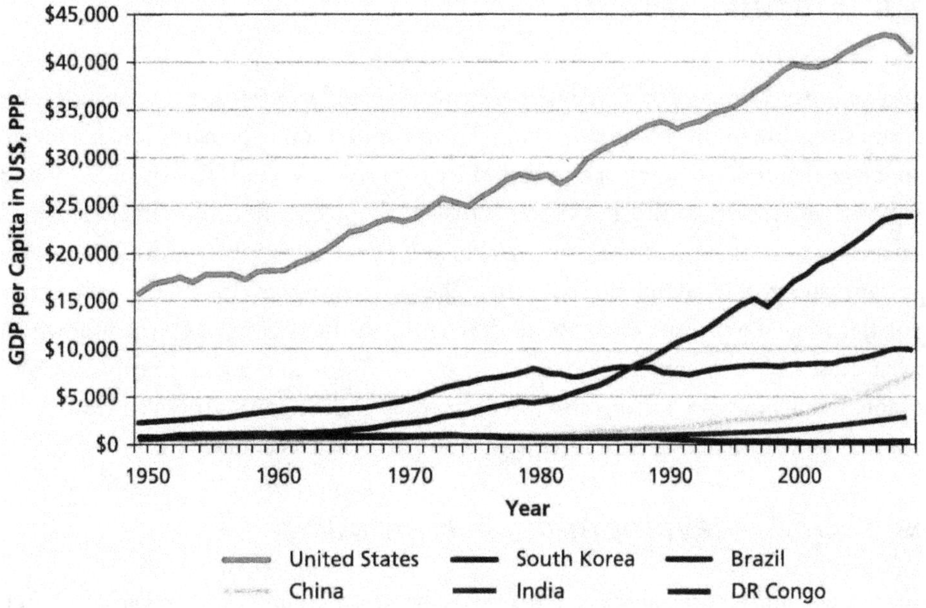

Source: Data compiled from Gapminder, vwww.gapminder.org/.

much of sub-Saharan Africa, where most economies have shown signs of life only in the last decade. In between these two extremes lies a myriad of patterns. For example, Latin America and much of the Middle East enjoyed rapid industrial growth in the first three decades following World War II, only to collapse into economic stagnation for two decades before re-emerging in the new millennium. In sharp contrast, giants China and India were late bloomers, beginning their dramatic and ongoing economic expansions in the late 1970s and early 1980s. As a result of this unevenness, the developing world now features a much more diverse array of living standards than it did in the 1950s. Figure 5.1.2 exemplifies this diversity and some of these regional patterns by showing the post-1950 trends in prosperity levels for the four countries of Figure 5.1.1 plus two more, Brazil and South Korea.

Figure 5.1.2 demonstrates that living standards have improved outside the West since 1950, but it also exemplifies the large and ongoing gap between the West and the South. The West itself continued to grow during this time period, and its head start as of 1950 was vast, accrued over nearly two centuries. Figure 5.1.2 depicts how far China, even after three decades of blazing economic growth, would have to go to ever catch up with the per-person incomes of the United States. Moreover, as exemplified by the DR Congo case, some LDCs have experienced little to no growth since 1950. Extremely poor countries, which economist Paul Collier categorizes as the "bottom billion,"[19] are almost exclusively in Africa, although they also include Afghanistan, Haiti, Myanmar, and North Korea. Because of these laggards, the ratio in incomes of the richest and poorest countries has ballooned to more than one hundred to one.

Goals and Organization: Who or What Causes Global Poverty?

This textbook has two primary goals. The first is to provide readers with a rich description of political, economic, and social life in the developing world. **Description** means the narration of a piece of reality to create an image and understanding of it in the reader's or listener's mind. To that end, this book defines and portrays various features of the global South that distinguish it from the developed world, giving empirical data—that is, facts, histories, summaries, and other observable information—that capture many important aspects of less developed countries. The second goal is to lay out the various explanations for why global income inequalities exist. Stated differently, the book focuses on the following question: Who or what caused less developed countries to be poor? This is thus a goal of **explanation,** meaning argumentation about how one factor causes or influences another one. Any well-reasoned argument about why and how a particular factor causes another one is called a **theory**.

Causes of Underdevelopment: A Framework

Many readers might consider social science theories to be overly complicated and abstract. In fact, however, people engage in theoretical thinking about cause and effect all the time. Consider the following example. In 1948, its year of independence from Japanese occupation, Korea had a GDP per capita of just US$660. In 1960, its year of independence, Nathalie's DR Congo had a higher GDP per capita of US$870. By 2009, however, South Korea had a GDP per capita that was sixty-seven times that of DR Congo's. Why did this reversal of economic fortunes occur? Even if they know little about South Korea and DR Congo, most people can surely think of some plausible possibilities to answer this "why" question. Perhaps there is something about the countries' natural resources, leadership, climate, culture, or treatment by foreign powers that caused the difference in average wealth to emerge. The many plausible answers to this question about cause and effect are examples of theory.

The West, the South, or the Natural World?

Decades of scholarship on economic growth and global poverty have yielded a huge number of theories about why global poverty and inequalities between wealthy and poor nations exist and persist. Scholars from numerous disciplines—economics, sociology, anthropology, political science, geography, history, genetics, archaeology, physiology—have weighed in on this important question, blaming poverty on everything from tropical diseases to the International Monetary Fund. To give readers some means to navigate this complex scholarly terrain, this book provides an easy-to-remember, threefold scheme for categorizing and understanding the various theoretical answers to the question "who causes global poverty?": the West, the South, and the natural world. This categorization is evident in the parts of this book and throughout most of the end-of-chapter case studies.

Did the West cause today's LDCs to be poor? This category attributes underdevelopment in the developing world to international factors, namely those originating in foreign lands and particularly in Western Europe and the United States. Through the international slave trade, colonialism, globalization, and foreign aid, the West may have created disadvantageous contexts for development or even directly impoverished other parts of the world. Alternatively, are factors indigenous to the South itself the cause of global wealth disparities? This category attributes underdevelopment to origins that are internal to LDCs. A large body of scholarship indicts the domestic factors that are part of an LDCs own leadership, institutions, or culture, such as economic policy, laws and customs, and degree of internal harmony. Scholarship within this tradition attributes underdevelopment to factors such as undemocratic rule, corruption, weak property rights, a failure to embrace free markets, poor treatment of women and girls, civil conflict and violence, state failure, and rigid identities. Finally, do factors in the natural world that are beyond human design explain global poverty? This third and final category attributes economic underdevelopment to various aspects of geography and the physical environment, such as climate, topographical terrain, land productivity, and disease burdens.

Thinking about Theory

In thinking about theory and the threefold classification scheme, several points are in order. First, readers should reject the temptation to conclude that a single theory could successfully explain why some countries are rich and why some are poor. Reality is far too complex to be monocausal. For example, the brief history of economic development given in the preceding section might indicate that the question of why some countries are poor today may need two answers. A country is an LDC today because (1) it was left behind by the rise of the West during the first Industrial Revolution and (2) it has failed to rise as quickly as South Korea in the post-1950 world. The causes behind the relative distancing in livelihoods between European and non-European countries in the nineteenth century may be different from those behind the failure of so many countries to replicate the South Korean skyrocket since 1950.

Second, readers must understand that no amount of logic, empirical observation, or sophisticated statistical manipulation will ever prove a theory to be accurate or inaccurate. There are always overlooked theories and factors that could be the source of the true impact on development. For example, one could attribute the differences in prosperity levels between DR Congo and Great Britain to the fact that one was colonized and the other was a colonizer. But the differences between the two do not stop there. Great Britain is far from the equator while DR Congo is on it. Great Britain is a democracy while DR Congo is not. Great Britain has a relatively unified national identity while DR Congo does not. In fact, the list of differences between the two is infinite, so isolating the one or ones exerting the causal effect is impossible. For this reason, readers should remember the adage that "correlation does not mean causation." That said, readers can certainly use their own logical and observational faculties to arrive at conclusions about which theories are more or less useful for understanding the causes of underdevelopment.

Third, as with any categorization, the threefold classification has oversimplifying imperfections. For example, one explanation for Africa's underdevelopment is that many of its countries have numerous ethnic groups that struggle to cooperate and get along. This seemingly attributes the cause of underdevelopment to the South, meaning a domestic factor. However, African countries' high levels of ethnic diversity are partly due to the West, an international factor. European colonizers drew the national borders for much of the continent and, in doing so, grouped together many ethnic groups that had little in common. Rather than getting overly hung up on whether the theory attributes ultimate cause to the South or the

West, readers should simply think of the classification as a useful, albeit imperfect, tool that helps them more easily understand and remember the various theories.

Finally, this textbook will avoid the emotion and ideology that often accompanies debates over the causes of underdevelopment. In practice, millions find there to be much at stake in considering what causes global poverty, since the answer allows one to assign blame for impoverishment. For example, Zimbabwe's president Robert Mugabe repeatedly deflects blame for his leadership of a country in economic decline by retorting that the roots of its plight lie in the past sins of Western colonialism and white-minority rule. *Shaping the Developing World* stays away from explicitly making moral judgments or casting blame for global inequality, although readers will surely see the ethical implications of many of the theories discussed within. [...]

WHY IS THE DEMOCRATIC REPUBLIC OF CONGO THE POOREST COUNTRY ON EARTH?

In 2009, the average citizen in Nathalie's Democratic Republic of Congo (DR Congo, named Zaire from 1971 to 1997) had a living standard equivalent to what a U.S. citizen would have if he or she had one dollar per day to spend. This figure made it the poorest country in the world and one of just a few countries whose living standards were lower in 2009 than they were in 1960.[20] All of this is true despite the fact that DR Congo is huge (it has the largest land area in sub-Saharan Africa), rich in topography (it contains the world's second-largest rain forest and Africa's second-largest river), and flush with natural resources (such as diamonds and the coltan found in most cell phones). In contrast, South Korea is tiny and poor in resources, and it was actually poorer than DR Congo as recently as 1950. Why is DR Congo, a country with so much potential, still so poor? Table 5.1.5 provides some possible answers that are described in greater detail in this case study.

Table 5.1.5. **Development Comparison: DR Congo and South Korea**

Indicator	DR Congo	South Korea
GDP per capita at PPP	US$329	US$27,541
Population in poverty	73 percent	<1 percent
Human Development Index	.286 (187th of 187)	.897 (15th of 187)
Number of languages spoken	216	1
Persons removed through Atlantic slave trade	~1,000,000	0
Malaria cases per 100,000 people, 2008	37,400	8

Sources: Data compiled from the World Bank, World Development Indicators, 2011 and 2008, http://data.worldbank.org/sites/default/files/wdi-final.pdf; United Nations Development Programme, "Human Development Report 2010," http://hdr.undp.org/en/reports/global/hdr2010/, 161; Human Development Index; Ethnologue.com; and Nathan Nunn, "The Long-Term Effects of Africa's Slave Trades," *Quarterly Journal of Economics 123*, no. 1 (2008): 139–176.

The South: Kleptocracy and Cultural Fragmentation

One set of possible answers lies in DR Congo's political leadership and the makeup of its society. Five years after achieving independence from Belgium in 1960, a young army officer named Joseph Mobutu staged a successful coup d'état, installed himself as president, and remained in that post for thirty-two authoritarian years. In office, Mobutu, who later renamed himself Mobuto Sese Seko, established one of history's most corrupt regimes. Telling his state employees to "go ahead and steal, as long as you don't take too much,"[21] Mobutu himself followed only the first half of this advice. Mobutu treated state funds as his own, amassing numerous palaces and mansions, many of them in Europe and some containing 14,000-bottle wine cellars, discotheques, private zoos, and doors so large they required two men to open.[22] Mobutu also allowed his political allies and even opponents to participate in the plundering, keeping them quiescent to his otherwise ineffective rule. The means to wealth were not talent and hard work, but theft of taxpayers. Under Mobutu, DR Congo was considered the paradigmatic kleptocracy: government by those who steal.

In the interest of Zaireanizing (based on his own renaming of the country) the economy and redistributing wealth from rich Europeans to Zairian citizens, Mobutu expropriated most of Zaire's foreign-owned firms and farms. He kept some of the assets for himself and handed the rest over to Zairian public officials and other elites. In doing so, he gave agricultural land and factories to individuals not because they were good farmers or industrial managers, but because they were his cronies or leaders of important ethnic groups. Economic collapse ensued. Prices rose and store shelves emptied because the new Zairian owners of many businesses were not knowledgeable or motivated enough to produce goods and services as productively as the previous owners. The experience of expropriation discouraged future investment by both foreigners and Zairians. Between 1973 and Mobutu's departure from power in 1997, the average income in Zaire declined by two-thirds.[23]

Another possible answer resides in the fact that Congolese citizens have little cultural unity. Congolese identify more with their ethnolinguistic group, of which there are more than 200, than they do with the DR Congo as a nation. There is little sense of national identity, with one set of scholars characterizing this reality by saying that "there is no Congo."[24] This lack of national unity has erupted on multiple occasions into violent conflict that has had major economic costs. For example, in its first year of independence in 1960, the Congo nearly disintegrated into four separate countries as three different regions declared their desire to secede based largely around ethnic nationalist claims. The Congolese military eventually reunified the country, but only after years of violently repressing secessionist movements. More recently, the Great War of Africa (1998–2003), the deadliest war in the continent's history, occurred on Congolese soil when militias claiming to represent disillusioned ethnic groups in the far eastern corner of the country attempted to march all the way to Kinshasa in the west to overthrow the incumbent government. The conflict killed an estimated 5.4 million people and cost billions of dollars in lost economic activity.[25]

The West: Stolen Aid, Colonial Abuse, and Slavery

Mobutu didn't act alone. The West was complicit in his kleptomania. Soon after independence, Belgian and American intelligence agencies intervened in Congolese politics to place Mobutu in power over

U.S. president Ronald Reagan (1981–1989) shakes hands with Zairian president Mobutu Sese Seku (1965–1997). Despite years of inept and corrupt rule that impoverished his country, Mobutu received millions of dollars of aid from the United States and other Western countries simply because he was seen as a reliable bulwark against communism in Africa.

other leaders they saw as overly friendly with the Soviet Union. In the interest of keeping him in power, the United States, France, and Belgium granted Mobutu $1 billion in foreign aid over his thirty-two-year reign. Much of the aid ended up in the Swiss bank accounts of Mobutu and his cronies, and little was actually used to build schools, health clinics, or roads. The International Monetary Fund also extended eleven different bailout packages to Mobutu despite knowing that the funds were misused and ineffective in stabilizing the economy. Amidst all of the theft, U.S. president Ronald Reagan still called one of the world's most prolific thieves a "voice of good sense and goodwill"[26] because of his anticommunist credentials.

The West's complicity in the plundering of the Congo did not begin with the rise of Mobutu. Nearly a century earlier, King Leopold II of Belgium initiated his own reign of terror in pursuit of what he called "a slice of this magnificent African cake."[27] a reign that stripped the Congo of natural and human resources. Leopold, who from 1885 to 1908 was the sole proprietor of the Congo Free State, implemented a brutal system of forced labor and looting that contemporary Arthur Conan Doyle called "the greatest crime which has ever been committed in the history of the world."[28] Leopold's armed security apparatus, the Force Publique, required native villagers to periodically collect quotas of ivory or rubber that were to be exported to Europe. These quotas grew increasingly difficult to fill as nearby reserves became exhausted, and when villagers failed to deliver a sufficient amount, they were whipped with strips of dried hippopotamus hide, had their hands chopped off, or were shot. Under Leopold, the population loss in the Congo Free State was an estimated 10 million people, and countless hours of labor and troves of natural resources were taken with no compensation in return.[29] Leopold and other Western powers even bear some responsibility for DR Congo's deep cultural divisions, since it was they who arbitrarily drew the colony's and eventual country's borders. In drawing the borders at a conference in Berlin in 1884 and 1885, they consulted no Congolese citizens and paid no heed to the fact that they were uniting more than 200 different ethnic groups into a single political territory.

Leopold's colonization of the Congo actually occurred relatively recently in the history of Western contact with Africa. As early as the sixteenth century, men and women residing in the territory that is today the DR Congo were being captured and shipped across the Atlantic Ocean to become slaves in the New World. Slavery was devastating not just to the slaves themselves, but also to the African economies they left behind. Between 1400 and 1900, almost 1 million people were forcibly removed from DR Congo territory.[30] This dramatic loss of human capital, often in exchange for destructive or unproductive imports such as guns, clothing, and seashells, kept the Congo's population growth and density low in a time when other continents were developing urban centers that were hotbeds of productivity and innovation.

The Natural World: Geography and the Resource Curse

Clearly, Congolese leaders and Western personnel have ravaged both the human and natural richness of the Congo for centuries. Is it possible, however, that all of this exploitation has been just a sideshow to the ultimate cause of DR Congo's poverty: geography? Beneath its flashy mineral wealth and its superlative river and rain forest lies a natural context that is quite detrimental to economic growth. First, DR Congo is wet—too wet: The country has more thunderstorms than any other in the world. This leeches its soils of their minerals and makes it impossible to grow all but a few crops.[31] Second, DR Congo has the largest number of malaria cases in the world, and the disease is the country's top killer. Like Nathalie, the average Congolese child suffers six to ten bouts *every year*, and 200,000 Congolese children die from malaria annually.[32] At best, children heal in a few days, yet during that time they have missed out on some schooling, may have drawn an adult caregiver away from work, and have probably experienced stunted brain development.

Nature also may have cursed the DR Congo in a more paradoxical way: by endowing it with a vast quantity of valuable natural resources. Although perhaps done with some hyperbole, one source estimated DR Congo's underground mineral wealth to be worth $24 trillion, more than the GDP of the United States or Europe.[33] DR Congo has the world's largest deposits of cobalt and coltan, and it also contains rich underground stores of copper, diamonds, and gold. Yet instead of making it rich, this mineral wealth fuels DR Congo's recurring political violence and conflict. For example, some of the violent domestic and foreign militias that marauded DR Congo during the Great War looted mines and used their booty to finance themselves. Moreover, few investors care to build up DR Congo's industrial base since its minerals sector remains so attractive.

All told, this long list of explanations for DR Congo's underdevelopment would seem to suggest that the odds are stacked heavily against the world's poorest country. But are all of these explanations equally plausible, and is the picture this one-sided? This textbook will give readers the tools to answer these questions in an informed way.

Thinking Critically about Development

- Some of these explanations for the Congo's poverty focus on individual people, such as Mobutu and Leopold, while others stress broader and less ephemeral factors, such as culture and climate. Generally speaking, which approach is more convincing? In other words, if the Congo had had better-intentioned colonial and postcolonial leaders, would it be wealthier today, or would this not have mattered?

- Is it possible that some of the factors listed as sources of Congolese underdevelopment, such as deaths from malaria and number of languages spoken, are more a *result* of underdevelopment than its cause?
- Is the comparison between DR Congo and South Korea useful for deciphering cause and effect, or are the countries too different from one another?

KeyTerms

agricultural revolution
description
explanation
gross domestic product
human capital
Industrial Revolution
infrastructure
less developed country (LDC)
physical capital
political regime
theory
underdevelopment

Suggested Readings

Banerjee, Abhijit Vinayak, Roland Benabou, and Dilip Mookherjee, eds. *Understanding Poverty.* New York: Oxford University Press, 2006.

Cameron, Rondo, and Larry Neal. *A Concise Economic History of the World: From Paleolithic Times to the Present.* New York: Oxford University Press, 2002.

Hochschild, Adam. *King Leopold's Ghost: A Story of Greed, Terror, and Heroism in Colonial Africa.* Boston: Mariner Books, 1998.

Smith, Dan. *The Penguin State of the World Atlas.* 9th ed. New York: Penguin Books, 2012.

Wrong, Michela. *In the Footsteps of Mr. Kurtz: Living on the Brink of Disaster in Mobutu's Congo.* New York: Harper Collins, 2001.

World Bank *Atlas of Global Development.* 3rd ed. Washington, D.C.: World Bank Publications, 2011.

Web Resources

Gapminder, www.gapminder.org
World Development Indicators, http://data.worldbank.org/sites/default/files/wdi-finaI.pdf
World Banke-Atlas, http://data.worldbank.org/products/data-visualization-tools/eatlas

Notes

1. The individuals described in these vignettes are fictional, although parts of their stories are compiled from nonfictional accounts.
2. All six of these regional categories are the designations used by the World Bank. The need to specify high income, instead of just OECD, is that the OECD now contains a few countries, such as Chile and Mexico, which are not strictly high income and are part of the traditionally defined developing world. The need for designating OECD, instead of just high income, in the category label is that there are a number of countries that only recently reached high-income status, such as Kuwait and Saudi Arabia, which are not part of the traditionally defined West or developed world. In the end, the "high-income OECD" category contains the following countries: Australia, Austria, Belgium, Canada, Czech Republic, Denmark, Estonia, Finland, France, Germany, Greece, Hungary, Iceland, Ireland, Italy, Israel, Japan, South Korea, Luxembourg, the Netherlands, New Zealand, Norway, Poland, Portugal, Slovak Republic, Slovenia, Spain, Sweden, Switzerland, United Kingdom, and United States.
3. Unless otherwise noted, regional averages are calculated using country population weights.
4. Matthew Ridley, *The Rational Optimist: How Prosperity Evolves* (New York: Harper, 2010), 22.
5. Branko Milanovic, *The Haves and the Have-Nots: A Brief and Idiosyncratic History of Global Inequality* (New York: Basic Books, 2011).
6. Statistics in this paragraph are from the World Bank's World Development Indicators, http://data.worldbank.org/data-catalog/world-development-indicators.
7. International Labour Organization, "Key Indicators of the Labour Market Dataset," October 16, 2011, www.ilo.org/empelm/what/WCMS_114240/lang--en/index.htm.
8. Abhijit V. Banerjee and Esther Duflo, *Poor Economics: A Radical Rethinking of the Way to Fight Global Poverty* (New York: Public Affairs, 2011), 160.
9. All data in this and the previous paragraph are from Gapminder, www.gapminder.org.
10. World Bank, *World Development Report 2008: Agriculture for Development,* 2007, http://siteresources.worldbank.org/INTWDR2008/Resources/WDR_00_book.pdf, 45.
11. William J. Bernstein, *The Birth of Plenty: How the Prosperity of the Modern World Was Created* (New York: McGraw-Hill, 2004), 193.
12. Angus Maddison, *Monitoring the World Economy, 1820–1992.* (Paris: OECD, 1995).
13. Gapminder, www.gapminder.org.
14. Milanovic, *The Haves and Have-Nots,* 102.
15. Benjamin M. Friedman, *The Moral Consequences of Economic Growth* (New York: Vintage Books, 2006), 354.
16. Charles Kenny, *Getting Better: Why Global Development is Succeeding—and How We Can Improve the World Even More* (New York: Basic Books, 2011), 19.

17. "The New Middle Classes Rise Up," *The Economist,* September 3, 2011, 23–24.

18. "Technology Quarterly: Making Data Dance," *The Economist,* December 11, 2010, 25.

19. Paul Collier, *The Bottom Billion: Why the Poorest Countries Are Failing and What Can Be Done About It* (Oxford: Oxford University Press, 2007).

20. Gapminder, www.gapminder.org.

21. MichelaWrong, *In the Footsteps of Mr. Kurtz: Living on the Brink of Disaster in Mobutu's Congo* (New York: Harper Collins, 2001), 99.

22. Ibid.

23. World Bank, World Development Indicators, http://data.world-bank.org/sites/default/files/wdi-finaI.pdf.

24. Jeffrey Herbst and Greg Mills, "There Is No Congo," *Foreign Policy,* March 18, 2009.

25. Joe Bavier, "Congo War-Driven Crisis Kills 45,000 a Month: Study," Reuters, January 22, 2008, www.reuters.com/article/2008/01/22/us-con go-democratic-death-idUSL2280201220080122.

26. Heidi Kriz, "When He Was King," Metroactive: News and Issues, May 22–28, 1997, http://www.metroactive.com/papers/metro/05.22.97/cover/mobutu-9721.html.

27. Thomas Pakenham, *The Scramble for Africa: White Man's Conquest of the Dark Continent from 1876 to 1912* (New York: Random House, 1991), 22.

28. Adam Hochschild, *King Leopold's Ghost: A Stoiy of Greed, Terror, and Heroism in Colonial Africa* (Boston: Mariner Books, 1998), 271.

29. Ibid.

30. Nathan Nunn, "The Long-Term Effects of Africa's Slave Trades," *Quarterly Journal of Economics* 122, no. 1 (2008): 139–176.

31. World Lightning Map, Geology.com, http://geology.com/articles/lightning-map.shtml.

32. Miriam Mannak, "Malaria Remains Biggest Killer," Inter Press Service, October 27, 2008, http://www.ipsnews.net/2008/10/health-dr-congo-malaria-remains-biggest-killer/.

33. M. J. Morgan, "DR Congo's S24 Trillion Fortune," The Free Library, February 1, 2009, www.thefreelibrary.com/DR+Congo's+S24+trillion+fortune.-a0193800184.

United Nations Human Development Report 1990

People are the real wealth of a nation. The basic objective of development is to create an enabling environment for people to enjoy long, healthy and creative lives. This may appear to be a simple truth. But it is often forgotten in the immediate concern with the accumulation of commodities and financial wealth.

Technical considerations of the means to achieve human development—and the use of statistical aggregates to measure national income and its growth—have at times obscured the fact that the primary objective of development is to benefit people. There are two reasons for this. First, national income figures, useful though they are for many purposes, do not reveal the composition of income or the real beneficiaries. Second, people often value achievements that do not show up at all, or not immediately, in higher measured income or growth figures: better nutrition and health services, greater access to knowledge, more secure livelihoods, better working conditions, security against crime and physical violence, satisfying leisure hours, and a sense of participating in the economic, cultural and political activities of their communities. Of course, people also want higher incomes as one of their options. But income is not the sum total of human life.

This way of looking at human development is not really new. The idea that social arrangements must be judged by the extent to which theypromote "human good" goes back at least to Aristotle. He also warned against judging societies merely by such things as income and wealth that are sought not for themselves but desired as means to other objectives. "Wealth is evidently not the good we are seeking, for it is merely useful and for the sake of something else."

Aristotle argued for seeing "the difference between a good political arrangement and a bad one" in terms of its successes and failures in facilitating people's ability to lead "flourishing lives". Human beings as the real end of all activities was a recurring theme in the writings of most of the early philosophers. Emmanuel Kant observed: "So act as to treat humanity, whether in their own person or in that of any other, in every case as an end withal, never as means only."

The same motivating concern can be found in the writings of the early leaders of quantification in economics—William Petty, Gregory King, François Quesnay, Antoine Lavoisier and Joseph Lagrange, the grandparents of GNP and GDP. It is also clear in the writings of the leading political economists—Adam Smith, David Ricardo, Robert Malthus, Karl Marx and John Stuart Mill.

But excessive preoccupation with GNP growth and national income accounts has obscured that powerful perspective, supplanting a focus on ends by an obsession with merely the means.

Recent development experience has once again underlined the need for paying close attention to the link between economic growth and human development—for a variety of reasons.

- Many fast-growing developing countries are discovering that their high GNP growth rates have failed to reduce the socioeconomic deprivation of substantial sections of their population.
- Even industrial nations are realizing that high income is no protection against the rapid spread of such problems as drugs, alcoholism, AIDS, homelessness, violence and the breakdown of family relations.
- At the same time, some low-income countries have demonstrated that it is possible to achieve high levels of human development if they skilfully use the available means to expand basic human capabilities.
- Human development efforts in many developing countries have been severely squeezed by the economic crisis of the 1980s and the ensuing adjustment programmes.

Human development is the process of enlarging people's choices

Recent development experience is thus a powerful reminder that the expansion of output and wealth is only a means. The end of development must be human well-being. How to relate the means to the ultimate end should once again become the central focus of development analysis and planning.

Table 5.2.1. GNP per Capita and Selected Social Indicators

Country	GNP per Capita (US$)	Life Expectancy (Years)	Adult Literacy (%)	Infant Mortality (per 1.000 live births)
Modest GNP per Capita with High Human Development				
Sri Lanka	400	71	87	32
Jamaica	940	74	82	18
Costa Rica	1,610	75	93	18
High GNP per Capita with Modest Human Development				
Brazil	2,020	65	78	62
Oman	5,810	57	30	40
Saudi Arabia	6,200	64	55	70

How can economic growth be managed in the interest of the people? What alternative policies and strategies need to be pursued if people, not commodities, are the principal focus of national attention? This Report addresses these issues.

Defining Human Development

Human development is a process of enlarging people's choices. The most critical ones are to lead a long and healthy life, to be educated and to enjoy a decent standard of living. Additional choices include political freedom, guaranteed human rights and self respect—what Adam Smith called the ability to mix with others without being "ashamed to appear in publick" (Box 5.2.1).

It is sometimes suggested that income is a good proxy for all other human choices since access to income permits exercise of every other option. This is only partly true for a variety of reasons:

- Income is a means, not an end. It may be used for essential medicines or narcotic drugs. Well-being of a society depends on the uses to which income is put, not on the level of income itself.
- Country experience demonstrates several cases of high levels of human development at modest income levels and poor levels of human development at fairly high income levels.
- Present income of a country may offer little guidance to its future growth prospects. If it has already invested in its people, its potential income may be much higher than what its current income level shows, and vice versa.

BOX 5.2.1. HUMAN DEVELOPMENT DEFINED

Human development is a process of enlarging people's choices. In principle, these choice can be infinite and change over time. But at all levels of development, the three essential ones are for people to lead a long and healthy life, to acquire knowledge and to have access to resources needed for a decent standard of living. If these essential choices are not available, many other opportunities remain inaccessible.

But human development does not end there. Additional choices, highly valued by many people, range from political, economic and social freedom to opportunities for being creative and productive, and enjoying personal selfrespect and guaranteed human rights.

Human development has two sides: the formation of human capabilities—such as improved health, knowledge and skills—and the use people make of their acquired capabilities—for leisure, productive purposes or being active in cultural, social and political affairs. If the scales of human development do not finely balance the two sides, considerable human frustration may result.

According to this concept of human development, income is clearly only one option that people would like to have, albeit an important one. But it is not the sum total of their lives. Development must, therefore, be more than just the expansion of income and wealth. Its focus must be people.

- Multiplying human problems in many industrial, rich nations show that high income levels, by themselves, are no guarantee for human progress.

The simple truth is that there is no automatic link between income growth and human progress. The main preoccupation of development analysis should be how such a link can be created and reinforced.

The term *human development* here denotes both the *process* of widening people's choices and the *level* of their achieved wellbeing. It also helps to distinguish clearly between two sides of human development. One is the formation of human capabilities, such as improved health or knowledge. The other is the use that people make of their acquired capabilities, for work or leisure.

This way of looking at development differs from the conventional approaches to economic growth, human capital formation, human resource development, human welfare or basic human needs. It is necessary to delineate these differences clearly to avoid any confusion:

- GNP growth is treated here as being necessary but not sufficient for human development. Human progress may be lacking in some societies despite rapid GNP growth or high per capita income levels unless some additional steps are taken.
- Theories of human capital formation and human resource development view human beings primarily as means rather than as ends. They are concerned only with the supply side—with human beings as instruments for furthering commodity production. True, there is a connection, for human beings *are* the active agents of all production. But human beings are more than capital goods for commodity production. They are also the ultimate ends and beneficiaries of this process. Thus, the concept of human capital formation (or human resource development) captures only one side of human development, not its whole.
- Human welfare approaches look at human beings more as the beneficiaries of the development process than as participants in it. They emphasise distributive policies rather than production structures.
- The basic needs approach usually concentrates on the bundle of goods and services that deprived population groups need: food, shelter, clothing, health care and water. It focuses on the provision of these goods and services rather than on the issue of human choices.

Human development, by contrast, brings together the production and distribution of commodities and the expansion and use of human capabilities. It also focusses on choices—on what people should have, be and do to be able to ensure their own livelihood. Human development is, moreover, concerned not only with basic needs satisfaction but also with human development as a participatory and dynamic process. It applies equally to less developed and highly developed countries.

Human development as defined in this Report thus embraces many of the earlier approaches to human development. This broad definition makes it possible to capture better the complexity of human life—the many concerns people have and the many cultural, economic, social and political differences in people's lives throughout the world.

The broad definition also raises some questions: Does human development lend itself to measurement and quantification? Is it operational? Can it be planned and monitored?

Measuring Human Development

In any system for measuring and monitoring human development, the ideal would be to include many variables, to obtain as comprehensive a picture as possible. But the current lack of relevant comparable statistics precludes that. Nor is such comprehensiveness entirely desirable. Too many indicators could produce a perplexing picture—perhaps distracting policymakers from the main overall trends. The crucial issue therefore is of emphasis.

The Key Indicators

This Report suggests that the measurement of human development should for the time being focus on the three essential elements of human life—longevity, knowledge and decent living standards.

For the first component—longevity—life expectancy at birth is the indicator. The importance of life expectancy lies in the common belief that a long life is valuable in itself and in the fact that various indirect benefits (such as adequate nutrition and good health) are closely associated with higher life expectancy. This association makes life expectancy an important indicator of human development, especially in view of the present lack of comprehensive information about people's health and nutritional status (Box 5.2.2).

BOX 5.2.2. WHAT PRICE HUMAN LIFE?

The use of life expectancy as one of the principal indicators of human development rests on three considerations: the intrinsic value of longevity, its value in helping people pursue various goals and its association with other characteristics, such as good health and nutrition.

The importance of life expectancy relates primarily to the value people attach to living long and well. That value is easy for theorists to underestimate in countries where longevity is already high. Indeed, when life expectancy is very high, the challenge of making the lives of the old and infirm happy and worthwhile may be regarded by some as an exacting task. For the less fortunate people of the world, however, life is battered by distress, deprivation and the fear of premature death. They certainly attach a higher value to longer life expectancy.

Longevity also helps in the pursuit of some of life's other most valued goals. Living long may not be people's only objective, but their other plans and ambitions clearly depend on having a reasonable life span to develop their abilities, use their talents and carry out their plans.

A long life correlates closely with adequate nutrition, good health and education and other valued achievements. Life expectancy is thus a proxy measure for several other important variables in human development.

For the second key component—knowledge—literacy figures are only a crude reflection of access to education, particularly to the good quality education so necessary for productive life in modern society. But literacy is a person's first step in learning and knowledge-building, so literacy figures are essential in any measurement of human development. In a more varied set of indicators, importance would also have to be attached to the outputs of higher levels of education. But for basic human development, literacy deserves the clearest emphasis.

The third key component of human development—command over resources needed for a decent living—is perhaps the most difficult to measure simply. It requires data on access to land, credit, income and other resources. But given the scarce data on many of these variables, we must for the time being make the best use of an income indicator. The most readily available income indicator—per capita income—has wide national coverage. But the presence of nontradable goods and services and the distortions from exchange rate anomalies, tariffs and taxes make per capita income data in nominal prices not very useful for international comparisons. Such data can, however, be improved by using purchasing-power-adjusted real GDP per capita figures, which provide better approximations of the relative power to buy commodities and to gain command over resources for a decent living standard.

A further consideration is that the indicator should reflect the diminishing returns to transforming income into human capabilities. In other words, people do not need excessive financial resources to ensure a decent living. This aspect was taken into account by using the logarithm of real GDP per capita for the income indicator.

All three measures of human development suffer from a common failing: they are averages that conceal wide disparities in the overall population. Different social groups have different life expectancies. There often are wide disparities in male and female literacy. And income is distributed unevenly.

The case is thus strong for making distributional corrections in one form or another (Box 5.2.3). Such corrections are especially important for income, which can grow to enormous heights. The inequality possible in respect of life expectancy and literacy is much more limited: a person can be literate only once, and human life is finite.

Reliable and comparable estimates of inequality of income are hard to come by, however. Even the Gini coefficient, probably the most widely used measure of income inequality, is currendy available for fewer than a quarter of the 130 countries in the Human Development Indicators at the end of this Report—and many of those estimates are far from dependable. Distributional data for life expectancy and literacy by income group are not being collected, and those available on rural-urban and male- female disparities are still too scant for international comparisons.

The conceptual and methodological problems of quantifying and measuring human development become even more complex for political freedom, personal security, interpersonal relations and the physical environment. But even if these aspects largely escape measurement now, analyses of human development must not ignore them. The correct interpretation of the data on quantifiable variables depends on also keeping in mind the more qualitative dimensions of human life. Special effort must go into developing a simple quantitative measure to capture the many aspects of human freedom.

BOX 5.2.3. WHAT NATIONAL AVERAGES CONCEAL

Averages of per capita income often conceal widespread human deprivation. Look at Panama, Brazil, Malaysia and Costa Rica in the table below. That is the order of their ranking by GNP percapita.

If the GNP figures are corrected for variations in purchasing power in different countries, the ranking shifts somewhat—to Brazil, Panama. Malaysia and Costa Rica.

But if distributional adjustments are made using each country's Gini coefficient, the original ranking reverses to Costa Rica, Malaysia, Brazil, Panama.

The average value of literacy, life expectancy and other indicators can be similarly adjusted. There is a great deal of technical literature on the subject, but the basic approach is simple. If inequality is seen as reducing the value of average achievement as given by an unweighted mean, that average value can be adjusted by the use of inequality measures. Such distributional corrections can make a significant difference to evaluations of country performance.

Country	GNP per Capita (US$) 1987	Real GDP per Capita (PPP$) 1987	Gini Coefficient of Inequality	Distribution-Adjusted GDP per Capita (PPP$)
Panama	2,240	4,010	.57	1,724
Brazil	2,020	4,310	.57	1,852
Malaysia	1,810	3,850	.48	2,001
Costa Rica	1,610	3,760	.42	2,180

Attainments and Shortfalls

Progress in human development has two perspectives. One is attainment: what has been achieved, with greater achievements meaning better progress. The second is the continuing shortfall from a desired value or target.

In many ways the two perspectives are equivalent—the greater the attainments, the smaller the shortfalls. But they also have some substantive differences. Disappointment and dismay at low performance often originate in the belief that things could be much better, an appraisal that makes the concept of a shortfall from some acceptable level quite central. Indeed, human deprivation and poverty inevitably invoke shortfalls from some designated value, representing adequacy, acceptability or achievability.

The difference between assessing attainments and shortfalls shows up more clearly in a numerical example. Performances often are compared in percentage changes: a 10-year rise in life expectancy from 60 years to 70 years is a 17% increase, but a 10-year rise in life expectancy from 40 years to 50 years is a 25% increase. The less the attainment already achieved, the higher the percentage value of the same absolute increase in life expectancy.

Raising a person's life expectancy from 40 years to 50 years would thus appear to be a larger achievement than going from 60 years to 70 years. In fact, raising life expectancy from the terribly low level of 40 years to 50 years is achievable through such relatively easy measures as epidemic control. But improving life expectancy from 60 years to 70 years may often be a much more difficult and more creditable accomplishment. The shortfall measure of human progress captures this better than the attainment measure does.

Taking once again the example of life expectancy, if 80 years is the target for calculating shortfalls, a rise of life expectancy from 60 years to 70 years is a 50% reduction in shortfall—halving it from 20 years to 10 years. That is seen as a bigger achievement than the 25% reduction in shortfall (from 40 years to 30 years) when raising life expectancy from 40 years to 50 years.

The shortfall thus has two advantages over the attainment in assessing human progress. It brings out more clearly the difficulty of the tasks accomplished, and it emphasises the magnitude of the tasks that still lie ahead.

The Human Development Index

People do not isolate the different aspects of their lives. Instead, they have an overall sense of well-being. There thus is merit in trying to construct a composite index of human development.

Past efforts to devise such an index have not come up with a fully satisfactory measure [...]. They have focussed either on income or on social indicators, without bringing them together in a composite index. Since human beings are both the means and the end of development, a composite index must capture both these aspects. This Report carries forward the search for a more appropriate index by suggesting an index that captures the three essential components of human life—longevity, knowledge and basic income for a decent living standard. Longevity and knowledge refer to the formation of human capabilities, and income is a proxy measure for the choices people have in putting their capabilities to use.

The construction of the human development index (HDI) starts with a deprivation measure (Box 5.2.4). For life expectancy, the target is 78 years, the highest average life expectancy attained by any country. The literacy target is 100%. The income target is the logarithm of the average poverty line income of the richer countries, expressed in purchasing-power-adjusted international dollars. Human development indexes for 130 countries with more than a million people are presented in the Human Development Indicators, Table 1. Those for another 32 countries with fewer than a million people are in the Human Development Indicators, Table 25.

Country Ranking by HDI and GNP

The human development index ranks countries very differently from the way GNP per capita ranks them. The reason is that GNP per capita is only one of life's many dimensions, while the human development index captures other dimensions as well.

BOX 5.2.4. CONSTRUCTING A HUMAN DEVELOPMENT INDEX

Human deprivation and development have many facets, so any index of human progress should incorporate a range of indicators to capture this complexity. But having too many indicators in the index would blur its focus and make it difficult to interpret and use. Hence the need for compromise—to balance the virtues of broad scope with those of retaining sensitivity to critical aspects of deprivation.

This Report has chosen three types of deprivation as the focus of attention: people's deprivation in life expectancy, literacy and income for a decent living standard. Each measure could have been further refined (especially by making distributional adjustments) if there had been adequate comparable data. But in the absence of such data, the focus here represents a move in the right direction—away from the narrow and misleading attention to only one dimension of human life, whether economic or social.

The first two indicators—life expectancy and adult literacy—are commonly used concepts. But the third—the purchasing power to buy commodities for satisfying basic needs—is not as well understood. The GNP figures typically used for international comparisons do not adequately account for national differences in purchasing power or the distorting effect of official exchange rates. To overcome these inadequacies, we use here the purchasing-power-adjusted GDP estimates developed in the International Price Comparison Project, a collaborative effort of the UN Statistical Office, the World Bank, EUROSTAT, OECD, ECE and ESCAP, now being expanded by USAID. And since there are diminishing returns in the conversion of income into the fulfilment of human needs, the adjusted GDP per capita figures have been transformed into their logarithms.

To construct a composite index, a *minimum* value (the maximum deprivation set equal to one) and a *desirable* or *adequate* value (no deprivation set equal to zero) had to be specified for each of the three indicators.

The minimum values were chosen by taking the lowest 1987 national value for each indicator. For life expectancy at birth, the minimum value was 42 years, in Afghanistan, Ethiopia and Sierra Leone. For adult literacy, it was 12%, in Somalia. For the purchasing-power-adjusted GDP per capita, the value was $220 (log value 2.34), in Zaire.

The values of desirable or adequate achievement were Japan's 1987 life expectancy at birth of 78 years, an adult literacy rate of 100%, and the average official "poverty line" income in nine industrial countries, adjusted by purchasing power parities, of $4,861. The nine countries are Australia, Canada, the Federal Republic of Germany, the Netherlands, Norway, Sweden, Switzerland, the United Kingdom and the United States.

The minimum and desirable or adequate values are the end-points of a scale indexed from one to zero for each measure of deprivation. Placing a country at the appropriate point on each scale and averaging the three scales gives its average human deprivation index, which when subtracted from 1 gives the human development index (HDI). [. . .].

Figure 5.2.1. GNP per Capita and the HDI

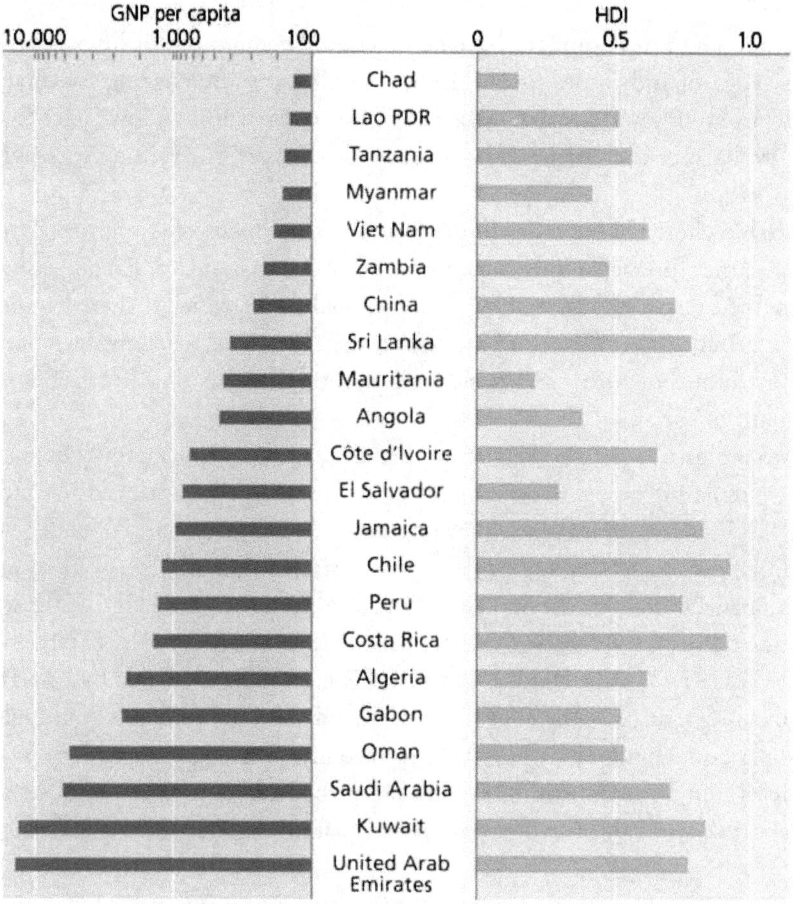

Sri Lanka, Chile, Costa Rica, Jamaica, Tanzania and Thailand, among others, do far better on their human development ranking than on their income ranking, showing that they have directed their economic resources more towards some aspects of human progress. But Oman, Gabon, Saudi Arabia, Algeria, Mauritania, Senegal and Cameroon, among others, do considerably worse on their human development ranking than on their income ranking, showing that they have yet to translate their income into corresponding levels of human development.

To stress again an earlier point, the human development index captures a few of people's choices and leaves out many that people may value highly—economic, social and political freedom (Box 5.2.5), and protection against violence, insecurity and discrimination, to name but a few. The HDI thus has limitations. But the virtue of broader coverage must be weighed against the inconvenience of complicating the basic picture it allows policymakers to draw. These tradeoffs pose a difficult issue that future editions of the *Human Development Report* will continue to discuss.

Figure 5.2.2. Ranking of Countries' GNP per Capita and HDI

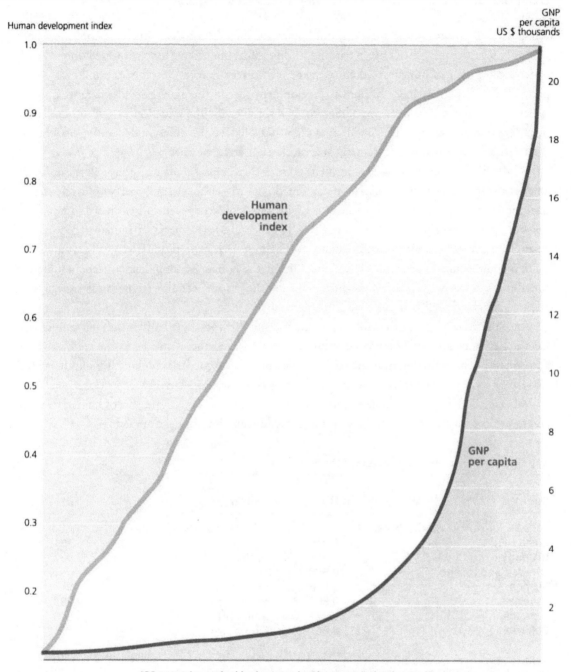

130 countries ranked by human development index (green line)
and by GNP per capita (black line)

The chart shows two separate distributions of countries. The upper curve represents their ranking according to the human development index while the lower curve shows their ranking according to GNP per capita. The two curves reveal that the disparity among countries is much greater in income than in human development. There is no automatic link between the level of per capita income in a country and the level of its human development.

BOX 5.2.5. FREEDOM AND HUMAN DEVELOPMENT

Human development is incomplete without human freedom. Throughout history, people have been willing to sacrifice their lives to gain national and personal liberty. We have witnessed only recently an irresistible wave of human freedom sweep across Eastern Europe, South Mrica and many other parts of the world. Any index of human development should therefore give adequate weight to a society's human freedom in pursuit of material and social goals. The valuation we put on similar human development achievements in different countries will be quite different depending on whether they were accomplished in a democratic or an authoritarian framework.

While the need for qualitative judgement is clear, there is no simple quantitative measure available yet to capture the many aspects of human freedom—free elections, multiparty political systems, uncensored press, adherence to the rule of law, guarantees of free speech and so on. To some extent, however, the human development index (HDI) captures some aspects of human freedom. For example, if the suppression of people suppresses their creativity and productivity, that would show up in income estimates or literacy levels. In addition, the human development concept, adopted in this Report, focusses on people's capabilities or, in other words, people's strength to manage their affairs—which, after all, is the essence of freedom.

For illustrative purposes, the table below shows a selection of countries (within each region) that have achieved a high level of human development (relative to other countries in the region) within a reasonably democratic political and social framework. [...] countries ranking high in their HDI also have a more democratic framework—and vice versa—with some notable exceptions.

What is needed is considerable empirical work to quantify various indicators of human freedom and to explore further the link between human freedom and human development.

Top 15 Countries in Democratic Human Development

Country	HDI	Country	HDI
Latin America and the Caribbean		*Middle East and North Africa*	
Costa Rica	0.916	Turkey	0.751
Uruguay	0.916	Tunisia	0.657
Trinidad and Tobago	0.885		
Mexico	0.876	*Sub-Saharan Africa*	
Venezuela	0.861	Mauritius	0.788
Jamaica	0.824	Botswana	0.646
Colombia	0.801	Zimbabwe	0.576
Asia			
Malaysia	0.800		
Sri Lanka	0.789		
Thailand	0.783		

Slumdog Tourism

by Kennedy Odede

AUG. 9, 2010
Nairobi, Kenya
Slum tourism has a long history—during the late 1800s, lines of wealthy New Yorkers snaked along the Bowery and through the Lower East Side to see "how the other half lives."

But with urban populations in the developing world expanding rapidly, the opportunity and demand to observe poverty firsthand have never been greater. The hot spots are Rio de Janeiro, Mumbai—thanks to "Slumdog Millionaire," the film that started a thousand tours—and my home, Kibera, a Nairobi slum that is perhaps the largest in Africa.

Slum tourism has its advocates, who say it promotes social awareness. And it's good money, which helps the local economy.

But it's not worth it. Slum tourism turns poverty into entertainment, something that can be momentarily experienced and then escaped from. People think they've really "seen" something—and then go back to their lives and leave me, my family and my community right where we were before.

I was 16 when I first saw a slum tour. I was outside my 100-square-foot house washing dishes, looking at the utensils with longing because I hadn't eaten in two days. Suddenly a white woman was taking my picture. I felt like a tiger in a cage. Before I could say anything, she had moved on.

When I was 18, I founded an organization that provides education, health and economic services for Kibera residents. A documentary filmmaker from Greece was interviewing me about my work. As we made our way through the streets, we passed an old man defecating in public. The woman took out her video camera and said to her assistant, "Oh, look at that."

For a moment I saw my home through her eyes: feces, rats, starvation, houses so close together that no one can breathe. I realized I didn't want her to see it, didn't want to give her the opportunity to judge my community for its poverty—a condition that few tourists, no matter how well intentioned, could ever understand.

Other Kibera residents have taken a different path. A former schoolmate of mine started a tourism business. I once saw him take a group into the home of a young woman giving birth. They stood and watched as she screamed. Eventually the group continued on its tour, cameras loaded with images of a woman in pain. What did they learn? And did the woman gain anything from the experience?

To be fair, many foreigners come to the slums wanting to understand poverty, and they leave with what they believe is a better grasp of our desperately poor conditions. The expectation, among the visitors and the tour organizers, is that the experience may lead the tourists to action once they get home.

But it's just as likely that a tour will come to nothing. After all, looking at conditions like those in Kibera is overwhelming, and I imagine many visitors think that merely bearing witness to such poverty is enough.

Nor do the visitors really interact with us. Aside from the occasional comment, there is no dialogue established, no conversation begun. Slum tourism is a one-way street: They get photos; we lose a piece of our dignity.

Slums will not go away because a few dozen Americans or Europeans spent a morning walking around them. There are solutions to our problems—but they won't come about through tours.

Kennedy Odede, the executive director of Shining Hope for Communities, a social services organization, is a junior at Wesleyan University.

CHAPTER SIX

Culture and Identity

In the prehistoric past, people formed small bands and tribes for survival. Identity derived from the band or the tribe and common needs for water, food, and shelter held it together. Many bands subdivided and reunited seasonally based on the availability of food in the natural environment. When hunting and gathering did not yield enough food for the group, bands subdivided. The more resources available, the larger the band might become. Over time, the cultivation of grain and the domestication of livestock enabled humans to form larger and more complex societies. As communities become more complex and more integrated, culture and identity remain central to how people understand the world and their ability to act in it. In this chapter, readers consider what culture and identity mean today.

The study of culture and identity has multiple disciplinary homes including anthropology, sociology, cultural studies, and psychology. Anthropologists study cultural variations and how humans make meaning from the world they live in. According to the American Anthropological Association, anthropology is "the study of what makes us human."[1] It is interesting to think that although humans need the same things to survive, the way they meet these needs varies tremendously. This is a broad field composed of four subfields, each of which applies theories to its distinctive methodologies. The fields include archaeology, biological anthropology, cultural anthropology, and linguistic anthropology. Sociology differs from anthropology in focusing on society instead of culture. While anthropology encompasses all dimensions of humanity including evolutionary origins and physiology, sociology concentrates on social relationships and the societal structures that result. Sociology provides tools that contribute to understanding social, economic, and political processes in a global context, in the words of the American Sociological Association.[2] Some sociologists have been adopting anthropology's methodology of participant observation, bringing the two fields closer together. Psychology differs from both sociology and anthropology in its object: the study of the human mind. Psychology also differs in method because it relies more heavily on the experimental method. Control over variables, measurement, and cause and effect relationships—which tend to be more experimental—are highly valued. Like anthropology and sociology, it has many subfields for considering human mental processes and behavior.

---

1   http://www.americananthro.org/AdvanceYourCareer/Content.aspx?ItemNumber=2150
2   http://www.asanet.org/topics

The topic of culture taken up in this chapter is connected to themes explored in previous chapters in a number of ways. Notably, the development of the modern state system (Chapter Two) entailed drawing borders based on power and authority more than culture or the natural environment. This process generated new tensions and conflicts among people. Colonial powers often drew political borders in a way that strengthened their political power and split the colonized people into multiple political entities. Thus, European expansion created categories of people who belonged and people for whom there were grounds (ethnic, tribal, religious) for exclusion. Ethnicity is an important part of this process (Nash 1989: 1). People of different ethnic backgrounds who previously had no need to cooperate were brought into close contact—and sometimes competition—in the state system. Uniting diverse peoples within a set of new borders brings culture and politics into dynamic tension.

Culture

The concept of culture has a deep intellectual history. Cultural theorist Raymond Williams famously noted that "culture" is one of the most complicated words in the English language (Williams 1976: 87). The word began its life referring to the cultivation of the soil, but developed many more meanings over time. As colleges and universities developed in Europe in the sixteenth century, culture came to be used to refer to the cultivation of *people* through education (OED Online n.d.). Then, in eighteenth-century Europe, culture was used as an evolutionary concept that predicted betterment and refinement. Preceding the Industrial Revolution, the concept was thought to apply only to the culture of Europeans in higher socioeconomic brackets (Beldo 2010: 145). When imperialism brought Europeans into contact with non-European peoples, however, the word culture began to encompass the varying customs of people from east to west (OED Online n.d.). The idea that peoples would change in a one-directional process that would make them more like western Europeans was heavily influenced by Herbert Spencer. Readers may be familiar with Spencer as the English philosopher, polymath, sociologist, and political theorist who was enormously influential in the Victorian era. Anthropologists rejected this notion, however, in favor of seeing culture in a more relativistic way. Cultural relativism has been praised as a basis for greater tolerance and criticized as incoherent and uncritical.

About two decades ago, anthropologists began to question whether there were ever discrete, iso-latable cultures. As mentioned in Chapter One, globalization has shown how culture is not something that is "pure" or homogeneous but rather something that is hybrid. It can be difficult to draw precise boundaries between two cultures. As you can imagine, questioning the core concept provoked a disciplinary crisis. Linguistic anthropologists suggest we think of culture as a process rather than a thing that humans possess. For better or worse, however, the word culture has remained a noun.

It is through culture that people come to categorize their experiences and assign meanings to them. In the words of Michael Herzfeld (2000: 1), culture is a form of common sense that can be studied comparatively. By common sense, he meant the set of shared and unstated assumptions that make a community tick. This includes the beliefs and practices that are accepted as true or correct without reflection or analysis.

Culture can only partially constrain one's way of interpreting the world. Empirical research on language and perception suggests that one's culture or worldview makes certain ways of interpreting and dealing with reality easier and therefore more likely than others. One way cultural diversity has been studied is through the use of color terms. The number of color terms in a culture's language varies widely from two words to hundreds of them. Scientific studies in which subjects are shown chips with colors on them demonstrate that people with few color words in their language are still able to see and make subtle distinctions between colors, whether or not there is a word in their language to describe the difference. One of the conclusions social scientists have made from this is that humans see the same reality but categorize it in different ways cross culturally. And when the categories cease to be effective, cultures evolve to encompass new ways of seeing and categorizing.

Culture is learned in a variety of ways, including enculturation, acculturation, and assimilation. Enculturation refers to the process of learning to live in the society of which one is a part. Learning takes place through both informal (watching and participating in daily activities) and formal (schools, lessons, internships) learning. How is this different from socialization? As used by sociologists, socialization refers to the process through which cultural traditions are passed from one generation to the next. Enculturation focuses on the largely unconscious and embodied processes through which infants and children learn to be adult members of their society (Nanda 1994: 133). This kind of deep learning shapes behavior that is only sometimes reflected upon. We are talking about how one moves, speaks, eats, and stands. As such, enculturation informs the attitudes that are taken as unquestionable and the behaviors that feel most natural. Eye contact provides a more specific example. In some cultures, direct eye contact is a measure of honesty and straightforwardness. In other cultures, direct eye contact is considered aggressive.

Acculturation is the process of cultural and psychological change that results from the interaction of two or more cultures (Berry 2005). Acculturation takes place in response to direct and first-hand contact, in what is often a two-way process. The effects of acculturation can be seen at individual and societal levels. At the societal level, acculturation results in changes to cultural practices and social structures and institutions. For example, is it acceptable to marry on the basis of love, or is it the practice that the family is to arrange the marriage of a couple? Another example is provided by the Sioux of North America. After horses were brought by the Spanish, the Sioux absorbed the horse into their native culture and religion. So fully was the horse integrated that it is now difficult to imagine Sioux culture without the animal.

At the individual level, acculturation means a person learns to live in a different culture. Exchange programs, internships in foreign countries, and study abroad require one to become acculturated in order to function. Acculturation may include dietary practices, habits of dress, and learning the language. Of course, not everyone acculturates in the same way. Attitudes toward one's own and other groups, as well as behavior, exhibit significant variation (Berry 2005: 704). Failing to acculturate can be the source of considerable tension. One example is provided by a Chinese exchange student who did not feel welcomed by his host family and asked to be moved to a different family. Discussion revealed the source of the misunderstanding: cold food. In the family's steady fare of cereal, sandwiches, and salads, cooked foods were sparse. For the Chinese student, cold food was a clear sign the family did not care about him. Once the family's intent to welcome him was clarified, the student felt more amenable to eating cold foods. The family understood that hot foods were the norm for their guest and made some modification to their dietary practices.

Assimilation occurs when a culture loses its distinctive attributes and its members become indistinguishable from other members of the dominant society. Assimilation is different from acculturation because it takes place not just as a result of contact, but as a result of asymmetrical power relations. Throughout history, there have been frequent attempts to compel groups to assimilate. In a 1894 speech entitled "True Americanism," Teddy Roosevelt stated that Americans have a right and a duty to insist that immigrants become like other Americans. In the first half of the twentieth century, intensive attempts were made to assimilate the tribes of North America. Children were placed in boarding schools where they were prevented from learning their native language. The children were compelled to adopt European manners, clothing, and religion. By the middle of the twentieth century, however, a strong ethos of multicultural inclusionism, created more latitude and tolerance for cultural differences.

Identity

Identity is defined as "the qualities, beliefs, etc., that make a particular person or group different from others."[3] The way one experiences identity is, however, much more complicated because of intersectionality—the fact that as individuals, people have religious, racial, ethnic, gender, and sexual identities that result in patterns of privilege and disadvantage. There are of course many kinds of identity: individual, group, social, ethnic, racial, and political to name only a few. One may speak of identity formation, identity crisis, identity politics. But what is at the core of these different types of identity?

There are two complementary aspects of identity. The first is similarity. Here, identity refers to qualities one shares with others. To provide the basis of an identity, these qualities are durable. One can be Ethiopian in Addis Ababa, Paris, or New York. The second aspect of identity is that it is a means to distinguish oneself (or one's group) from others. The ability to differentiate oneself from others, and the fact that people do this routinely, would not be possible without the first usage of identity. The two irreducible components of identity are therefore similarity and difference.

Image 6.1. Self-Identity

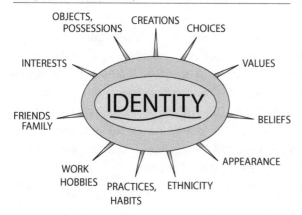

When identities are reduced to stereotypes, they may become the source of conflict. In the context of competition over scarce resources, simplified representations become exacerbated and turn into obstacles to the resolution of conflict. A central concern of contemporary social sciences with regard to identity is to understand phenomena such as xenophobia, racism, and terrorism. Understanding these phenomena would go part of the way to identifying how to overcome the beliefs and behaviors that are detrimental to a peaceful and cohesive world (Image 6.1).

---

3   Merriam Webster Dictionary, http://www.merriam-webster.com/dictionary/identity.

The Self

Have you ever seen a flier on your campus inviting you to be a subject in a psychological study? Behavioral scientists (experimental branches of psychology, cognitive science, and allied fields) have long published research based on large samples of individuals drawn from Western, educated, democratic, and relatively prosperous societies. In fact, the majority of the data are based on American undergraduates. From the psychological experimental perspective, variation across human populations was believed to be too insignificant to modify the experiment design.

The individuals taken to be representative are, however, "WEIRD" (Western, Educated, Industrialized, Rich, and Democratic) (Henrich, Heine, and Norenzayan 2010). According to Henrich et al., American college students are "outliers" in fields of spatial reasoning, moral reasoning, self-concepts, ideas of fairness, and so on. Henrich and his colleagues found that while the behavioral sciences draw on a limited demographic of the human populations, researchers in these fields tend to believe their findings to be universal. If one reads the word "humans" or "people" in a university textbook, it is likely to be based on research in which the subjects are disproportionately young, educated, and North American (2010: 63). Now, under some circumstances, there are good arguments for choosing WEIRD individuals as subjects. But for the most part, the differences are too significant to take the WEIRD individuals as illuminating of the world's population as a whole.

A brief consideration of the self will demonstrate potential differences more concretely. When asked to describe yourself, what categories would you use? Would it be according to your taste in music, your friends, or your faith? The way people describe themselves varies a great deal across cultures. While people in the Western industrialized countries are likely to describe themselves as free, autonomous, and unique individuals, people in many other parts of the world, especially societies that are less individualistic, describe themselves in terms of their social relationships. A specific example of this broad and yet significant generalization can be found by comparing Japan and the United States. Cousins's research shows that in a controlled environment, Japanese subjects used more social role and relationship statements to describe themselves while American subjects used more abstract and decontextualized psychological descriptors for themselves (1989: 124). Cousins's research suggests this is explained by divergent cultural conceptions of the self, not differences in cognitive ability.

Human beings develop different thinking styles depending on their cultural contexts. In a different experiment that focused on the reasoning styles of Chinese Americans and European Americans, subjects were asked to state which two of three objects go together: a panda, a monkey, and a banana. The respondents from Asian countries typically select the monkey and the banana. These objects relate to each other in an environment: monkeys eat bananas. The researchers suggest that their bilingual Chinese subjects organize objects in a more relational and less categorical way, whether tested in Chinese or English. The responses of Chinese from the mainland and Taiwan, as well as from Hong Kong and Singapore, were all consistent with the central finding. By contrast, the Americans with some type of European ancestry typically state it is the monkey and the panda that go together because both are animals. This reflects a less contextual and more analytical thinking style in which objects are evaluated independently of their context (Ji, Zhang, and Nisbett 2004).

These culturally conditioned styles of thinking come to shape what is considered normal. Culturally specific disorders further demonstrate important human variation. Latah is a condition in which a person is highly sensitive to being startled. When surprised, individuals with Latah may scream, curse, break into uncontrollable laughter, or have dancing movements. While Latah has been categorized as a "disorder," medical anthropologists argue that it is a normal part of Malay-Indonesian culture and not something people seek treatment for. Rather, Latah is a culturally-conditioned habit that serves as a coping strategy for stress. Anthropologists also dispute whether it is wholly involuntary. There is some evidence that individuals are conditioned to have Latah and that the responses work to distinguish classes of people (Bartholomew 1994). Another instructive example can be found in depression. Cross-cultural research provides abundant evidence that how a depressive mood, or dysphoria (sadness, hopelessness, unhappiness, lack of pleasure with things in the world and relationships), is interpreted in radically different ways around the globe. Buddhists find that taking pleasure from things of the world and social relationships is the basis of all suffering. Intentional dysphoria is prerequisite to finding peace and salvation. For Shi'ite Muslims in Iran, grief is linked to recognizing the experience of living in an unjust world. Willingness to accept dysphoria shows a person has depth of character and openness to religious experience. And while the Kaluli of Papua New Guinea place a great deal of importance on the full outward expression of grief and sadness, Balinese do not share this value. They place a higher value on exhibiting a level mood (Kleinman and Good 1985: 3).

Given such wide variability—and disagreement—about the limits of normalcy, both the field of psychiatry and international organizations such as the World Health Organization have become increasingly sensitive to how accurate understanding of differences may contribute to improving the diagnosis, classification, and treatment of disorders.

Gender

Gender is an especially significant component of selfhood, and it has undergone significant definitional transformation. In the policymaking world, the word gender became a politically correct way to refer to women. Gender is better thought of as a system. Like other identity categories, gender is a social structure that shapes both individual identities and the contexts in which they operate. As Cohn explains "gender is not simply a set of ideas about male and female people and their proper relations to each other; gender is, more broadly, a way of categorizing, ordering, and symbolizing power, of hierarchically structuring relationships among different categories of people, and different human activities symbolically associated with masculinity or femininity" (Cohn 2013: 3). In other words, just as class, race, and caste are systems of power, so too is gender.

Scholars' ideas about gender as an identity have changed significantly in the past few decades. Early Western conceptions based primarily on psychoanalytic thinking viewed the development of a gender identity as something that was a product of childhood family relationships. More recent conceptualizations of gender posit that gender is something people do, not something that they are. Judith Butler argues that instead of "having" gender identities that are established and fixed at an early age, gender is something that is produced, enacted, and performed on a daily basis in a way that is fluid (Butler 1990). In her view, there is no identity behind the behavior that is thought to be expressing a gender. Rather, it is the acts or the behavior that constitutes gender. It could be said that a stable gender is the effect, not the source of culturally shaped activities. Butler calls this conceptualization performativity.[4] Butler sees gender, and categories such as "women" and "men," as complicated by other dimensions of identity such as sexuality, ethnicity, and class.

Perspectives on the "Clash of Civilizations"

Perhaps one of the hottest and longstanding debates about culture and identity can be found in the notion that there will be a "clash of civilizations". At the end of the Cold War, Samuel Huntington projected there would be a new world order in which culture and religion would be the source of conflict. His book, *The Clash of Civilizations and the Remaking of World Order*, describes how tensions would be based not on political and ideological divisions like the ones between the United States and the Soviet Union, but on culture and religion.

> It is my hypothesis that the fundamental source of conflict in this new world will not be primarily ideological or primarily economic. The great divisions among humankind and the dominating source of conflict will be cultural .... The fault lines between civilizations will be the battle lines of the future. (1993: 22)

Huntington perceived a shift from a time when the world was divided between a set of wealthy and primarily democratic countries that took their cues from the United States, and the communist countries that took their lead from the Soviet Union. A great deal of the conflict between these the U.S.S.R. and the U.S., he points out, was acted out through less developed countries, and typically newly independent countries.

Huntington's book was important because it came to frame debates about how to think about the post-Cold War world. His thesis has been vigorously debated on a number of grounds. It also inspired a large number of books refuting the thesis and calling it a myth. Books with titles like *The Myth of the Clash of Civilizations* (Bottici 2010), and *The Fear of Barbarians: Beyond the Clash of Civilizations* (Todorov 2010) give you the flavor of the debate.

One major criticism of his thesis is methodological: the notion of "civilizations" upon which he based his argument was ill defined. The seven or eight civilizations he names treat enormous geographic areas as monolithic, closed, and homogeneous entities. The civilizations are Sinic (China, Vietnam, and Korea), Japanese, Hindu, Islamic, Orthodox, Western (centered in Europe and North America), Latin American, and African. You may notice immediately that some are named according to religion, some by continent, and others by political borders. Halliday (1996) points out that Huntington neglected the internal dynamics, plurality, and complexities of Islam and the Muslim world in particular. Thus the methodology oversimplifies and does not give adequate attention to the differences within the regions or the collaboration between them.

Huntington's position on Islam made his ideas especially controversial. In *The Clash of Civilizations*, Huntington clearly portrayed Islam as a threat to the West. He argued Islamic cultures are incapable of creating democracy, and suggested that any attempt to spread democracy to Muslim regions would

---

4   https://www.youtube.com/watch?v=Bo7o2LYATDc

end in failure. The book expresses the Machiavellian idea that differences between civilizations must be manipulated in the interests of the (threatened) West. This suggests an antagonistic way of looking at the world, influenced by political realism (studied in Chapter Two). The clash of civilizations idea assumes conflict is inevitable and is primarily motivated by fear.

A third set of criticisms has to do with the policy implications of faulty methodology and realist assumptions. Noam Chomsky suggests that Huntington framed the Islamic threat in such a way as to continue to increase defense spending, even in the absence of the Cold War. Ikenberry (1997) worried that the thesis could act as a self-fulfilling prophesy: misperceived threats create tensions that may erupt in conflict or justify interventions. These scholars suggest unfavorable policy could be the outcome of the thesis.

The approach to cultural differences taken by Lila Abu-Lughod in her well known 2002 article republished in this volume (as well as members and scholars of diaspora discussed below) are diametrically opposed. Abu-Lughod explores why there is frequently a turn to culture to explain the September 11, 2001 attacks. She argues the sudden interest in the culture and the religion of the Middle Eastern region, and the role of women distracted people from examining the history of the region and the United States' role in the development of a repressive regime. Blaming culture is not particularly useful because it takes the place of a historical and geopolitical accounting of why a situation evolves as it does. She reminds readers that the United States supported conservative groups in Afghanistan to weaken the Soviet intervention, and these groups later evolved into the Taliban. This speaks directly to the Clash of Civilizations debate. Blaming Islam misses the point that the United States had a role in creating the situation. Treating countries as separate and autonomous is misleading because foreign intervention has played an important role.

Abu-Lughod argues that "rescuing" Afghan women from the Taliban and its veiling requirement was an important part of the rhetoric surrounding the war on terror. To support her argument, she quotes First Lady Laura Bush as stating that "The fight against terrorism is also a fight for the rights and dignity of women" (US Government cited in Abu-Lughod 2002: 3). Abu-Lughod counters the First Lady's claim that Afghan women welcomed liberation by Americans by noting how presumptive and paternalistic is this stance. She recommends not using any language that describes other cultures as fundamentally alien, as Huntington does. Although head coverings were treated as symbols of Afghan women's oppression, the fact that they did not take them off when the Taliban were defeated demonstrates the meaning of various head coverings is intricately—and variably—connected to socioeconomic status, religion, gender, class, and cultural norms. (Abu-Lughod. Lila. 2002 "Do Muslim Women Really Need Saving? Anthropological Reflections on Cultural Relativism and its Others" American Anthropologist Vol 104, Issue 3, 783–790.)

Flows: Diaspora

While culture and identity are certainly contextual, this is not to insist that they are necessarily rooted in a specific place. Readers may be familiar with diasporas such as the Jewish Diaspora, the Palestinian Diaspora, or the African Diaspora. A diaspora is a dispersed population whose origin is somewhere besides the place they reside. So, for example, the African Diaspora refers to the dispersal of African people as a result of the transatlantic Slave Trade. The term is also used to refer to the postcolonial migration to Europe of people from the Caribbean and West African countries like Ghana and Nigeria, influencing the cultures of both places.

Diaspora studies question whether there is inevitably a link between people and specific places. The idea that there is necessarily a homology between culture, people, nation, and a particular terrain is certainly behind a great deal of societal conflict. More to the point, under conditions of globalization, people are increasingly living lives that are not tied to any particular place and this has implications for how culture and identity are negotiated.

According to William Safran, to be considered a diaspora, a community must have certain characteristics. The group must be displaced from a homeland or center to at least *two* peripheral areas. They maintain a vision, myth, or memory about their previous homeland. The people in the group believe that they are not fully accepted by the societies in which they live outside their homeland. They often believe the ancestral home to be the ideal homeland and may have ideas that they or their ancestors will return there.

Diasporas tend to provoke a complex of emotions and attitudes focused on the advantages of staying and the dream of returning (Uehling 2013: n.p.). This challenges traditional notions in the social sciences that people are either socially rooted or displaced because members of a diaspora are both. There is an imagined utopia of the original homeland that is intensified by the hardship of minority status.

Stuart Hall (1990) was one of the first to develop the notion of diaspora. He explored how Afro-Caribbean film and photography of the diaspora defied the perceived power of White Europeans. Cultural theorists and art historians put forward the idea that, in many ways, the identity of "the West" depended on conceiving of blackness as fundamentally different (Mercer 2016: 2). This masks the interdependence in the relationship between colonizer and colonized (Mercer 2016: 2).

The assumption that becoming modern was the same as the process of becoming Western—and relinquishing an authentic ethnic or cultural identity—is gradually being undermined by attention to the ways that colonized groups in general and indigenous ones in particular have exercised choice in adopting some cultural practices and rejecting others. This has led to a thesis that it would be better to think of multiple modernities, rather than there being a single modernity that spread. From this perspective, the notion that modernity started in the West and then subsequently spread to the African continent, Asia, etc, is too simplistic (Mercer 2016: 6). For example, Bell et al. (1996) suggest that photographic studios in Africa (and their argument does not identify any particular African countries) began to experiment and thrive at the same time as photographic technology was developing in other parts of the world.

At an aesthetic level, modernism is inherently multicultural. A few snapshots of modern art can reveal the extent of the interdependence. Malevich created a monochromatic painting based on his interpretation of Indian mysticism and Vedic philosophy; Picasso incorporated African masks he saw at a Paris ethnographic museum; and Gauguin, among others, played with colors and religious symbolism from Tahiti. Examined as cultural appropriation today, these examples show that transnational flows and exchanges as well as influences and inspirations, are multidirectional.

While this volume is confined to a single semester course, continued engagement with international studies will provide more perspectives and additional tools for understanding the complex dynamics between culture, economics and politics.

References

Abu-Lughod, Lila. 2002. "Do Muslim Women Really Need Saving? Anthropological Reflections on Cultural Relativism and its Others," *American Anthropologist* Vol 104(3) September 2002, 783–790.

Barber, Benjamin. 2003. *Jihad vs. McWorld*. New York: Corgi.

Bartholomew, R. E. 1994. "Disease, Disorder, or Deception? Latah as Habit in a Malay Extended Family. *Journal of Nervous and Mental Disorders* 182 (6): 331–338.

Beldo, Les. 2010. "Concept of Culture." In H. James Birx (ed.), *21st Century Anthropology: A Reference Handbook (Volume 1)*. Thousand Oaks, CA: SAGE, 144–152.

Bell, Clare, Okwui Enwezor, Danielle Tilkin, and Octavio Zaya, eds. 1996. *In/sight: African Photographers, 1940 to the Present*. Exhibition catalogue. New York: Guggenheim Museum.

Berry, John W. 2005. "Acculturation: Living Successfully in Two Cultures." *International Journal of Intercultural Relations* 29 (2005): 697–712.

Bottici, Chiar. 2010. *The Myth of the Clash of Civilizations*. London, New York: Routledge.

Butler, Judith. 1990 [1999]. *Gender Trouble: Feminism and the Subversion of Identity*. New York: Routledge.

Cohn, Carol. 2013. *Women and Wars*. Cambridge: Polity Press.

Cousins, Steven D. 1989. "Culture and Self Perception in Japan and the United States." *Journal of Personality and Social Psychology* 56 (1): 124–131.

Eriksen, Thomas Hyland. 2014. Globalization: The Key Concepts (2nd ed.). London and New Delhi: Bloomsbury.

Hall, Stuart. 1990. *Cultural Identity and Diaspora: Identity, Community, Culture, Difference*. Lawrence and Wishart.

Halliday, Fred. 1996. *Islam and the Myth of Confrontation*. New York: St. Martin's Press.

Henrich, Joseph, Steven Heine, and Ara Norenzayan. 2010. "The Weirdest People in the World?" *Behavioral and Brain Sciences* 3: 61–135.

Herzfeld, Michael. 2001. *Anthropology: Theoretical Practice in Culture and Society*. London: Blackwell.

Huntington, Samuel P. 1993. "The Clash of Civilizations?" *Foreign Affairs* 72 (3): 21–49.

Huntington, Samuel P. 1996. *The Clash of Civilizations and the Remaking of World Order*. New York: Simon & Schuster.

Ikenberry, John G. 1997. "Just Like the Rest." *Foreign Affairs* 76 (2): 163.

Ji, Li-Jun, Zhiyong Zhang, and Richard Nisbett. 2004. "Is It Culture or Is It Language? Examination of Language Effects in Cross-Cultural Research on Categorization." *Journal of Personality and Social Psychology* 87 (1): 57–65.

Kleinman, Arthur, and Byron Good. "Introduction." In Arthur Kleinman and Byron Good (eds.), *Culture and Depression: Studies in the Anthropology and Cross-Cultural Psychiatry of Affect and Disorder*. Berkeley and Los Angeles: University of California Press, 1–42.

Lee, Robert. 1999. *The Clash of Civilizations: An Intrusive Gospel in Japanese Civilization* Harrisburg, PA: Trinity Press.

Nanda, Serena. 1994. *Cultural Anthropology*. Belmont, CA: Wadsworth.

Nash, Manning. 1989. *The Cauldron of Ethnicity in the Modern World*. Chicago: University of Chicago Press.

OED Online. N.D. "culture, n." Oxford University Press. http://www.oed.com/view/Entry/45746?isAdvanced=false& result=1&rskey=mUIaGG& [accessed December 13, 2013].

Todorov, Tzvetan. 2010. *The Fear of Barbarians: Beyond the Clash of Civilizations*, Translated by Andrew Brown. Cambridge, Polity Press.

Uehling, Greta. 2013. "Diaspora" in Encyclopedia of the World's Minorities Carl Skutsch, ed. New York and London: Routledge [online accessed July 4, 2018]

Williams, Raymond. 1976. *Keywords: A Vocabulary of Culture and Society*. New York: Oxford University Press.

Readings

In "Identity, Community, and Selfhood: Understanding the Self in Relations to Contemporary Youth Cultures," Sarah Riley explores the changes to culture and identity as a result of the shift from an industrial economy to an information economy. Riley explores how young people in Britain manage identities in response to forces such as consumerism and the contemporary emphasis on individual responsibility. She argues that young people build identities out of consumption practices and leisure activities more than the traditional sources such as work and location. Riley explores the stress activated by having multiple identities in a globalized world. She argues that subjectivity is changing in the direction of fractured and multiple selves that must be continually negotiated across real and virtual spaces.

Amin Maalouf provides a discussion of identity from a personal perspective. The introduction to his book "In the Name of Identity: Violence and the Need to Belong" explores the complexity of identity to demonstrate that everyone is to a some extent a composite of identities and allegiances. Maalouf suggests that it is risky to think of ourselves as harboring a singular identity "deep down inside" because this can become the basis of prejudice. He contends that the language we use to explain our identities to one another is important

In "Do Muslim Women Really Need Saving" Lila Abu-Lughod explores the tendency to reify culture, making it seem more bounded than it really is. This thinking contributes to overlooking the external forces that influence how people in any given country come to live. She argues that cultural others should be acknowledged as different, without resorting to the extreme form of cultural relativism that explains everything in terms of culture. She suggests that readers not be too quick to make assumptions about what people who are Muslim, in particular, want. This discussion provides a foundation for exploring the politics of the head scarf with sensitivity to its varied meanings. Abu-Lughod, Lila. 2002. "Do Muslim Women Really Need Saving? Anthropological Reflections on Cultural Relativism and its Others," American Anthropologist, vol. 104, no. 3, pp. 783–790.

In "The Next Hot Sound," **Benjamin Shingler** introduces readers to a genre called "Powwow step" that mixes various musical genres like hip hop, reggae, and dub step into an original and hybrid form that includes traditional Native dance music. This is a classic example of the concept of hybridity. Shingler explores this hybridity through the work of A Tribe Called Red based in Ottawa. As indigenous artists, they feel it is important to speak out in favor of greater political self-determination for indigenous people. Shingler sees this band as working, by means of the hybridity of their chosen genre, to break down stereotypes, just as authors Saucedo (Chapter One), Adichie (Chapter Five), and Odede (Chapter Five) have sought to dismantle other stereotypes. Shingler, Benjamin. 2013. "The Next Hot Sound? Powwow Step, Aboriginal Hip-Hop." *Aljazeera America*, November 28, http://america.aljazeera. com/articles/2013/11/28/the-next-hot-soundyouhearwillbepowwowstepaboriginalhiphop.html.

Online Resource

Shingler, Benjamin. 2013. "The Next Hot Sound? Powwow Step, Aboriginal Hip-Hop." *Aljazeera America*, November 28, http://america.aljazeera.com/articles/2013/11/28/the-next-hot-soundyouhearwillbe-powwowstepaboriginalhiphop.html.

Image Credit

Image 6.1: https://engaged-brains.wikispaces.com/Self+Identity.

Identity, Community, and Selfhood: Understanding the Self in Relation to Contemporary Youth Cultures

by Sarah Riley

The context for this paper are the changes in the structures and institutions of advanced industrial societies over the past 50 years that include the decline in manufacturing industries, changes in family structures and increases in communication media. These changes have resulted in profound shifts in how we make sense of ourselves. Young people must attempt to accomplish and negotiate an expectation of multiple identity management within a context of powerful social forces that include consumerism and a neo-liberal emphasis on risk, responsibility and individualism. This paper explores these three factors—consumption, multiplicity and neo-liberalism—in the shaping of young people's identity in relation to contemporary youth cultures.

Leisure and Consumption

Traditional anchors for identity, such as occupation or region, now compete with, or are replaced by, identities based upon consumption, lifestyle and leisure (Giddens, 1991). Leisure-based activities have increasingly become important indicators of who we are and our place in society, including how we understand civic and political participation. A series of shifts have occurred which have further strengthened the relationships between consumption and identity for young people. These include delaying responsibilities associated with adulthood and independent living, an increase in communication media, and developments in advertising and marketing.

The cost of living and of higher education are two factors that have led to British youth delaying their participation in responsibilities associated with adulthood, such as independent living, home ownership or parenthood. Depending on their socio-economic status, on average, young people remain either financially dependent on their parents, or contribute financially to the parental home, until their late twenties (Parker, Aldridge & Measham, 1998). Without the need to pay for mortgages or children this delayed access to adult responsibilities means that young people often have more time and money for leisure than had previous generations.

The ability to consume has been further enhanced through developments in technology that have given young people unprecedented access to information on a multitude of consumption and leisure practices and to the people and communities who participate in them. Such technologies include the internet, increases in the number of television channels, and changes in publishing that have reduced production costs, making specialist smaller readership magazines commercially viable.

Young people are also targeted by those interested in commercially exploiting youth markets, including, for example, regional governments who have seen young adults' consumption in bars and clubs as the solution to city centre regeneration (Chatterton & Hollands, 2003). A range of aggressive and insidious marketing techniques have been developed and used to target young people, including, for example, giving popular children free products to promote to their peer group. So while there has always been a complex interaction between the media, consumer interests and 'authentic' youth culture (Riley & Cahill, 2005) young people today experience unprecedented exposure to commercial pressures (see, for example, discussions of 'ethnographic marketing', 'viral advertising' and 'KGOY' (Kids growing older younger).

Branding and other marketing practices have intimately linked identity with consumption. For example, young men may identify as a 'rebel' by buying particular clothes rather than having participated in any act considered rebellious (Gill, Henwood & McClean, 2005). There is considerable debate over the agency young people have regarding consumption and identity. Young people are not necessarily passive consumers and while they may be attracted to particular identities associated with branded materials they may take these items and rework them in various ways, including parody. Others argue however, that the notion of agency is itself an illusion of discourses of consumption, or at the very least, subversion through consumption has limitations. (For an example of the debates on agency and consumption in relation to young women and sexualised clothing see Duit & van Zoonen (2006, 2007) and Gill (2007)).

The relationships between traditional anchors of identity and those produced through consumption and leisure are also disputed. Indeed, analyses of 'changing times' tend to be anecdotal, with limited empirical work available (www.identities.org.uk). It is likely, however, that young people's subjectivities are constructed through a variety of identities shaped by 'traditional' orientations to class, region, family and gender, and more 'liquid', flexible ones orienting around leisure-based activities, such as sports or shopping. Thus, leisure and consumption-based identities may not have replaced traditional anchors for identity, rather, when young people had access to them these identities may sit alongside each other, being drawn upon when contextually relevant (Riley, Griffin & Morey, 2008). Having access to, and being able to participate in, both traditional and liquid identities is subject to a complex interaction of personal and social variables, but is linked to social inequality. For example, working class children are more likely to have a TV in their bedroom, increasing the amount of advertising to which they are subjected (Mayo, 2005).[1]

---

1   Although this effect may be negated by the steady increase in young people's private access to the internet.

Multiplicity

As well as opening up opportunities for leisure and consumption increases in communication media have offered a plethora of ways of understanding ourselves. In having access to, for example, history programmes about life in ancient Egypt, soap operas with evil twins, or channels dedicated to extreme sports, young people grow up in a world in which they have literally seen it all before. Thus, the proliferation and globalisation of near instant forms of technological communication make available a dynamically-shifting range of stories and forms of knowledge that can inform young people's identity management. Subjectivity, then, is not considered to be constructed from pre-formed essences which exist independently outside of time, talk or other social activity, but are constantly (re)produced in interaction, constructed from the range of subject positions available to the individual, which may be contradictory or only partially formed.

Developments in communication technologies have intensified relationships between subjectivity and technology. There has always been a link between subjectivity and technology, for example using a hammer allows a person to experience their arm as a lever (Burkitt, 1999). However, distinctions between bodies, selves and technology have increasingly blurred, leading analysts to talk of cyborg as a metaphor for understanding contemporary subjectivity in which the boundaries between organism and machine are transgressed and from which new senses of self emerge (Gergen, 1991). For example, mobile phones can give us the sense of never being alone, of carrying with us the potential of always being able to connect to others.

For contemporary young people, exposed to and consuming a range of communication media, consumption and leisure practices, the traditional move from identifying with one's family to one's peer group is now one that is likely to involve multiple peer groups. It is therefore more appropriate to think of youth cultures in the plural in order to foreground the multiplicity of identities that orient around the notion of youth and to think of young people moving dynamically between these communities. In previous eras, subcultures, such as hippies or punks, bestowed meaningfulness on those who clearly identified with one group, locating authenticity in those who most closely approximated the permanent alternative lifestyle that reflected the norms associated with this group (McKay, 1998). Now such an understanding of authenticity may be less valued and meaningfulness may be as easily located in temporary, fluid and multiple identities, identities facilitated through technology and consumption practices. So while some people may still strongly identify with one group, others adopt a more playful pick-andmix approach, moving through a kaleidoscope of fractured scenes and taste cultures (Muggleton & Weinzierl, 2004).

While youth cultures have multiplied and fractured, other, homogenising forces have come into play, including the globalisation of youth cultures and the blurring of adult and youth activities. Communication technologies have aided the globalisation and commercialisation of youth cultures, working as homogenising forces that enable youth cultures to be formed and communicated almost instantly in more or less similar ways across the world (see, for example, Studdert's (2006) discussion on African Chelsea football club supporters). There has also been a blurring of adult and youth interests and activities. Just as young people delay taking on adult responsibilities and so extend their adolescence into adulthood, older generations too have been less inclined to relinquish youthful activities. The music video game 'Guitar Hero', for example, recently advertised itself as cross-generational entertainment for parents and their teenage children to use while queuing together for a festival. Successful movement across these boundaries is not, however, a given. Instead, scenes usually fracture and multiply to accommodate niche markets, for example 'Baby Raves'—electronic dance music daytime events held for parents with small children.

Having a range of identities has traditionally been understood as psychologically healthy, since a person can maintain positive self esteem by drawing on other aspects of self if one aspect experiences failure (see, for example, work on Social Identity Theory by Tajfel & Turner, 1986). The increase in opportunities to experience multiple identities may therefore be considered to have positive potential. Creating different identities, such as online avatars or Bluetooth monikers, allow people to construct different senses of selves that represent or allow them to engage in different behaviours and activities. For example, different DJ names can represent different types of music played by that person, freeing the DJ from being pigeon-holed while also allowing him/herself to communicate to his/her potential audience what kind of music to expect on a particular night. However, concern has been raised that the number of identities a person may be expected to dynamically and, in a 24 hour culture, perpetually, move through, can create over-demanding situations, causing stress. Furthermore, some understandings will inevitably clash with others, so that multiplicity is associated with contradiction. For example, young women are expected to both have 'girl power' and to be heterosexually attractive, thereby reproducing traditional expectations of femininity (for examples, see Gill 2006, or http://www.lse.ac.uk/collections/newFemininities/).

Problems associated with consumption are also implicated in the management of multiple identities, since these different aspects of self are often facilitated through the ability to consume. Participation requires, for example, entrance to clubs, appropriate clothes, or technological equipment. School children regularly use social networking sites after school to communicate with each other, creating social exclusion for those without access to the internet at home. Thus, there are significant structural inequalities in the ability to adopt a playful 'pick-and-mix' stance. Indeed significant inequalities may be produced at the most basic level of self-storying, since the most excluded in society may struggle even to tell one, let alone, multiple narratives about themselves.

Neo-Liberalism

The need to story oneself with multiple narratives, whether drawn from traditional- or consumption-based identity markers, is particularly relevant because of the dominance of neo-liberalism. Identity has always been an important marker for young people, and engaging in leisure and consumption, such as in choices around appearance and clothes, has played a significant role in this. What is different for today's youth is the tightening of meaning around identity and consumption that has been facilitated through neo-liberal rhetoric of risk, responsibility and individualism.

Neo-liberalism describes the idea that people are encouraged to see themselves as if they are autonomous, rational, risk-managing subjects, responsible for their own destinies and called "to render one's life knowable and meaningful through a narrative of free choice and autonomy—however constrained one might actually be" (Gill, 2006, p.260; see also Kelly, 2006). From this position, the social context in which a person lives is reduced to their immediate interpersonal relations, and any personal, social or health problems, and their attendant solutions, are located within the individual. Neo-liberalism allows people to make sense of themselves in individualistic and psychological terms, understanding their consumption practices as freely chosen markers of their identity (Cronin, 2003). Neo-liberal rhetoric of individual choice and responsibility now dominates much of post-industrial sense making about what it means to be a good person. Such changes have been identified as powerful new forms of governance (Rose, 1989). For example, being asked to work excessive and low paid hours may not be considered exploitation but accounted for in terms of a worker's psychological characteristic of being a helpful person (Walkerdine, 2002). Thus, young people are developing their sense of self in a context in which wider discourses in society encourage them to understand themselves through psychological and individual discourses, rather than those that are communal or sociological.

Neo-liberal subjectivity has been associated with an increased focus on the body as an important site for identity management. For example, there has been a coupling between neo-liberal values of rationality and responsibility and the cultural valuing of slenderness, so that a slender and toned body has come to represent a person who has rational control over their appetites and who acts responsibly in relation to maintaining a healthy body. These associations mean that body size has come not just to signify physical health, but also mental health and morality (Riley, et al, 2008).

The relationship between the body and identity may be particularly important for young people, given that in comparison to adults, young people tend to have less control over other aspects of their lives. Young people may employ a range of body modification techniques, from dieting and weight training to cosmetic surgery or body art. As an example, body art, an umbrella term for a variety of practices including tattoos and piercings, has become increasingly popular as a way of articulating personal and social identities (Riley & Cahill, 2005) and with continued developments in technology and cosmetic surgery may produce ever more creative forms of body modification (for example, the use of implants to create horns).

Youth cultures are often associated with pleasure and hedonism, and the body is central to these issues. For example, electronic music dance culture (also known as 'rave') employs technologies such as sound systems, lasers, electronically manufactured music and 'designer' drugs to produce hyper real communal and embodied experiences (Wilson, 2006). These experiences allow participants to develop identities and experiences of self that may be incorporated into neo-liberal narratives of self. Neo-liberal rhetoric can also be employed to justify such pleasures, as it can be argued that the individual has the right and freedom to engage in escapism through extreme but pleasurable intoxication (Riley, Morey & Griffin, 2008). Given the excessive weekend drinking seen across Britain's city centres such a 'culture of intoxication', in which people collectively seek and celebrate a loss of control, may be considered normalised for many young people (Measham & Brain, 2005). Paradoxically then, neo-liberal rights and responsibilities discourses may be employed to justify embodied, communal, intoxicated and even 'mad' selves, selves that are the antithesis of the rational neo-liberal subject.

Neo-Tribalism

Neo-liberalism has arguably come to dominate much of contemporary western thinking about subjectivity, however, it is not without competing discourses. For example, sociologist Michel Maffesoli, while also emphasising the informal and local, argues that contemporary social organisation is highly social. Maffesoli's theory of neo-tribalism challenges notions of society as increasingly alienated and individualistic and instead characterises daily life as a continuous movement through a range of small and potentially temporary groups that are distinguished by shared lifestyles, values and understandings of what is appropriate behaviour (Maffesoli, 1996). These groups give a sense of belonging and identity, examples of which include gathering to watch football in a bar, participants on service user websites or regular commuters sharing public transport. What distinguishes neo-tribal social formation from traditional social groupings is that people belong to a variety of groups, many of them by choice, so that neo-tribal memberships are plural, temporary, fluid and often elective (Riley, Griffin & Morey, *in submission*).

Within neo-tribal theory people are understood as moving dynamically through a series of groups, some more partially formed than others, which are in the person's locality. However, technologies such as the internet make the notion of being 'local' relative, since people may share physical or virtual proximity. That neo-tribes are distinguished by the grouping, however temporary in time or space, of people who share lifestyles, values and understandings of what is appropriate behaviour leads Maffesoli to analyse such groups as engaged in moments of 'sovereignty over one's own existence'. Neo-tribal gatherings provide sovereignty because they create temporary pockets of freedom to engage in behaviours and values associated with that group, which may be different from the values and expected behaviours of other groups (that participants may or may not also be members of). For example, a person may shout aggressively when watching football in a bar, but would not raise their voice at a family meal.

Creating spaces in which to practice one's group values requires a turning away from other groups in order to 'do your own thing'. The resultant lack of engagement with other groups, in particular more dominant groups, often leads to youth cultures being constructed as problematic. First, because it is read as a sign of young people failing to engage with adult groups or adult led activities deemed good for the young people. Second, these groups are often understood as challenging the dominant culture or celebrating values at odds with the dominant culture, creating moral panics that construct young people as 'folk devils'. However, analyses of these groups often show a complex blending of values that both reflect and challenge dominant values. For example, pro-ana websites, which are created by young women to promote the concept of anorexia as a lifestyle choice, are an example of young women engaging in valued practices of being pro-active and employing technological skills. However, they are applying themselves to the promotion of a cause that can lead to serious illness or death. Similarly, setting up an illegal rave requires the bringing together of a diverse set of resources that include entrepreneurial, organisational, musical and electrical engineering skills, skills used to facilitate parties that are unlicensed, held on other people's property and involve high levels of illicit drug use.

Dominant values themselves are, of course, constantly being negotiated and Maffesoli (1996) argues that there is currently a general move by the 'masses' away from the institutional power and rational organisations that defined the modern age to a zeitgeist that celebrates sociality, proximity, emotional attachments and hedonistic values. Thus, when groups create opportunities to practice sovereignty over their existence they are creating spaces in which to engage in values that orient around sociality, emotionality and hedonism. In relating neo-tribalism to young people, it may be useful to recognise the similarities between Maffesoli's concept of sovereignty and Hakim Bey's 'Temporary Autonomous Zones' (TAZ), a term he uses to describe transitory unsanctioned self-governing sites (Bey, 1991). In coming together to participate in acts of sociality and hedonism, TAZs or neo-tribal gatherings can be understood as providing sites of resistance to a neo-liberal sensibility based on rationality, rights, responsibility and individualism.

The creation of temporary and fluid spaces in which to participate in one's own values, can be understood as an emerging form of political engagement, an 'everyday politics' that focuses on the local, informal or personal, rather than engaging with official organisations and institutional power. Personal lives have been used previously as the basis for political activism (examples being the 'identity politics' of feminism, gay/lesbian liberation and black power). However, such forms of political activism, like traditional political activities, often focus on a social change agenda. What distinguishes the new personalised form of politics is that the focus is on creating temporary spaces in which to participate in ones' own values and associated behaviours—to be able to 'do your own thing'—thus participants do not necessarily need to engage with other groups or organisations of governance. Everyday politics is thus about creating spaces in which to live out alternative values, shifting political participation to the 'everyday' individual or informal group level.

An 'everyday politics' may be particularly relevant for young people because of a perceived lack of attention from those involved in traditional politics to issues of concern for young people (e.g., the environment). Furthermore, as Harris argues, when young people engage with state institutions to effect social change, their action problematically works to both endorse these systems and to locate themselves in a subordinate position within them: "young people may well have their own ideas about how states and citizenry should operate, and to ask to be included or to participate in the current order is to endorse a system that may be fundamentally at odds with these other visions. Further, it is to accept one's subordinate position as a fringe dweller who can only ever hope to be invited or asked to participate, but who can never do the inviting themselves" (2001, p.187). Like Maffesoli, Harris argues that one solution is not to engage with institutions associated with governance and power, but to create one's own spaces of autonomy. Harris's (2001) work on girlzines is such an example. Harris (ibid.) argued that the young women involved used internet magazines to create their own space from which to negotiate, redefine and reclaim politics, citizenship and novel gender subjectivities. Harris's work suggests that leisure and entertainment based activities can provide sites for young people to engage in practices that relate to participation and citizenship, providing the opportunity to produce 'counter stories' that act as "forms of politics, often misrecognised as entertainment" (Harris, Carney & Fine, 2001, p.12). Neo-liberalism is implicated in 'everyday politics' since neo-liberal rhetoric of focusing on the personal through discourses of individual choice and personal responsibility provides the ideological context in which locating political participation at the individual or informal group level makes sense. However, arguments for these forms of political engagement are controversial and empirical work is scattered and underdeveloped (a special issue of 'Youth' on everyday politics edited by Anita Harris is currently underway; also see Riley et al., *in submission*).

Implications

Adolescence and early adulthood are traditionally conceptualised as making up an important time in identity development. Today's youth experience this time in a context in which the culturally dominant model of the self is of an autonomous, rational, psychological subject who bears ultimate responsibility for the self and who must manage multiple identities, many of which are made available through consumption and technology.

This context provides a range of opportunities for pleasurable and playful engagement with identity, allowing the young people who can take these opportunities to construct a sense of place in the world. However, this construction of self also creates certain stressors. First, locating every success or failure at the personal or psychological level absents other ways of making sense of oneself and masks the impact of structural inequalities on life 'choices'. Second, the constant pressure to (re)make yourself and manage multiplicity is both demanding and requires the management of contradictory identities. Third, structural inequalities mean that some people do not have the resources to do this kind of identity management.

In masking the impact of structural inequalities neo-liberalism sets the scene for a shift towards a personalising of politics. Locating oneself at the personal and psychological level, coupled with a general move away from engaging with traditional institutional power, creates the context in which it may make sense for young people to focus their political energies on informal acts, such as recycling or benefit gigs for small charities. This shift can be read as reflecting an alienation from traditional politics that is a part of the contemporary British political landscape (Colman & Gøtze, 2001; Harris, 2001), or more positively, as a sign of a zeitgeist swing away from one form of political engagement to another (Maffesoli, 1996).

Although neo-liberalism has come to dominate our understanding of the subject it is one concept amongst many. One alternative to neo-liberalism that also has political potential is neo-tribalism (Maffesoli, 1996). Neo-tribalism argues that our identities are made from moving through a variety of local groups to which we have an emotional attachment, these groups are conceptualised as creating temporary pockets of sovereignty in which to celebrate values of hedonism and sociality. Youth cultures can be conceptualised as neo-tribes, in which young people carve out temporal spaces in which to practice particular sets of values and behaviours. In creating these spaces neo-tribes can be considered as new forms of political participation, since they allow alternative values systems to survive. Young people may therefore create their own neo-tribes in which to celebrate identities that offer an alternative to the rational risk managing neo-liberal subject, the 'culture of intoxication' being one such example.

The moral panic that ensued from today's culture of intoxication is part of a long history of representing 'youth as problem' and can be seen to inform tensions around how contemporary young people appropriate space and technology. While being youthful is a valued commodity, young people themselves are often represented as deviant, representations that are classed and gendered—sexually active females, criminally active males, for example (Griffin, 1993). (For a contemporary example, see the very particular and narrow reading of youth in the World Bank's World Development Report, which locates solutions to problematic youth in formal institutions, absenting the possibilities that youth cultures themselves provide positive spaces for identity development (Luttrell-Rowland, 2007)).

Hedonistic youth cultures can, however, be analysed as attempts to use pleasure as a vehicle for creating positive social alternatives. Rave culture, for example, exhorts the values of PLUR—peace, love, unity and respect (Wilson, 2006). Similarly, excessive weekend drinking in city centres has been analysed as a sign that working class youth have the confidence to use these public spaces in a way that previous generations did not (Chatterton & Hollands, 2003).

However, such forms of resistance may reinforce the overall dominance of neo-liberalism. For example, engaging in intoxicated excesses at the weekend may release tension created by the stress of being a neo-liberal subject, facilitating participants to return to work on Monday. Participants of hedonistic resistance to neo-liberalism often account for their behaviour with neo-liberal rhetoric of rights and risk, arguing that if one is ultimately responsible for oneself then one also has a right to do what one wants with that self (Riley, Morey & Griffin, 2008). There is therefore a complex interaction between alternative and dominant discourses of self since one may be enabled by the other. Young people may be snatching spaces to be 'free' but they are using the masters' tools to do so. Thus, while neo-tribal memberships provide participants with a sense of belonging they may not challenge the neo-liberal construction of self as a project. Furthermore, neo-tribalism still requires the subject to manage multiplicity (in this case of group/tribal based identities) with the attendant stressors of multiplicity described above. Neo-liberal constructions of the self and multiple subjectivities are thus likely to continue into the future as significant ways of understanding oneself and place in the world.

There are examples of young people participating in collective action, a recent example being the anti-Iraq war 'Not in My Name' campaign. However, it has been argued that the impact of locating responsibility at the personal level has reduced young people's ability to make collective challenges since they are less likely to be exposed to discourses of collective experience and struggle, including, for example, those of feminism (McRobbie, 2008). Neo-liberalism may also foster a culture in which the social contract between citizen and government is weakened—if successes or failures are reduced to the interpersonal, then the citizen owes the state nothing.

The proliferation and globalisation of near instant forms of technological communication combined with the multiple and fragmented nature of social lives means that we have available to us an ever shifting kaleidoscope of understandings from which we can draw on in the (re)production of neo-liberal subjectivities. These subjectivities are reduced to their immediate interpersonal relations, to the realm of the personal and psychological, but not necessarily to the private. Communication technologies allow the self to be (re)produced in the public sphere, for example though entries in social network sites such as Facebook, blogs or personal and work websites. Just as every aspect of life can already be seen on TV, so we replay it back using technology to make partial and fractured narratives of ourselves that span space and time. See, for example, 'FutureMe.org', an online resource for sending emails to yourself in the future. The 'best' of these messages are made public in an anonymous form for entertainment. Indeed it may be that communication technologies are creating a situation where people understand aspects of themselves as only truly meaningful when offered up for the consumption of others. It is possible therefore that communication technologies, such as Web 2.0, are creating a new shift in which the private may only be meaningfully experienced when in the public.

Developments in technology are likely to enhance this process. For example, the ability to store a life-time of video on an iPod will allow an individual to consume their own life experiences (Cliff, O'Malley & Taylor, 2008). Fear of social exclusion if one doesn't participate in these technologies, plus surveillance technology, such as CCTV and the use of finger print scanners to ID children in schools,[2] means that there is only limited opt out from these forms of technology. Furthermore, communication technologies do not provide unlimited ways of self-storying. Rather the technologies themselves and the cultural valuing of particular traits create powerful scaffolding around which people build their self-narratives. For example, there are international internet dating websites that require participants to describe the colour of their hair and eyes, despite these being primarily defining features for Caucasian people. Similarly, research on online gaming shows that participants regularly create avatars that fulfil conventional definitions of heterosexually attractive gendered attributes (for example, women create female avatars that have slender, toned bodies) (Waskul & Edgley, 2000).

In the future young people will therefore have to negotiate a self that is splintered off into a series of surfaces that reflect both the technologies that enable them and the cultural mores in which they are located. Sociologist Norbert Elias argued that changes in social structures during the Middle Ages led to a shift in human subjectivity in which the public and private became compartmentalised. Responses to actions such as public defecation changed, so that people moved these behaviours to the private sphere. These changes led to a shift in consciousness in which thoughts could also become private, making, for example, the experience of 'repressed anger' a possibility, since previously anger was a public act and not a private experience (that one may or may not express). Changes in contemporary social organisation, enabled through communication technologies, have the potential to create similar radical changes in subjectivity. Notably, a fractured and multiple self experienced in the public sphere and reflected through technology across a range of temporal physical and virtual locations.

Already the internet has produced a situation in which aspects of our selves are created through technology and distributed across time and space. Some of these selves have connections to each other, as in the past selves communicating with future selves as via FutureMe.org. With other selves the connections to the original source(s) are broken or new connections are made, such as forgotten photographs uploaded onto public domains and re-appropriated by friends, colleagues or people unknown. An example of reappropriation I found was a young girl's homepage that had a photograph of another (attractive) child on it, with the explanation that 'she looks a bit like me'. It may be that young people will experience fractured and multiple subjectivity in the same way that they are encouraged to consider high street clothing—as tools of identity to be temporarily appropriated, experienced and then cast off in favour of some new look or experience. Future subjectivity may therefore be conceptualised as a collection of multiple, diffuse selves existing across time and space, that have differing degrees of relationships with each other and perhaps no longer needing to be held together by the concept of a 'core self'.

It is likely, therefore, that in the future young people will need to find ways to exist in the plural. In a preferable future they will be able to develop a sense of being valued and of having opportunities to participate positively in the many social worlds that will be potentially available to them. Schools and other educational institutions will have a duty to help facilitate this.

---

2   This is being used for example at a City Academy in Bristol to replace taking the register and for ordering lunch.

One way to increase young people's access to traditional and liquid identities from which to story themselves would be through the creation of more personalised education. In the same way that technologies are enabling increasingly more individually tailored medical interventions, a personalised educational system could be developed in which each student would in effect be their own portfolio manager, managing themselves as a project. The aim for educationalists would be to help young people identify their values, interests and talents and to find ways of using these to develop the various skills they need to become critical and engaged citizens who feel valuated and located in their world.

By drawing on young people's own interests educators may use leisure and consumption as a way to excite them about education, creating holistic ways to develop young people's understanding and engagement with their world.[3] Pop music, for example, is often a key site for young people's interest and identity. Music technologies now allow people to compose music without needing knowledge of musical theory. Creating music with this technology can be used as a starting point for students to gain a sense of self-efficacy, from which they might develop their education holistically, exploring a range of associated subjects including musical theory, sociopolitical history and practical learning through organising and performing in a concert. It may therefore be an advantage to blur education with entertainment, particularly given the expectation, at least in some sections of society, that work should be enjoyable (Tapscott, 2008).

Future education may require different relations of authority between educational institutions and their students. Already communication technologies have reduced teachers' control over pupils. For example, school pupils have created a mobile phone ring tone that their teachers cannot hear by recording the 'mosquito', a high pitched noise used to keep teenagers away from public amenities like late night shops. Technologies are likely to increase young people's autonomy, like some contemporary adults they may work (or study) from home, or in the future, they may use biologically embedded technologies only viewable to themselves (Cliff, O'Malley & Taylor, 2008). A personalised education system that incorporates the values and interests of the student is likely to enhance self-motivated study and create more egalitarian relationships with educational institutions. However, respecting the values and interests of students may bring challenges, given that youth cultures are often a complex blend of dominant and counter cultural values. After all, one can confidently predict that young people will sometimes do things not expected or approved of by their elders.

Communication technologies mean that educators and students can draw from a huge range of resources of expertise. For example, lectures from world renowned academics are available on 'YouTube'. The role of future educators in a personalised educational setting would then be to help young people identify which sites may help them develop the skills they most need to meet their educational interests, values and needs. Educators would also have the role of helping students make links between their personal portfolios and the wider world. For example, identifying transferable skills, connections to the job market and developing critical analytical skills that would help them negotiate their way through their virtual and physical worlds. One way to do this is for students to be encouraged to explore the power of

---

3   See Gergen with Wortham (2001) for a discussion of social constructionist approach to education, which includes the principles of making education relevant to student's lives, taking a holistic approach, encouraging reflexivity and making links to activities and actions outside the classroom.

language in structuring the way people understand their world, so that students can critically evaluate the texts that they use through the analytics of argument, reflection and doubt (Gergen with Wortham, 2001; Postman, 1995). Postman (1995), for example, argues for a curriculum that constructs knowledge as historically multiple, borrowed and intermingled. Such a curriculum would introduce plurality and set a framework for understanding one's own multiplicity, contradictions and socio-historic context.

Drawing on Postman would allow future educators to help young people develop a critical framework to negotiate and manage both their personal and social identities, while challenging some of the individualism of neo-liberalism and allowing young people to explore the impact of taking up particular identities in particular ways. This approach would prepare young people to both positively engage with the requirements of neo-liberal subjectivity, while also having the critical skills to explore alternative discourses, such as those associated with collective identities or spirituality.

In helping young people locate themselves as persons in relationships, embedded in a range of local and global communities educators would act as 'community enablers'. An example of using communication technologies to develop positive social identity based narratives comes from California, where young Hispanic pupils, living in a context in which their families have lower socio-economic status in comparison to their white counterparts, worked with Web 2.0 technology to produce positive narratives of their ethnic identity, which were then shared between themselves and with their wider community (Rodriguez, 2007). A similar project could, for example, be used with young people in the UK who struggle to find positive self-narratives in their communities (for example, young unemployed working class men in post-industrial Britain (Winlow, 2001)).

Helping young people form positive relationships with their community could be enabled through setting assessments that connect individuals together to demonstrate the values and necessity of group cohesion. Efficacy of group work would be further enhanced if assessments were directly linked to involvement in community action, either in the school or wider community, so that young people were encouraged to consider themselves has having meaningful connections to their communities (see action research and social constructionist approaches in education, e.g., Gergen with Wortham, 2001; Reason and Bradbury, 2008). Such projects would explicitly or implicitly teach students about social citizenship, and have the potential to tap into neo-tribal values of sociality, emotionality and the pleasures associated with creating pockets of sovereignty over one's own existence.

Neo-tribal theory argues that as people move in and out of the various groups to which they are affiliated their understanding of what is right and acceptable behaviour becomes relative, since it shifts for each group (Maffesoli, 1996). This form of relativist morality replaces the universal distinction between 'right' and 'wrong' on which modernist notions of morality are based. Maffesoli's argument is that such a relativist perspective facilitates tolerance, since it allows for, and indeed normalises, a diversity of values and practices across different communities and social groups. If this hypothesis is correct it would be possible for educators to help young people identify their various memberships and to facilitate pride and positive identities in these memberships, without the need to negatively construct out-groups. An ideal outcome of neo-tribalism, then, is to enjoy confidence in one's own memberships while maintaining an interest in others, a standpoint that may protect young people from being attracted to more fundamentalist orientated identities that provide a sense of security through the creation of a negative 'Other'.

Future educators could therefore value and work with what students bring to their classes, facilitate successful management of the self as a project and act as community enablers. In a preferable future they would also take on the role of protector. Young people will need protection and guidance in terms of managing their public selves, including the implications of how they present themselves online, as well as managing the stresses of multiple identities (which may include class related expectations of over- or under-achievement). Students will need support in how to engage with technology without getting lost or consumed by it. Young people will also need to be protected against bullying facilitated by technology (e.g., mass 'hate' texts), privacy invasions (by both individuals and government institutions) and virulent advertising.

A preferable future then, is one where schools are fun, interesting, relevant and safe. Places where it is recognised that young people bring a range of interests and values to their educational setting, which are engaged with in order to facilitate the development of positive personal and social identities. A personalised portfolio model of education in which the educator acts as a facilitator may help students gain the skills for successful management of the self as a project, so that they may enjoy the rights and responsibilities attached to neo-liberal subjectivity. However, educators would also need to provide alternative discourses to neo-liberalism, helping young people develop critical faculties and to explore other ways of understanding themselves, in particular as persons in relationships embedded in communities. Educators will also need to act as protective stewards, shielding young people from some of the more aggressive and insidious aspects of technology, surveillance and commercialisation, helping young people develop skills to safely negotiate their identities across the various mediums they will inhabit.

References

Bey, H. (1991) *T.A.Z.: The Temporary Autonomous Zone, Ontological Anarchy, Poetic Terrorism*. New York, Autonomedia.

Burkitt, I. (1999) *Bodies of Thought: Embodiment, Identity and Modernity*. London, Sage.

Chatterton, P. and Hollands, R. (2003) *Urban nightscapes. Youth Cultures, Pleasure Spaces and Corporate Power*. London, Routledge.

Cliff, D., O'Malley and Taylor, J. (2008) Beyond Current Horizon's paper.

Colman, S. and Gøtze, J. (2001) '*Bowling Together: On line Public Engagement in Policy Deliberation*. London, Hansard Society.

Duits, L. and van Zoonen, L. (2006) Headscarves and Porno-Chic: Disciplining Girls' Bodies in the European Multicultural Society. *European Journal of Women's Studies*, 13 (2), pp103–117.

Duits, L. and van Zoonen, L. (2007) Who's Afraid of Female Agency? A Rejoinder to Gill'. *European Journal of Women's Studies*, 14 (2), pp161–1

Gergen, K. (1991) *The Saturated Self*. New York, Basic Books.

Gergen, K.J. with Wortham, S. (2001) Social Constructionism and Pedagogical Practice. In: Gergen, K.J., *Social Constructionism in Context*. London, Sage.

Giddens, A. (1991) *Modernity and self-identity: Self and society in the late modern age.* Stanford, Stanford University Press.

Gill, R. (2006) *Gender and the Media.* London, Polity Press.

Gill, R. (2007) Critical respect: The difficulties and dilemmas of agency and 'choice' for feminism: A reply to Duits and van Zoonen. *European Journal of Women's Studies*, 14 (1), pp.65–76.

Gill, R., Henwood, K. and McClean, C. (2005) Body projects and the regulation of normative masculinity. *Body & Society*, 11, pp37–62.

Griffin, Chris (1993) *Representations of Youth: The study of Youth and Adolescence in Britain and America.* Cambridge, Polity.

Greener, T. and Hollands, R. (2006) 'Beyond subculture and post-subculture? The case of virtual psy-trance' *Journal of Youth Studies*, 9 (4), pp393–418.

Harris, A. (2001) 'Dodging and waving: Young women countering the stories of youth and citizenship', *International Journal of Critical Psychology*, 4 (2), pp183–199.

Harris, A., Carney, S. and Fine, M. (2001) Counter work: Introduction to 'Under the covers: Theorising the Politics of Counter Stories'. *International Journal of Critical Psychology*, 4 (2), pp6–18.

Kelly, P. (2006) 'The entrepreneurial self and 'youth at-risk': Exploring the horizons of identity in the twenty-first century', *Journal of Youth Studies*, 9 (1), pp17–3.

Luttrell-Rowland, M. (2007) Gang soldiers and 'Idle Girls': Constructions of youth and development in world bank discourse. *Research in Comparative and International Education*, 2 (3), pp230–241.

McKay, G. (1998) *DIY Culture: Party and Protest in Nineties Britain.* London and New York, Verso

McRobbie, A. (2008) *Displacement Feminism.* London, Sage.

Maffesoli, M. (1996) *The Time of the Tribes: The Decline of Individualism in Mass Society.* London, Sage.

Mayo, E. (2005) *Shopping Generation.* London, National Consumer Council.

Measham, F. and Brain, K. (2005) 'Binge' drinking, British alcohol policy and the new culture of intoxication. *Crime, Media, Culture*, 1 (3), pp262–283

Muggleton, D. and Weinzier, L. (2004) *The Post-Subcultural Reader.* New York, Berg.

Postman, N, (1995) *The End of Education: Redefining the Value of School.* New York, Alfred Knopf.

Reason, P. and Bradbury, H. (2008) *Handbook of Action Research.* London, Sage.

Riley, S., Burns, M., Frith, H., Wiggins, S. and Markula, P. (2008) *Critical Bodies: Representations, Identities and Practices of Weight and Body Management.* London, Palgrave.

Riley, S.C.E. and Cahill, S. (2005) Managing meaning & belonging: Young women's negotiation of authenticity in Body Art. *Journal of Youth Studies*, 8 (3), pp261–279.

Riley, S., Griffin, C. and Morey, Y. (2008) *Reverberating Rhythms: Social Identity and Political Participation in Clubland.* End of Award Report, ESRC, *ref.RES-000-22-1171.*

Riley, S., Morey, Y. and Griffin, C. (2008). Ketamine: The Divisive Dissociative. A Discourse Analysis of the Constructions of Ketamine by Participants of a Free Party (Rave) Scene. *Addiction, Research and Theory*, 16 (3), pp217–230.

Riley, S., Griffin, C. and Morey, Y. The case for 'everyday politics': evaluating neo-tribal theory as a way to understand alternative forms of political participation, using Electronic Dance Culture as an example. *Sociology, in submission*.

Rodriguez, M. (2007) Transnationalism through the eyes of young people. Paper presented at the BSA seminar *Young people, new technologies and political engagement*, University of Surrey, 24–25th July.

Rose, N. (1989) *Inventing our Selves: Psychology, Power and Personhood*. Cambridge, Cambridge University Press.

Studdert, D. (2006) *Conceptualising community: Beyond State and Individual*. London, PalgraveMacMillan.

Tajfel, H. and Turner, J.C. (1986). The social identity theory of inter-group behavior. In: Worchel, S. and Austin, L.W. eds. *Psychology of Intergroup Relations*. Chicago, Nelson-Hall.

Tapscott, D. (2008) *Generation Expects*. Guardian, 8th November, p.1. 'Work' section

Walkerdine V ed (2002) *Challenging Subjects: Critical Psychology for a New Millennium*. London, Palgrave MacMillan.

Waskul, D., Douglass, M. and C. Edgley. (2000) 'Cybersex: Outercourse and the Enselfment of the Body', *Symbolic Interaction*, 23 (4), pp375–397.

Wilson, B. (2006) *Fight, Flight or Chill. Subcultures, Youth and Rave into the Twenty-First Century*. Montreal & Kingston, McGill-Queen's University Press.

Winlow, S. (2001) Badfellas: *Crime, Tradition and New Masculinities*. London, Berg.

In the Name of Identity: Violence and the Need to Belong

by Amin Maalouf

Introduction

How many times, since I left Lebanon in 1976 to live in France, have people asked me, with the best intentions in the world, whether I felt "more French" or "more Lebanese"? And I always give the same answer: "Both!" I say that not in the interests of fairness or balance, but because any other answer would be a lie. What makes me myself rather than anyone else is the very fact that I am poised between two countries, two or three languages and several cultural traditions. It is precisely this that defines my identity. Would I exist more authentically if I cut off a part of myself?

To those who ask the question, I patiently explain that I was born in Lebanon and lived there until I was 27; that Arabic is my mother tongue; that it was in Arabic translation that I first read Dumas and Dickens and *Gulliver's Travels;* and that it was in my native village, the village of my ancestors, that I experienced the pleasures of childhood and heard some of the stories that were later to inspire my novels. How could I forget all that? How could I cast it aside? On the other hand, I have lived for 22 years on the soil of France; I drink her water and wine; every day my hands touch her ancient stones; I write my books in her language; never again will she be a foreign country to me.

So am I half French and half Lebanese? Of course not. Identity can't be compartmentalised. You can't divide it up into halves or thirds or any other separate segments. I haven't got several identities: I've got just one, made up of many components in a mixture that is unique to me, just as other people's identity is unique to them as individuals.

Sometimes, after I've been giving a detailed account of exactly why I lay claim to all my affiliations, someone comes and pats me on the shoulder and says "Of course, of course—but what do you really feel, deep down inside?"

For a long time I found this oft-repeated question amusing, but it no longer makes me smile. It seems to reflect a view of humanity which, though it is widespread, is also in my opinion dangerous. It presupposes that "deep down inside" everyone there is just one affiliation that really matters, a kind of "fundamental truth" about each individual, an "essence" determined once and for all at birth, never to change thereafter. As if the rest; all the rest a person's whole journey through time as a free agent; the beliefs he acquires in the course of that journey; his own individual tastes, sensibilities and affinities; in short his life itself counted for nothing. And when, as happens so often nowadays, our contemporaries are exhorted to "assert their identity," they are meant to seek within themselves that same alleged fundamental allegiance, which is often religious, national, racial or ethnic, and having located it they are supposed to flaunt it proudly in the face of others.

Anyone who claims a more complex identity is marginalised. But a young man born in France of Algerian parents clearly carries within him two different allegiances or "belongings," and he ought to be allowed to use both. For the sake of argument I refer to two "belongings," but in fact such a youth's personality is made up of many more ingredients. Within him, French, European and other western influences mingle with Arab, Berber, African, Muslim and other sources, whether with regard to language, beliefs, family relationships or to tastes in cooking and the arts. This represents an enriching and fertile experience if the young man in question feels free to live it fully if he is encouraged to accept it in all its diversity. But it can be traumatic if whenever he claims to be French other people look on him as a traitor or renegade, and if every time he emphasises his ties with Algeria and its history, culture and religion he meets with incomprehension, mistrust or even outright hostility.

The situation is even more difficult on the other side of the Rhine. I'm thinking of the case of a Turk who might have been born near Frankfurt 30 years ago and who has always lived in Germany. He speaks and writes German better than the language of his ancestors. Yet for the society of his adopted country he isn't a German, while for that of his origins he is no longer completely a Turk. Common sense dictates that he should be able to claim both allegiances. But at present neither the law nor people's attitudes allows him to accept his composite identity tranquilly.

I have quoted the first examples that came to mind, but I could have used many others. For instance, that of someone born in Belgrade of a Serbian mother and a Croatian father. That of a Hutu woman married to a Tutsi, or vice versa. Or that of an American with a black father and a Jewish mother.

It may be said that these are special cases. I don't agree. The handful of people I've cited are not the only ones with a complex identity. Every individual is a meeting ground for many different allegiances, and sometimes these loyalties conflict with one another and confront the person who harbours them with difficult choices. In some cases the situation is obvious at a glance; others need to be looked at more closely.

Is there any citizen of present-day Europe who doesn't sense a kind of tug-of-war, an inevitably ever-increasing conflict between on the one hand his affiliation to an ancient country like France, Spain, Denmark or England, and, on the other, his allegiance to the continental entity that is in the process of forming? And there are many dedicated "Europeans," from the Basque country to Scodand, who at the same time feel a strong and fundamental attachment to a particular region and its people, its history and its language. Can anyone in the United States even today assess his place in society without reference to his earlier connections, whether they be African, Hispanic, Irish, Jewish, Italian, Polish or other?

That said, I'm prepared to admit that the first examples I cited are to a certain extent special. All the people concerned in them are arenas for allegiances currently in violent conflict with one another: they live in a sort of frontier zone criss-crossed by ethnic, religious and other fault lines. But by virtue of this situation—peculiar rather than privileged—they have a special role to play in forging links, eliminating misunderstandings, making some parties more reasonable and others less belligerent, smoothing out difficulties, seeking compromise. Their role is to act as bridges, go-betweens, mediators between the various communities and cultures. And that is precisely why their dilemma is so significant: if they themselves cannot sustain their multiple allegiances, if they are continually being pressed to take sides or ordered to stay within their own tribe, then all of us have reason to be uneasy about the way the world is going.

I talk of their being "pressed" and "ordered"—but by whom? Not just by fanatics and xenophobes of all kinds, but also by you and me, by each and all of us. And we do so precisely because of habits of thought and expression deeply rooted in us all; because of a narrow, exclusive, bigoted, simplistic attitude that reduces identity in all its many aspects to one single affiliation, and one that is proclaimed in anger.

I feel like shouting aloud that this is how murderers are made—it's a recipe for massacres! That may sound somewhat extreme, but in the pages that follow I shall try to explain what I mean.

My Identity, My Allegiances

A life spent writing has taught me to be wary of words. Those that seem clearest are often the most treacherous. "Identity" is one of those false friends. We all think we know what the word means and go on trusting it, even when it's slyly starting to say the opposite.

Far be it from me to want to keep on redefining the idea of identity. It has been the fundamental question of philosophy from Socrates's "Know thyself!" through countless other masters down to Freud. To approach it anew today would call for more qualifications than I possess and for very much greater temerity. The task I set myself is more modest. I want to try to understand why so many people commit crimes nowadays in the name of religious, ethnic, national or some other kind of identity. Has it always been like this since time immemorial, or is the present era influenced by hitherto unknown factors? Sometimes what I say may seem rather simplistic. If so it's because I want to set my argument out as calmly, patiently and fairly as possible, without resorting to jargon or unwarranted shortcuts.

What's known as an identity card carries the holder's family name, given name, date and place of birth, photograph, a list of certain physical features, the holder's signature and sometimes also his fingerprints—a whole array of details designed to prove without a shadow of doubt or confusion that the bearer of the document is so-and-so, and that amongst all the millions of other human beings there isn't one—not even his double or his twin brother—for whom he could be mistaken.

My identity is what prevents me from being identical to anybody else.

Defined in this way the word identity reflects a fairly precise idea—one which in theory should not give rise to confusion. Do we really need lengthy arguments to prove that there are not and cannot be two identical individuals? Even if in the near future someone manages, as we fear they may, to "clone" human beings, the clones would at best be identical only at the time of their "birth"; as soon as they started to live they would start being different.

Each individual's identity is made up of a number of elements, and these are clearly not restricted to the particulars set down in official records. Of course, for the great majority these factors include allegiance to a religious tradition; to a nationality—sometimes two; to a profession, an institution, or a particular social milieu. But the list is much longer than that; it is virtually unlimited. A person may feel a more or less strong attachment to a province, a village, a neighbourhood, a clan, a professional team or one connected with sport, a group of friends, a union, a company, a parish, a community of people with the same passions, the same sexual preferences, the same physical handicaps, or who have to deal with the same kind of pollution or other nuisance.

Of course, not all these allegiances are equally strong, at least at any given moment. But none is entirely insignificant, either. All are components of personality—we might almost call them "genes of the soul" so long as we remember that most of them are not innate.

While each of these elements may be found separately in many individuals, the same combination of them is never encountered in different people, and it's this that gives every individual richness and value and makes each human being unique and irreplaceable.

It can happen that some incident, a fortunate or unfortunate accident, even a chance encounter, influences our sense of identity more strongly than any ancient affiliation. Take the case of a Serbian man and a Muslim woman who met 20 years ago in a cafe in Sarajevo, fell in love and got married. They can never perceive their identity in the same way as does a couple that is entirely Serbian or entirely Muslim; their view of religion and mother country will never again be what it was before. Both partners will always carry within them the ties their parents handed down at birth, but these ties will henceforth be perceived differently and accorded a different importance.

Let us stay in Sarajevo and carry out an imaginary survey there. Let us observe a man of about 50 whom we see in the street.

In 1980 or thereabouts he might have said proudly and without hesitation, "I'm a Yugoslavian!" Questioned more closely, he could have said he was a citizen of the Federal Republic of Bosnia-Herzegovina, and, incidentally, that he came from a traditionally Muslim family.

If you had met the same man twelve years later, when the war was at its height, he might have answered automatically and emphatically, "I'm a Muslim!" He might even have grown the statutory beard. He would quickly have added that he was a Bosnian, and he would not have been pleased to be reminded of how proudly he once called himself a Yugoslavian.

If he was stopped and questioned now, he would say first of all that he was a Bosnian, then that he was a Muslim. He'd tell you he was just on his way to the mosque, but he'd also want you to know that his country is part of Europe and that he hopes it will one day be a member of the Union.

How will this same person want to define himself if we meet him in the same place 20 years hence? Which of his affiliations will he put first? The European? The Islamic? The Bosnian? Something else again? The Balkan connection, perhaps?

I shan't risk trying to predict. All these factors are part of his identity. He was born to a family that was traditionally Muslim; the language he speaks links him to the Southern Slavs, who were once joined together in a single state, but are so no longer; he lives on land which belonged sometimes to the Ottoman and sometimes to the Austrian Empire, and which played a part in the major dramas of European history.

In every era one or other of his affiliations swelled up, so to speak, in such a way as to eclipse all the others and to appear to represent his whole identity. In the course of his life he'll have heard all kinds of fables. He'll have been told he was a proletarian pure and simple. Or a Yugoslavian through and through. Or, more recently, a Muslim. For a few difficult months he'll even have been made to think he had more in common with the inhabitants of Kabul than with those of Trieste!

In every age there have been people who considered that an individual had one overriding affiliation so much more important in every circumstance to all others that it might legitimately be called his "identity." For some it was the nation, for others religion or class. But one has only to look at the various conflicts being fought out all over the world today to realise that no one allegiance has absolute supremacy. Where people feel their faith is threatened, it is their religious affiliation that seems to reflect their whole identity. But if their mother tongue or their ethnic group is in danger, then they fight ferociously against their own coreligionists. Both the Turks and the Kurds are Muslims, though they speak different languages; but does that make the war between them any less bloody? Hutus and Tutsis alike are Catholics, and they speak the same language, but has that stopped them slaughtering one another? Czechs and Slovaks are all Catholics too, but does that help them live together?

I cite all these examples to underline the fact that while there is always a certain hierarchy among the elements that go to make up individual identities, that hierarchy is not immutable; it changes with time, and in so doing brings about fundamental changes in behaviour.

Moreover, the ties that count in people's lives are not always the allegedly major allegiances arising out of language, complexion, nationality, class or religion. Take the case of an Italian homosexual in the days of fascism. I imagine that for the man himself that particular aspect of his personality had up till then been important, but not more so than his professional activity, his political choices or his religious beliefs. But suddenly state repression swoops down on him and he feels threatened with humiliation, deportation or death. It's the recollection of certain books I've read and films I've seen that leads me to choose this example. This man, who a few years earlier was a patriot, perhaps even a nationalist, was no longer able to exult at the sight of the Italian army marching by; he may even have come to wish for its defeat. Because of the persecution to which he was subjected, his sexual preferences came to outweigh his other affiliations, among them even the nationalism which at that time was at its height. Only after the war, in a more tolerant Italy, would our man have felt entirely Italian once more.

The identity a person lays claim to is often based, in reverse, on that of his enemy. An Irish Catholic differentiates himself from Englishmen in the first place in terms of religion, but vis-à-vis the monarchy he will declare himself a republican; and while he may not know much Gaelic, at least he will speak his own form of English. A Catholic leader who spoke with an Oxford accent might seem almost a traitor.

One could find dozens of other examples to show how complex is the mechanism of identity: a complexity sometimes benign, but sometimes tragic. I shall quote various instances in the pages that follow, some briefly and others in more detail. Most of them relate to the region I myself come from—the Middle East, the Mediterranean, the Arab world, and first and foremost Lebanon. For that is a country where you are constantly having to question yourself about your affiliations, your origins, your relationships with others, and your possible place in the sun or in the shade.

I sometimes find myself "examining my identity" as other people examine their conscience. As you may imagine, my object is not to discover within myself some "essential" allegiance in which I may recognise myself. Rather the opposite: I scour my memory to find as many ingredients of my identity as I can. I then assemble and arrange them. I don't deny any of them.

I come from a family which originated in the southern part of the Arab world and which for centuries lived in the mountains of Lebanon. More recently, by a series of migrations, it has spread out to various other parts of the world, from Egypt to Brazil and from Cuba to Australia. It takes pride in having always been at once Arab and Christian, and this probably since the second or third century ad—that is, long before the rise of Islam and even before the West was converted to Christianity.

The fact of simultaneously being Christian and having as my mother tongue Arabic, the holy language of Islam, is one of the basic paradoxes that have shaped my own identity. Speaking Arabic creates bonds between me and all those who use it every day in their prayers, though most of them by far don't know it as well as I do. If you are in central Asia and meet an elderly scholar outside a Timuride *medersa,* you need only address him in Arabic for him to feel at ease. Then he will speak to you from the heart, as he'd never risk doing in Russian or English.

This language is common to us all—to him, to me and to more than a billion others. On the other hand, my being a Christian—regardless of whether I am so out of deep religious conviction or merely for sociological reasons—also creates a significant link between me and the two billion or so other Christians in the world. There are many things in which I differ from every Christian, every Arab and every Muslim, but between me and each of them there is also an undeniable kinship, in one case religious and intellectual and in the other linguistic and cultural.

That said, the fact of being at once an Arab and a Christian puts one in a very special situation: it makes you a member of a minority—a situation not always easy to accept. It marks a person deeply and permanently. I cannot deny that it has played a decisive part in most of the decisions I have had to make in the course of my own life, including my decision to write this [text].

Thus, when I think about either of these two components of my identity separately, I feel close either through language or through religion to a good half of the human race. But when I take the same two elements together, I find myself face to face with my own specificity.

I could say the same thing about other ties. I share the fact that I'm French with 60 million or so others; the fact that I'm Lebanese with between eight and ten million, if you include the diaspora; but with how many do I share the fact that I'm both French and Lebanese? With a few thousand, at most.

Every one of my allegiances links me to a large number of people. But the more ties I have the rarer and more particular my own identity becomes.

If I went into my origins in more detail I'd have to say I was born into what is known as the Melchite or Greek Catholic community, which recognises the authority of the Pope while retaining some Byzantine rites. Seen from a distance, this affiliation is no more than a detail, a curiosity; but seen from close to, it is a defining aspect of my identity. In a country like Lebanon, where the more powerful communities have fought for a long time for their territory and their share of power, members of very small minorities like mine have seldom taken up arms, and have been the first to go into exile. Personally, I always declined to get involved in a war that struck me as absurd and suicidal; but this judgemental attitude, this distant way of looking at things, this refusal to fight, are not unconnected with the fact that I belong to a marginalised community.

So I am a Melchite. But if anyone ever bothered to look my name up in the administrative records—which in Lebanon, as you may imagine, classify people in terms of their religious persuasion—they would find me mentioned not among the Melchites, but in the register of Protestants. Why? It would take too long to explain. All I need say here is that in our family there were two rival family traditions, and that throughout my childhood I was a witness to this tug-of-war. A witness, and sometimes even the bone of contention too. If I was sent to the French school run by the Jesuit fathers it was because my mother, a determined Catholic, wanted to remove me from the Protestant influence prevailing at that time in my father's family, where the children were traditionally sent to British or American schools. It was because of this conflict that I came to speak French, and it was because I spoke French that during the war in Lebanon I went to live in Paris rather than in New York, Vancouver or London. It was for this reason, too, that when I started to write I wrote in French.

Shall I set out even more details about my identity? Shall I mention my Turkish grandmother, or her husband, who was a Maronite Christian from Egypt? Or my other grandfather, who died long before I was born and who I am told was a poet, a freethinker, perhaps a freemason, and in any case violently anti-clerical? Shall I go back as far as the great-great-great-uncle who was the first person to translate Molière into Arabic and to have his translation staged in 1848 in an Ottoman theatre?

No, there's no need to go on. I'll merely ask: how many of my fellow men share with me all the different elements that have shaped my identity and determined the main outlines of my life? Very few. Perhaps none at all. And that is what I want to emphasise: through each one of my affiliations, taken separately, I possess a certain kinship with a large number of my fellow human beings; but because of all these allegiances, taken together, I possess my own identity, completely different from any other.

I scarcely need exaggerate, at all to say that I have some affiliations in common with every other human being. Yet no one else in the world has all or even most of the same allegiances as I do. Out of all the dozens of elements I can put forward, a mere handful would be enough to demonstrate my own particular identity, different from that of anybody else, even my own father or son.

I hesitated a long time before writing the pages that lead up to this one. Should I really start the [text] by describing my own situation at such length?

On the one hand, I wanted to use the example with which I was most familiar to show how, by adducing a few affiliations, one could simultaneously declare one's ties with one's fellow human beings and assert one's own uniqueness. On the other hand, I was well aware that the more one analyses a special case the more one risks being told that it *is* only a special case.

But in the end I took the plunge, in the belief that any person of goodwill trying to carry out his or her own "examination of identity" would soon, like me, discover that that identity is a special case. Mankind itself is made up of special cases. Life is a creator of differences. No "reproduction" is ever identical. Every individual without exception possesses a composite identity. He need only ask himself a few questions to uncover forgotten divergences and unsuspected ramifications, and to see that he is complex, unique and irreplaceable.

That is precisely what characterises each individual identity: it is complex, unique and irreplaceable, not to be confused with any other. If I emphasise this point it's because of the attitude, still widespread but in my view highly pernicious, which maintains that all anyone need do to proclaim his identity is simply say he's an Arab, or French, or black, or a Serb, or a Muslim, or a Jew. Anyone who sets out, as I have done, a number of affiliations, is immediately accused of wanting to "dissolve" his identity in a kind of undifferentiated and colourless soup. And yet what I'm trying to say is exactly the opposite: not that all human beings are the same, but that each one is different. No doubt a Serb is different from a Croat, but every Serb is also different from every other Serb, and every Croat is different from every other Croat. And if a Lebanese Christian is different from a Lebanese Muslim, I don't know any two Lebanese Christians who are identical, nor any two Muslims, any more than there are anywhere in the world two Frenchmen, two Africans, two Arabs or two Jews who are identical. People are not interchangeable, and often in the same family, whether it be Rwandan, Irish, Lebanese, Algerian or Bosnian, we find, between two brothers who have lived in the same environment, apparently small differences which make them act in diametrically opposite ways in matters relating to politics, religion and everyday life. These differences may even turn one of the brothers into a killer, and the other into a man of dialogue and conciliation.

Few would object explicitly to what I've been saying. Yet we all behave as if it were not true. Taking the line of least resistance, we lump the most different people together under the same heading. Taking the line of least resistance, we ascribe to them collective crimes, collective acts and opinions. "The Serbs have massacred ...," "The English have devastated ...," "The Jews have confiscated ...," "The Blacks have torched ...," "The Arabs refuse ...." We blithely express sweeping judgements on whole peoples, calling them "hardworking" and "ingenious," or "lazy," "touchy," "sly," "proud," or "obstinate." And sometimes this ends in bloodshed.

I know it is not realistic to expect all our contemporaries to change overnight the way they express themselves. But I think it is important for each of us to become aware that our words are not innocent and without consequence: they may help to perpetuate prejudices which history has shown to be perverse and deadly.

For it is often the way we look at other people that imprisons them within their own narrowest allegiances. And it is also the way we look at them that may set them free.

The Next Hot Sound? Powwow Step, Aboriginal Hip-Hop

by Benjamin Shingler

Perhaps best exemplified by the group A Tribe Called Red, powwow step is more than just a music genre November 28, 2013 5:00AM ET

Once you hear it, it makes total sense: a blend of hip-hop, reggae and dub-step, with elements of the traditional dance music of Native American powwows.

It's powwow step, a powerful, catchy sound that has carried the aboriginal DJ crew A Tribe Called Red from Ottawa, Canada, to sold-out venues worldwide.

"All we really did was match up dance music with dance music," Ian Campeau, a member of the group, said modestly.

But there's much more to the rise of A Tribe Called Red, which hasn't shied away from political issues as Canada wrestles with its brutal treatment of indigenous peoples through history. The three-man crew is part of a new generation of artists who are helping redefine how aboriginal culture is viewed by the wider Canadian public and articulate the need for greater aboriginal self-determination.

A Tribe Called Red has been a vocal supporter of the grass-roots protest movement known as Idle No More, spoken out against an Ottawa-area youth football team called the Redskins (the team decided to drop the name this fall) and denounced fans who showed up in aboriginal headdress at their shows.

"We don't have a luxury of saying, 'OK, we're going to just be a band,'" said Bear Witness, another member of the crew, sipping on a coffee at a Montreal hotel.

"But that's not who we are," he said. "We're indigenous artists. I have moments where I feel weak and I don't want to have to take this on and carry this kind of weight all the time. But it's not a choice. It's reality, and it's a responsibility."

Music to Bear Witness By

A day earlier, Bear, Campeau (aka DJ NDN, which stands for "never die native") and fellow crew member Dan General (aka DJ Shub) performed at a trendy club on the same block, in the heart of Montreal's downtown.

Although their set didn't start until well past midnight, the crowd was ready to dance—no, more like jump—to the beat, a mass of waving hands and bopping heads.

Onstage, the three men stood in a line before an impressive collection of laptops, turntables and mixers, systemically overlapping traditional vocals and drums with electronic bass music.

One of the biggest cheers came when the group began one of its catchiest tracks, "Electric Powwow," with a sample from a Louis CK rant on the absurdity of the term "Indian."

Another strong track, "Braves," reworks the tune best known as the rally song of baseball's Atlanta Braves, the tomahawk chop.

"At first the results seem gimmicky," The Guardian said in a review of the group's new album, "Nation II Nation," "but soon the care and determination with which this trio have undertaken to project and protect this traditional musical form becomes apparent."

At the show, screens set up on either side of stage rework stereotypical depictions of Native Americans in everything from silent films to cartoons.

The group's imagery, like its music, forces the audience to rethink the perception of what it means to be aboriginal.

At one point, the time-traveling DeLorean from "Back to the Future 3" pops onto the screen and is chased down by a group of natives on horseback. The scene is played in a choppy loop, with the colors distorted.

"At its root, it's about looking at the one-dimensional misrepresentation of aboriginal people in the media and examining it and digging deeper below the surface level," said Bear, a self-described "media-obsessed person" responsible for the group's footage.

A Museum Exhibit

Bear, a Cayuga tribal member from Six Nations, is also one of the artists featured in an exhibit at Montreal's Musee d'Art Contemporain, "Beat Nation: Art, Hip Hop and Aboriginal Culture." The exhibit, originally assembled for a small gallery in Vancouver, is now making its way across the country.

It's an eclectic mix of paintings, sculpture, installation and video that juxtapose stereotypes about Canada's indigenous people with contemporary reality.

At the entrance, a multimedia piece called "dubyadubs" features footage of Iron Eyes Cody—an actor of Italian descent who played Native Americans in Hollywood films—accompanied by electronic music.

The piece, put together by the Montreal-based DJ madeskimo, who has Inuit roots, includes samples of Hindi music—another nod to the wrongheaded notion of the Indian propagated by the first European explorers.

Elsewhere in the exhibit, the image of thunderbird—a mythical creature frequently depicted in aboriginal art of the Pacific Northwest—is reimagined as an urban landmark, buzzing in neon light.

Inherent in much of the work is the case for the right of Canada's aboriginal people to determine their own future and regain control of their territories—an argument that was thrust into the mainstream during last year's Idle No More protests, said Tania Willard, one of the curators of the exhibit, who lives on a reserve near Kamloops, British Columbia.

While the exhibit is a significant step in the mainstream acceptance of contemporary aboriginal art, Willard said she was careful not to present it "as some kind of new moment where aboriginal people were all of a sudden embracing new media."

For many years, "we've advocated and fought to get inside the galleries," she said.

Over the years, there has been some criticism from older community members who see the infusion of hip-hop into aboriginal culture as a break from tradition toward mainstream assimilation.

But like all artists, Willard said, those featured in the exhibit are exposed to a "pluralist, multi-influence kind of world" and don't want to be "limited by a specific ethnographic lens."

"We're complete and total people living in this world, and we have many influences," she said.

How Many People from K-Town?

In the case of A Tribe Called Red, Bear said, the group makes an effort to use powwow songs in a way that honors the roots of indigenous culture.

"I know that there's people out there who are traditional and really serious about what powwow is and may not appreciate what we're doing, but that hasn't been something we've been confronted with," Bear said.

"People within the powwow community haven't come and told us to stop doing what we're doing."

If anything, the group's entry into the mainstream seems to have helped bridge a divide between aboriginal and nonaboriginal people.

In the summer of 1990, Campeau points out, a Mohawk community near Montreal, Kanesatake, was involved in a dispute with the nearby town of Oka. The situation became known as the Oka crisis.

Real estate developers wanted to extend a golf course onto an ancestral burial ground of the Mohawk nation. The Mohawks barricaded a road leading to the development in protest, and the government countered with an intervention from police and, eventually, the Canadian military.

Now, two decades after that ugly episode, a lot of residents of the Mohawk territory closest to Montreal, Kahnawake, remain upset about the conflict, and some still rarely go to the city, said Campeau, who is an Ojibway from the Nipissing First Nation.

But A Tribe Called Red said more made the trip to see the band's latest Montreal show than on previous occasions. (The question "How many people from K-Town are in the house?" got a huge cheer.)

"Now that we're playing in bigger shows, it seems they're more comfortable," Campeau said.

"Maybe they want to claim us as their own."

Do Muslim Women Really Need Saving? Anthropological Reflections on Cultural Relativism and its Others

by Lila Abu-Lughod

What are the ethics of the current "War on Terrorism, a war that justifies itself by purporting to liberate, or save, Afghan women? Does anthropology have anything to offer in our search for a viable position to take regarding this rationale for war?

I was led to pose the question of my title in part because of the way I personally experienced the response to the U.S. war in Afghanistan. Like many colleagues whose work has focused on women and gender in the Middle East, I was deluged with invitations to speak—not just on news programs but also to various departments at colleges and universities, especially women's studies programs. Why did this not please me, a scholar who has devoted more than 20 years of her life to this subject and who has some complicated personal connection to this identity? Here was an opportunity to spread the word, disseminate my knowledge, and correct misunderstandings. The urgent search for knowledge about our sister "women of cover" (as President George Bush so marvelously called them) is laudable and when it comes from women's studies programs where "transnational feminism" is now being taken seriously, it has a certain integrity (see Safire 2001).

My discomfort led me to reflect on why, as feminists in or from the West, or simply as people who have concerns about women's lives, we need to be wary of this response to the events and aftermath of September 11, 2001. I want to point out the minefields—a metaphor that is sadly too apt for a country like Afghanistan, with the world's highest number of mines per capita—of this obsession with the plight of Muslim women. I hope to show some way through them using insights from anthropology, the discipline whose charge has been to understand and manage cultural difference. At the same time, I want to remain critical of anthropology's complicity in the reification of cultural difference.

Cultural Explanations and the Mobilization of Women

It is easier to see why one should be skeptical about the focus on the "Muslim woman" if one begins with the U.S. public response. I will analyze two manifestations of this response: some conversations I had with a reporter from the PBS *NewsHour with Jim Lehrer* and First Lady Laura Bush's radio address to the nation on November 17, 2001, The presenter from the *NewsHour* show first contacted me in October to see if I was willing to give some background for a segment on Women and Islam, I mischievously asked whether she had done segments on the women of Guatemala, Ireland, Palestine, or Bosnia when the show covered wars in those regions; but I finally agreed to look at the questions she was going to pose to panelists, The questions were hopelessly general. Do Muslim women believe "x"? Are Muslim women "y"? Does Islam allow "z" for women? I asked her: If you were to substitute Christian or Jewish wherever you have Muslim, would these questions make sense? I did not imagine she would call me back. But she did, twice, once with an idea for a segment on the meaning of Ramadan and another time on Muslim women in politics. One was in response to the bombing and the other to the speeches by Laura Bush and Cherie Blair, wife of the British Prime Minister.

What is striking about these three ideas for news programs is that there was a consistent resort to the cultural, as if knowing something about women and Islam or the meaning of a religious ritual would help one understand the tragic attack on New York's World Trade Center and the U.S. Pentagon, or how Afghanistan had come to be ruled by the Taliban, or what interests might have fueled U.S. and other interventions in the region over the past 25 years, or what the history of American support for conservative groups funded to undermine the Soviets might have been, or why the caves and bunkers out of which Bin Laden was to be smoked "dead or alive," as President Bush announced on television, were paid for and built by the CIA.

In other words, the question is why knowing about the "culture" of the region, and particularly its religious beliefs and treatment of women, was more urgent than exploring the history of the development of repressive regimes in the region and the U.S. role in this history. Such cultural framing, it seemed to me, prevented the serious exploration of the roots and nature of human suffering in this part of the world. Instead of political and historical explanations, experts were being asked to give religio-cultural ones. Instead of questions that might lead to the exploration of global interconnections, we were offered ones that worked to artificially divide the world into separate spheres—recreating an imaginative geography of West versus East, us versus Muslims, cultures in which First Ladies give speeches versus others where women shuffle around silently in burqas.

Most pressing for me was why the Muslim woman in general, and the Afghan woman in particular, were so crucial to this cultural mode of explanation, which ignored the complex entanglements in which we are all implicated, in sometimes surprising alignments. Why were these female symbols being mobilized in this "War against Terrorism" in a way they were not in other conflicts? Laura Bush's radio address on November 17 reveals the political work such mobilization accomplishes. On the one hand, her address collapsed important distinctions that should have been maintained. There was a constant slippage between the Taliban and the terrorists, so that they became almost one word—a kind of hyphenated monster identity: the Taliban-and-the-terrorists. Then there was the blurring of the very separate causes in Afghanistan of women's continuing malnutrition, poverty, and ill health, and their more recent exclusion under the Taliban from employment, schooling, and the joys of wearing nail polish. On the other hand, her speech reinforced chasmic divides, primarily between the "civilized people throughout the world" whose hearts break for the women and children of Afghanistan and the Taliban-and-the-terrorists, the cultural monsters who want to, as she put it, "impose their world on the rest of us."

Most revealingly, the speech enlisted women to justify American bombing and intervention in Afghanistan and to make a case for the "War on Terrorism" of which it was allegedly a part. As Laura Bush said, "Because of our recent military gains in much of Afghanistan, women are no longer imprisoned in their homes. They can listen to music and teach their daughters without fear of punishment. The fight against terrorism is also a fight for the rights and dignity of women" (U.S. Government 2002).

These words have haunting resonances for anyone who has studied colonial history. Many who have worked on British colonialism in South Asia have noted the use of the woman question in colonial policies where intervention into sati (the practice of widows immolating themselves on their husbands' funeral pyres), child marriage, and other practices was used to justify rule. As Gayatri Chakravorty Spivak (1988) has cynically put it: white men saving brown women from brown men. The historical record is full of similar cases, including in the Middle East. In Turn of the Century Egypt, what Leila Ahmed (1992) has called "colonial feminism" was hard at work. This was a selective concern about the plight of Egyptian women that focused on the veil as a sign of oppression but gave no support to women's education and was professed loudly by the same Englishman, Lord Cromer, who opposed women's suffrage back home.

Sociologist Marnia Lazreg (1994) has offered some vivid examples of how French colonialism enlisted women to its cause in Algeria, She writes:

> Perhaps the most spectacular example of the colonial appropriation of women's voices, and the silencing of those among them who had begun to take women revolutionaries ... as role models by not donning the veil, was the event of May 16, 1958 [just four years before Algeria finally gained its independence from France after a long bloody struggle and 130 years of French control—L.A.]. On that day a demonstration was organized by rebellious French generals in Algiers to show their determination to keep Algeria French. To give the government of France evidence that Algerians were in agreement with them, the generals had a few thousand native men bused in from nearby villages, along with a few women who were solemnly unveiled by French women ... Rounding up Algerians and bringing them to demonstrations of loyalty to France was not in itself an unusual act during the colonial era. But to unveil women at a well-choreographed ceremony added to the event a symbolic dimension that dramatized the one constant feature of the Algerian occupation by France: its obsession with women. [Lazreg 1994:135]

Lazreg (1994) also gives memorable examples of the way in which the French had earlier sought to transform Arab women and girls. She describes skits at awards ceremonies at the Muslim Girls' School in Algiers in 1851 and 1852, In the first skit, written by "a French lady from Algiers," two Algerian Arab girls reminisced about their trip to France with words including the following:

Oh! Protective France: Oh! Hospitable France! ...
Noble land, where I felt free
Under Christian skies to pray to our God: ...
God bless you for the happiness you bring us!
And you, adoptive mother, who taught us
That we have a share of this world,
We will cherish you forever! [Lazreg 1994:68–69]

These girls are made to invoke the gift of a share of this world, a world where freedom reigns under Christian skies. This is not the world the Taliban-and-the-terrorists would "like to impose on the rest of us."

Just as I argued above that we need to be suspicious when neat cultural icons are plastered over messier historical and political narratives, so we need to be wary when Lord Cromer in British-ruled Egypt, French ladies in Algeria, and Laura Bush, all with military troops behind them, claim to be saving or liberating Muslim women.

Politics of the Veil

I want now to look more closely at those Afghan women Laura Bush claimed were "rejoicing" at their liberation by the Americans. This necessitates a discussion of the veil, or the burqa, because it is so central to contemporary concerns about Muslim women. This will set the stage for a discussion of how anthropologists, feminist anthropologists in particular, contend with the problem of difference in a global world. In the conclusion, I will return to the rhetoric of saving Muslim women and offer an alternative.

It is common popular knowledge that the ultimate sign of the oppression of Afghan women under the Taliban-and-the-terrorists is that they were forced to wear the burqa. Liberals sometimes confess their surprise that even though Afghanistan has been liberated from the Taliban, women do not seem to be throwing off their burqas. Someone who has worked in Muslim regions must ask why this is so surprising, Did we expect that once "free" from the Taliban they would go "back" to belly shirts and blue jeans, or dust off their Chanel suits? We need to be more sensible about the clothing of "women of cover, and so there is perhaps a need to make some basic points about veiling.

First, it should be recalled that the Taliban did not invent the burqa. It was the local form of covering that Pashtun women in one region wore when they went out. The Pashtun are one of several ethnic groups in Afghanistan and the burqa was one of many forms of covering in the subcontinent and Southwest Asia that has developed as a convention for symbolizing women's modesty or respectability. The burqa, like some other forms of "cover" has, in many settings, marked the symbolic separation of men's and women's spheres, as part of the general association of women with family and home, not with public space where strangers mingled.

Twenty years ago the anthropologist Hanna Papanek (1982), who worked in Pakistan, described the burqa as "portable seclusion." She noted that many saw it as a liberating invention because it enabled women to move out of segregated living spaces while still observing the basic moral requirements of separating and protecting women from unrelated men. Ever since I came across her phrase portable seclusion, I have thought of these enveloping robes as "mobile homes," Everywhere, such veiling signifies belonging to a particular community and participating in a moral way of life in which families are paramount in the organization of communities and the home is associated with the sanctity of women.

The obvious question that follows is this: If this were the case, why would women suddenly become immodest? Why would they suddenly throw off the markers of their respectability, markers, whether burqas or other forms of cover, which were supposed to assure their protection in the public sphere from the harassment of strange men by symbolically signaling to all that they were still in the inviolable space of their homes, even though moving in the public realm? Especially when these are forms of dress that had become so conventional that most women gave little thought to their meaning.

To draw some analogies, none of them perfect, why are we surprised that Afghan women do not throw off their burqas when we know perfectly well that it would not be appropriate to wear shorts to the opera? At the time these discussions of Afghan women's burqas were raging, a friend of mine was chided by her husband for suggesting she wanted to wear a pantsuit to a fancy wedding; "You know you don't wear pants to a WASP wedding," he reminded her. New Yorkers know that the beautifully coiffed Hasidic women, who look so fashionable next to their dour husbands in black coats and hats, are wearing wigs. This is because religious belief and community standards of propriety require the covering of the hair. They also alter boutique fashions to include high necks and long sleeves. As anthropologists know perfectly well, people wear the appropriate form of dress for their social communities and are guided by socially shared standards, religious beliefs, and moral ideals, unless they deliberately transgress to make a point or are unable to afford proper cover. If we think that U.S. women live in a world of choice regarding clothing, all we need to do is remind ourselves of the expression, "the tyranny of fashion."

What had happened in Afghanistan under the Taliban is that one regional style of covering or veiling, associated with a certain respectable but not elite class, was imposed on everyone as "religiously" appropriate, even though previously there had been many different styles, popular or traditional with different groups and classes—different ways to mark women's propriety, or, in more recent times, religious piety. Although I am not an expert on Afghanistan, I imagine that the majority of women left in Afghanistan by the time the Taliban took control were the rural or less educated, from nonelite families, since they were the only ones who could not emigrate to escape the hardship and violence that has marked Afghanistan's recent history, If liberated from the enforced wearing of burqas, most of these women would choose some other form of modest headcovering, like all those living nearby who were not under the Taliban—their rural Hindu counterparts in the North of India (who cover their heads and veil their faces from affines) or their Muslim sisters in Pakistan.

Even *The New York Times* carried an article about Afghan women refugees in Pakistan that attempted to educate readers about this local variety (Fremson 2001). The article describes and pictures everything from the now-iconic burqa with the embroidered eyeholes, which a Pashtun woman explains is the proper dress for her community, to large scarves they call chadors, to the new Islamic modest dress that wearers refer to as *hijab*. Those in the new Islamic dress are characteristically students heading for professional careers, especially in medicine, just like their counterparts from Egypt to Malaysia. One wearing the large scarf was a school principal; the other was a poor street vendor. The telling quote from the young street vendor is, "If I did [wear the burqa] the refugees would tease me because the burqa is for 'good women' who stay inside the home" (Fremson 2001:14). Here you can see the local status associated with the burqa—it is for good respectable women from strong families who are not forced to make a living selling on the street.

The British newspaper *The Guardian* published an interview in January 2002 with Dr. Suheila Siddiqi, a respected surgeon in Afghanistan who holds the rank of lieutenant general in the Afghan medical corps (Goldenberg 2002). A woman in her sixties, she comes from an elite family and, like her sisters, was educated. Unlike most women of her class, she chose not to go into exile. She is presented in the article as "the woman who stood up to the Taliban" because she refused to wear the burqa. She had made it a condition of returning to her post as head of a major hospital when the Taliban came begging in 1996, just eight months after firing her along with other women. Siddiqi is described as thin, glamorous, and confident. But further into the article it is noted that her graying bouffant hair is covered in a gauzy veil. This is a reminder that though she refused the burqa, she had no question about wearing the chador or scarf.

Finally, I need to make a crucial point about veiling. Not only are there many forms of covering, which themselves have different meanings in the communities in which they are used, but also veiling itself must not be confused with, or made to stand for, lack of agency. As I have argued in my ethnography of a Bedouin community in Egypt in the late 1970s and 1980s (1986), pulling the black head cloth over the face in front of older respected men is considered a voluntary act by women who are deeply committed to being moral and have a sense of honor tied to family. One of the ways they show their standing is by covering their faces in certain contexts. They decide for whom they feel it is appropriate to veil.

To take a very different case, the modern Islamic modest dress that many educated women across the Muslim world have taken on since the mid-1970s now both publicly marks piety and can be read as a sign of educated urban sophistication, a sort of modernity (e.g., Abu-Lughod 1995, 1998; Brenner 1996; El Guindi 1999; MacLeod 1991; Ong 1990). As Saba Mahmood (2001) has so brilliantly shown in her ethnography of women in the mosque movement in Egypt, this new form of dress is also perceived by many of the women who adopt it as part of a bodily means to cultivate virtue, the outcome of their professed desire to be close to God.

Two points emerge from this fairly basic discussion of the meanings of veiling in the contemporary Muslim world, First, we need to work against the reductive interpretation of veiling as the quintessential sign of women's unfreedom, even if we object to state imposition of this form, as in Iran or with the Taliban. (It must be recalled that the modernizing states of Turkey and Iran had earlier in the century banned veiling and required men, except religious clerics, to adopt Western dress.) What does freedom mean if we accept the fundamental premise that humans are social beings, always raised in certain social and historical contexts and belonging to particular communities that shape their desires and understandings of the world? Is it not a gross violation of women's own understandings of what they are doing to simply denounce the burqa as a medieval imposition? Second, we must take care not to reduce the diverse situations and attitudes of millions of Muslim women to a single item of clothing. Perhaps it is time to give up the Western obsession with the veil and focus on some serious issues with which feminists and others should indeed be concerned.

Ultimately, the significant political-ethical problem the burqa raises is how to deal with cultural "others." How are we to deal with difference without accepting the passivity implied by the cultural relativism for which anthropologists are justly famous—a relativism that says it's their culture and it's not my business to judge or interfere, only to try to understand. Cultural relativism is certainly an improvement on ethnocentrism and the racism, cultural imperialism, and imperiousness that underlie it; the problem is that it is too late not to interfere. The forms of lives we find around the world are already products of long histories of interactions.

I want to explore the issues of women, cultural relativism, and the problems of "difference" from three angles. First, I want to consider what feminist anthropologists (those stuck in that awkward relationship, as Strathem [1987] has claimed) are to do with stiange political bedfellows, I used to feel torn when I received the e-mail petitions circulating for the last few years in defense of Afghan women under the Taliban. I was not sympathetic to the dogmatism of the Taliban; I do not support the oppression of women. But the provenance of the campaign worried me. I do not usually find myself in political company with the likes of Hollywood celebiities (see Hirschkind and Mahmood 2002). I had never received a petition from such women defending the Tight of Palestinian women to safety from Isiaeli bombing or daily harassment at checkpoints, asking the United States to reconsider its support for a government that had dispossessed them, closed them out from work and citizenship rights, refused them the most basic freedoms. Maybe some of these same people might be signing petitions to save African women from genital cutting, or Indian women from dowry deaths. However, I do not think that it would be as easy to mobilize so many of these American and European women if it were not a case of Muslim men oppressing Muslim women—women of cover for whom they can feel sorry and in relation to whom they can feel smugly superior. Would television diva Oprah Winfrey host the Women in Black, the women's peace group from Israel, as she did RAWA, the Revolutionary Association of Women of Afghanistan, who were also granted the *Glamour Magazine* Women of the Year Award? What are we to make of post-Taliban "Reality Tours" such as the one advertised on the internet by Global Exchange for March 2002 under the title "Courage and Tenacity: A Women's Delegation to Afghanistan"? The rationale for the $1,400 tour is that "with the removal of the Taliban government, Afghan women, for the first time in the past decade, have the opportunity to reclaim their basic human rights and establish their role as equal citizens by participating in the rebuilding of their nation." The tour's objective, to celebrate International Women's Week, is "to develop awareness of the concerns and issues the Afghan women are facing as well as to witness the changing political, economic, and social conditions which have created new opportunities for the women of Afghanistan" (Global Exchange 2002).

To be critical of this celebration of women's rights in Afghanistan is not to pass judgment on any local women's organizations, such as RAWA, whose members have courageously worked since 1977 for a democratic secular Afghanistan in which women's human rights are respected, against Soviet-backed regimes or U.S.-, Saudi-, and Pakistani-supported conservatives, Their documentation of abuse and their work through clinics and schools have been enormously important.

It is also not to fault the campaigns that exposed the dreadful conditions under which the Taliban placed women. The Feminist Majority campaign helped put a stop to a secret oil pipeline deal between the Taliban and the U.S. multinational Unocal that was going forward with U.S. administration support. Western feminist campaigns must not be confused with the hypocrisies of the new colonial feminism of a Republican president who was not elected for his progressive stance on feminist issues or of administrations that played down the terrible record of violations of women by the United State's allies in the Northern Alliance, as documented by Human Rights Watch and Amnesty International, among others. Rapes and assaults were widespread in the period of infighting that devastated Afghanistan before the Taliban came in to restore order.

It is, however, to suggest that we need to look closely at what we are supporting (and what we are not) and to think carefully about why. How should we manage the complicated politics and ethics of finding ourselves in agreement with those with whom we normally disagree? I do not know how many feminists who felt good about saving Afghan women from the Taliban are also asking for a global redistribution of wealth or contemplating sacrificing their own consumption radically so that African or Afghan women could have some chance of having what I do believe should be a universal human right—the right to freedom from the structural violence of global inequality and from the ravages of war, the everyday rights of having enough to eat, having homes for their families in which to live and thrive, having ways to make decent livings so their children can grow, and having the strength and security to work out, within their communities and with whatever alliances they want, how to live a good life, which might very well include changing the ways those communities are organized.

Suspicion about bedfellows is only a first step; it will not give us a way to think more positively about what to do or where to stand. For that, we need to confront two more big issues. First is the acceptance of the possibility of difference. Can we only free Afghan women to be like us or might we have to recognize that even after "liberation" from the Taliban, they might want different things than we would want for them? What do we do about that? Second, we need to be vigilant about the rhetoric of saving people because of what it implies about our attitudes.

Again, when I talk about accepting difference, I am not implying that we should resign ourselves to being cultural relativists who respect whatever goes on elsewhere as "just their culture." I have already discussed the dangers of "cultural" explanations; "their" cultures are just as much part of history and an interconnected world as ours are. What I am advocating is the hard work involved in recognizing and respecting differences—precisely as products of different histories, as expressions of different circumstances, and as manifestations of differently structured desires. We may want justice for women, but can we accept that there might be different ideas about justice and that different women might want, or choose, different futures from what we envision as best (see Ong 1988)? We must consider that they might be called to personhood, so to speak, in a different language.

Reports from the Bonn peace conference held in late November to discuss the rebuilding of Afghanistan revealed significant differences among the few Afghan women feminists and activists present. RAWA's position was to reject any conciliatory approach to Islamic governance. According to one report I read, most women activists, especially those based in Afghanistan who are aware of the realities on the ground, agreed that Islam had to be the starting point for reform. Fatima Gailani, a U.S.-based advisor to one of the delegations, is quoted as saying. "If I go to Afghanistan today and ask women for votes on the promise to bring them secularism, they are going to tell me to go to hell." Instead, according to one report, most of these women looked for inspiration on how to fight for equality to a place that might seem surprising. They looked to Iran as a country in which they saw women making significant gains within an Islamic framework—in part through an Islamically oriented feminist movement that is challenging injustices and reinterpreting the religious tradition.

The situation in Iran is itself the subject of heated debate within feminist circles, especially among Iranian feminists in the West (e.g., Mir-Hosseini 1999; Moghissi 1999; Najmabadi 1998, 2000). It is not clear whether and in what ways women have made gains and whether the great increases in literacy, decreases in birthrates, presence of women in the professions and government, and a feminist flourishing in cultural fields like writing and filmmaking are because of or despite the establishment of a so-called Islamic Republic. The concept of an Islamic feminism itself is also controversial. Is it an oxymoron or does it refer to a viable movement forged by brave women who want a third way?

One of the things we have to be most careful about in thinking about Third World feminisms, and feminism in different parts of the Muslim world, is how not to fall into polarizations that place feminism on the side of the West. I have written about the dilemmas faced by Arab feminists when Western feminists initiate campaigns that make them vulnerable to local denunciations by conservatives of various sorts, whether Islamist or nationalist, of being traitors (Abu-Lughod 2001). As some like Afsaneh Najmabadi are now arguing, not only is it wrong to see history simplistically in terms of a putative opposition between Islam and the West (as is happening in the United States now and has happened in parallel in the Muslim world), but it is also strategically dangerous to accept this cultural opposition between Islam and the West, between fundamentalism and feminism, because those many people within Muslim countries who are trying to find alternatives to present injustices, those who might want to refuse the divide and take from different histories and cultures, who do not accept that being feminist means being Western, will be under pressure to choose, just as we are: Are you with us or against us?

My point is to remind us to be aware of differences, respectful of other paths toward social change that might give women better lives. Can there be a liberation that is Islamic? And, beyond this, is liberation even a goal for which all women or people strive? Are emancipation, equality, and rights part of a universal language we must use? To quote Saba Mahmood, writing about the women in Egypt who are seeking to become pious Muslims. "The desire for freedom and liberation is a historically situated desire whose motivational force cannot be assumed a priori, but needs to be reconsidered in light of other desires, aspirations, and capacities that inhere in a culturally and historically located subject" (2001:223). In other words, might other desires be more meaningful for different groups of people? Living in close families? Living in a godly way? Living without war? I have done fieldwork in Egypt over more than 20 years and I cannot think of a single woman I know, from the poorest rural to the most educated cosmopolitan, who has ever expressed envy of U.S. women, women they tend to perceive as bereft of community, vulnerable to sexual violence and social anomie, driven by individual success rather than morality, or strangely disrespectful of God.

Mahmood (2001) has pointed out a disturbing thing that happens when one argues for a respect for other traditions. She notes that there seems to be a difference in the political demands made on those who work on or are trying to understand Muslims and Islamists and those who work on secular-humanist projects. She, who studies the piety movement in Egypt, is consistently pressed to denounce all the harm done by Islamic movements around the world—otherwise she is accused of being an apologist. But there never seems to be a parallel demand for those who study secular humanism and its projects, despite the terrible violences that have been associated with it over the last couple of centuries, from world wars to colonialism, from genocides to slavery. We need to have as little dogmatic faith in secular humanism as in Islamism, and as open a mind to the complex possibilities of human projects undertaken in one tradition as the other.

Beyond the Rhetoric of Salvation

Let us return, finally, to my title, "Do Muslim Women Need Saving?" The discussion of culture, veiling, and how one can navigate the shoals of cultural difference should put Laura Bush's self-congratulation about the rejoicing of Afghan women liberated by American troops in a different light. It is deeply problematic to construct the Afghan woman as someone in need of saving. When you save someone, you imply that you are saving her from something. You are also saving her to something. What violences are entailed in this transformation, and what presumptions are being made about the superiority of that to which you are saving her? Projects of saving other women depend on and reinforce a sense of superiority by Westerners, a form of arrogance that deserves to be challenged. All one needs to do to appreciate the patronizing quality of the rhetoric of saving women is to imagine using it today in the United States about disadvantaged groups such as African American women or working-class women. We now understand them as suffering from structural violence. We have become politicized about race and class, but not culture.

As anthropologists, feminists, or concerned citizens, we should be wary of taking on the mantles of those 19th-century Christian missionary women who devoted their lives to saving their Muslim sisters. One of my favorite documents from that period is a collection called *Our Moslem Sisters*, the proceedings of a conference of women missionaries held in Cairo in 1906 (Van Sommer and Zwemer 1907). The subtitle of the book is *A Cry of Need from the Lands of Darkness Interpreted by Those Who Heard It.* Speaking of the ignorance, seclusion, polygamy, and veiling that blighted women's lives across the Muslim world, the missionary women spoke of their responsibility to make these women's voices heard. As the introduction states, "They will never cry for themselves, for they are down under the yoke of centuries of oppression" (Van Sommer and Zwemer 1907:15). "This book," it begins, "with its sad, reiterated story of wrong and oppression is an indictment and an appeal. It is an appeal to Christian womanhood to right these wrongs and enlighten this darkness by sacrifice and service" (Van Sommer and Zwemer 1907:5).

One can hear uncanny echoes of their virtuous goals today, even though the language is secular, the appeals not to Jesus but to human rights or the liberal West. The continuing currency of such imagery and sentiments can be seen in their deployment for perfectly good humanitarian causes. In February 2002, I received an invitation to a reception honoring an international medical humanitarian network called Médecins du Monde/Doctors of the World (MdM). Under the sponsorship of the French Ambassador to the United States, the Head of the delegation of the European Commission to the United Nations, and a member of the European Parliament, the cocktail reception was to feature an exhibition of photographs under the clichéd title "Afghan Women: Behind the Veil."

The invitation was remarkable not just for the colorful photograph of women in flowing burqas walking across the barren mountains of Afghanistan but also for the text, a portion of which I quote:

> For 20 years MdM has been ceaselessly struggling to help those who are most vulnerable. But increasingly, thick veils cover the victims of the war. When the Taliban came to power in 1996, Afghan Women became faceless. To unveil one's face while receiving medical care was to achieve a sort of intimacy, find a brief space for secret freedom and recover a little of one's dignity. In a country where women had no access to basic medical care because they did not have the right to appear in public, where women had no right to practice medicine, MdM's program stood as a stubborn reminder of human rights … . Please join us in helping to lift the veil.

Although I cannot take up here the fantasies of intimacy associated with unveiling, fantasies reminiscent of the French colonial obsessions so brilliantly unmasked by Alloula in *The Colonial Harem* (1986). I can ask why humanitarian projects and human rights discourse in the 21st century need rely on such constructions of Muslim women.

Could we not leave veils and vocations of saving others behind and instead train our sights on ways to make the world a more just place? The reason respect for difference should not be confused with cultural relativism is that it does not preclude asking how we, living in this privileged and powerful part of the world, might examine our own responsibilities for the situations in which others in distant places have found themselves. We do not stand outside the world, looking out over this sea of poor benighted people, living under the shadow—or veil—of oppressive cultures; we are part of that world, Islamic movements themselves have arisen in a world shaped by the intense engagements of Western powers in Middle Eastern lives.

A more productive approach, it seems to me, is to ask how we might contribute to making the world a more just place. A world not organized around strategic military and economic demands; a place where certain kinds of forces and values that we may still consider important could have an appeal and where there is the peace necessary for discussions, debates, and transformations to occur within communities. We need to ask ourselves what kinds of world conditions we could contribute to making such that popular desires will not be overdetermined by an overwhelming sense of helplessness in the face of forms of global injustice. Where we seek to be active in the affairs of distant places, can we do so in the spirit of support for those within those communities whose goals are to make women's (and men's) lives better (as Walley has argued in relation to practices of genital cutting in Africa, [1997])? Can we use a more egalitarian language of alliances, coalitions, and solidarity, instead of salvation?

Even RAWA, the now celebrated Revolutionary Association of the Women of Afghanistan, which was so instrumental in bringing to U.S. women's attention the excesses of the Taliban, has opposed the U.S. bombing from the beginning. They do not see in it Afghan women's salvation but increased hardship and loss. They have long called for disarmament and for peacekeeping forces. Spokespersons point out the dangers of confusing governments with people, the Taliban with innocent Afghans who will be most harmed. They consistently remind audiences to take a close look at the ways policies are being organized around oil interests, the arms industry, and the international drug trade. They are not obsessed with the veil, even though they are the most radical feminists working for a secular democratic Afghanistan. Unfortunately, only their messages about the excesses of the Taliban have been heard, even though their criticisms of those in power in Afghanistan have included previous regimes. A first step in hearing their wider message is to break with the language of alien cultures, whether to understand or eliminate them. Missionary work and colonial feminism belong in the past. Our task is to critically explore what we might do to help create a world in which those poor Afghan women, for whom "the hearts of those in the civilized world break, can have safety and decent lives.

Lila Abu-Lughod Department of Anthropology, Columbia University, New York, NY 10027

Notes

Acknowledgments. I want to thank Page Jackson, Fran Mascia-Lees, Tim Mitchell, Rosalind Morris, Anupama Rao, and members of the audience at the symposium "Responding to War," sponsored by Columbia University's Institute for Research on Women and Gender (where I presented an earlier version), for helpful comments, references, clippings, and encouragement.

References Cited

Abu-Lughod, Lila
1986   Veiled Sentiments: Honor and Poetry in a Bedouin Society. Berkeley: University of California Press.
1995   Movie Stars and Islamic Moralism in Egypt. Social Text 42:53–67.
1998   Remaking Women: Feminism and Modernity in the Middle East. Princeton; Princeton University Press.
2001   Orientalism and Middle East Feminist Studies. Feminist Studies 27(1):101–113.
Ahmed, Leila
1992   Women and Gender in Islam. New Haven, CT: Yale University Press,

Alloula, Malek
1986   The Colonial Harem, Minneapolis: University of Minnesota Press.

Brenner, Suzanne
1996   Reconstructing Self and Society: Javanese Muslim Women and "the Veil." American Ethnologist 23(4):673–697.

El Guindi, Fadwa
1999   Veil: Modesty, Privacy and Resistance. Oxford: Berg.

Fremson, Ruth
2001   Allure Must Be Covered. Individuality Peeks Through. New York Times. November 4: 14.

Global Exchange
2002   Courage and Tenacity: A Women's Delegation to Afghanistan. Electronic document, http://www.globalexchange.org/tours/auto/2002-03-05_CourageandTenacityAWomensDele.html. Accessed February 11.

Goldenberg, Suzanne
2002   The Woman Who Stood Up to the Taliban. The Guardian, January 24, Electronic document, http://222.guardian.co.uk/afghanistan/story/0,1284,63840.

Hirschkind, Charles, and Saba Mahmood
2002   Feminism, the Taliban, and the Politics of Counter-Insurgency. Anthropological Quarterly, Volume 75(2): 107–122.

Lazreg, Marnia
1994   The Eloquence of Silence: Algerian Women in Question. New York: Routledge.

MacLeod, Arlene
1991   Accommodating Protest. New York; Columbia University Press.

Mahmood, Saba
2001   Feminist Theory, Embodiment, and the Docile Agent: Some Reflections on the Egyptian Islamic Revival, Cultural Anthropology 16(2):202–235.

Mir-Hosseini, Ziba
1999   Islam and Gender: The Religious Debate in Contemporary Iran. Princeton: Princeton University Press,

Moghissi, Haideh
1999   Feminism and Islamic Fundamentalism, London: Zed Books.

Najmabadi, Afsaneh
1998   Feminism in an Islamic Republic. *In* Islam, Gender and Social Change. Yvonne Haddad and John Esposito, eds. Pp. 59–84. New York: Oxford University Press.
2000   (Un)Veiling Feminism. Social Text 64:29–15.

Ong, Aihwa
1988   Colonialism and Modernity: Feminist Re-Presentations of Women in Non-Western Societies. Inscriptions 3–4:79–93.
1990   State Versus Islam: Malay Families, Women's Bodies, and the Body Politic in Malaysia. American Ethnologist 17(2):258–276.

Papanek, Hanna
1982   Purdah in Pakistan: Seclusion and Modem Occupations for Women. *In* Separate Worlds. Hanna Papanek and Gail Minault, eds. Pp. 190–216. Columbus, MO: South Asia Books.
Safire, William
2001   "On Language. " New York Times Magazine, October 28: 22.
Spivak, Gayatri Chakravorty
1988   Can the Subaltern Speak? *In* Marxism and the Interpretation of Culture. Cary Nelson and Lawrence Grossberg, eds. Pp. 271–313. Urbana: University of Illinois Press.
Strathern, Marilyn
1987   An Awkward Relationship: The Case of Feminism and Anthropology. Signs 12:276–292.
U.S. Government
1907   Our Moslem Sisters: A Cry of Need from Lands of Darkness Interpreted by Those Who Heard It. New York: Fleming H. Reveil Co.
2002   Electronic document, http://www.whitehouse.gov/news/releases/2001/11/20011117. Accessed January 10.
Walley, Christine
1997   Searching for "Voices": Feminism, Anthropology, and the Global Debate over Female Genital Operations. Cultural Anthropology 12(3):405–438.

CPSIA information can be obtained
at www.ICGtesting.com
Printed in the USA
LVHW05s1912030918
589034LV00016B/144/P